Cocos2d-x Game Development Blueprints

Build a plethora of games for various genres using one of the most powerful game engines, Cocos2d-x

Karan Sequeira

BIRMINGHAM - MUMBAI

Cocos2d-x Game Development Blueprints

First published: July 2015

Production reference: 1220715

Published by Packt Publishing Ltd.
Livery Place
35 Livery Street
Birmingham B3 2PB, UK.

ISBN 978-1-78398-526-5

www.packtpub.com

Credits

Author
Karan Sequeira

Reviewers
Harrison
Carlos Piñan
Germán González Rodríguez

Commissioning Editor
Ashwin Nair

Acquisition Editor
Kevin Colaco

Content Development Editor
Shweta Pant

Technical Editor
Madhunikita Sunil Chindarkar

Copy Editor
Roshni Banerjee

Project Coordinator
Shipra Chawhan

Proofreader
Safis Editing

Indexer
Priya Sane

Production Coordinator
Komal Ramchandani

Cover Work
Komal Ramchandani

About the Author

Karan Sequeira is a budding game developer with 4 years of experience in the mobile game development industry. He started out as a JavaScript programmer, developing HTML5 games, and fell in love with C++ when he moved to Cocos2d-x. He has a handful of games on the iOS and Android app stores and is currently working for an organization in the in-flight entertainment industry. He is extremely passionate about learning new technologies and dreams about building an artificially intelligent super computer that can fall in love.

I am deeply grateful to the amazing folks at Packt Publishing, who presented me with a wonderful opportunity and supported me unceasingly. I owe a lot to the developers of Cocos2d-x and its ever-growing community of developers. But most of all, I am blessed to have a loving and encouraging family as well as friends who have been patient through all the times I've ditched them for this book.

About the Reviewers

Harrison is one of the core developers of Cocos2d-x. As a maintainer of this broadly used game engine, he has been working on the v2.x and v3.x versions since 2013, focusing on rendering modules. In addition to this, he is experienced on desktop game developing, including game logic, rendering, animation, and particle systems. In his own words, "Cocos2d-x is making progress, I hope my team and I can provide a good engine for all developers—code less, enjoy more!"

Carlos Piñan is a software engineer with 5 years of experience and is dedicated to game development and Android development. He contributes libraries to the Cocos2d-x communities and contributes to the Android community as well. He is a speaker at different events and is a trainer for Android apps.

He contributes to algorithm books and other Cocos2d-x books as well.

I would like to thank my family for always believing in me and my friends at Vitrum for being a great team.

Germán González Rodríguez is a software engineer with a master's degree in telecommunications engineering and over 7 years' experience working as a game, app, and web developer on the PC, Mac, iOS, and Android platforms. He has had a passion for programming video games since an early age. In school, he checked out hundreds of library books and typed in thousands of lines of BASIC code to make text adventures on his father's old 386 computer.

After he finished his degree, he worked for an independent video game developing company called Lemon Team in Alicante, Spain, until he became a freelance software engineer. In that time, he successfully shipped games on the App Store, Google Play Store, Amazon Appstore, and Windows Store with more than 2,000,000 combined installations for companies such as Amazon Games Studios and Fresh Games.

At present, he lives in the US and tries to promote sustainability practices as a game developer in the nonprofit organization Cool Choices, which is based in Madison, Wisconsin.

I would like to thank my wife, Patricia, for her love, support, and patience. I love you.

I would also like to thank my parents for always being there. I am who I am today because of you.

---

www.PacktPub.com

Support files, eBooks, discount offers, and more

For support files and downloads related to your book, please visit www.PacktPub.com.

Did you know that Packt offers eBook versions of every book published, with PDF and ePub files available? You can upgrade to the eBook version at www.PacktPub.com and as a print book customer, you are entitled to a discount on the eBook copy. Get in touch with us at service@packtpub.com for more details.

At www.PacktPub.com, you can also read a collection of free technical articles, sign up for a range of free newsletters and receive exclusive discounts and offers on Packt books and eBooks.

https://www2.packtpub.com/books/subscription/packtlib

Do you need instant solutions to your IT questions? PacktLib is Packt's online digital book library. Here, you can search, access, and read Packt's entire library of books.

Why subscribe?

- Fully searchable across every book published by Packt
- Copy and paste, print, and bookmark content
- On demand and accessible via a web browser

Free access for Packt account holders

If you have an account with Packt at www.PacktPub.com, you can use this to access PacktLib today and view 9 entirely free books. Simply use your login credentials for immediate access.

Table of Contents

Preface

Cocos2d-x offers you, as a game developer, an open source engine that enables you to effortlessly build powerful 2D games and publish them on a multitude of popular platforms. In today's fast-paced world, what more could a game developer need?

This book gets you started by introducing the continually evolving HTML5 platform and familiarizes you with the Cocos2d-html5 framework.

This book is written to get you well versed with the many versatile features of Cocos2d-x, by demonstrating the creation of nine different games—from arcade style games to new age physics games and from simple puzzle games to strategic tower defense games! All the while, focusing on gameplay and letting Cocos2d-x do all the heavy lifting for you.

For the finale, you will learn how to build your games for Android and Windows Phone 8, bringing you to a full circle on Cocos2d-x.

What this book covers

Chapter 1, A Colorful Start, introduces the HTML5 version of the Cocos2d family by creating a simple and colorful puzzle game. You will learn how to set up your environment to develop using the Cocos2d-html5 engine. You also get familiar with the various actions you can use to get things done in an instant.

Chapter 2, How to Fly a Dragon!, concludes your HTML5 journey and will show you how to use sprite sheets, how to implement simple gravity, and use rectangular collision detection.

Chapter 3, Not Just a Space Game, shows you how to create a multiplatform Cocos2d-x project. You will also learn to create a level-based arcade game where you learn how to parse XML, play particle effects, and extend the engine by inheriting from its primary classes.

Chapter 4, Back to the Drawing Board, shows you just how easy it is to make a game that completely uses primitive drawing for its entities. You will also learn how to implement simple accelerometer controls and how to add difficulty progression to an endless game.

Chapter 5, Let's Get Physical!, guides you through the process of using Box2D to build a physics game. You will also learn about state machines and object pools.

Chapter 6, Creativity with Textures, shows you how to fire OpenGL commands and render your own sprite. You will also learn to use Box2D to make a picturesque side-scroller game.

Chapter 7, Old is Gold!, introduces you to the Tiled map editor and the basics of a tile-based game. You will also learn how to implement a reusable tile-based collision detection algorithm.

Chapter 8, Box2D Meets RUBE, introduces you to RUBE, which is a powerful physics editor. You will use it to create levels for a slingshot type physics game. You will also learn about ray casting and how to implement explosions in Box2D.

Chapter 9, The Two Towers, shows you how easy it is to implement a tower defense game in Cocos2d-x. In the process, you will learn how to implement scalable architectures for your enemies and towers. You will also learn how a simple gesture recognizer works and how you can control the speed of your gameplay.

Chapter 10, Cross-platform Building, shows you how to set up your environment and build one of your games on Android and Windows Phone 8.

What you need for this book

The source bundle will contain all the source code and project files to run each game. However, you will need to install the following software to run the games:

- A computer running Windows, Linux, or Mac OS. However, you will need a computer running Windows 8 in order to build on Windows Phone 8.
- WebStorm, or a similar JavaScript editor, and at least one browser to run the HTML5 games in the first two chapters.
- Microsoft Visual Studio to run the projects on Windows PC and Windows Phone and Eclipse to run the projects on Android.

Who this book is for

This book is written for people who have basic experience in Cocos2d-x and want to use it to implement a wide variety of high-quality games. The book revisits some of the basic concepts, but we hit the ground running. As such, some basic understanding of Cocos2d-x is recommended. In addition, since the first couple of chapters are on Cocos2d-html5, some knowledge of JavaScript is strongly recommended.

Conventions

In this book, you will find a number of text styles that distinguish between different kinds of information. Here are some examples of these styles and an explanation of their meaning.

Code words in text, database table names, folder names, filenames, file extensions, pathnames, dummy URLs, user input, and Twitter handles are shown as follows: " If you expand the `Classes` folder inside `pumpkindefenseComponent`, you will notice that the actual sources are missing."

A block of code is set as follows:

```
createTileData:function(){
  this.tileData = [];
  // generate tile data randomly
  for(var i = 0; i < (NUM_COLS * NUM_ROWS); ++i){
    this.tileData[i] = 1 + Math.floor(Math.random() *
      MAX_COLOURS);
  }
}
```

Any command-line input or output is written as follows:

```
export NDK_ROOT=/Android/android-ndk-r10
```

New terms and **important words** are shown in bold. Words that you see on the screen, for example, in menus or dialog boxes, appear in the text like this: " By default, you will see a whole lot of packages selected, out of which **Android SDK Platform-tools** and **Android SDK Build-tools** are necessary."

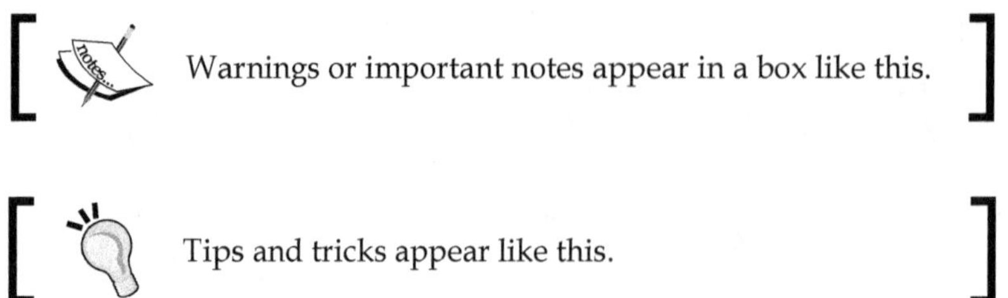

Warnings or important notes appear in a box like this.
Tips and tricks appear like this.

Reader feedback

Feedback from our readers is always welcome. Let us know what you think about this book—what you liked or disliked. Reader feedback is important for us as it helps us develop titles that you will really get the most out of.

To send us general feedback, simply e-mail `feedback@packtpub.com`, and mention the book's title in the subject of your message.

If there is a topic that you have expertise in and you are interested in either writing or contributing to a book, see our author guide at `www.packtpub.com/authors`.

Customer support

Now that you are the proud owner of a Packt book, we have a number of things to help you to get the most from your purchase.

Downloading the example code

You can download the example code files from your account at `http://www.packtpub.com` for all the Packt Publishing books you have purchased. If you purchased this book elsewhere, you can visit `http://www.packtpub.com/support` and register to have the files e-mailed directly to you.

Downloading the color images of this book

We also provide you with a PDF file that has color images of the screenshots/diagrams used in this book. The color images will help you better understand the changes in the output. You can download this file from `https://www.packtpub.com/sites/default/files/downloads/52650S_ColorImages.pdf`.

Errata

Although we have taken every care to ensure the accuracy of our content, mistakes do happen. If you find a mistake in one of our books—maybe a mistake in the text or the code—we would be grateful if you could report this to us. By doing so, you can save other readers from frustration and help us improve subsequent versions of this book. If you find any errata, please report them by visiting `http://www.packtpub.com/submit-errata`, selecting your book, clicking on the **Errata Submission Form** link, and entering the details of your errata. Once your errata are verified, your submission will be accepted and the errata will be uploaded to our website or added to any list of existing errata under the Errata section of that title.

To view the previously submitted errata, go to `https://www.packtpub.com/books/content/support` and enter the name of the book in the search field. The required information will appear under the **Errata** section.

Piracy

Piracy of copyrighted material on the Internet is an ongoing problem across all media. At Packt, we take the protection of our copyright and licenses very seriously. If you come across any illegal copies of our works in any form on the Internet, please provide us with the location address or website name immediately so that we can pursue a remedy.

Please contact us at `copyright@packtpub.com` with a link to the suspected pirated material.

We appreciate your help in protecting our authors and our ability to bring you valuable content.

Questions

If you have a problem with any aspect of this book, you can contact us at `questions@packtpub.com`, and we will do our best to address the problem.

1
A Colorful Start

We start the journey of game development in Cocos2d-x with a simple, fun, and colorful game. Let's call it **ColourSmash**. This will serve as a revision of the basic features of the engine and will get us started with some fun development. We will be using the HTML5 version of Cocos2d for this project—`Cocos2d-html5-v2.2.3` to be specific. So all the coding in this chapter, and the next, will be done in JavaScript.

Here's what you'll learn in this chapter:

- How and where to use `cc.Scene` and `cc.Layer`
- How to optimize rendering with a batch node
- How to use actions and easing
- How to get touches
- How to schedule callbacks

An overview of ColourSmash

The game we will discuss here is one of the many famous puzzle games found online. The basic idea of the game is simple: click on a colored tile and all adjacent tiles of the same color disappear. As you may have guessed, the game world consists of a set of colorful tiles. You keep clicking tiles and they disappear. What makes it fun is a bunch of tiles disappearing together yields you a bonus!

This is a glimpse of what we should have at the end of this chapter:

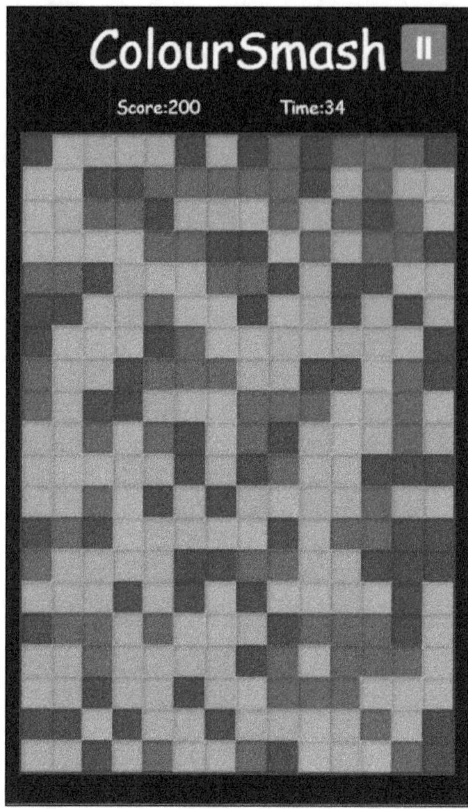

Setting up the environment for Cocos2d-html5

Before we actually begin developing this game, let's spend some time setting up an environment for our HTML5 games. Since these are HTML5 games, they will essentially run in a web browser—be it on a computer or a mobile device. You are free to run these games in a browser of your choice. My personal favorite is Google Chrome!

Since we will be using JavaScript to develop the game, I would definitely recommend brushing up on some basic JavaScript coding principles before diving into the code. You can visit the following URL for some help:

`http://jstherightway.org/`

Moving on, here is the list of software that you will require to run the tests/samples in the Cocos2d-html5 source as well as the Cocos2d-html5 games we'll develop:

- Cocos2d-html5 source (version 2.2.3 at the time of writing this chapter) can be found at `http://cdn.Cocos2d-x.org/Cocos2d-html5-v2.2.3.zip`
- WebStorm (optional) at `https://confluence.jetbrains.com/display/WI/Previous+WebStorm+Releases`
- WampServer (optional and for Windows only) can be downloaded from `http://www.wampserver.com/en/`

The first software on the list is, of course, the source of the Cocos2d-html5 engine, without which we won't be able to move a single web-based muscle.

The next software on the list is WebStorm, which is a powerful JavaScript editor that provides features such as code completion, code refactoring, debugging, and many others. Of course, this does not impact our chapter in anyway. You can choose to use any editor of your choice.

The last item on the list is WampServer, which is optional and is valid only for developers working on a Windows machine. WampServer provides a web server that can serve files over HTTP. This is especially useful if you want to test your game on wireless devices connected to the same network as your development machine.

Once you've downloaded the above software, move to the next section where we will create a sample project.

Creating a project in Cocos2d-html5

Creating a project in Cocos2d-html5 is as simple as copying a readymade template and renaming it to what you want to call your game. If you've downloaded and extracted the archive of the Cocos2d-html5 source, navigate to the `template` folder inside it. Your file explorer should show you something like this:

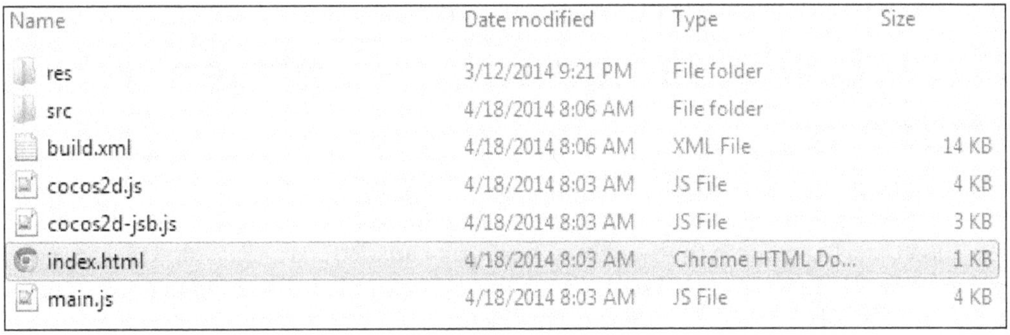

Name	Date modified	Type	Size
res	3/12/2014 9:21 PM	File folder	
src	4/18/2014 8:06 AM	File folder	
build.xml	4/18/2014 8:06 AM	XML File	14 KB
cocos2d.js	4/18/2014 8:03 AM	JS File	4 KB
cocos2d-jsb.js	4/18/2014 8:03 AM	JS File	3 KB
index.html	4/18/2014 8:03 AM	Chrome HTML Do...	1 KB
main.js	4/18/2014 8:03 AM	JS File	4 KB

If you run the `index.html` file you see in the `template` folder, you'll realize that it is nothing but a `hello world` project. This is exactly what we need to get us started. To create a new project in Cocos2d-html5, follow these steps:

1. Copy all the files within the `template` folder.
2. Create a folder in the root directory of the Cocos2d-html5 engine. The engine's root with the folder for ColourSmash is shown in the following screenshot:

Name	Date modified	Type	Size
cocos2d	4/23/2014 3:23 PM	File folder	
ColourSmash	5/18/2015 10:01 PM	File folder	
extensions	4/23/2014 3:23 PM	File folder	
external	4/23/2014 3:23 PM	File folder	
HelloHTML5World	7/28/2014 9:59 AM	File folder	
lib	4/23/2014 3:18 PM	File folder	
licenses	12/23/2013 12:14 ...	File folder	
samples	4/23/2014 3:23 PM	File folder	
template	4/23/2014 3:23 PM	File folder	
tools	4/23/2014 3:23 PM	File folder	
AUTHORS.txt	4/18/2014 8:06 AM	Text Document	7 KB
CHANGELOG.txt	4/23/2014 3:07 PM	Text Document	18 KB
index.html	4/18/2014 8:03 AM	Chrome HTML Do...	4 KB
README.mdown	4/18/2014 8:06 AM	MDOWN File	2 KB

3. Now, paste all the files that you copied from the `template` folder into the folder you just created.

That's it! You have created your first project in Cocos2d-html5. Now, it's time to get acquainted with the different kinds of files located in the project's directory.

Getting acquainted with the project structure

The main backbone files required for any Cocos2d-html5 game are the `index.html`, `main.js`, and `cocos2d.js` files. These are exactly the files you will see in your project's root directory. In addition to these three files, you can also see a file called `build.xml` and another file called `cocos2d-jsb.js`. Take a look at the following table for a brief description of what these files are responsible for:

File	Description
`index.html`	This is the main HTML page that will be displayed on any device's browser. This is where your game will run. This is also the file you must double-click on in order to launch the game in a browser.
`main.js`	This file could be compared to the `AppDelegate` class from Cocos2d-x. It is the starting point of our game and is where the director is informed of which the game's first scene should be.
`cocos2d.js`	This file is the main configuration file and is the only source file that gets linked to your HTML page. This file is responsible for invoking the engine's main loader. Any sources that go into your game need to be listed in this file.
`cocos2d-jsb.js`	This JavaScript source file is required to boot JavaScript bindings and is not required for Cocos2d-html5. You could delete this file if you don't intend on using JavaScript bindings.
`build.xml`	You can compress your entire game's source code into a single file using the Google Closure Compiler that is provided under the `tools` directory of the Cocos2d-html5 source. This file is the input to the Ant build command that invokes the compiler. To run this, you will need Ant and JRE installed on your machine.
`resources.js`	This file contains a JSON object that lists all the resources that you will need to run the game. You must ensure that each and every resource (image, plist, font, audio, and so on) is included in this file. Not doing so will most certainly crash your application. The engine will then load all the files listed in this file into the browser's memory. Therefore, you will still need to load the textures, sprite frames and animations into their respective caches.

Now that we have a basic understanding of the structure of a typical Cocos2d-html5 project, it is time to create our very first scene in ColourSmash.

Creating the first scene – the main menu

Our first scene happens to be the opening screen of the game—the main menu. It is what the users will see when the game has finished loading. This scene is defined in `mainmenu.js` in the source for this project. This is what it looks like:

```
var MainMenu = cc.Layer.extend({

  init:function () {
    this._super();

    return true;
  }
```

```
});

var MainMenuScene = cc.Scene.extend({
  onEnter:function () {
    this._super();
    var layer = new MainMenu();
    layer.init();
    this.addChild(layer);
  }
});
```

As you can see, we have two entities here; an object called `MainMenu`, which is of type `cc.Layer`, and a class called `MainMenuScene`, which extends the `cc.Scene` class. Understandably, if you've worked on Cocos2d-x before, this is the way the various screens within a game are structured into scenes and layers. If you do need to brush up on some Cocos2d node graph basics, feel free to pay a visit to the following link:

`http://www.cocos2d-x.org/wiki/Scene_Graph`

Now that we have created a `cc.Scene` class and a `cc.Layer` class, it's time to create some basic UI elements. We add a title and a play button to our main menu and add some color to the background. Hence, the following code is added to the `init` function of `MainMenu`:

```
// create a coloured layer as background
var background = cc.LayerColor.create(cc.c4b(25, 0, 51, 255), this.
screenSize.width, this.screenSize.height);
this.addChild(background);

// create a label to display the name of the game
var titleLabel = cc.LabelTTF.create("ColourSmash", "Comic Sans MS",
64);
titleLabel.setPosition(cc.p(this.screenSize.width * 0.5, this.
screenSize.height * 0.8));
this.addChild(titleLabel, 1);

// create a play button to move to the game world
var playButton = cc.MenuItemSprite.create(cc.Sprite.create(s_Play));
playButton.setCallback(this.onPlayClicked, this);
playButton.setPosition(cc.p(this.screenSize.width * 0.5, this.
screenSize.height * 0.5));

// create a menu that will contain the button above
var menu = cc.Menu.create(playButton);
menu.setPosition(0,0);
this.addChild(menu, 1);
```

Notice how the callback is set for the play button. In Cocos2d-html5, we need not specify the kind of function pointer that we're setting into the callback. Since all functions are objects in JavaScript, we need to pass the handler function, and the class it belongs to, as parameters to the `setCallback` function. The handler function that will take us to the `GameWorld` is given as follows:

```
onPlayClicked:function(){
  // ask the director to change the running scene
  cc.Director.getInstance().replaceScene(cc.TransitionFade.create(0.5,
new GameWorldScene()));
}
```

An important difference in the API of Cocos2d-x and Cocos2d-html5 is the absence of selector types in the latter. Whether a function has to be passed as a `schedule_selector`, a `callfunc_selector`, or a `menu_selector`, the API requires only the reference to the function.

The code for the play button's callback is pretty straightforward. It just tells the director to replace the current scene with `GameWorldScene` and include a smooth fade transition.

That completes a simple version of our `MainMenu`, but how will this scene be displayed in the first place? To answer that question, we navigate to the bottom of the `main.js` file and pass an object of our `MainMenuScene` class as an argument to the `cocos2dApp` class' constructor:

```
var myApp = new cocos2dApp(MainMenuScene);
```

This will set `MainMenuScene` as the first scene that will be displayed when the web application has loaded.

Downloading the example code

You can download the example code files from your account at `http://www.packtpub.com` for all the Packt Publishing books you have purchased. If you purchased this book elsewhere, you can visit `http://www.packtpub.com/support` and register to have the files e-mailed directly to you.

Moving on to the game world

We will add another scene to represent the actual game play, which will contain its own `cc.Layer` called `GameWorld`. This class is defined in the `gameworld.js` file in the source bundle for this chapter. Every scene that you define must be added to the list of sources in `cocos2d.js` and `build.xml` if you plan on using the closure compiler to compress your source files.

For this game, all we need is a small, white, square-shaped image like this:

We will use this white image and manually set different RGB values for the sprites to create our grid of colorful tiles. Don't forget to add this to the `resources.js` file so that it is preloaded and can be used in the game.

Now that we have our sprites, we can actually start building our grid. Let's define a few constants before we do that. You're right, JavaScript does not have a concept of constants, however, for the purposes of our understanding, we will name and consider these quantities as constants. Here is the declaration of the constants in the `gameworld.js` file:

```
var MAX_COLOURS = 4;
// maximum number of colours we can use
var TILE_SIZE = 32;
// size in points of each tile (same as tile.png)
var NUM_COLS = 14;
// maximum number of columns
var NUM_ROWS = 20;
// maximum number of rows
var GAMEPLAY_OFFSET = cc.p(TILE_SIZE/2, TILE_SIZE);
// offset so that game is not stuck to the bottom-left
var SCORE_PER_TILE = 10;
// score when a tile is cleared
var BONUS = [50, 40, 30, 20, 10];
// number of tiles used to trigger bonuses eg. Bonus if 50 tiles
collected in one shot

// define an object that we can use an enumeration for our colour
types
var E_COLOUR_TYPE = {
  E_COLOUR_NONE:0,
  E_COLOUR_RED:1,
```

```
    E_COLOUR_GREEN:2,
    E_COLOUR_BLUE:3,
    E_COLOUR_YELLOW:4
  };
```

We have defined a constant `GAMEPLAY_OFFSET`. This is a convenient variable that specifies how many points should be added to our grid so that it appears in the center of the game world. We have also defined another quantity `E_COLOUR_TYPE`, which will act as enum to represent our color types. Since JavaScript is a weak-typed language, we cannot really create enumerations like in C++, which is a strong-typed language. The best we can do is to simulate a normal JavaScript object so that we can have the convenience of an enum, as done in the preceding code snippet.

Declaring and initializing the variables

Let's declare the members of the `GameWorld` class and define the `init` method that will be called when this scene is created:

```
// member variable declarations
// save screenSize for fast access
screenSize:null,
// array to represent the colour type for each tile
tileData:null,
// array to hold each tile's sprite
tileSprites:null,
// batch rendering
spriteBatchNode:null,
// arrays to support game logic
tilesToRemove:null,
tilesToShift:null,
// score and time
score:0,
scoreLabel:null,
time:0,
timeLabel:null,
// buttons and popups
pauseButton:null,
popup:null,
isGameOver:false,

init:function () {
  this._super();
```

```
        this.screenSize = cc.Director.getInstance().getWinSize();

        this.tilesToRemove = [];
        this.tilesToShift = [];
        this.createBackground();
        this.createTileData();
        this.createTileSprites();
        this.createHUD();
        this.doCountdownAnimation();

        return true;
    },
```

Right on top, we have two arrays named `tileData` and `tileSprites` to hold our data and sprites respectively. Then, we have our sprite batch node that will be used for optimized rendering. Next, you can see arrays that we will use to find and remove tiles when a user makes a move. Last but not the least, we have our HUD elements and menu buttons.

Creating the background

Let's begin filling up the `GameWorld` by creating the background, which will contain the play area for the game, the title of the game, and a pause button. The code is as follows:

```
    createBackground:function(){
        // same as main menu
        var background = cc.LayerColor.create(cc.c4b(25, 0, 51, 255), this.
    screenSize.width, this.screenSize.height);
        this.addChild(background);

        // generate vertices for the gameplay frame
        var vertices = [];
        vertices[0] = cc.pAdd(GAMEPLAY_OFFSET, cc.p(-1, -1));
        vertices[1] = cc.pAdd(GAMEPLAY_OFFSET, cc.p(-1, (NUM_ROWS * TILE_
    SIZE)+1));
        vertices[2] = cc.pAdd(GAMEPLAY_OFFSET, cc.p((NUM_COLS * TILE_
    SIZE)+1, (NUM_ROWS * TILE_SIZE)+1));
        vertices[3] = cc.pAdd(GAMEPLAY_OFFSET, cc.p((NUM_COLS * TILE_
    SIZE)+1, -1));
        // use new DrawingPrimitive class
        var gamePlayFrame = cc.DrawNode.create();
        // pass vertices, fill colour, border width and border colour to get
    a nice bordered, coloured rectangle
```

```
  gamePlayFrame.drawPoly(vertices, cc.c4f(0.375, 0.375, 0.375, 1), 2,
cc.c4f(0.4, 0, 0, 1));
  // must add the DrawNode else it won't be drawn at all
  this.addChild(gamePlayFrame);

  // label to show the title of the game
  var titleLabel = cc.LabelTTF.create("ColourSmash", "Comic Sans MS",
52);
  titleLabel.setPosition(cc.p(this.screenSize.width * 0.5, this.
screenSize.height * 0.95));
  this.addChild(titleLabel);

  // menu containing a button to pause the game
  this.pauseButton = cc.MenuItemSprite.create(cc.Sprite.create(s_
Pause));
  this.pauseButton.setCallback(this.onPauseClicked, this);
  this.pauseButton.setPosition(cc.p(this.screenSize.width * 0.9, this.
screenSize.height * 0.95));
  this.pauseButton.setEnabled(false);
  var pauseMenu = cc.Menu.create(this.pauseButton);
  pauseMenu.setPosition(cc.POINT_ZERO);
  this.addChild(pauseMenu,1);
},
```

We've used a `cc.LayerColor` class to create a simple, colored background that is of the same size as the screen. Next, we make use of the new primitive drawing class called `cc.DrawNode`. This class is much faster and simpler than the `cc.DrawingPrimitive` class. We will use it to draw a filled rectangle with a colored border of some thickness. This rectangle will act as a visual container for our tiles.

To do this, we generate an array of vertices to represent the four points that compose a rectangle and pass it to the `drawPoly` function along with the color to fill, border width, and border color. The `cc.DrawNode` object is added to `GameWorld` just like any other `cc.Node`. This is one of the major differences between the `cc.DrawNode` and the older `cc.DrawingPrimitives`. We don't need to manually draw our primitives on every frame inside the `draw` function either. This is handled by the `cc.DrawNode` class. In addition, we can run most kinds of `cc.Action` objects the `cc.DrawNode`. We will discuss more on actions later. For now, all that's left is to add a label for the game's title and a pause button to launch the pause menu.

Creating the tiles

Now that we have defined the background and play area, let's create the tiles and their respective sprites. The code is as follows:

```
createTileData:function(){
        this.tileData = [];
        // generate tile data randomly
        for(var i = 0; i < (NUM_COLS * NUM_ROWS); ++i){
            this.tileData[i] = 1 + Math.floor(Math.random() * MAX_
COLOURS);
        }
    },
```

Based on a random value, one of the four predefined color types are chosen from the `E_COLOUR_TYPE` enum and saved into the `tileData` array. The code is as follows:

```
createTileSprites:function(){
  // create the batch node passing in path to the texture & initial
capacity
  // initial capacity is slightly more than maximum number of sprites
  // this is because new tiles may be added before old tiles are
removed
  this.spriteBatchNode = cc.SpriteBatchNode.create(s_Tile, NUM_COLS *
NUM_ROWS + NUM_ROWS);
  this.addChild(this.spriteBatchNode);

  this.tileSprites = [];
  for(var i = 0; i < (NUM_COLS * NUM_ROWS); ++i){
  this.createTileSprite(i);
  }
},
```

Looking at the `createTileSprites` function, we have created a `cc.SpriteBatchNode` object and added it to the game world. The `cc.SpriteBatchNode` class offers a great way to optimize rendering, as it renders all its child sprites in one single draw call. For a game like ours where the grid is composed of 280 sprites, we save on 279 draw calls! The only prerequisite of the `cc.SpriteBatchNode` class is that all its children sprites use the same texture. Since all our tile sprites use the same image, we fulfill this criterion.

We create the sprite batch node and pass in the path to the image and the initial capacity as parameters. You can see that the initial capacity is slightly more than the maximum number of tiles in the grid. This is done to prevent unnecessary resizing of the batch node later in the game.

> It's a good idea to create a sprite batch node with a predefined capacity. If you fail to do this, the sprite batch node class will have to allocate more memory at runtime. This is computationally expensive, since the texture coordinates will have to be computed again for all existing child sprites.

Great! Let's write the `createTileSprite` function where we will create each sprite object, give them a color, and give them a position:

```
createTileSprite:function(tileId){
  // create sprite with the image
  this.tileSprites[tileId] = cc.Sprite.create(s_Tile);
  // set colour based on the tile's data
  this.tileSprites[tileId].setColor(this.getColourForTile(this.
tileData[tileId]));
  // set colour based on the tile's index
  this.tileSprites[tileId].setPosition(this.
getPositionForTile(tileId));
  // save the index of the tile as user data
  this.tileSprites[tileId].setUserData(tileId);
  // add the sprite to the batch node
  this.spriteBatchNode.addChild(this.tileSprites[tileId]);
},
```

The `createTileSprite` function, which is called in a loop, creates a sprite and sets the respective position and color. The position is calculated based on the tile's ID within the grid, in the function `getPositionForTile`. The color is decided based on the `E_COLOUR_TYPE` value of the corresponding cell in the `tileData` array in the `getColourForTile` function.

Please refer to the code bundle for this chapter for the implementation of these two functions. Notice how the `tileId` value for each tile sprite is saved as user data. We will make good use of this data a little later in the chapter.

Creating the Heads-Up Display

A **Heads-Up Display (HUD)** is the part of the game's user interface that delivers information to the user. For this game, we have just two pieces of information that we need to tell the user about, that is, the score and the time left. As such, we initialize these variables and create respective labels and add them to `GameWorld`. The code is as follows:

```
createHUD:function(){
  // initialise score and time
```

```
    this.score = 0;
    this.time = 60;

    // create labels for score and time
    this.scoreLabel = cc.LabelTTF.create("Score:" + this.score, "Comic
Sans MS", 18);
    this.scoreLabel.setPosition(cc.p(this.screenSize.width * 0.33, this.
screenSize.height * 0.875));
    this.addChild(this.scoreLabel);
    this.timeLabel = cc.LabelTTF.create("Time:" + this.time, "Comic Sans
MS", 18);
    this.timeLabel.setPosition(cc.p(this.screenSize.width * 0.66, this.
screenSize.height * 0.875));
    this.addChild(this.timeLabel);
  },
```

The countdown timer

A countdown timer is quite common in many time-based games. It serves the purpose of getting the user charged-up to tackle the level, and it also prevents the user from losing any time because the level started before the user could get ready.

Let's take a look at the following code:

```
doCountdownAnimation:function(){
  // create the four labels
  var labels = [];
  for(var i = 0; i < 4; ++i)
  {
    labels[i] = cc.LabelTTF.create("", "Comic Sans MS", 52);
    // position the label at the centre of the screen
    labels[i].setPosition(cc.p(this.screenSize.width/2, this.
screenSize.height/2));
    // reduce opacity so that the label is invisible
    labels[i].setOpacity(0);
    // enlarge the label
    labels[i].setScale(3);
    this.addChild(labels[i]);
  }

  // assign strings
  labels[0].setString("3");
  labels[1].setString("2");
```

```
    labels[2].setString("1");
    labels[3].setString("Start");

    // fade in and scale down at the same time
    var fadeInScaleDown = cc.Spawn.create(cc.FadeIn.create(0.25),
  cc.EaseBackOut.create(cc.ScaleTo.create(0.25, 1)));
    // stay on screen for a bit
    var waitOnScreen = cc.DelayTime.create(0.75);
    // remove label and cleanup
    var removeSelf = cc.RemoveSelf.create(true);

    for(var i = 0; i < 4; ++i)
    {
      // since the labels should appear one after the other,
      // we give them increasing delays before they appear
      var delayBeforeAppearing = cc.DelayTime.create(i);
      var countdownAnimation = cc.Sequence.create(delayBeforeAppearing,
  fadeInScaleDown, waitOnScreen, removeSelf);
      labels[i].runAction(countdownAnimation);
    }

    // after the animation has finished, start the game
    var waitForAnimation = cc.DelayTime.create(4);
    var finishCountdownAnimation = cc.CallFunc.create(this.
  finishCountdownAnimation, this);
    this.runAction(cc.Sequence.create(waitForAnimation,
  finishCountdownAnimation));
  },

  finishCountdownAnimation:function(){
    // start executing the game timer
    this.schedule(this.updateTimer, 1);
    // finally allow the user to touch
    this.setTouchEnabled(true);
    this.pauseButton.setEnabled(true);
  },
```

We declare an array to hold the labels and run a loop to create the four labels. In this loop, the position, opacity, and scale for each label is set. Notice how the scale of the label is set to `3` and opacity is set to `0`. This is because we want the text to scale down from large to small and fade in while entering the screen. Finally, add the label to `GameWorld`. Now that the labels are created and added the way we want, we need to dramatize their entry and exit. We do this using one of the most powerful features of the Cocos2d-x engine—actions!

Actions are lightweight classes that you can run on a node to transform it. Actions allow you to move, scale, rotate, fade, tint, and do much more to a node. Since actions can run on any node, we can use them with everything from sprites to labels and from layers to even scenes!

We use the `cc.Spawn` class to create our first action, `fadeInScaleDown`. The `cc.Spawn` class allows us to run multiple finite time actions at the same time on a given node. In this case, the two actions that need to be run simultaneously are `cc.FadeIn` and `cc.ScaleTo`. Notice how the `cc.ScaleTo` object is wrapped by a `cc.EaseBackOut` action. The `cc.EaseBackOut` class is inherited from `cc.ActionEase`. It will basically add a special easing effect to the `cc.ActionInterval` object that is passed into it.

Easing actions are a great way to make transformations in the game much more aesthetically appealing and fun. They can be used to make simple actions look elastic or bouncy, or give them a sinusoidal effect or just a simple easing effect. To best understand what `cc.EaseBackOut` and other `cc.ActionEase` actions do, I suggest that you check out the Cocos2d-x or Cocos2d-html5 test cases.

Next, we create a `cc.DelayTime` action called `waitOnScreen`. This is because we want the text to stay there for a bit so the user can read it. The last and final action to be run will be a `cc.RemoveSelf` action. As the name suggests, this action will remove the node it is being run on from its parent and clean it up. Notice how we have created the array as a function variable and not a member variable. Since we use `cc.RemoveSelf`, we don't need to maintain a reference and manually delete these labels.

The `cc.RemoveSelf` action is great for special effects in the game. Special effects may include simple animations or labels that are added, animate for a bit, and then need to be removed. In this way, you can create a node, run an action on it, and forget about it!

Examples may include simple explosion animations that appear when a character collides in the game, bonus score animations, and so on.

These form our three basic actions, but we need the labels to appear and disappear one after another. In a loop, we create another `cc.DelayTime` action and pass an incremental value so that each label has to wait just the right amount of time before its `fadeInScaleDown` animation begins. Finally, we chain these actions together into a `cc.Sequence` object named `countdownAnimation` so that each action is run one after another on each of the labels. The `cc.Sequence` class allows us to run multiple finite time actions one after the other on a given node.

The countdown animation that has just been implemented can be achieved in a far more efficient way using just a single label with some well designed actions. I will leave this for you as an exercise (hint: make use of the `cc.Repeat` action).

Once our countdown animation has finished, the user is ready to play the game, but we need to be notified when the countdown animation has ended. Thus, we add a delay of 4 seconds and a callback to the `finishCountdownAnimation` function. This is where we schedule the `updateTimer` function to run every second and enable touch on the game world.

Let's get touchy...

Touch events are broadcasted to all `cc.Layers` in the scene graph that have registered for touch events by calling `setTouchEnabled(true)`. The engine provides various functions that offer different kinds of touch information.

For our game, all we need is a single touch. So, we shall override just the `onTouchesBegan` function that provides us with a set of touches. Notice the difference in the name of the function versus Cocos2d-x API. Here is the `onTouchesBegan` function from the `gameworld.js` file:

```
onTouchesBegan:function (touches, event) {
  // get touch coordinates
  var touch = cc.p(touches[0].getLocation().x, touches[0].
getLocation().y);
  // calculate touch within the grid
  var touchWithinGrid = cc.pSub(touch, GAMEPLAY_OFFSET);
  // calculate the column touched
  var col = Math.floor(touchWithinGrid.x / TILE_SIZE);
  // calculate the row touched
  var row = Math.floor(touchWithinGrid.y / TILE_SIZE);
  // calculate the id of the touched tile
  var touchedTile = row * NUM_COLS + col;

  // simple bounds checking to ignore touches outside of the grid
  if(col < 0 || col >= NUM_COLS || row < 0 || row >= NUM_ROWS)
  return;

  // disable touch so that the subsequent functions have time to
execute
  this.setTouchEnabled(false);
  this.findTilesToRemove(col, row, this.tileData[touchedTile]);
  this.updateScore(touch);
```

```
    this.removeTilesWithAnimation();
    this.findTilesToShift();
},
```

Once we have got the point of touch, we calculate exactly where the touch has occurred within the grid of tiles and subsequently the column, row, and exact tile that has been touched. Equipped with this information, we can actually go ahead and begin coding the core gameplay.

An important thing to notice is how touch is disabled here. This is done so that the subsequent animations are given enough time to finish. Not doing this would result in a few of the tiles staying on screen and leaving blank spaces. You are encouraged to comment this line to see exactly what happens in this case.

The core gameplay

The core gameplay will consist of the following steps:

1. Finding the tile/s to be removed
2. Removing the tile/s with an awesome effect
3. Finding and shifting the tiles above into the recently vacated space with an awesome effect
4. Adding new tiles
5. Adding score and bonus
6. Ending the game when the time has finished

We will go over each of these separately and in sufficient detail, starting with the recursive logic to find which tiles to remove. To make it easy to understand what each function is actually doing, there are screenshots after each stage.

Finding the tiles

The first step in our gameplay is finding the tiles that should be cleared based on the tile that the user has touched. This is done in the `findTilesToRemove` function as follows:

```
findTilesToRemove:function(col, row, tileColour){
  // first do bounds checking
  if(col < 0 || col >= NUM_COLS || row < 0 || row >= NUM_ROWS)
  return;
```

```
    // calculate the ID of the tile using col & row
    var tileId = row * NUM_COLS + col;

    // now check if tile is of required colour
    if(this.tileData[tileId] != tileColour)
    return;

    // check if tile is already saved
    if(this.tilesToRemove.indexOf(tileId) >= 0)
    return;

    // save the tile to be removed
    this.tilesToRemove.push(tileId);

    // check up
    this.findTilesToRemove(col, row+1, tileColour);

    // check down
    this.findTilesToRemove(col, row-1, tileColour);

    // check left
    this.findTilesToRemove(col-1, row, tileColour);

    // check right
    this.findTilesToRemove(col+1, row, tileColour);
  },
```

The `findTilesToRemove` function is a recursive function that takes a column, row, and target color (the color of the tile that the user touched). The initial call to this function is executed in the `onTouchesBegan` function.

A simple bounds validation is performed on the input parameters and control is returned in case of any invalidation. Once the bounds have been validated, the ID for the given tile is calculated based on the row and column the tile belongs to. This is the index of the specific tile's data in the `tileData` array. The tile is then pushed into the `tilesToRemove` array if its color matches the target color and if it hasn't already been pushed. What follows then are the recursive calls that check for matching tiles in the four directions: up, down, left, and right.

Before we proceed to the next step in our gameplay, let's see what we have so far. The red dot is the point the user touched and the tiles highlighted are the ones that the `findTilesToRemove` function has found for us.

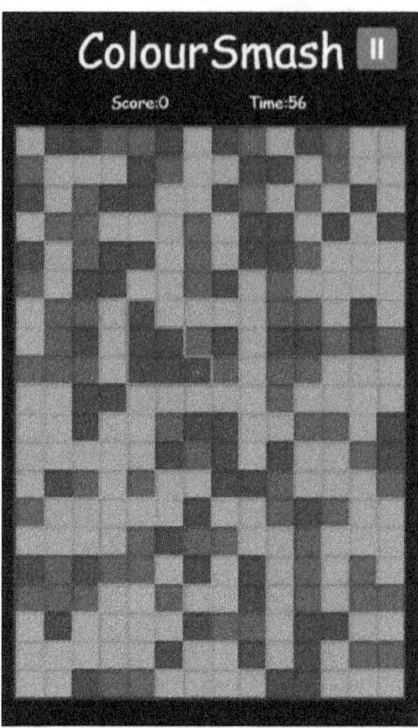

Removing the tiles

The next logical step after finding the tiles that need to be removed is actually removing them. This happens in the `removeTilesWithAnimation` function from the `gameworld.js` file:

```
removeTilesWithAnimation:function(){
  for(var i = 0; i < this.tilesToRemove.length; ++i)
  {
    // first clear the tile's data
    this.tileData[this.tilesToRemove[i]] = E_COLOUR_TYPE.E_COLOUR_
NONE;
    // the tile should scale down with easing and then remove itself
    this.tileSprites[this.tilesToRemove[i]].runAction(cc.Sequence.
create(cc.EaseBackIn.create(cc.ScaleTo.create(0.25, 0.0)),
cc.RemoveSelf.create(true)));
    // nullify the tile's sprite
    this.tileSprites[this.tilesToRemove[i]] = null;
  }
```

```
    // wait for the scale down animation to finish then bring down the
tiles from above
    this.spriteBatchNode.runAction(cc.Sequence.create(cc.DelayTime.
create(0.25), cc.CallFunc.create(this.bringDownTiles, this)));
  },
```

The first order of business in this function would be to clear the data used to represent the tile, so we set it to `E_COLOUR_NONE`. Now comes the fun part—creating a nice animation sequence for the exit of the tile. This will consist of a scale-down animation wrapped by a neat `cc.EaseBackIn` ease effect.

Now, all we need to do is nullify the tile's sprite since the engine will take care of removing and cleaning up the sprite for us by virtue of the `cc.RemoveSelf` action. This animation will take time to finish, and we must wait, so we create a sequence consisting of a delay (with a duration the same as the scale-down animation) and a callback to the `bringDownTiles` function. We run this action on the `spriteBatchNode` object.

Let's see what the game looks like after the `removeTilesWithAnimation` function has executed:

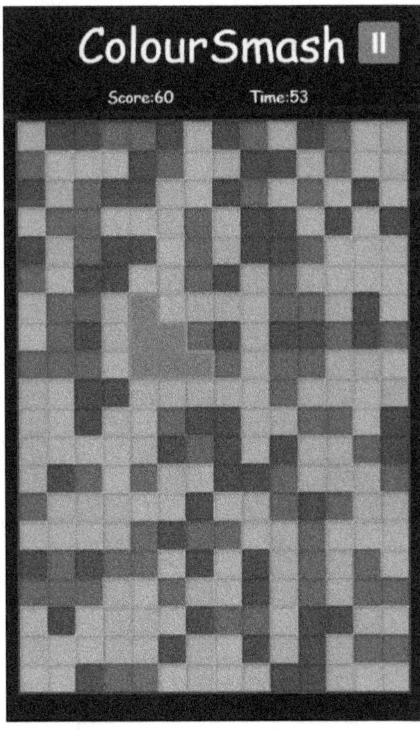

Finding and shifting tiles from above

As you can see in the preceding screenshot, we're left with a big hole in our gameplay. We now need the tiles above to fall down and fill this hole. This happens in the `findTilesToShift` function from the `gameworld.js` file:

```
findTilesToShift:function(){
  // first sort the tiles to be removed, in descending order
  this.tilesToRemove.sort(function(a, b){return b-a});

  // for each tile, bring down all the tiles belonging to the same
column that are above the current tile
  for(var i = 0; i < this.tilesToRemove.length; ++i)
  {
    // calculate column and row for the current tile to be removed
    var col = Math.floor(this.tilesToRemove[i] % NUM_COLS);
    var row = Math.floor(this.tilesToRemove[i] / NUM_COLS);

    // iterate through each row above the current tile
    for(var j = row+1; j < NUM_ROWS; ++j)
    {
      // each tile gets the data of the tile exactly above it
      this.tileData[(j-1) * NUM_COLS + col] = this.tileData[j * NUM_
COLS + col];
      // each tile now refers to the sprite of the tile exactly above
it
      this.tileSprites[(j-1) * NUM_COLS + col] = this.tileSprites[j *
NUM_COLS + col];
      // null checking...this sprite may have already been nullified
by removeTilesWithAnimation
      if(this.tileSprites[(j-1) * NUM_COLS + col])
      {
        // save the new index as user data
        this.tileSprites[(j-1) * NUM_COLS + col].setUserData((j-1) *
NUM_COLS + col);
        // save this tile's sprite so that it is animated, but only if
it hasn't already been saved
        if(this.tilesToShift.indexOf(this.tileSprites[(j-1) * NUM_COLS
+ col]) == -1)
        this.tilesToShift.push(this.tileSprites[(j-1) * NUM_COLS +
col]);
      }
    }
```

```
        // after shifting the whole column down, the tile at the top of
the column will be empty
        // set the data to -1...-1 means empty
        this.tileData[(NUM_ROWS-1) * NUM_COLS + col] = -1;
        // nullify the sprite's reference
        this.tileSprites[(NUM_ROWS-1) * NUM_COLS + col] = null;
    }
},
```

Before actually shifting anything, we use some JavaScript trickery to quickly sort the tiles in descending order. Now within a loop, we find out exactly which column and row the current tile belongs to. Then, we iterate through every tile above the current tile and assign the data and sprite of the above tile to the data and sprite of the current tile.

Before saving this tile's sprite into the `tilesToShift` array, we check to see if the sprite hasn't already been nullified by the `removeTilesWithAnimation` function. Notice how we set the user data of the tile's sprite to reflect its new index. Finally, we push this sprite into the `tilesToShift` array, if it hasn't already been pushed.

Once this is done, we will have a single tile right at the top of the grid that is now empty. For this empty tile, we set the data to `-1` and nullify the sprite's reference. This same set of instructions continues for each of the tiles within the `tilesToRemove` array until all tiles have been filled with tiles from above. Now, we need to actually communicate this shift of tiles to the user through a smooth bounce animation. This happens in the `bringDownTiles` function in the `gameworld.js` file as follows:

```
bringDownTiles:function(){
    for(var i = 0; i < this.tilesToShift.length; ++i)
    {
        // the tiles should move to their new positions with an awesome
looking bounce
        this.tilesToShift[i].runAction(cc.EaseBounceOut.create(cc.
MoveTo.create(0.25, this.getPositionForTile(this.tilesToShift[i].
getUserData()))));
    }
    // wait for the movement to finish then add new tiles
    this.spriteBatchNode.runAction(cc.Sequence.create(cc.DelayTime.
create(0.25), cc.CallFunc.create(this.addNewTiles, this)));
},
```

In the `bringDownTiles` function, we loop over the `tilesToShift` array and run a `cc.MoveTo` action wrapped by a `cc.EaseBounceOut` ease action. Notice how we use the user data to get the new position for the tile's sprite. The tile's index is stored as user data into the sprite so that we could use it at any time to calculate the tile's correct position.

Once again, we wait for the animation to finish before moving forward to the next set of instructions. Let's take a look at what the game world looks like at this point. Don't be surprised by the **+60** text there, we will get to it soon.

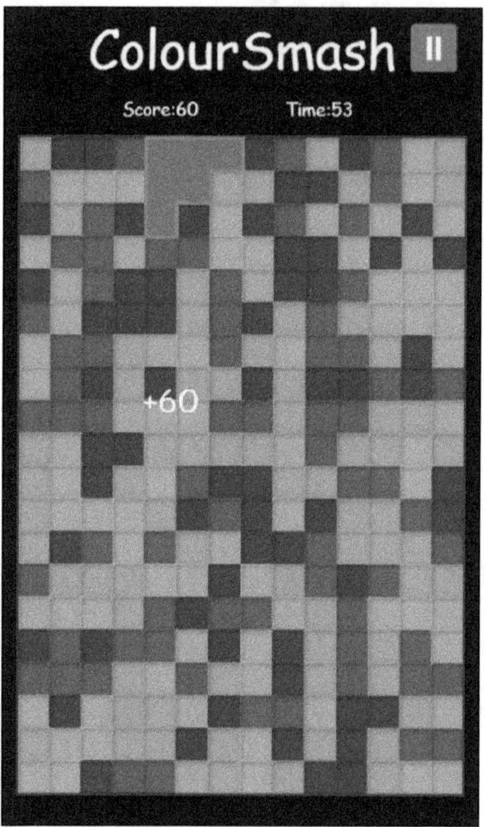

Adding new tiles

We have successfully managed to find and remove the tiles the user has cleverly targeted, and we have also shifted tiles from above to fill in the gaps. Now we need to add new tiles so the game can continue such that there are no gaps left. This happens in the `addNewTiles` function in the `gameworld.js` file as follows:

```
addNewTiles:function(){
```

```
    // first search for all tiles having value -1...-1 means empty
    var emptyTileIndices = [], i = -1;
    while( (i = this.tileData.indexOf(-1, i+1)) != -1){
    emptyTileIndices.push(i);
    }

    // now create tile data and sprites
    for(var i = 0; i < emptyTileIndices.length; ++i)
    {
    // generate tile data randomly
    this.tileData[emptyTileIndices[i]] = 1 + Math.floor(Math.random() *
  MAX_COLOURS);
    // create tile sprite based on tile data
    this.createTileSprite(emptyTileIndices[i]);
    }

    // animate the entry of the sprites
    for(var i = 0; i < emptyTileIndices.length; ++i)
    {
      // set the scale to 0
      this.tileSprites[emptyTileIndices[i]].setScale(0);
      // scale the sprite up with a neat easing effect
      this.tileSprites[emptyTileIndices[i]].runAction(cc.EaseBackOut.
  create(cc.ScaleTo.create(0.125, 1)));
    }

    // the move has finally finished, do some cleanup
    this.cleanUpAfterMove();
  },
```

We start by finding the indices where new tiles are required. We use some JavaScript trickery to quickly find all the tiles having data `-1` in our `tileData` array and push them into the `emptyTileIndices` array.

Now we need to simply loop over this array and randomly generate the tile's data and the tile's sprite. However, this is not enough. We need to animate the entry of the tiles we just created. So, we scale them down completely and then run a scale-up action with an ease effect.

We have now completed a single move that the user has made and it is time for some cleanup. Here is the `cleanUpAfterMove` function of `gameworld.js`:

```
  cleanUpAfterMove:function(){
    // empty the arrays
    this.tilesToRemove = [];
```

```
    this.tilesToShift = [];
    // enable touch so the user can continue playing, but only if the
  game isn't over
    if(this.isGameOver == false)
    this.setTouchEnabled(true);
  },
```

In the cleanup function, we simply empty the `tilesToRemove` and `tilesToShift` arrays. We enable the touch so that the user can continue playing. Remember that we had disabled touch in the `onTouchesBegan` function. Of course, touch should only be enabled if the game has not ended.

This is what the game world looks like after we've added new tiles:

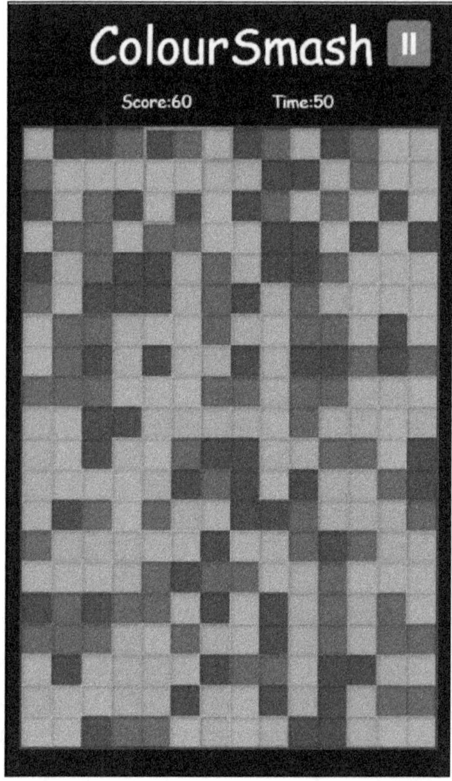

Adding score and bonus

So the user has taken the effort to make a move, the tiles have gone, and new ones have arrived, but the user hasn't been rewarded for this at all. So let's give the user some positive feedback in terms of their score and check if the user has made a move good enough to earn a bonus.

All this magic happens in the `updateScore` function in the `gameworld.js` file as follows:

```
updateScore:function(point){
  // count the number of tiles the user just removed
  var numTiles = this.tilesToRemove.length;

  // calculate score for this move
  var scoreToAdd = numTiles * SCORE_PER_TILE;

  // check if a bonus has been achieved
  for(var i = 0; i < BONUS.length; ++i)
  {
    if(numTiles >= BONUS[i])
    {
      // add the bonus to the score for this move
      scoreToAdd += BONUS[i] * 20;
      break;
    }
  }

  // display the score for this move
  this.showScoreText(scoreToAdd, point);
  // add the score for this move to the total score
  this.score += scoreToAdd;
  // update the total score label
  this.scoreLabel.setString("Score:" + this.score);
  // run a simple action so the user knows the score is being added
  // use the ease functions to create a heart beat effect
  this.scoreLabel.runAction(cc.Sequence.create(cc.EaseSineIn.
create(cc.ScaleTo.create(0.125, 1.1)), cc.EaseSineOut.create(cc.
ScaleTo.create(0.125, 1))));
},
```

We calculate the score for the last move by counting the number of tiles removed in the last move. Remember that this function is called right after the `findTilesToRemove` function in `onTouchesBegan`, so `tilesRemoved` still has its data. We now compare the number of tiles removed with our bonus array `BONUS`, and add the respective score if the user managed to remove more than the predefined tiles to achieve a bonus.

This score value is added to the total score and the corresponding label's string is updated. However, merely setting the string to reflect the new score is not enough in today's games. It is very vital to get the users' attention and remind them that they did something cool or earned something awesome. Thus, we run a simple and subtle scale-up/scale-down animation on the score label. Notice how the ease actions are used here. This results in a heartbeat effect on the otherwise simple scaling animation.

We notify the score achieved in each move to the user using the `showScoreText` function:

```
// this function can be used to display any message to the user
// but we will use it to display the score for each move
showScoreText:function(scoreToAdd, point){
  // create the label with the score & place it at the respective
point
  var bonusLabel = cc.LabelTTF.create("+" + scoreToAdd, "Comic Sans
MS", 32);
  bonusLabel.setPosition(point);
  // initially scale it down completely
  bonusLabel.setScale(0);
  // give it a yellow colour
  bonusLabel.setColor(cc.YELLOW);
  this.addChild(bonusLabel, 10);

  // animate the bonus label so that it scales up with a nice easing
effect
  bonusLabel.runAction( cc.Sequence.create(cc.EaseBackOut.create(cc.
ScaleTo.create(0.125, 1)),
  cc.DelayTime.create(1),
  // it should stay on screen so the user can read it
  cc.EaseBackIn.create(cc.ScaleTo.create(0.125, 0))
  // scale it back down with a nice easing effect
  cc.RemoveSelf.create(true) ));
  // its task is finished, so remove it with cleanup
},
```

The preceding function can be used to display any kind of text notification to the user. For the purpose of our game, we will use it only to display the score in each move. The function is quite simple and precise. It creates a label with the string passed as a parameter and places it at the position passed as a parameter. This function also animates the text so it scales up with some easing, stays for some time so the user registers it, scales down again with easing, and finally removes the text.

It seems as if we have almost finished our first game, but there is still a vital aspect of this game that is missing—the timer. What was the point of running a scheduler every second? Well let's take a look.

Updating the timer

We scheduled the timer as soon as the countdown animation had finished by calling the `updateTimer` function every second, but what exactly are we doing with this `updateTimer` function?

Let's take a look at the code:

```
updateTimer:function(){
  // this is called every second so reduce the time left by 1
  this.time --;
  // update the time left label
  this.timeLabel.setString("Time:" + this.time);

  // the user's time is up
  if(this.time<= 0)
  {
    // game is now over
    this.isGameOver = true;
    // unschedule the timer
    this.unschedule(this.updateTimer);
    // stop animating the time label
    this.timeLabel.stopAllActions();
    // disable touch
    this.setTouchEnabled(false);
    // disable the pause button
    this.pauseButton.setEnabled(false);
    // display the game over popup
    this.showGameOverPopup();
  }
```

```
    else if(this.time == 5)
    {
      // get the user's attention...there are only 5 seconds left
      // make the timer label scale up and down so the user knows the
  game is about to end
      // use the ease functions to create a heart beat effect
      var timeUp = cc.Sequence.create(cc.EaseSineIn.create(cc.ScaleTo.
  create(0.125, 1.1)), cc.EaseSineOut.create(cc.ScaleTo.create(0.125,
  1)));
      // repeat this action forever
      this.timeLabel.runAction(cc.RepeatForever.create(timeUp));
    }
  },
```

At the start of the function, the time variable is decremented and the respective label's string is updated. Once the time is up, the `isGameOver` flag is enabled. We don't need the scheduler to call the `updateTimer` function anymore, so we unschedule it. We disable touch on the `GameWorld` layer and disable the pause button. Finally, we show a game-over popup.

We add a little more fun into the game by rapidly scaling up and down the time label when there are 5 seconds or less left in the game. Again, the ease actions are used cleverly to create a heartbeat effect. This will not only inform the users that the game is about to end, but also get them to hurry up and score as many points as possible.

This completes the flow of the game. The only thing missing is the pause popup, which is created in the `showPausePopup` function that gets called when the handler for the `pauseButton` object is executed. Both the pause and game-over popups contain two or more buttons that serve to restart the game or navigate to the main menu. The logic for creating these popups is pretty simplistic, so we won't spend time going over the details. Also, there are a few cool things to look at in the code for the `MainMenu` class in the `mainmenu.js` file. Some liveliness and dynamics have been added to an otherwise static screen. You should refer to your code bundle for the implementation.

Summary

You've learned a lot in this chapter by building ColourSmash. By now, you should be familiar with the structure and relationship of the `cc.Scene` and `cc.Layer`. This same structure will be used in the forthcoming projects, both in Cocos2d-html5 and Cocos2d-x.

We also made extensive use of a wide variety of actions, thereby understanding how powerful they make the Cocos2d-x engine. You have also understood the importance of easing while using actions. You learned how to register touches and how to run simple schedulers. There is still a lot to learn and a lot more fun ahead.

Our next game is similar to an extremely famous game that took the world by storm. You're surely in for a treat!

2

How to Fly a Dragon!

This is the story of a dragon trapped inside a castle. You might ask why would a mighty creature like a dragon be trapped inside a castle. Well, obviously because he has deformed wings that are too small to carry his weight! It's our duty to help this poor creature out of this horrendous castle! We will continue using Cocos2d-html5 to create this charming game about a dragon trying to escape the bounds of the castle, with the player tapping to help the dragon fly. We'll call this game **DragonDash**.

In this chapter, you'll learn:

- How to load a sprite sheet
- How to create and use a `cc.Animation`
- How to implement simple gravity and rectangular collision detection
- How to play HTML5 audio and persistently store data in the browser

This is what we will achieve by the end of this chapter:

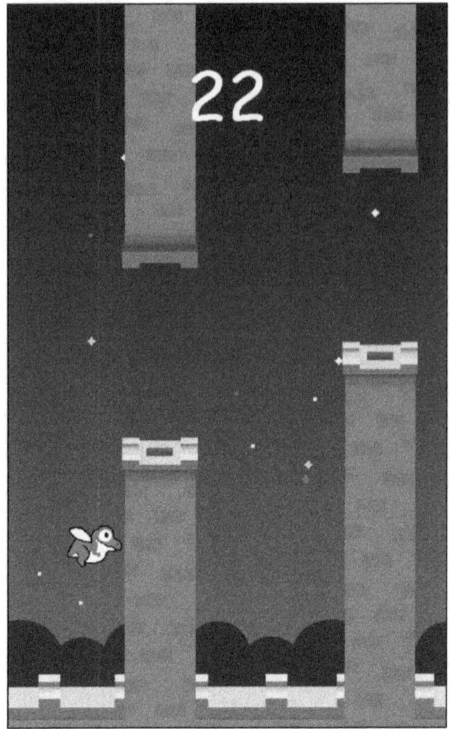

Getting to know sprite sheets

The first game we made was so simple that it just used a single image file. But the story of our dragon will need much more. So, we finally have enough art to actually collate it into a sprite sheet. As you may already know, a sprite sheet is an image that contains many other images. A sprite sheet needs a texture file and an information file to tell the engine where each individual image or frame lies within the texture. Since this is a fairly small game, you have just one sprite sheet that looks like this:

I created this sprite sheet and the corresponding plist using **Texture Packer**. Texture Packer is a great utility that helps you compose all of your sprite frames into a single sprite sheet. This is just one of the many things Texture Packer can do for you and your graphics artist. You can find Texture Packer and relevant information at the following URL:

`https://www.codeandweb.com/texturepacker`

You must load a sprite sheet into the `cc.SpriteFrameCache` if you intend to use its sprites. The code is as follows:

```
cc.SpriteFrameCache.getInstance().addSpriteFrames(
  "beautiful_dragon.plist");
```

In the preceding code, `"beautiful_dragon.plist"` is an example of a `.plist` file for a given sprite sheet. Don't bother about the syntax there. The code reads `getInstance` instead of `sharedSpriteFrameCache` that you're familiar with. It's among the few differences between the C++ and JavaScript versions of the engine.

Now that you've learned how to load sprite sheets, we can proceed with the creation of the scenes of this game. Similar to our first game, this is also composed of two scenes: the main menu / opening scene and the game world. So without further ado, let's define our fairy tale's main menu!

Creating a lively menu screen

The main menu needs to look something like this, but our dragon needs to be flying. Therefore, the castle wall and the backdrop should also move.

Judging from the screenshot, you already know that we will be covering a major chunk of the game just creating this screen. Well, what can you do, our little dragon always wants to fly! So let's take some time and analyze the various things we need to do in order to accomplish the lively fairy tale menu screen.

Here are the things we need to implement:

1. Create a dragon that can fly. Don't worry the frame animation takes care of that, we just need to move him!
2. Create an environment with a background, some stars, and two continuously scrolling layers with a parallax effect.
3. Create the basic UI.

Our first task dictates that we must create a dragon that can fly. This means our character must have an animation wherein it flaps its wings and some motion so that it moves upwards and downwards.

We will create the frame animation by hand. Don't worry, we won't be "drawing" the frames by hand. I meant creating the animation by specifying each frame. The code is as follows:

```
addDragonAnimation:function(){
  // push the frames that will make up the dragon's flying animation
  var spriteFrames = [];
  spriteFrames.push(cc.SpriteFrameCache.getInstance().
getSpriteFrame("dhch_1"));
  spriteFrames.push(cc.SpriteFrameCache.getInstance().
getSpriteFrame("dhch_2"));
  spriteFrames.push(cc.SpriteFrameCache.getInstance().
getSpriteFrame("dhch_3"));
  spriteFrames.push(cc.SpriteFrameCache.getInstance().
getSpriteFrame("dhch_2"));
  spriteFrames.push(cc.SpriteFrameCache.getInstance().
getSpriteFrame("dhch_1"));

  // create the animation with the array of sprite frames and delay
per frame
  var dragonAnimation = cc.Animation.create(spriteFrames, 0.1);
  // add the created animation to the cache with a name so it can be
reused
  cc.AnimationCache.getInstance().addAnimation(dragonAnimation,
"dragonFlying");
},
```

We start by pushing sprite frames into an array. Then, create a `cc.Animation` object, passing into the `create` function the array of frames and the amount of time each frame should stay on the screen. This is the frame rate of the animation. We then add the animation into the `cc.AnimationCache` because we will use it again in the game world. This technique of creating a `cc.Animation` has been demonstrated for understanding only. Of course, this is not how you will generally go about creating animations. There are neat little animation plists for that. We will cover this topic soon. For now, let's proceed by creating the sprite, setting its position, and adding it to a batch node in the `addDragon` function as follows:

```
addDragon:function(){
  // create sprite and add to the sprite batch node
  var dragonSprite = cc.Sprite.createWithSpriteFrameName("dhch_1");
  dragonSprite.setPosition(cc.p(this.screenSize.width * 0.2, this.
screenSize.height * 0.5));
```

```
    this.spriteBatchNode.addChild(dragonSprite, E_ZORDER.E_LAYER_
PLAYER);

    // fetch flying animation from cache & repeat it on the dragon's
sprite
    var animation = cc.AnimationCache.getInstance().
getAnimation("dragonFlying");
    dragonSprite.runAction(cc.RepeatForever.create(cc.Animate.
create(animation)));

    // create a hover movement and repeat it on the dragon's sprite
    var flySequence = cc.Sequence.create(cc.EaseSineOut.create(cc.
MoveBy.create(animation.getDuration()/2, cc.p(0, 10))),
cc.EaseSineOut.create(cc.MoveBy.create(animation.getDuration()/2,
cc.p(0, -10))));
    dragonSprite.runAction(cc.RepeatForever.create(flySequence));
},
```

Now that we've added the sprite to `spriteBatchNode`, we'll run the animation we just created by fetching it from the cache. Finally, the flying motion is implemented using a sequence of `cc.Actions`, just like you've seen in the previous chapter. Run these actions on a sprite repeatedly and our dragon begins to fly. Notice how the duration for `cc.MoveBy` is based on the duration of the animation. This is done so that the flapping of the dragon's wings synchronizes with its up-and-down flying motion. Okay, so we have a flying dragon now, but it looks like it's flying through a black hole! So let's create the environment.

Creating a fairy tale

Since we are dealing with a dragon here, it seems only fair that the environment should also be out of a fairy tale. Hence, we will build our environment with a castle, a midnight sky full of twinkling stars, and a few dark silhouettes. Since we will need this exact same environment in our other major scene, that is, the game world, it's a good idea to separate it out into another class. Thus, we have the `FairytaleManager` class defined in the `fairytaleManager.js` file:

```
var MAX_SCROLLING_SPEED = 6;
var CASTLE_SPRITE_Y = -50;
var SILHOUETTE_SPRITE_Y = 100;
var MAX_STARS = 15;
```

```
function FairytaleManager(parent)
{
  // save reference to GameWorld
  this.parent = parent;
  this.screenSize = parent.screenSize;
  // initialise variables
  this.castleSpriteSize = cc.SIZE_ZERO;
  this.castleSprites = [];
  this.lastCastleIndex = 0;
  this.silhouetteSpriteSize = cc.SIZE_ZERO;
  this.silhouetteSprites = [];
  this.lastSilhouetteIndex = 0;
}
```

First, we declare a few global quantities that we will require. The `constructor` function for `FairytaleManager` is fairly straightforward. We will maintain a reference of the parent, which could be either `MainMenu` or `GameWorld`. You will find arrays named `castleSprites` and `silhouetteSprites`. These arrays store the sprites for our magnificent, infinitely long castle walls and silhouettes. Don't tell the dragon that the castle is infinitely long just yet!

Let's take a look at the code:

```
FairytaleManager.prototype.init = function() {
  // this makes a nice midnight sky
  var background = cc.LayerGradient.create(cc.c4b(15, 15, 25, 255),
cc.c4b(84, 83, 104, 255));
  this.parent.addChild(background, E_ZORDER.E_LAYER_BG);

  this.createCastle();
  this.createSilhouette();
  this.createStars();
};
```

We also have an `init` function for convenience. This is where we begin to create our fairy tale environment—starting with the midnight blue sky, the castle, silhouettes, and the stars.

Building an infinitely long castle in 20 lines of code

Yes it is possible to build an infinitely long castle in 20 lines of code, especially when you have a powerful engine doing all the heavy lifting for you. Let's look at the `createCastle` function:

```
FairytaleManager.prototype.createCastle = function() {
  // record size of the castle wall sprite
  this.castleSpriteSize = cc.SpriteFrameCache.getInstance().
getSpriteFrame("dhbase").getOriginalSize();
  // initial position
  var nextPosition = this.castleSpriteSize.width * 0.5;
  // fill up one & a half screen
  while(nextPosition < this.screenSize.width * 1.5)
  {
    // create castle wall sprite and add it to the parent's batch node
    var castleSprite = cc.Sprite.createWithSpriteFrameName("dhbase");
    castleSprite.setPosition(cc.p(nextPosition, CASTLE_SPRITE_Y));
    this.parent.spriteBatchNode.addChild(castleSprite, E_ZORDER.E_
LAYER_CASTLE);
    // store this sprite...we need to update it
    this.castleSprites.push(castleSprite);
    // the next wall depends on this variable
    nextPosition += this.castleSpriteSize.width;
  }
  // we need this to position the next wall sprite
  this.lastCastleIndex = this.castleSprites.length-1;
};
```

We begin by recording the size of each sprite that will be tiled to form the castle wall into the `castleSpriteSize` variable. Then in a loop, we create sprites and position them next to each other so as to create the seamless castle wall.

Notice that we're adding these sprites to the `spriteBatchNode` of the parent class. We shall take advantage of the fact that we have just one texture here by batch rendering sprites together. Also, pay attention to the additional parameter we pass to the `addChild` function: the z-order. As you may know, the z-order dictates the order in which nodes will be rendered on the screen. Thus, a node with a smaller z-order is rendered before a node with a larger z-order. The z-order enum `E_ZORDER` is defined in `gameworld.js` as follows:

```
var E_ZORDER = {
  E_LAYER_BG:0,
```

```
    E_LAYER_STARS:2,
    E_LAYER_SILHOUETTE:4,
    E_LAYER_CASTLE:6,
    E_LAYER_TOWER:8,
    E_LAYER_PLAYER:10,
    E_LAYER_HUD:12,
    E_LAYER_POPUPS:14
};
```

Subsequently, we push the sprite into the array and increment the `nextPosition` variable so that the next wall is correctly positioned. Finally, store the index of the sprite placed at the end; we will use this shortly. A similar function, called `createSilhouette`, is also written to create the continuous chain of silhouettes. The technique used there is identical to the one used above, so I will skip explaining it.

The technique we just implemented to create a continuous, "tiled" layer of sprites in this chapter is implemented because of a limitation in the Cocos2d-html5 version of the engine. In the C++ version, one would normally modify the texture parameters of a sprite causing it to repeat a texture seamlessly within the sprite. But doing that involves setting some OpenGL parameters, as shown in the following code:

```
// setup the texture to repeat
  ccTexParamstex_params;
  tex_params.minFilter = GL_NEAREST;
  tex_params.magFilter = GL_NEAREST;
  tex_params.wrapS = GL_REPEAT;
  tex_params.wrapT = GL_REPEAT;
  sprite_->getTexture()->setTexParameters(&tex_params);
```

In HTML5, this would translate into WebGL (the JavaScript API for OpenGL) parameters. Since WebGL may not always be supported on the target device's browser, we cannot use that technique to repeat a texture within a sprite.

Adding the stars

We have a midnight sky, a castle, and some silhouettes. But how can there be a midnight sky without stars? Let's add some stars in the `createStars` function:

```
FairytaleManager.prototype.createStars = function() {
  // random number of stars...this night sky always changes
  var numStars = MAX_STARS + Math.floor(Math.random() * MAX_STARS);
  for(var i = 0; i < numStars; ++i)
  {
    var star = null;
```

```
      // either big star or small
      if(Math.random() > 0.5)
        star = cc.Sprite.createWithSpriteFrameName("dhstar1");
       else
         star = cc.Sprite.createWithSpriteFrameName("dhstar2");

       // random position
       var position = cc.p(Math.random() * this.screenSize.width, Math.
random() * this.screenSize.height);
       star.setPosition(position);
       // twinkle twinkle randomly star
       var duration = 1 + Math.random() * 2;
       var action = cc.RepeatForever.create(cc.Sequence.create(cc.
DelayTime.create(duration*2), cc.FadeOut.create(duration), cc.FadeIn.
create(duration)));
       star.runAction(action);
       // add this too the batch node as well
       this.parent.spriteBatchNode.addChild(star);
  }
};
```

We begin by randomly deciding the number of stars in our midnight sky. Then in a loop, we randomly decide between big (`"dhstar1"`) and small (`"dhstar2"`) stars and position them randomly as well. All that randomness must surely add a bit of fairy tale essence to our game. Finally, we repeat a random duration fade-in and fade-out sequence on each star for that magical touch. "Twinkle twinkle randomly stars!"

Well, it looks like we have a magical midnight sky full of stars and a magnificent castle. But the dragon looks quite silly flying without actually moving. So let's help him out by setting things into motion.

Setting things into motion

We'll need to move the castle and the silhouettes to create an illusion of the dragon flying. We do this by updating their position after every tick, as shown here:

```
FairytaleManager.prototype.update = function() {
  this.updateCastle();
  this.updateSilhouette();
};
```

The `update` function will be called from the parent layer (`MainMenu` or `GameWorld`) on every tick. It is here that you will have to move your castle and the backdrop. The `updateCastle` and `updateSilhouette` functions are identical, so I will discuss the `updateCastle` function only:

```
FairytaleManager.prototype.updateCastle = function(){
  for(var i = 0; i < this.castleSprites.length; ++i)
  {
    // first update the position based on the scroll speed
    var castleSprite = this.castleSprites[i];
    castleSprite.setPosition(castleSprite.getPositionX() - MAX_
SCROLLING_SPEED, castleSprite.getPositionY());

    // check if the sprite has gone completely out of the left edge of
the screen
    if(castleSprite.getPositionX() < (this.castleSpriteSize.width *
-0.5))
    {
      // reposition it after the last wall sprite
      var positionX = this.castleSprites[this.lastCastleIndex].
getPositionX() + this.castleSpriteSize.width - MAX_SCROLLING_SPEED;
      castleSprite.setPosition(positionX, castleSprite.
getPositionY());
      // this sprite now becomes the new last wall
      this.lastCastleIndex = i;
    }
  }
};
```

We loop through each sprite of the castle and shift them left by `MAX_SCROLLING_SPEED` pixels. Subsequently, we need to check if a castle sprite has gone completely out of the left edge of the screen. If it has, we need to reposition it at the right end of the screen, next to the sprite that is currently at the end. We already have a variable named `lastCastleIndex` that tells us that. After placing this sprite at the end, we also need to update the `lastCastleIndex` variable. It is worth noting that the `updateSilhouette` function scrolls the silhouette sprites at half the value of `MAX_SCROLLING_SPEED`. This is how we will create a perception of depth or parallax.

We achieved the illusion of an infinitely long castle. Okay, you can go ahead and tell the dragon about it now. It's time to start playing the game anyway.

On to the game world

You already set the environment up in the last two sections. Now we need to code in some gameplay. So we add towers that the dragon must dodge and add some gravity as well as touch controls. All this action happens in our second scene, which goes by the name `GameWorld` and is defined in the `gameworld.js` file. The following are the member variables of `gameworld.js`:

```
// variables
screenSize:null,
spriteBatchNode:null,
score:0,
scoreLabel:null,
mustAddScore:false,
tutorialSprite:null,
popup:null,
castleRoof:0,
hasGameStarted:false,
// managers
towerManager:null,
dragonManager:null,
fairytaleManager:null,
```

You might remember some of the variables declared in the preceding code from the previous chapter. In addition, you can see some variables that record the position of the castle roof, if the game has started and if a score needs to be added. Finally, you will find three variables that will reference our respective managers.

In our first game, we coded all the game logic straight into the `GameWorld` class. This time, we will create separate manager classes for each feature of the game. We have already discussed the `FairytaleManager`. Soon, we'll discuss the `TowerManager` and `DragonManager` classes. The `init` function of `GameWorld` is as follows:

```
init:function () {
  this._super();
  // enable touch
  this.setTouchEnabled(true);
  // store screen size for fast access
  this.screenSize = cc.Director.getInstance().getWinSize();

  // create and add the batch node
  this.spriteBatchNode = cc.SpriteBatchNode.create(s_SpriteSheetImg,
256);
  this.addChild(this.spriteBatchNode, E_ZORDER.E_LAYER_BG + 1);
```

```
    // set the roof of the castle
    this.castleRoof = 100;
    // create & init all managers
    this.towerManager = new TowerManager(this);
    this.towerManager.init();
    this.dragonManager = new DragonManager(this);
    this.dragonManager.init();
    this.fairytaleManager = new FairytaleManager(this);
    this.fairytaleManager.init();
    this.createHUD();

    this.scheduleUpdate();
    return true;
  },
```

First and foremost, enable touch and create the batch node into which you will add all your game's sprites. Next, set the `castleRoof` variable to `100`. This means the roof of the castle is considered to be 100 pixels from the bottom of the screen. Then, you create and initialize the three main managers, create the HUD, and schedule the `update` function.

The HUD for this game is quite simple. You can find the logic for it in the `createHUD` function. It consists of a score label and a sprite for the tutorial that looks like this:

The core gameplay

The core gameplay that will take place in our `GameWorld` scene consists of the following steps:

- Create
    - Creating the dragon
    - Creating the towers
    - Creating the fairy tale environment
- Update
    - Applying gravity and force to the dragon
    - Scrolling towers and keep them coming
    - Updating the fairy tale environment
- Collision detection

Creating the dragon

Let's define a few global "constants" that we will use repeatedly and the constructor of `DragonManager` in the `dragonManager.js` file:

```
var MAX_DRAGON_SPEED = -40;
var FLAP_FORCE = 13;
var ANIMATION_ACTION_TAG = 123;
var MOVEMENT_ACTION_TAG = 121;

function DragonManager(gameWorld)
{
  // save reference to GameWorld
  this.gameWorld = gameWorld;
  this.screenSize = gameWorld.screenSize;
  // initialise variables
  this.dragonSprite = null;
  this.dragonSpeed = cc.POINT_ZERO;
  this.dragonPosition = cc.POINT_ZERO;
  this.mustApplyGravity = false;
}
```

The constructor maintains a reference to `GameWorld` and `screenSize`, and it initializes the variables needed to create and update the dragon. Notice how `mustApplyGravity` has been set to `false`. This is because we don't want the dragon crashing into the castle walls as soon as the game starts. We wait for the user's touch before applying gravity.

Let's take a look at the following code:

```
DragonManager.prototype.init = function() {
  // create sprite and add to GameWorld's sprite batch node
  this.dragonSprite = cc.Sprite.createWithSpriteFrameName("dhch_1");
  this.dragonPosition = cc.p(this.screenSize.width * 0.2, this.
screenSize.height * 0.5);
  this.dragonSprite.setPosition(this.dragonPosition);
  this.gameWorld.spriteBatchNode.addChild(this.dragonSprite, E_
ZORDER.E_LAYER_PLAYER);

  // fetch flying animation from cache & repeat it on the dragon's
sprite
  var animation = cc.AnimationCache.getInstance().
getAnimation("dragonFlying");
  var repeatedAnimation = cc.RepeatForever.create(cc.Animate.
create(animation));
  repeatedAnimation.setTag(ANIMATION_ACTION_TAG);
  this.dragonSprite.runAction(repeatedAnimation);
```

```
    .
    .
    .
};
```

The `init` function is responsible for creating the dragon's sprite and giving the default hovering motion that we saw on the `MainMenu` screen. So, `dragonSprite` is created and added to `spriteBatchNode` of the `GameWorld` and positioned appropriately. We then fetch the flying animation from the `cc.AnimationCache` and run it repeatedly on `dragonSprite`. Consequently, the hovering motion runs just like on the `MainMenu` screen.

Setting tags for actions is a great way to avoid maintaining references to the various actions you may have running on a node. This way, you can get the object of a particular action by calling `yourNode.getActionByTag(actionsTag)` on the node running the action. You can also use `yourNode.stopActionByTag(actionsTag)` to stop the action without a reference to the respective action.

Creating the towers

At the top of the `towerManager.js` file, we will create a small `Tower` object to maintain the upper and lower sprites for the tower as well as its position:

```
function Tower(position)
{
    this.lowerSprite = null;
    this.upperSprite = null;
    this.position = position;
}
```

Next, we define the constructor of `TowerManager` as follows:

```
var VERT_GAP_BWN_TOWERS = 300;
function TowerManager(gameWorld)
{
  // save reference to GameWorld
  this.gameWorld = gameWorld;
  this.screenSize = gameWorld.screenSize;
  // initialise variables
  this.towers = [];
  this.towerSpriteSize = cc.SIZE_ZERO;
  this.firstTowerIndex = 0;
  this.lastTowerIndex = 0;
}
```

The upper and lower sprites for each tower will be separated vertically so that the user can help the dragon pass through. This gap is represented by `VERT_GAP_BWN_TOWERS`. The `TowerManager` constructor maintains a reference to `GameWorld` and records the value of `screenSize`. It also initializes the towers' array and the size for a tower's sprite. The last two variables are convenience variables that will point to the first and last tower, respectively.

Let's take a look at the following code:

```
TowerManager.prototype.init = function() {
  // record size of the tower's sprite
  this.towerSpriteSize = cc.SpriteFrameCache.getInstance().
getSpriteFrame("opst_02").getOriginalSize();

  // create the first pair of towers
  // they should be two whole screens away from the dragon
  var initialPosition = cc.p(this.screenSize.width*2, this.screenSize.
height*0.5);
  this.firstTowerIndex = 0;
  this.createTower(initialPosition);
  // create the remaining towers
  this.lastTowerIndex = 0;
  this.createTower(this.getNextTowerPosition());
  this.lastTowerIndex = 1;
  this.createTower(this.getNextTowerPosition());
  this.lastTowerIndex = 2;
};
```

We start by recording the size of a tower's sprite. Then, the first tower is placed a good distance away from the dragon. You don't want to overwhelm users as soon as they hit play. The distance in this case is two times the screens width. We then create three towers by calling the `createTower` function and passing in a position calculated in the `getNextTowerPosition` function. Observe how the `firstTowerIndex` and `lastTowerIndex` variables are set. Don't worry, you'll understand this soon.

Let's take a look at the following code:

```
TowerManager.prototype.createTower = function(position) {
  // create a new tower and add it to the array
  var tower = new Tower(position);
  this.towers.push(tower);

  // create lower tower sprite & add it to GameWorld's batch node
  tower.lowerSprite = cc.Sprite.createWithSpriteFrameName("opst_02");
```

```
  tower.lowerSprite.setPositionX(position.x);
  tower.lowerSprite.setPositionY( position.y + VERT_GAP_BWN_TOWERS *
-0.5 + this.towerSpriteSize.height * -0.5 );
  this.gameWorld.spriteBatchNode.addChild(tower.lowerSprite, E_
ZORDER.E_LAYER_TOWER);

  // create upper tower sprite & add it to GameWorld's batch node
  tower.upperSprite = cc.Sprite.createWithSpriteFrameName("opst_01");
  tower.upperSprite.setPositionX(position.x);
  tower.upperSprite.setPositionY( position.y + VERT_GAP_BWN_TOWERS *
0.5 + this.towerSpriteSize.height * 0.5 );
  this.gameWorld.spriteBatchNode.addChild(tower.upperSprite, E_
ZORDER.E_LAYER_TOWER);
};
```

First, you create a `Tower` object and push it into the towers' array. You then create the lower and upper sprites for the tower. Both lower and upper sprites will have the same *x* coordinate but different *y* coordinates. The bit of arithmetic here basically creates a vertical gap between the towers and adjusts them according to their anchor points. Finally, the sprites are added into `spriteBatchNode` of `GameWorld`. Now, let's spend some time understanding the `getNextTowerPosition` function, as this will be used to dynamically generate the positions of the towers making our dragon's journey that much more challenging and fun.

Let's take a look at the following code:

```
TowerManager.prototype.getNextTowerPosition = function() {
  // randomly select either above or below last tower
  var isAbove = (Math.random() > 0.5);
  var offset = Math.random() * VERT_GAP_BWN_TOWERS * 0.75;
  offset *= (isAbove) ? 1:-1;

  // new position calculated by adding to last tower's position
  var newPositionX = this.towers[this.lastTowerIndex].position.x +
this.screenSize.width*0.5;
  var newPositionY = this.towers[this.lastTowerIndex].position.y +
offset;

  // limit the point to stay within 30-80% of the screen
  if(newPositionY >= this.screenSize.height * 0.8)
    newPositionY -= VERT_GAP_BWN_TOWERS;
  else if(newPositionY <= this.screenSize.height * 0.3)
    newPositionY += VERT_GAP_BWN_TOWERS;
```

```
    // return the new tower position
    return cc.p(newPositionX, newPositionY);
};
```

First, we choose whether the tower calling this function should be positioned above or below the last tower. Then, an offset or gap is calculated with a random factor of `VERT_GAP_BWN_TOWERS`. This offset is added to the last tower's *y* coordinate and half of the screen's width is added to the last tower's *x* coordinate to get the position for the next tower. By last tower I mean the tower that is currently most to the right or last in line. Finally, we clamp the *y* coordinate to stay between 30-80 percent of the screen. Otherwise, we would have to fly our dragon out of the screen or straight into the castle. I'm sure the dragon would not like the latter.

I shall skip the environment creation since we have already covered it for the `MainMenu` screen.

The update loop

The game will be updated after every tick in the `update` function of `GameWorld` because we called `scheduleUpdate` in the `init` function of `GameWorld`. This is where we need to call the `update` functions of our respective manager classes. The code is as follows:

```
update:function(deltaTime) {
    // update dragon
    this.dragonManager.update();
    // update towers only after game has started
    if(this.hasGameStarted)
    this.towerManager.update();
    // update environment
    this.fairytaleManager.update();
    this.checkCollisions();
},
```

We must update all our managers and check collisions after every tick. That is what our update loop will consist of. Notice how the `update` function of the `TowerManager` class is called only once the game has started. This is because we still want the environment and the dragon to be active while users comprehend the tutorial. But we don't want the towers to start appearing before users have had enough time to understand what they need to do.

Updating the dragon

The `update` function of the `DragonManager` class will be responsible for applying gravity, updating the dragon's position, and checking for collisions between the dragon and the roof of the castle.

Let's take a look at the code:

```
DragonManager.prototype.update = function() {
  // calculate bounding box after applying gravity
  var newAABB = this.dragonSprite.getBoundingBox();
  newAABB.setY(newAABB.getY() + this.dragonSpeed.y);

  // check if the dragon has touched the roof of the castle
  if(newAABB.y <= this.gameWorld.castleRoof)
  {
    // stop downward movement and set position to the roof of the 
castle
    this.dragonSpeed.y = 0;
    this.dragonPosition.y = this.gameWorld.castleRoof + newAABB.
getHeight() * 0.5;

    // dragon must die
    this.dragonDeath();
    // stop the update loop
    this.gameWorld.unscheduleUpdate();
  }
  // apply gravity only if game has started
  else if(this.mustApplyGravity)
  {
    // clamp gravity to a maximum of MAX_DRAGON_SPEED & add it
    this.dragonSpeed.y = ( (this.dragonSpeed.y + GRAVITY) < MAX_
DRAGON_SPEED ) ? MAX_DRAGON_SPEED : (this.dragonSpeed.y + GRAVITY);
  }

  // update position
  this.dragonPosition.y += this.dragonSpeed.y;
  this.dragonSprite.setPosition(this.dragonPosition);
};
```

We start by calling the `getBoundingBox()` function of the `dragonSprite` class that will return a `cc.Rect` to represent the sprite's bounding box. We use this bounding box to check for collisions with the roof of the castle. If a collision has occurred, we stop the dragon from falling and instead position it right on top of the castle roof. We then tell the dragon to die by calling `dragonDeath` and unscheduling the `update` function of the `GameWorld` class. If no collision is found, the game should continue normally. So, apply some gravity to the dragon's speed. Finally, update the dragon's position based on the speed.

Updating the towers

The `update` function of the `TowerManager` class is responsible for scrolling the towers from right to left and repositioning them once they leave the left edge of the screen. The code is as follows:

```
TowerManager.prototype.update = function(){
  var tower = null;
  for(var i = 0; i < this.towers.length; ++i)
  {
    tower = this.towers[i];
    // first update the position of the tower
    tower.position.x -= MAX_SCROLLING_SPEED;
    tower.lowerSprite.setPosition(tower.position.x, tower.lowerSprite.
getPositionY());
    tower.upperSprite.setPosition(tower.position.x, tower.upperSprite.
getPositionY());

    // if the tower has moved out of the screen, reposition them at
the end
    if(tower.position.x < this.towerSpriteSize.width * -0.5)
    {
      this.repositionTower(i);
      // this tower now becomes the tower at the end
      this.lastTowerIndex = i;
      // that means some other tower has become first
      this.firstTowerIndex = ((i+1) >= this.towers.length) ? 0:(i+1);
    }
  }
};
```

The `update` function of the `TowerManager` class is quite straightforward. You start by moving each tower `MAX_SCROLLING_SPEED` pixels to the left. If a tower has gone outside the left edge of the screen, reposition it at the right edge. Pay attention to how the `lastTowerIndex` and `firstTowerIndex` variables are set. The last tower is important to us because we need to know where to place subsequent towers. The first tower is important to us because we need it for collision detection.

Collision detection

Our dragon would really love to just keep flying and not run into anything, but that doesn't mean we don't check for collisions. The code is as follows:

```
checkCollisions:function() {
  // first find out which tower is right in front
  var frontTower = this.towerManager.getFrontTower();

  // fetch the bounding boxes of the respective sprites
  var dragonAABB = this.dragonManager.dragonSprite.getBoundingBox();
  var lowerTowerAABB = frontTower.lowerSprite.getBoundingBox();
  var upperTowerAABB = frontTower.upperSprite.getBoundingBox();

  // if the respective rects intersect, we have a collision
  if(cc.rectIntersectsRect(dragonAABB, lowerTowerAABB) || cc.rectInter
sectsRect(dragonAABB, upperTowerAABB))
  {
    // dragon must die
    this.dragonManager.dragonDeath();
    // stop the update loop
    this.unscheduleUpdate();
  }
  else if( Math.abs(cc.rectGetMidX(lowerTowerAABB) -
cc.rectGetMidX(dragonAABB)) <= MAX_SCROLLING_SPEED/2 )
  {
    // increment score once the dragon has crossed the tower
    this.incrementScore();
  }
},
```

Since the dragon can only collide with the tower that is in the front, there is no point checking for collisions with all the towers. After asking the `TowerManager` class for the tower in the front, we proceed to read the bounding box rectangles for the dragon and the tower's lower and upper sprites. We then check for an intersection between the dragon and the tower's rectangles. If a collision is found, we tell the dragon to die by calling the `dragonDeath` method of the `DragonManager` class and unscheduling the `update` function of the `GameWorld` class. If the dragon manages to clear the tower, we increment the score by one in the `incrementScore` function.

Flying the dragon

Now that we have created our dragon, the towers and the environment we are ready to begin playing when the user taps the screen. We record touches in the `onTouchesBegan` function as follows:

```
onTouchesBegan:function (touches, event) {
  this.hasGameStarted = true;
  // remove the tutorial only if it exists
  if(this.tutorialSprite)
  {
    // fade it out and then remove it
    this.tutorialSprite.runAction(cc.Sequence.create(cc.FadeOut.
create(0.25), cc.RemoveSelf.create(true)));
    this.tutorialSprite = null;
  }
  // inform DragonManager that the game has started
  this.dragonManager.onGameStart();
  // fly dragon...fly!!!
  this.dragonManager.dragonFlap();
},
```

Right at the beginning of the function, we set the `hasGameStarted` flag to `true`. Remember how we need this flag to be `true` in order to call the `update` function of the `TowerManager` class? We proceed to fade out and remove the tutorial sprite. The `if` condition is there to prevent the tutorial sprite from being removed repeatedly on every touch. We must also inform the `DragonManager` class that the game has begun so that it can start applying gravity to the dragon. Finally, every touch must push the dragon a bit upwards in the air, so we call the `dragonFlap` function of the `DragonManager` class, as shown here:

```
DragonManager.prototype.dragonFlap = function() {
  // don't flap if dragon will leave the top of the screen
  if(this.dragonPosition.y + FLAP_FORCE >= this.screenSize.height)
```

```
    return;

    // add flap force to speed
    this.dragonSpeed.y = FLAP_FORCE;

    cc.AudioEngine.getInstance().playEffect(s_Flap_mp3);
};
```

Our dragon is really charming, so we won't ever let him go off the screen. Hence, we return from this function if a flap will cause the dragon to exit the top of the screen. If all is okay, we simply add some force to the vertical component of the dragon's speed. That is pretty much all it takes to simulate the simplest form of gravity on an object. We call the `playEffect` function to play an effect. We will discuss HTML5 audio in our last section. For now, all you need to know is that the engine takes care of playing the sound for us so that it works almost everywhere.

Farewell dear dragon

Well, a collision has occurred and our dragon must now miserably fall to his death. If only you had played better and helped him through a few more towers. Let's see how our dragon dies in the `dragonDeath` function:

```
DragonManager.prototype.dragonDeath = function() {
  // fall miserably to the roof of the castle
  var rise = cc.EaseSineOut.create(cc.MoveBy.create(0.25, cc.p(0,
this.dragonSprite.getContentSize().height)));
  var fall = cc.EaseSineIn.create(cc.MoveTo.create(0.5, cc.p(this.
screenSize.width * 0.2, this.gameWorld.castleRoof)));
  // inform GameWorld that dragon is no more :(
  var finish = cc.CallFunc.create(this.gameWorld.onGameOver, this.
gameWorld);
  // stop the frame based animation...dragon can't fly once its dead
  this.dragonSprite.stopAllActions();
  this.dragonSprite.runAction(cc.Sequence.create(rise, fall, finish));

  cc.AudioEngine.getInstance().playEffect(s_Crash_mp3);
};
```

The preceding function is called when the dragon touches the castle roof in the `update` function of the `DragonManager` class and also when the dragon collides with a tower in the `checkCollisions` function of the `GameWorld` class. At this stage, the `update` function of the `GameWorld` class has been unscheduled. So we animate the dragon to fall to the castle roof with some easing and call the `onGameOver` function of the `GameWorld` class after that has happened. We also play a horrendous sound effect.

Saving a high score using LocalStorage

For a game like this where users are constantly driven to improve their score, it goes without saying that you need to store the user's best score persistently. Even though this game is running in a browser, we can still store data persistently. To accomplish this, we make use of HTML5 LocalStorage. Cocos2d-html5 provides a wrapper, although it is just as easy accessing LocalStorage with the `window.localStorage.setItem` or `window.localStorage.getItem` command.

HTML5 LocalStorage stores data in key/value pairs and a web page can only access data stored by itself. Thus our game's data is safe with the browser. This data has no expiry date and will not be destroyed even if the browser is closed. The only exception is if the user chooses to clear the browser's cache. Data is not persistent if the user chooses to browse in private or incognito mode.

We shall store our high-score data with a key specified by the `HIGHSCORE_KEY` variable defined at the top of `gameworld.js`. When the main menu is displayed, we check to see whether data exists for `HIGHSCORE_KEY`. The code is as follows:

```
// set default value for high score
// this will be executed only the first time the game is launched
// local storage stores data persistently
if(sys.localStorage.getItem(HIGHSCORE_KEY) == null)
sys.localStorage.setItem(HIGHSCORE_KEY, "0");
```

The `getItem` function returns `null` if no such data is available. Thus, we store a default high-score value of `0`. Subsequently, if a new high score is achieved, it must be stored in a similar fashion. This is done in the `showGameOverPopup` function in `GameWorld`:

```
// fetch old high score from browser's local storage
var oldHighScore = parseInt(sys.localStorage.getItem(HIGHSCORE_KEY));

var highScoreLabel = cc.LabelTTF.create("Your Best:" + oldHighScore,
"Comic Sans MS", 60);
highScoreLabel.setPosition(cc.p(this.screenSize.width*0.5, this.
screenSize.height*0.5));
this.popup.addChild(highScoreLabel);
```

```
// check if new high score has been achieved
if(this.score > oldHighScore)
{
  // save the new high score
  sys.localStorage.setItem(HIGHSCORE_KEY, this.score+"");

  // animate the button suggesting that a new high score has been
achieved
  highScoreLabel.runAction(cc.Sequence.create(cc.DelayTime.create(1),
  cc.EaseSineIn.create(cc.ScaleTo.create(0.25, 1.1)),
  cc.CallFunc.create( function(nodeExecutingAction, data){
nodeExecutingAction.setString("Your Best:" + this.score); }, this ),
  cc.EaseSineOut.create(cc.ScaleTo.create(0.25, 1))));
}
```

Let's make some HTML5 noise

Unlike our first game, we do have a few sounds for our dragon's story. HTML5 audio is still quite primitive on mobile browsers, but it is satisfactory on desktop browsers and it is a developing specification.

For the purpose of our game, we need only two effects: one for the flapping of dragon's wings and another when he crashes into a tower. You've already seen how to play these effects. These sounds must be listed in the `resources.js` file and must also be preloaded. We preload them in `mainmenu.js` with the following commands:

```
cc.AudioEngine.getInstance().preloadEffect(s_Flap_mp3);
cc.AudioEngine.getInstance().preloadEffect(s_Crash_mp3);
```

Summary

With the story of this little dragon, you learned a lot more about the engine. We loaded our first sprite sheet and understood what happens under the hood of animations by creating one by ourselves. You also learned how to repeat textures seamlessly. We then added some simple gravity and implemented rectangular collision detection. Finally, we discussed how to persistently store data in a web browser and play sounds using HTML5 audio. My best score at the time of writing this chapter was 103. Why don't you try and beat me?

In the next chapter, we'll be creating a space game. So fasten your seat belts, here we go!

3

Not Just a Space Game

After playing around a bit with Cocos2d-html5, it's finally time to get down and dirty with the good old C++ version of the engine. So, you will be using Cocos2d-x for this chapter and all the subsequent chapters. In this chapter, we will use actions for almost everything we need and get creative with some particle effects. You will also learn how to include progression in a game by creating a few levels.

We will cover the following topics in this chapter:

- How to use the awesome Cocos2d-x project creator tool to create a cross-platform project
- How to create a custom sprite by extending `CCSprite`
- How to use a particle system
- How to parse an XML file using `tinyxml2`

An overview of SpaceCraze

As the last survivor of an elite space combat team, you are faced with the grueling task of making your way back home. In order to do that, however, you must destroy every enemy battleship you encounter and smash your way home.

The controls in this game are straightforward: players must touch to navigate their ship left or right. Both player and enemies will have the ability to shoot bullets to bring destruction upon each other, and bullets for both player and enemies will be fired automatically.

In addition to enemies, there will also be a few obstacles that players will inevitably have to destroy. However, just killing all enemies will be enough to clear a given stage. Also, the player will be blessed with three lives. In this version of the game, we have just five levels, but I urge you design many more on your own. Here is a glimpse of the first level of the game just to get you a bit excited:

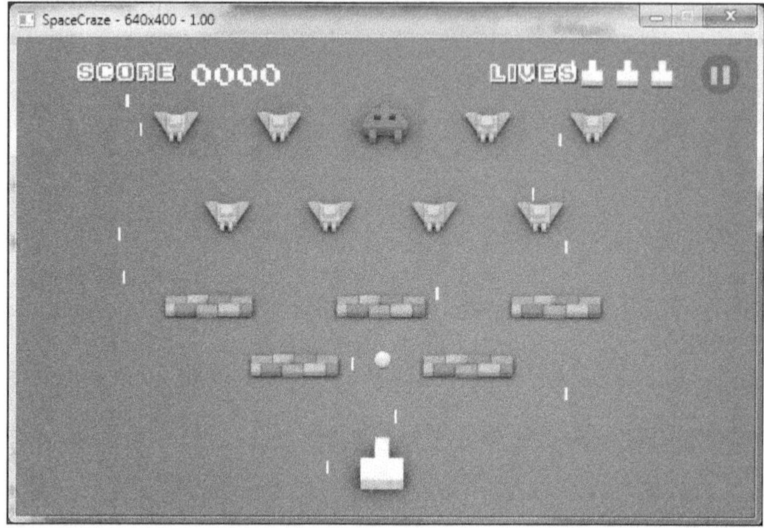

Creating a project

The first order of business will be creating a project file for SpaceCraze. If you have worked with Cocos2d-x before, you know that earlier we had to use separate scripts and batch files to create projects for the various platforms supported by the engine. It was a cumbersome task at that. So, the brilliant guys from the Cocos2d-x community have come up with a unified solution that will create all your required project files in one shot. They call it, quite simply, the **project-creator** tool.

You can find project-creator inside the `tools` folder of Cocos2d-x. In the `project-creator` folder, you will find a Python executable by the name of `create_project.py`. This is the executable that we will use to create a cross-platform Cocos2d-x project. As a prerequisite, you will need Python installed on your machine before running `create_project.py`. The script has instructions on how it should be used but I will go over it just this once.

To create a cross-platform Cocos2d-x project, follow these steps:

1. Navigate to the `project-creator` folder by typing the following command into the terminal:

   ```
   cd PATH_TO_COCOS2DX/tools/project-creator/
   ```

   Here, `PATH_TO_COCOS2DX` is the location of Cocos2d-x on your filesystem.

2. To create your project, type the following command into the terminal:

   ```
   ./create_project.py -project SpaceCraze -package com.karanseq.
   SpaceCraze -language cpp
   ```

You specified the project name, package name, and programming language for this project in the preceding steps—`SpaceCraze`, `com.karanseq.SpaceCraze`, and `cpp`, respectively. If you did everything right, your terminal window should look something like this:

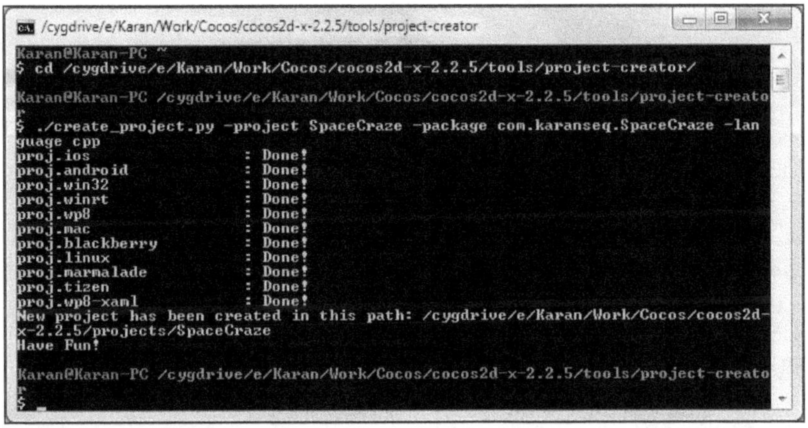

So, we've used the brilliantly written script to create our first Cocos2d-x project. You must have noticed the number of platforms you can deploy to! Notice how the newly-created project is placed inside the projects folder within Cocos2d-x-2.2.5. When you download the source code for this chapter and subsequent Cocos2d-x chapters, be sure to place the project inside the `projects` folder. It may not exist when you first set up the engine; in that case, you should simply create it.

Defining the global variables of the game

Every game we make henceforth will have a common header file included and global data defined in a separate class. This class has been made for convenience only and—technically—you can choose not to have it at all. However, all the enums, constants, and macros used in the game will be stored here, so be sure to include it in the sources where needed.

Let's take a look at the `GameGlobals.h` file:

```
#ifndef GAME_GLOBALS_H_
#define GAME_GLOBALS_H_

#include "cocos2d.h"
#include "SimpleAudioEngine.h"

USING_NS_CC;

using namespace std;

#define SCREEN_SIZE GameGlobals::screen_size_
#define SOUND_ENGINE CocosDenshion::SimpleAudioEngine::sharedEngine()
#define MAX_STARS 15
#define BULLET_MOVE_DURATION 1.5f
#define MAX_BULLETS 25
#define MAX_LEVELS 5

// enum used for proper z-ordering
enum E_ZORDER
{
  E_LAYER_BACKGROUND = 0,
  E_LAYER_FOREGROUND = 2,
  E_LAYER_ENEMIES_BRICKS = 4,
  E_LAYER_BULLETS = 6,
  E_LAYER_PLAYER = 8,
  E_LAYER_HUD = 10,
  E_LAYER_POPUP = 12,
};

class GameGlobals
{
public:
  GameGlobals(void){};
  ~GameGlobals(void){};
```

```
    // initialise common global data here...called when application
finishes launching
    static void Init();
    // load initial/all game data here
    static void LoadData();

    // save screen size for fast access
    static CCSize screen_size_;

    // function takes comma separated string & returns vector of values
    static vector<float> GetFloatListFromString(string input);
    // function takes comma separated string & returns CCPoint
    static CCPoint GetPointFromString(string input);
};

#endif // GAME_GLOBALS_H_
```

First, we included all headers that will be required and we also declared the namespaces we will be using throughout the project. We then defined all the pre-processor directives that will be needed, starting with the familiar `SCREEN_SIZE` that points to the `screen_size_` variable from `GameGlobals`. We also created a convenience macro `SOUND_ENGINE` to fetch the singleton object of the class `SimpleAudioEngine`.

The constants that follow define the maximum number of stars in the background, the default duration for bullet movement, the maximum number of bullets currently on screen, and the maximum number of levels in SpaceCraze. Next up, we have an enum named `E_ZORDER` that will basically specify the order of rendering for this game.

Now if you look at the members of the class `GameGlobals`, you will notice that they're all static. That's simply because these functions are basic helpers to the game and the variables are basic data banks, and it's convenient to have them available to the entire codebase. After the constructor and destructor, you have an `Init` function that will load default values for the member variables. `LoadData` is responsible for loading all our spritesheets and sounds. Last but not the least, we have a few helper functions: one that will return a `vector` of `float` values from a comma-separated string and another that will return a `CCPoint` from a comma-separated string. Let's quickly define these methods so we can then actually begin with the game.

The implementation `GameGlobals.cpp` file looks like this:

```
#include "GameGlobals.h"

CCSize GameGlobals::screen_size_ = CCSizeZero;

void GameGlobals::Init()
{
  screen_size_ = CCDirector::sharedDirector()->getWinSize();
  LoadData();
}

void GameGlobals::LoadData()
{
  // add Resources folder to search path. This is necessary when
releasing for win32
  CCFileUtils::sharedFileUtils()->addSearchPath("Resources");

  // load sprite sheet/s
  CCSpriteFrameCache::sharedSpriteFrameCache()->addSpriteFramesWithFil
e("spacetex.plist");

  // load sound effects & background music
  SOUND_ENGINE->preloadEffect("blast_brick.wav");
  SOUND_ENGINE->preloadEffect("blast_enemy.wav");
  SOUND_ENGINE->preloadEffect("blast_player.wav");
  SOUND_ENGINE->preloadEffect("game_over.wav");
  SOUND_ENGINE->preloadEffect("level_complete.wav");
  SOUND_ENGINE->preloadEffect("shoot_enemy.wav");
  SOUND_ENGINE->preloadEffect("shoot_player.wav");
}

// function takes comma separated string & returns vector of values
vector<float> GameGlobals::GetFloatListFromString(string input)
{
  vector<float> result;
  result.clear();

  if(input == "")
  return result;
```

```
    stringstream ss(input);
    float i;
    while (ss >> i)
    {
      result.push_back(i);
      if (ss.peek() == ',')
      ss.ignore();
    }
    return result;
  }

  // function takes comma separated string & returns CCPoint
  CCPoint GameGlobals::GetPointFromString(string input)
  {
    CCPoint point = CCPointZero;
    if(input == "")
    return point;
    vector<float> list = GetFloatListFromString(input);
    point.x = list[0];
    point.y = list[1];
    return point;
  }
```

We assigned a default value for the screen size and specified the default constructor and destructor. Inside the `Init` function, we saved the screen size from `CCDirector` and finally called the `LoadData` function.

In the `LoadData` function, we added the `Resources` path to the search paths inside `CCFileUtils`. This points `CCFileUtils` to our resources. Then, we loaded our sprite sheet and all our sound effects.

Finally, we defined our helper functions, starting with the `GetFloatListFromString` function. This function uses the functions inside `std::string` to turn an input string such as `"10,20,30,40,50"` into `std::vector` containing float values such as `{10.0f, 20.0f, 30.0f, 40.0f, 50.0f}`.

The `GetPointFromString` function uses `GetFloatListFromString` to return a `CCPoint` from an input string. Alright, things are about to get exciting now! The first thing you get to learn is how to extend `CCSprite` and create your own version of it!

Creating your own Sprite

As you go about developing different types of games, you may find that you need to store some more information regarding the entities or objects in your game. Such a situation has arisen for this particular game as well. For SpaceCraze, we will need to manipulate the size of each of our entities' sprites: player, enemy and brick. In addition to size, we will also need to manipulate the `boundingBox` function. Why do we need to change the bounding box you wonder? Just take a look at a shot of the player's sprite frame shown here:

Notice how the texture here includes a shadow for styling. This would cause the bounding box for the player's sprite to include the shadow. Consequently, our collisions would look visually incorrect with the player getting shot without the enemy bullet actually making contact with the body of the player's ship.

So without further ado, let's get to the header file of the class that we shall conveniently name `CustomSprite`:

```
#ifndef CUSTOM_SPRITE_H_
#define CUSTOM_SPRITE_H_

#include "GameGlobals.h"

class CustomSprite : public CCSprite
{
public:
  CustomSprite() : size_(CCSizeZero) {}
  virtual ~CustomSprite();

  // returns and autorelease CustomSprite
  static CustomSprite* createWithSpriteFrameName(const char* frame_
name);

  // override CCSprite's boundingBox method
  virtual CCRect boundingBox();
```

```
    // add a customized CCSize used for the boundingBox
    CC_SYNTHESIZE(CCSize, size_, Size);
};

#endif // CUSTOM_SPRITE_H_
```

You can clearly see how `CustomSprite` publicly inherits from `CCSprite`. Within the header file, we have the constructor and destructor. You can see how the constructor initializes a variable called `size_` to `CCSizeZero`. I am sure you're looking for this variable within the class, but are you looking close enough?

The `size_` variable is wrapped neatly within the `CC_SYNTHESIZE` macro function at the bottom of the header file. Jump to the definition of `CC_SYNTHESIZE` and you will see that the macro simply declares a `protected` variable of a given type (first parameter) with the given name (second parameter), and it goes one step ahead to create `public accessor/getter` and `mutator/setter` functions of the specified name (third parameter).

Next, we have a `static` function that returns a pointer to `CustomSprite` and has a very familiar name. That's right, `createWithSpriteFrameName` belongs to the `CCSprite` class and we will be borrowing the same name to create our `CustomSprite` class. This function will receive the name of the sprite frame that `CustomSprite` will use.

Last but not the least, you can see the `virtual` function `boundingBox()` that we will be over-riding in our `CustomSprite` class. Let's take a look at the implementation of the class in `CustomSprite.cpp` file:

```
#include "CustomSprite.h"

CustomSprite::~CustomSprite()
{}

CustomSprite* CustomSprite::createWithSpriteFrameName(
  const char* frame_name)
{
  CustomSprite* sprite = new CustomSprite();
  if(sprite && sprite->initWithSpriteFrameName(frame_name))
  {
    sprite->autorelease();
    return sprite;
  }
  CC_SAFE_DELETE(sprite);
```

```
    return NULL;
}

CCRect CustomSprite::boundingBox()
{
  // return bounding box based on our own size_ variable
  return CCRectMake(m_obPosition.x - size_.width/2,
    m_obPosition.y - size_.height/2, size_.width, size_.height);
}
```

We started the `staticcreateWithSpriteFrameName` function by creating a new `CustomSprite` object. We then called the `initWithSpriteFrameName` function of `CCSprite`, which returns either `true` or `false` based on successful or unsuccessful initialization, respectively. If all is well, we mark the `CustomSprite` object as `autorelease` and return it. If all is not well, we delete the `CustomSprite` object and return `NULL`. The `CC_SAFE_DELETE` function is yet another useful macro. You will find a multitude of such macros in the `CCPlatformMacros.h` file located inside `cocos2dx/platform/`.

Finally, we have the over-ridden `boundingBox` function. As you may have guessed, we create and return a custom `CCRect` based on the `size_` value of the `CustomSprite`. All right! With a customized `CCSprite` on our shoulders, we can begin creating our crazy space game world.

On to the game world...

We have a lot of work to do, so let's quickly list the main tasks at hand:

- Create
    - Create the level by parsing an XML file containing level data
    - Create the player
    - Create the HUD
- Move the enemies
- Update
    - Fire player and enemy bullets
    - Collision detection
    - Level completion and game over conditions

However, before we complete all these tasks, we need to define the classes for our three major game play entities: player, enemy, and brick.

The Player class

Our `Player` entity inherits from `CustomSprite` and can die and come back to life, but only twice. The third time it dies, the game is over! Let's take a look at the significant functions that make our `Player` entity brave and enduring:

```
void Player::Enter()
{
  // initially position the player below the screen
  setPosition(ccp(SCREEN_SIZE.width * 0.5, SCREEN_SIZE.height *
-0.1));

  // animate the move into the screen
  CCActionInterval* movement = CCEaseBackOut::create(CCMoveTo::create(
  1.0f, ccp(SCREEN_SIZE.width * 0.5, SCREEN_SIZE.height * 0.1)));
  CCActionInstant* movement_over = CCCallFunc::create(this,
  callfunc_selector(Player::EnterFinished));
  runAction(CCSequence::createWithTwoActions(movement, movement_
over));
}

void Player::EnterFinished()
{
  // player has entered, now start the game
    game_world_->StartGame();
}
```

We called the `Enter` function of `Player` at the time of level creation. Here, we placed the player outside the screen and ran an action to move him in. No game can start without the player, so we called the `StartGame` function of `GameWorld` only after the animation is over in the callback function `EnterFinishe`.

Now let's move on to the death logic by looking at the following code:

```
void Player::Die()
{
  // first reduce lives
  lives_ = (--lives_ < 0) ? 0 : lives_;

  // respawn only if there are lives remaining
  is_respawning_ = (lives_ > 0);

  // animate the death :(
```

```
    CCActionInterval* death = CCSpawn::createWithTwoActions(
    CCFadeOut::create(0.5f), CCScaleTo::create(0.5f, 1.5f));
    // call the appropriate callback based on lives remaining
    CCActionInstant* after_death = (lives_ <= 0) ? (
    CCCallFunc::create(this, callfunc_selector(
    Player::OnAllLivesFinished))) : (CCCallFunc::create(
    this, callfunc_selector(Player::Respawn)));
    runAction(CCSequence::createWithTwoActions(death, after_death));

    // play a particle...a sad one :(
    CCParticleSystemQuad* explosion =
    CCParticleSystemQuad::create("explosion.plist");
    explosion->setAutoRemoveOnFinish(true);
    explosion->setPosition(m_obPosition);
    game_world_->addChild(explosion);

    SOUND_ENGINE->playEffect("blast_player.wav");
}
```

Our `Player` entity isn't invincible: it does get hit and must die. However, it does have three chances to defeat the enemies. The `Die` function starts by reducing the number of lives left. Then, we decide whether the `Player` entity can respawn based on how many lives there are left. If there are any lives left, we call the `Respawn` function or else the `OnAllLivesFinished` function after the death animation is over.

In addition to the scaling and fading animation, we also played a cool particle effect where the player died. We used the `CCParticleSystemQuad` class to load a particle effect from an external `.plist` file. I happened to generate this file online from a cool web app available at `http://onebyonedesign.com/flash/particleeditor/`.

Notice how we called the `setAutoRemoveOnFinish` function and passed in `true`. This causes the particle to be removed by the engine after it has finished playing. We also played a sound effect on the death of the `Player` entity.

Now, take a look at the following code:

```
void Player::Respawn()
{
  // reset the position, opacity & scale
  setPosition(ccp(SCREEN_SIZE.width * 0.5,
  SCREEN_SIZE.height * 0.1));
  setOpacity(255);
  setScale(0.0f);

  // animate the respawn
  CCSpawn* respawn = CCSpawn::createWithTwoActions(
```

```
    CCScaleTo::create(0.5f, 1.0f), CCBlink::create(1.0f, 5));
    CCCallFunc* respawn_complete = CCCallFunc::create(
    this, callfunc_selector(Player::OnRespawnComplete));
    runAction(CCSequence::createWithTwoActions(respawn,
    respawn_complete));
}

void Player::OnRespawnComplete()
{
  is_respawning_ = false;
}

void Player::OnAllLivesFinished()
{
  // player is finally dead...for sure...game is now over
  game_world_->GameOver();
}
```

The `Respawn` function places the player back at the initial position, resets the opacity and scale parameters. Then a cool blinking animation is run with a callback to `OnRespawnComplete`.

The `OnAllLivesFinished` function simply informs `GameWorld` to wind up the game—our player is no more!

The Enemy class

The `Player` entity is brave and tough for sure, but the enemies are no less malicious. That's right, I said enemies and we have three different kinds in this game. The `Enemy` class inherits from `CustomSprite`, just like the `Player` class. Let's look at the constructor and see how they're different:

```
Enemy::Enemy(GameWorld* game_world, const char* frame_name)
{
  game_world_ = game_world;
  score_ = 0;

  // different enemies have different properties
  if(strstr(frame_name, "1"))
  {
    bullet_name_ = "sfbullet3";
    particle_color_ = ccc4f(0.5255, 0.9373, 0, 1);
    bullet_duration_ = BULLET_MOVE_DURATION * 3;
    size_ = CCSizeMake(50, 35);
  }
```

```
    else if(strstr(frame_name, "2"))
    {
      bullet_name_ = "sfbullet1";
      particle_color_ = ccc4f(0.9569, 0.2471, 0.3373, 1);
      bullet_duration_ = BULLET_MOVE_DURATION * 1.5;
      size_ = CCSizeMake(50, 50);
    }
    else if(strstr(frame_name, "3"))
    {
      bullet_name_ = "sfbullet2";
      particle_color_ = ccc4f(0.9451, 0.8157, 0, 1);
      bullet_duration_ = BULLET_MOVE_DURATION * 0.8;
      size_ = CCSizeMake(55, 55);
    }
  }
```

The properties for each `Enemy` entity are based on the `frame_name` passed in to the constructor. These properties are `bullet_name_`, which is the sprite frame name for the bullets that this enemy will shoot; `particle_color_`, which stores the color of the particle played when this enemy dies; `bullet_duration_`, which stores the amount of time this enemy's bullet takes to reach the edge of the screen; and finally, the size of this enemy used while checking collisions. Now let's take a look at what happens when an enemy dies in the `Die` function:

```
int Enemy::Die()
{
  // do this so that the movement action stops
  stopAllActions();

  // play an animation when this enemy is hit by player bullet
  CCActionInterval* blast = CCScaleTo::create(0.25f, 0.0f);
  CCRemoveSelf* remove = CCRemoveSelf::create(true);
  runAction(CCSequence::createWithTwoActions(blast, remove));

  // play a particle effect
  // modify the start & end color to suit the enemy
  CCParticleSystemQuad* explosion =
  CCParticleSystemQuad::create("explosion.plist");
  explosion->setStartColor(particle_color_);
  explosion->setEndColor(particle_color_);
  explosion->setAutoRemoveOnFinish(true);
  explosion->setPosition(m_obPosition);
  game_world_->addChild(explosion);
```

```
    SOUND_ENGINE->playEffect("blast_enemy.wav");

    // return score_ so it can be credited to the player
    return score_;
}
```

We first called `stopAllActions` because all enemies will keep moving as a group across the screen from side to side as soon as the game starts. We then created a `CCSequence` that will animate and remove the enemy.

Similar to the `Player` class, the `Enemy` class also gets a cool particle effect on death. You can see that we used the same particle `.plist` file and changed the start and end color of the particle system. Basically, you can set and get every single property that comprises a particle system and tweak it to your needs or use them to start from scratch if you don't have a `.plist` file. There are also plenty of readymade particle systems in the engine that you can use and tweak.

Next, we played a sound effect when the enemy is killed. Finally, we returned the score that must be rewarded to the player for bravely slaying this enemy.

The Brick class

If it wasn't enough that there were multiple waves of enemies, the player must also deal with bricks blocking the player's line of sight. The `Brick` class also inherits from `CustomSprite` and is very similar to the `Enemy` class; however, instead of a `Die` function, it has a `Crumble` function that looks like this:

```
int Brick::Crumble()
{
  // play an animation when this brick is hit by player bullet
  CCActionInterval* blast = CCScaleTo::create(0.25f, 0.0f);
  CCRemoveSelf* remove = CCRemoveSelf::create(true);
  runAction(CCSequence::createWithTwoActions(blast, remove));

  SOUND_ENGINE->playEffect("blast_brick.wav");

  // return score_ so it can be credited to the player
  return score_;
}
```

We run a simple scale-down animation, remove the brick, play a sound effect, and return the score back to the calling function. That wraps up our three basic entities. Let's go ahead and see how these are linked to a level's XML file.

Parsing the level file

The first task on our list is parsing an XML file that will contain data about our enemies, bricks, and even the player. The level file for the first level, whose screenshot you saw at the start of this chapter, is given as follows:

```
<Level player_fire_rate="1.0">
<Enemy Setmove_duration="3.0" fire_rate="5.0">
<Enemy name="sfenmy1" score="25" position="280,650" />
<Enemy name="sfenmy1" score="25" position="460,650" />
<Enemy name="sfenmy2" score="50" position="640,650" />
<Enemy name="sfenmy1" score="25" position="820,650" />
<Enemy name="sfenmy1" score="25" position="1000,650" />
<Enemy name="sfenmy1" score="25" position="370,500" />
<Enemy name="sfenmy1" score="25" position="550,500" />
<Enemy name="sfenmy1" score="25" position="730,500" />
<Enemy name="sfenmy1" score="25" position="910,500" />
</EnemySet>
<BrickSet>
<Brick name="sfbrick1" score="10" position="300,350" />
<Brick name="sfbrick2" score="10" position="364,350" />
<Brick name="sfbrick1" score="10" position="450,250" />
<Brick name="sfbrick2" score="10" position="514,250" />
<Brick name="sfbrick1" score="10" position="600,350" />
<Brick name="sfbrick2" score="10" position="664,350" />
<Brick name="sfbrick1" score="10" position="750,250" />
<Brick name="sfbrick2" score="10" position="814,250" />
<Brick name="sfbrick1" score="10" position="900,350" />
<Brick name="sfbrick2" score="10" position="964,350" />
</BrickSet>
</Level>
```

Let's take some time to understand what the data in this XML represents. The root of the XML document is the `Level` tag. A given level contains a set of enemies and bricks represented by the `EnemySet` and `BrickSet` tags, respectively. The enemies and bricks contained within the `EnemySet` and `BrickSet` tags are represented by the `Enemy` and `Brick` tags, respectively. Now, we go over the attributes of these tags briefly in the following table:

Tag	Attribute	Description
`Level`	`player_fire_rate`	This is the rate at which a player fires bullets.
`EnemySet`	`move_duration`	This is the amount of time before which the entire set of enemies move.

Tag	Attribute	Description
EnemySet	fire_rate	This is the rate at which a bullet is fired from any one of the enemies.
Enemy and Brick	name	This is the sprite frame name to represent the given enemy/brick. It also serves as type of enemy.
Enemy&Brick	score	This is the score credited to the player when this enemy/brick is hit.

Now that we have understood what a level file can consist of, it's time to use a versatile XML parsing library named `tinyxml2`. You can find documentation and references on `tinyxml2` at `http://grinninglizard.com/tinyxml2docs/index.html`. The best thing is how simple and lightweight the library actually is! So let's go ahead and see how to use `tinyxml2` to actually parse this file inside the `CreateLevel` function of `GameWorld`:

```
void GameWorld::CreateLevel()
{
  // create the environment
  BackgroundManager* background_manager =
    BackgroundManager::create();
  addChild(background_manager, E_LAYER_BACKGROUND);

  // create & add the batch node
  sprite_batch_node_ =
    CCSpriteBatchNode::create("spacetex.png", 128);
  addChild(sprite_batch_node_);

  // initialize score & state machine flags
  score_ = score_to_carry_;
  has_game_started_ = false;
  has_game_stopped_ = false;
  is_game_paused_ = false;
  // initialize enemy position variables
  left_side_enemy_position_ = SCREEN_SIZE.width/2;
  right_side_enemy_position_ = SCREEN_SIZE.width/2;
```

Before we did any parsing and creates levels, we created and added `BackgroundManager` and `CCSpriteBatchNode` with the texture of our sprite sheet and the maximum number of child sprites. The `BackgroundManager` class will take care of creating the environment for SpaceCraze. We then initialized some member variables for our current level. The score that the player begins the current level with, is stored in `score_`. The next three variables are flags that are used to maintain the state of the game. The last two variables represent the left-most and right-most enemies that we will use when we move the enemies.

Now, let's take a look at the following code:

```
// generate level filename
  char level_file[16] = {0};
  sprintf(level_file, "Level%02d.xml", current_level_);

  // fetch level file data
  unsigned long size;
  char* data = (char*)CCFileUtils::sharedFileUtils()->
  getFileData(level_file, "rb", &size);

  // parse the level file
  tinyxml2::XMLDocument xml_document;
  tinyxml2::XMLError xml_result = xml_document.Parse(data, size);

  CC_SAFE_DELETE(data);

  // print the error if parsing was unsuccessful
  if(xml_result != tinyxml2::XML_SUCCESS)
  {
    CCLOGERROR("Error:%d while reading %s", xml_result, level_file);
    return;
  }

  // save player data
  tinyxml2::XMLNode* level_node = xml_document.FirstChild();
  player_fire_rate_ = level_node->ToElement()->
  FloatAttribute("player_fire_rate");

  // create set of enemies
  tinyxml2::XMLNode* enemy_set_node = level_node->FirstChild();
  CreateEnemies(enemy_set_node);

  // create set of bricks
  tinyxml2::XMLNode* brick_set_node =
  enemy_set_node->NextSibling();
  CreateBricks(brick_set_node);

  CreatePlayer();

  CreateHUD();

  // everything created, start updating
  scheduleUpdate();
}
```

In the preceding code, we used `tinyxml2` to parse the level file. We started by generating the path of the level file based on the number of the current level. We then asked `CCFileUtils` to return the data of the level file. We must delete the memory allocated to the `char*` by the name of `data` to avoid a memory leak in the game.

We must declare a object of class `XMLDocument` named `xml_document` and call the `Parse` function on it, providing the `char*` data and its size as parameters. We then checked for successful parsing of the XML document and printed an error message if unsuccessful. Now that we have our XML data parsed and ready to use, we save the root node of the document into the `level_node` variable by calling the `FirstChild` method on the `xml_document`. We can now painlessly extract the `player_fire_rate` attribute using the `FloatAttribute` function of the `XMLElement` class.

> While using `tinyxml2`, keep in mind the difference between `XMLNode` and `XMLElement`. The former is used when one wants to iterate through an `XMLDocument`. The latter is used to extract values and attributes for a given tag within the `XMLDocument`.

Creating enemies

Let's take a look at how the `CreateEnemies` function uses the `enemy_set_node` to generate the enemies for a given level:

```
void GameWorld::CreateEnemies(tinyxml2::XMLNode* enemy_set)
{
  // save enemy movement & firing information
  enemy_movement_duration_ = enemy_set->ToElement()->
  FloatAttribute("move_duration");
  enemy_fire_rate_ = enemy_set->ToElement()->
  FloatAttribute("fire_rate");

  // create array to hold enemies
  enemies_ = CCArray::create();
  enemies_->retain();

  // create array to hold enemy bullets
  enemy_bullets_ = CCArray::createWithCapacity(MAX_BULLETS);
  enemy_bullets_->retain();

  // iterate through <EnemySet> and create Enemy objects
  tinyxml2::XMLElement* enemy_element = NULL;
  for(tinyxml2::XMLNode* enemy_node = enemy_set->FirstChild();
  enemy_node != NULL; enemy_node = enemy_node->NextSibling())
  {
```

```
        enemy_element = enemy_node->ToElement();
        // Enemy sprite frame name taken from "name" attribute of <Enemy>
        Enemy* enemy = Enemy::createWithSpriteFrameName(this,
        enemy_element->Attribute("name"));
        // Enemy score taken from "score" attribute of <Enemy>
        enemy->setScore(enemy_element->IntAttribute("score"));
        // add Enemy to batch node & array
        sprite_batch_node_->addChild(enemy, E_LAYER_ENEMIES_BRICKS);
        enemies_->addObject(enemy);

        // Enemy position taken from "position" attribute of <Enemy>
        CCPoint position = GameGlobals::GetPointFromString(
        string(enemy_element->Attribute("position")));
        enemy->setPosition(position);

        // save enemies at the left & right extremes
        left_side_enemy_position_ = (position.x <
        left_side_enemy_position_) ? position.x : left_side_enemy_
    position_;
        right_side_enemy_position_ = (position.x >
        right_side_enemy_position_) ? position.x : right_side_enemy_
    position_;

        // save size of largest enemy
        CCSize size = enemy->getContentSize();
        max_enemy_size_.width = (size.width >
        max_enemy_size_.width) ? size.width:max_enemy_size_.width;
        max_enemy_size_.height = (size.height >
        max_enemy_size_.height) ? size.height:max_enemy_size_.height;
      }
    }
```

Before creating any enemies, the `move_duration` and `fire_rate` attributes are stored into the `enemy_movement_duration` and `enemy_fire_rate` variables, respectively. We then created and retained two `CCArrays:enemies_` and `enemy_bullets_` to store the enemies and enemy bullets, respectively.

Then, in a loop, we iterated through the `EnemySet` and created an object of the `Enemy` class to represent all the enemies in this level. We then set the score for each `Enemy` entity before adding it to the `sprite_batch_node_` object and the `enemies_` object respectively. Then, we positioned this `Enemy` entity based on the `position` attribute and one of our helper functions from `GameGlobals`. We also saved the position of the left-most and right-most enemies and also the size of the largest enemy's sprite. We will use these values while moving the enemies.

Creating bricks

Now, we will create bricks by iterating through the `BrickSet` tag. This is taken care of by the `CreateBricks` function, as shown in the following code:

```
void GameWorld::CreateBricks(tinyxml2::XMLNode* brick_set)
{
  // create array to hold bricks
  bricks_ = CCArray::create();
  bricks_->retain();

  // iterate through <BrickSet> and create Brick objects
  tinyxml2::XMLElement* brick_element = NULL;
  for(tinyxml2::XMLNode* brick_node = brick_set->FirstChild();
  brick_node != NULL; brick_node = brick_node->NextSibling())
  {
    brick_element = brick_node->ToElement();
    // Brick sprite frame name taken from "name" attribute of <Brick>
    Brick* brick = Brick::createWithSpriteFrameName(
    brick_element->Attribute("name"));
    // Brick score taken from "score" attribute of <Brick>
    brick->setScore(brick_element->IntAttribute("score"));
    // Brick position taken from "position" attribute of <Brick>
    brick->setPosition(GameGlobals::GetPointFromString(string(
    brick_element->Attribute("position"))));
    // add Brick to batch node & array
    sprite_batch_node_->addChild(brick, E_LAYER_ENEMIES_BRICKS);
    bricks_->addObject(brick);
  }
}
```

Just as in the `CreateEnemies` function, we started by creating and retaining an object of class CCArray named `bricks_`, to hold all the `Brick` objects. We then iterated through the `brick_set` and created the `Brick` objects, set their score and position, and finally added them to the `sprite_batch_node_` object and to the `bricks_` object respectively.

Creating the player

Now, we will create the `Player` entity in the `CreatePlayer` function:

```
void GameWorld::CreatePlayer()
{
  // create & add Player to batch node
  player_ = Player::createWithSpriteFrameName(this, "sfgun");
```

```
    sprite_batch_node_->addChild(player_, E_LAYER_PLAYER);

    // create array to hold Player bullets
    player_bullets_ = CCArray::createWithCapacity(MAX_BULLETS);
    player_bullets_->retain();

    // initialize Player properties
    player_->setLives(lives_to_carry_);
    player_->setIsRespawning(false);
    // tell Player to move into the screen
    player_->Enter();
}
```

In the `CreatePlayer` function, we created an object of the class `Player` and added it to the `sprite_batch_node_` object. We also created and retained a `CCArray` to hold the player's bullets for this level. Finally, we initialized the player's attributes and called the `Enter` function.

Creating HUD elements

The last thing we need to write before we complete our `CreateLevel` function is the `CreateHUD` function:

```
void GameWorld::CreateHUD()
{
    // create & add "score" text
    CCSprite* score_sprite =
      CCSprite::createWithSpriteFrameName("sfscore");
    score_sprite->setPosition(ccp(SCREEN_SIZE.width*0.15f,
      SCREEN_SIZE.height*0.925f));
    sprite_batch_node_->addChild(score_sprite, E_LAYER_HUD);

    // create & add "lives" text
    CCSprite* lives_sprite =
      CCSprite::createWithSpriteFrameName("sflives");
    lives_sprite->setPosition(ccp(SCREEN_SIZE.width*0.7f,
      SCREEN_SIZE.height*0.925f));
    sprite_batch_node_->addChild(lives_sprite, E_LAYER_HUD);

    // create & add score label
    char buf[8] = {0};
    sprintf(buf, "%04d", score_);
    score_label_ = CCLabelBMFont::create(buf, "sftext.fnt");
    score_label_->setPosition(ccp(SCREEN_SIZE.width*0.3f,
      SCREEN_SIZE.height*0.925f));
```

```
    addChild(score_label_, E_LAYER_HUD);

    // save size of life sprite
    CCSize icon_size = CCSpriteFrameCache::sharedSpriteFrameCache()->
      spriteFrameByName("sflifei")->getOriginalSize();
    // create array to hold life sprites
    life_sprites_ = CCArray::createWithCapacity(player_->getLives());
    life_sprites_->retain();

    // position life sprites some distance away from "life" text
    float offset_x = lives_sprite->getPositionX() +
      lives_sprite->getContentSize().width*1.5f + icon_size.width;
    for(int i = 0; i < player_->getLives(); ++i)
    {
      // position each life sprite further away from "life" text
      offset_x -= icon_size.width * 1.5f;
      CCSprite* icon_sprite = CCSprite::createWithSpriteFrameName("sfli
fei");
      icon_sprite->setPosition(ccp( offset_x, SCREEN_SIZE.
height*0.925f));
      // add life sprite to batch node & array
      sprite_batch_node_->addChild(icon_sprite, E_LAYER_HUD);
      life_sprites_->addObject(icon_sprite);
    }

    // create & add the pause menu containing pause button
    CCMenuItemSprite* pause_button = CCMenuItemSprite::create(
      CCSprite::createWithSpriteFrameName("sfpause"),
      CCSprite::createWithSpriteFrameName("sfpause"), this,
      menu_selector(GameWorld::OnPauseClicked));
    pause_button->setPosition(ccp(SCREEN_SIZE.width*0.95f,
      SCREEN_SIZE.height*0.925f));
    CCMenu* menu = CCMenu::create(pause_button, NULL);
    menu->setAnchorPoint(CCPointZero);
    menu->setPosition(CCPointZero);
    addChild(menu, E_LAYER_HUD);
}
```

We started by creating and adding `CCSprite` objects for the score and lives, respectively. Usually, labels are used for these kinds of HUD elements but we used sprite frames in this specific case.

Next, we created the `score` label using the `CCLabelBMFont` class that provides us with a label that uses a bitmap font. We need to supply the string that we want displayed along with the path to the `.fnt` file to the `create` function of the `CCLabelBMFont` class.

Use CCLabelBMFont when you have texts that need to be updated regularly. They update much faster as compared to CCLabelTTF. Additionally, CCLabelBMFont inherits from CCSpriteBatchNode—every character within the label can be accessed separately and hence can have different properties!

We also need to add sprites to represent how many lives the player had left. In the for loop, we created and added sprites to the sprite_batch_node_. We also added these sprites to a CCArray named life_sprites_ because we will need to remove them one by one as the player loses a life.

So, we finally created a CCMenu containing a CCMenuItemSprite for the pause button and added it to GameWorld. That sums up level creation and we are now ready to begin playing.

The start and stop functions

Now that we have created the level with enemies, bricks and a player, it's time to start playing. So let's see what happens in the StartGame function. Remember that this function is called from the Player class after the player has finished entering the screen. The code is as follows:

```
void GameWorld::StartGame()
{
  // call this function only once when the game starts
  if(has_game_started_)
    return;

  has_game_started_ = true;
  // start firing player & enemy bullets
  schedule(schedule_selector(GameWorld::FirePlayerBullet),
    player_fire_rate_);
  schedule(schedule_selector(GameWorld::FireEnemyBullet),
    enemy_fire_rate_);
  // start moving enemies
  StartMovingEnemies();
}
```

This function starts with a conditional that ensures it is called only once. We then scheduled two functions, FirePlayerBullet and FireEnemyBullet, at intervals of player_fire_rate_, and enemy_fire_rate_, respectively. Finally, we called StartMovingEnemies, which we will get to in a bit.

Now, let's take a look at the StopGame function:

```
void GameWorld::StopGame()
{
  has_game_stopped_ = true;
  // stop firing player & enemy bullets
  unschedule(schedule_selector(GameWorld::FirePlayerBullet));
  unschedule(schedule_selector(GameWorld::FireEnemyBullet));

  // stop Enemy movement
  CCObject* object = NULL;
  CCARRAY_FOREACH(enemies_, object)
  {
    CCSprite* enemy = (CCSprite*)object;
    if(enemy)
    {
      enemy->stopAllActions();
    }
  }
}
```

We first set has_game_stopped_ to true, which is important to the update function. We then unscheduled the functions responsible for firing the player and enemy bullets that we just saw using the unschedule function. Finally, we needed the enemies to stop moving too, so we iterated over the enemies_ array and called stopAllActions on each Enemy entity. What is important to know is that the StopGame function is called whenever the level is complete or the game is over.

Moving the enemies

Just to add some liveliness to the game, we move all the enemies across the screen from side to side. Let's take a look at the StartMovingEnemies function to get a clear idea:

```
void GameWorld::StartMovingEnemies()
{
  // compute maximum distance movable on both sides
  float max_distance_left = left_side_enemy_position_;
  float max_distance_right = SCREEN_SIZE.width -
    right_side_enemy_position_;
  // compute how much distance to cover per step
  float distance_per_move = max_enemy_size_.width*0.5;

  // calculate how many steps on both sides
```

```
    int max_moves_left = floor(max_distance_left / distance_per_move);
    int max_moves_right = floor(max_distance_right / distance_per_move);
    int moves_between_left_right = floor( (right_side_enemy_position_ -
      left_side_enemy_position_) / distance_per_move );

    CCActionInterval* move_left = CCSequence::createWithTwoActions(
      CCDelayTime::create(enemy_movement_duration_),
      CCEaseSineOut::create(CCMoveBy::create(0.25f,
      ccp(distance_per_move*-1, 0))));
    CCActionInterval* move_right = CCSequence::createWithTwoActions(
      CCDelayTime::create(enemy_movement_duration_),
      CCEaseSineOut::create(CCMoveBy::create(0.25f,
      ccp(distance_per_move, 0))));
    CCActionInterval* move_start_to_left = CCRepeat::create(
      move_left, max_moves_left);
    CCActionInterval* move_left_to_start = CCRepeat::create(
      move_right, max_moves_left);
    CCActionInterval* move_start_to_right = CCRepeat::create(
      move_right, max_moves_right);
    CCActionInterval* move_right_to_start = CCRepeat::create(
      move_left, max_moves_right);
    CCActionInterval* movement_sequence = CCSequence::create(
      move_start_to_left, move_left_to_start, move_start_to_right,
      move_right_to_start, NULL);

    // Move each Enemy
    CCObject* object = NULL;
    CCARRAY_FOREACH(enemies_, object)
    {
      CCSprite* enemy = (CCSprite*)object;
      if(enemy)
      {
        enemy->runAction(CCRepeatForever::create( (CCActionInterval*)
          movement_sequence->copy() ));
      }
    }
  }
```

We started by calculating the maximum distance the group of enemies can move both towards the left and the right. We also fixed the amount of distance to cover in one single step. We can now calculate how many steps it will take to reach the left and right edge of the screen and also how many steps are there between the left and right edges of the screen. Then, we created a sleuth of actions that will move the entire bunch of enemies repeatedly from side to side.

We defined the actions to move a single `Enemy` entity one step to the left and one step to the right into variables `move_left` and `move_right`, respectively. This movement needs to occur in steps, so the previous actions are a `CCSequence` of `CCDelayTime` followed by `CCMoveBy`. We then create four actions `move_start_to_left`, `move_left_to_start`, `move_start_to_right`, and `move_right_to_start` to take the entire group of enemies from their starting position to the left edge of the screen, then back to the starting position, then to the right edge of the screen and back to the start position. We created a `CCSequence` of these four actions and repeated them on every `Enemy` object in `enemies_`.

Fire the bullets!

Now that we have everything set in place, it's time for some fire power. The code for firing both player and enemy bullets is almost the same, so I will only go over the `FirePlayerBullet` and `RemovePlayerBullet` functions:

```
void GameWorld::FirePlayerBullet(float dt)
{
  // position the bullet slightly above Player
  CCPoint bullet_position = ccpAdd(player_->getPosition(),
    ccp(0, player_->getContentSize().height * 0.3));

  // create & add the bullet sprite
  CCSprite* bullet = CCSprite::createWithSpriteFrameName("sfbullet");
  sprite_batch_node_->addChild(bullet, E_LAYER_BULLETS);
  player_bullets_->addObject(bullet);

  // initialize position & scale
  bullet->setPosition(bullet_position);
  bullet->setScale(0.5f);

  // animate the bullet's entry
  CCScaleTo* scale_up = CCScaleTo::create(0.25f, 1.0f);
  bullet->runAction(scale_up);

  // move the bullet up
  CCMoveTo* move_up = CCMoveTo::create(BULLET_MOVE_DURATION,
    ccp(bullet_position.x, SCREEN_SIZE.height));
  CCCallFuncN* remove = CCCallFuncN::create(this, callfuncN_selector(
    GameWorld::RemovePlayerBullet));
  bullet->runAction(CCSequence::createWithTwoActions(move_up,
remove));

  SOUND_ENGINE->playEffect("shoot_player.wav");
}
```

We started by calculating the position of the bullet a bit above the player. We then created the player's bullet and added it to both `sprite_batch_node_` and `player_bullets_`. Next, we set the position and scale properties for the bullet sprite before running an action to scale it up. Finally, we created the action to move and the callback to `RemovePlayerBullet` once the move is finished. We ran a sequence of these two actions and played a sound effect to finish our `FirePlayerBullet` function.

Let's take a look at the following code:

```
void GameWorld::RemovePlayerBullet(CCNode* bullet)
{
  // remove bullet from list & GameWorld
  player_bullets_->removeObject(bullet);
  bullet->removeFromParentAndCleanup(true);
}
```

The `RemovePlayerBullet` function simply removes the bullet's sprite from the `sprite_batch_node_` and `player_bullets_` and is called when the bullet leaves the top edge of the screen or when it collides with an enemy or brick.

The update function

We call the `scheduleUpdate` function at the end of the `CreateLevel` function, thus we need to define an `update` function that will be called by the engine at every tick:

```
void GameWorld::update(float dt)
{
  // no collision checking if game has not started OR has stopped
    OR is paused
  if(!has_game_started_ || has_game_stopped_ || is_game_paused_)
    return;

  CheckCollisions();
}
```

You were expecting a bigger update function, weren't you? Well, when you have Cocos2d-x doing so much work for you, all you need to do is check for collisions. However, it is important that these collisions not be checked before the game has started, after it has stopped, or when it has been paused for obvious reasons. So, let's move ahead to collision detection in the next section.

Checking for collisions

Collision detection in this game will happen between the player's bullet and the enemies and bricks, and between the enemies' bullets and the player. Let's dive into the `CheckCollisions` function:

```
void GameWorld::CheckCollisions()
{
  CCObject* object = NULL;
  CCSprite* bullet = NULL;
  bool found_collision = false;

  // collisions between player bullets and bricks & enemies
  CCARRAY_FOREACH(player_bullets_, object)
  {
    bullet = (CCSprite*)object;
    if(bullet)
    {
      CCRect bullet_aabb = bullet->boundingBox();

      object = NULL;
      CCARRAY_FOREACH(bricks_, object)
      {
        CCSprite* brick = (CCSprite*)object;
        // rectangular collision detection between player bullet &
brick
        if(brick && bullet_aabb.intersectsRect(brick->boundingBox()))
        {
          // on collision, remove brick & player bullet
          RemoveBrick(brick);
          RemovePlayerBullet(bullet);
          found_collision = true;
          break;
        }
      }

      // found collision so stop checking
      if(found_collision)
        break;
```

```
        object = NULL;
        CCARRAY_FOREACH(enemies_, object)
        {
          CCSprite* enemy = (CCSprite*)object;
          // rectangular collision detection between player bullet &
enemy
          if(enemy && bullet_aabb.intersectsRect(enemy->boundingBox()))
          {
            // on collision, remove enemy & player bullet
            RemoveEnemy(enemy);
            RemovePlayerBullet(bullet);
            found_collision = true;
            break;
          }
        }

        // found collision so stop checking
        if(found_collision)
          break;
      }
    }

    // no collision checking with player when player is respawning
    if(player_->getIsRespawning())
      return;

      .
      .
      .
}
```

We first checked for collisions between the player bullets, enemies, and bricks. Thus, we iterated over `player_bullets_`. Within this loop, we iterated through `enemies_` and `bricks_`. Then, we called the `boundingBox` function that we had overridden in the `CustomSprite` class. Thus, we conducted a simple rectangular collision detection. If a collision was found, we called the `RemoveBrick` or `RemoveEnemy` function, followed by the function `RemovePlayerBullet`.

If the player wasn't respawning, we checked for collisions between the enemy bullets and the player in a similar way. If a collision was found, we told the player to die and called the `ReduceLives` function followed by the `RemoveEnemyBullet` function. The `ReduceLives` function simply removes one of the tiny life sprites from the HUD. This portion of the function has been left out and can be found in the source bundle for this chapter.

Let's quickly go over the functions we call when collisions occur under the different circumstances, starting with the `RemoveEnemy` and `RemoveBrick` functions:

```
void GameWorld::RemoveEnemy(CCSprite* enemy)
{
  // remove Enemy from array
  enemies_->removeObject(enemy);
  // tell Enemy to die & credit score
  AddScore(((Enemy*)enemy)->Die());

  // if all enemies are dead, level is complete
  if(enemies_->count() <= 0)
    LevelComplete();
}

void GameWorld::RemoveBrick(CCSprite* brick)
{
  // remove Brick from array
  bricks_->removeObject(brick);
  // tell Brick to crumble & credit score
  AddScore(((Brick*)brick)->Crumble());
}
```

The `RemoveEnemy` function first removes the enemy from `enemies_` and then tells the enemy to die. The score returned from the `Die` function of `Enemy` is then passed to the `AddScore` function, which basically updates the `score_` variable as well as the score label on the HUD. Finally, if all the enemies have been killed, the level is completed. The `RemoveBricks` function is virtually the same except there is no checking for level completion, as the player doesn't need to destroy all the bricks to complete a level.

Touch controls

So we have created the level, given the enemies some movement, implemented both enemy and player bullet firing, and implemented collision detection. But the `Player` is still stuck at the center of the screen. So, let's give him some movement and add some basic touch control:

```
void GameWorld::ccTouchesBegan(CCSet* set, CCEvent* event)
{
  CCTouch* touch = (CCTouch*)(*set->begin());
  CCPoint touch_point = touch->getLocationInView();
  touch_point = CCDirector::sharedDirector()->convertToGL(touch_
point);
```

```
  HandleTouch(touch_point);
}

void GameWorld::ccTouchesMoved(CCSet* set, CCEvent* event)
{
  CCTouch* touch = (CCTouch*)(*set->begin());
  CCPoint touch_point = touch->getLocationInView();
  touch_point = CCDirector::sharedDirector()->convertToGL(touch_
point);
  HandleTouch(touch_point);
}

void GameWorld::HandleTouch(CCPoint touch)
{
  // don't take touch when a popup is active & when player is
respawning
  if(is_popup_active_ || player_->getIsRespawning())
    return;

  player_->setPositionX(touch.x);
}
```

Both the `ccTouchesBegan` and `ccTouchesMoved` functions call the `HandleTouch` function with the converted touch point as parameter. The `HandleTouch` function then sets the player's *x* position to the touch's *x* position if there is no popup or if the player is not respawning.

Level complete and game over

A given level is complete when all enemies have been killed, and the game is over when all the player's lives are over. Let's see what happens in the `LevelComplete` and `GameOver` functions:

```
void GameWorld::LevelComplete()
{
  // tell player to leave screen
  player_->Leave();
  // stop game & update level variables
  StopGame();
  lives_to_carry_ = player_->getLives();
  score_to_carry_ = score_;
  // create & add the level complete popup
  LevelCompletePopup* level_complete_popup =
LevelCompletePopup::create(
    this, score_, player_->getLives());
```

```
    addChild(level_complete_popup, E_LAYER_POPUP);
    SOUND_ENGINE->playEffect("level_complete.wav");
  }
```

Now that the level is complete, we ask the player to leave the current level and stop the game. We need to carry forward the player's lives and score to the next level. Finally, we created and added the `LevelCompletePopup` and played a sound effect.

Let's take a look at the following code:

```
void GameWorld::GameOver()
{
  // stop game & reset level variables
  StopGame();
  current_level_ = 1;
  lives_to_carry_ = 3;
  score_to_carry_ = 0;
  // create & add the game over popup
  GameOverPopup* game_over_popup = GameOverPopup::create(this,
score_);
  addChild(game_over_popup, E_LAYER_POPUP);
  SOUND_ENGINE->playEffect("game_over.wav");
}
```

The player has lost all his lives so we must stop the game and reset the level number, lives, and score variables. We also added the `GameOverPopup` and played a sound effect.

With these last two functions, we have completed our third game in this book and our first Cocos2d-x game. I have skipped over some functionality in this chapter, for example, the animations on the `MainMenu`, the `BackgroundManager` class that takes care of the environment, and the `Popups` class. I urge you to go through the code bundle for this chapter to understand them.

Summary

SpaceCraze taught us a lot more about developing games with Cocos2d-x. We started the chapter with the awesome project-creator tool to create a cross-platform project. We then discussed how to extend the engine's most frequently used `CCSprite` class into our own `CustomSprite`. We then got creative by implementing a particle system. One of the important things you learned was storing and parsing our level data from XML files. This not only increases the scalability of the game, but also makes the level designer's job a lot easier. We also used actions for almost everything other than collision detection in this game. I'm sure you can see how much time, effort, and code we saved.

Our next game is sure to intrigue you. Want to know why? It's because we'll go back to the drawing board with primitive drawing and you will learn how to implement the really cool accelerometer control. Get ready!

4
Back to the Drawing Board

In our fourth game, we head back to the drawing board quite literally. We will create each element of the game using primitive drawing. Though that may seem a bit cumbersome to accomplish, Cocos2d-x makes it simple. Finally, we will add tilt controls to make this game even cooler!

In this chapter, you'll learn:

- How to use and extend the `CCDrawNode` class
- How to implement tilt controls
- How to add time-based difficulty progression

An introduction to Inverse Universe

This is yet another game set in space where you're surrounded by dark creatures that can destroy you by merely making contact. What makes matters worse is that you are absolutely powerless. The only way you can actually kill enemies is by the virtue of three wondrous power-ups: the bomb, the missile launcher, and the glorious shield.

The controls for this game are based on the accelerometer. Users will have to tilt their device to navigate the player ship. Inverse Universe is not about winning or losing; it is about survival. Thus, we won't be designing levels for this game like we did in the previous chapter. Instead, we will design difficulty levels in such a way that the game will get progressively more difficult as time goes by. This also lets the game stay open-ended and variable.

This is what you will have accomplished at the end of this chapter:

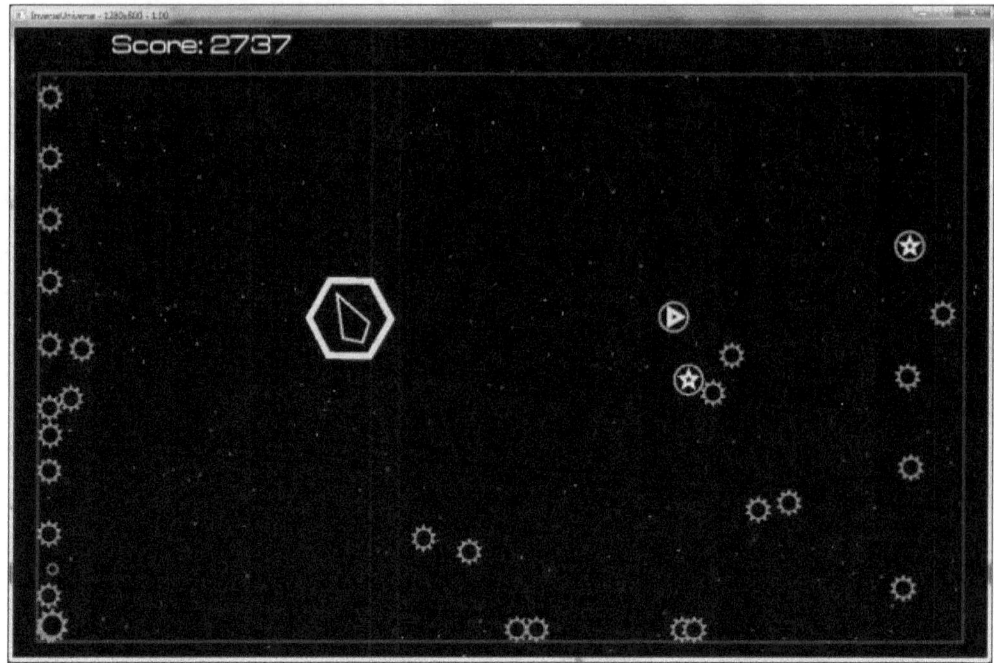

The CCDrawNode class

There are two ways to draw primitive shapes using the functionality provided by Cocos2d-x: one is using the various functions in `CCDrawingPrimitives` and the other way is using the `CCDrawNode` class. While the functions defined in `CCDrawingPrimitives` offer abundant variety, they also incur a performance penalty. The `CCDrawNode` class, on the other hand, provides just three different drawing functions and batches all its draw calls together to give much better performance. It also inherits from `CCNode` and thus we can run a few common actions on it! So, we will be using `CCDrawNode` to render our primitive shapes for this game.

Everything you saw in the preceding screenshot has been drawn using code—except for the score of course. All the main entities of our game, that is, the player, enemies, and power-ups, will inherit from `CCDrawNode` as you will see shortly. If you're confused about how primitive drawing can yield the preceding results, the following section will make things clearer.

Figuring out the geometry

The `CCDrawNode` class provides just three functions. These functions are `drawDot`, `drawSegment`, and `drawPolygon`, which enable you to draw a color-filled circle, a color-filled segment, and a color-filled polygon with a separate border, respectively. We will write a simple yet extremely resourceful function to help us with the generation of vertices for our game elements. However, before we write this utilitarian function, let's take a closer look at each element and the vertices they contain:

Game element	Visual	Visual with vertices
Player		
Enemy		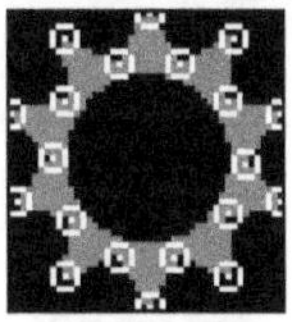
Shield	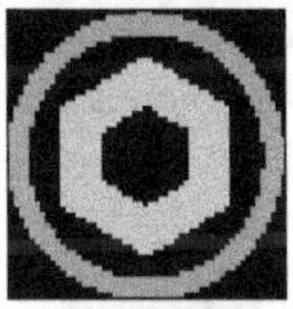	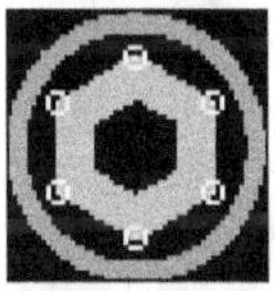
Bomb		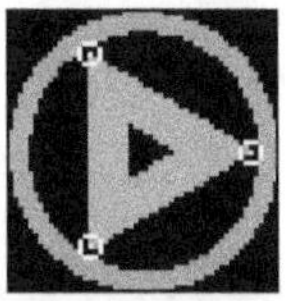
Missile launcher		

I have highlighted the vertices on each of these shapes to underline a basic geometrical object that we will use to our advantage in this game—the regular polygon. As most of you may know, a regular polygon is a polygon that is equiangular and equilateral. The interesting thing about a regular polygon is that we can use the parametric equation of a circle to get its vertices. This is exactly what the `GetRegularPolygonVertices` function from our helper class `GameGlobals` does. Let's take a look:

```
void GameGlobals::GetRegularPolygonVertices(vector<CCPoint> &vertices,
  int num_vertices, float circum_radius, float start_angle)
{
  vertices.clear();
  float delta_theta = 2 * M_PI / num_vertices;
  float theta = start_angle;
  for(int i = 0; i < num_vertices; ++i, theta += delta_theta)
  {
    vertices.push_back(CCPoint(circum_radius * cosf(theta),
      circum_radius * sinf(theta)));
  }
}
```

We passed in a `vector` of `CCPoint` that will actually hold the vertices along with the number of vertices, the radius of the encompassing circle, and the angle the first vertex will make with the x axis. The function then calculates the difference in angles between successive vertices of the polygon based on the number of vertices the polygon is supposed to have. Then, initializing `theta` with `start_angle`, we run a loop to generate each vertex using the parametric equation of the circle. To summarize, let's take a look at the output of this function:

```
GameGlobals::GetRegularPolygonVertices(vertices, 3, 50, 0)
```

This generates the vertices of the following triangle:

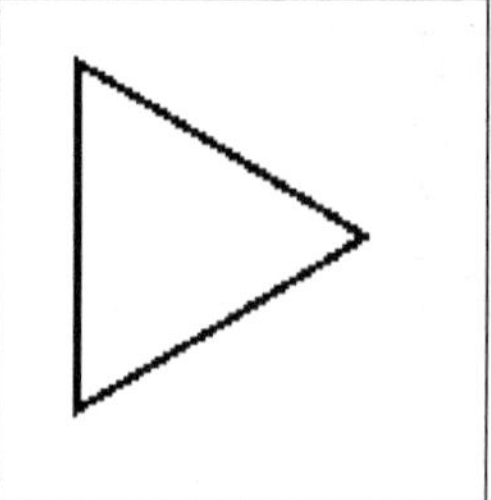

While `GameGlobals::GetRegularPolygonVertices(vertices, 3, 50, M_PI/2)` generates the vertices of the following triangle:

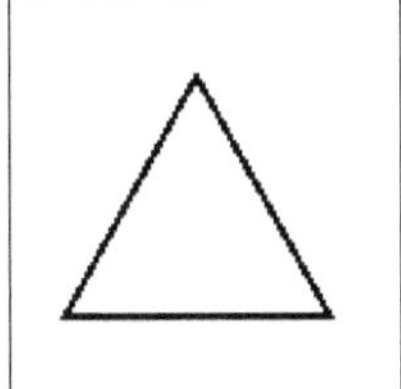

So, we have everything we need to draw most of the elements in our game. You can already fill in the blanks and see that the `Bomb`, which happens to be a power-up, can be summed up as a brown circle containing a green triangle. Similarly, the `Shield` power-up is a brown circle containing a cyan hexagon, but `MissileLauncher` and `Enemy` might not be that straightforward. We shall cross that bridge when we get there, but now we need to focus on the main elements of the game world.

Defining the elements of Inverse Universe

In this section, we will discuss the behavior of each element of the game in as much detail as possible, starting from the player, to the enemies and to each of the three power-ups. So, let's begin with the `Player` class.

The Player class

The `Player` class will inherit from `CCDrawNode` and will have a radius to be used for circular collision detection, a speed variable that will be set based on the input from the accelerometer, and a reference to `GameWorld`. Let's begin by defining the `init` function for the `Player` class:

```
bool Player::init()
{
  if(!CCDrawNode::init())
    return false;

  // generate vertices for the player
  CCPoint vertices[] = {CCPoint(PLAYER_RADIUS * 1.75f, 0),
    CCPoint(PLAYER_RADIUS * -0.875f, PLAYER_RADIUS),
    CCPoint(PLAYER_RADIUS * -1.75, 0), CCPoint(PLAYER_RADIUS *
-0.875f,
    PLAYER_RADIUS * -1)};
  // draw a green coloured player
```

```
    drawPolygon(vertices, 4, ccc4f(0, 0, 0, 0), 1.5f, ccc4f(0, 1, 0,
1));

    scheduleUpdate();
    return true;
}
```

The `init` function for the parent class is called first before defining the vertices that will make the player's ship. The variable `PLAYER_RADIUS` used to calculate the vertices has been defined in the `GameGlobals.h` file and is equivalent to 20 pixels. We then call the `drawPolygon` function, passing in the array of vertices, number of vertices, fill color, border thickness, and border color. We need all this to draw the player. Since this is a test of survival, our player must dodge enemies to prevent being destroyed but invariably death catches up to us all. The player dies in the following way in the `Die` function:

```
void Player::Die()
{
  // don't die if already dying
  if(is_dying_)
    return;

  is_dying_ = true;
  // stop moving
  speed_.x = 0;
  speed_.y = 0;

  float shake_duration = 0.5f;
  int num_shakes = 8;
  // create & animate the death and end the game afterwards
  CCActionInterval* shake = CCSpawn::createWithTwoActions(
    CCScaleTo::create(shake_duration, 1.2f), CCRepeat::create(
    CCSequence::createWithTwoActions(CCRotateBy::create(shake_
duration/(num_shakes*2),
    -20.0), CCRotateBy::create(shake_duration/(num_shakes*2), 20.0)),
num_shakes));
  CCActionInterval* shrink = CCEaseSineIn::create(CCScaleTo::create(0
.1f, 0.0f));
  CCActionInterval* death = CCSequence::create(shake, shrink, NULL);

  runAction(CCSequence::createWithTwoActions(death,
CCCallFunc::create(this,
  callfunc_selector(Player::Dead))));
  SOUND_ENGINE->playEffect("blast_player.wav");
}

void Player::Dead()
{
  game_world_->GameOver();
}
```

A collision may occur in every tick of the game loop thus we prevent the `Die` function from being called repeatedly by checking and immediately enabling the `is_dying_` flag. We then stop movement, animate the death with the help of a few composite actions, and also play a sound. The callback to the function `Dead` tells `GameWorld` to finish the game. There is more to the `Player` class than just this, but we will define the remaining behavior, such as the movement, when we get to the *Moving the player* section of this chapter.

The Enemy class

The enemies in this game are deadly creatures that follow the player throughout the game and get faster the longer they live. Let's give them their lethal characteristics by first defining their `init` function:

```
bool Enemy::init(GameWorld* instance)
{
  if(!CCDrawNode::init())
    return false;

  game_world_ = instance;
  CCPoint vertices[NUM_SPIKES*2];
  GenerateVertices(vertices);

  // draw the star shaped polygon filled with red colour
  drawPolygon(vertices, NUM_SPIKES*2, ccc4f(1, 0, 0, 1), 1.5f,
    ccc4f(1, 0, 0, 1));
  // draw a black hole in the middle
  drawDot(CCPointZero, ENEMY_RADIUS, ccc4f(0, 0, 0, 1));

  setScale(0.0f);

  return true;
}
```

We begin by calling the `init` function of the parent class and storing a reference to `GameWorld`. We then initialize an array of the type `CCPoint` and pass it into the `GenerateVertices` function. Here, `NUM_SPIKES` equals `10`. We then call the `drawPolygon` function followed by the `drawDot` function to create a red colour-filled polygon and a black colour-filled circle, giving the enemies their deadly appearance. Now let's take a look at the `GenerateVertices` function:

```
void Enemy::GenerateVertices(CCPoint vertices[])
{
```

```
    vector<CCPoint> inner_vertices, outer_vertices;
    // get two regular polygons, one smaller than the other and with a
      slightly advance rotation
    GameGlobals::GetRegularPolygonVertices(inner_vertices,
      NUM_SPIKES, ENEMY_RADIUS);
    GameGlobals::GetRegularPolygonVertices(outer_vertices, NUM_SPIKES,
      ENEMY_RADIUS * 1.5f, M_PI / NUM_SPIKES);

    // run a loop to splice the polygons together to form a star
    for(int i = 0; i < NUM_SPIKES; ++i)
    {
      vertices[i*2] = inner_vertices[i];
      vertices[i*2 + 1] = outer_vertices[i];
    }
  }
```

This function simply creates two `vectors` for the inner and outer vertices that make up the enemy's spiky appearance. Furthermore, you can see that we fill up these two vectors with vertices generated by the `GetRegularPolygonVertices` function that we defined earlier. Notice how the radius for the outer vertices is 1.5 times the radius for the inner vertices. We then run a loop and fill up the input array of `CCPoint` with inner and outer vertices, respectively. This order of inner vertex followed by outer vertex is important because otherwise we wouldn't get a properly filled polygon. You should reverse the order and see for yourself what happens to gain a better understanding of how the colour is filled inside a convex polygon.

Let's now give the enemies their behavior by defining the `Update` function:

```
  void Enemy::Update(CCPoint player_position, bool towards_player)
  {
    // no movement while spawning
    if(is_spawning_)
      return;

    // first find a vector pointing to the player
    CCPoint direction = ccpSub(player_position, m_obPosition);
    // normalize direction then multiply with the speed_multiplier_
    speed_ = ccpMult(direction.normalize(), speed_multiplier_ * (
      towards_player ? 1 : -1));

    // restrict movement within the boundary of the game
    CCPoint next_position = ccpAdd(m_obPosition, speed_);
    if(RECT_CONTAINS_CIRCLE(game_world_->boundary_rect_, next_position,
      ENEMY_RADIUS * 1.5f))
    {
```

```
      setPosition(next_position);
    }
    else
    {
      if(RECT_CONTAINS_CIRCLE(game_world_->boundary_rect_, CCPoint(
        next_position.x - speed_.x, next_position.y), ENEMY_RADIUS *
1.5f))
      {
        setPosition(ccp(next_position.x - speed_.x, next_position.y));
      }
      else if(RECT_CONTAINS_CIRCLE(game_world_->boundary_rect_, CCPoint(
        next_position.x, next_position.y - speed_.y), ENEMY_RADIUS *
1.5f))
      {
        setPosition(ccp(next_position.x, next_position.y - speed_.y));
      }
    }
  }
```

The `Update` function, called from the main update loop by `GameWorld`, is passed the player's position and whether the movement should be toward or away from the player. Why would such a deadly, fearless enemy be moving away from the player you wonder? Well, that happens when the player has the shield power-up enabled of course! Each enemy also has a spawning animation defined in the `Spawn` function, during which it is not supposed to move—hence the conditional and the return statements. We first calculate the speed for the enemy based on the direction towards or away from the player and a speed multiplier. Next, we perform some bounds checking and ensure that the enemy does not leave the boundary that is defined by `boundary_rect_` inside `GameWorld`. To perform this boundary check, we define a resourceful function in `GameGlobals.h` with the name `RECT_CONTAINS_CIRCLE`.

I'm sure you remember how the enemies are supposed to move faster the longer they live. This behavior is defined in the `Tick` function of the `Enemy` class:

```
void Enemy::Tick()
{
  // no ticking while spawning
  if(is_spawning_)
    return;

  ++ time_alive_;

  // as time increases, so does speed
  switch(time_alive_)
  {
```

```
      case E_SLOW:
        speed_multiplier_ = 0.5f;
        break;
      case E_MEDIUM:
        speed_multiplier_ = 0.75f;
        break;
      case E_FAST:
        speed_multiplier_ = 1.25f;
        break;
      case E_SUPER_FAST:
        speed_multiplier_ = 1.5f;
        break;
    }
  }
```

The speed multiplier that you saw inside the `Enemy::Update` function is given its value in the `Tick` function. We update the variable `time_alive_` that measures the seconds for which the enemy has been alive and, based on its value, assign a particular speed value to the `speed_multiplier_` variable so the enemy moves faster the longer that it lives. To enumerate the various speeds an enemy may move at, an enum by the name of `EEnemySpeedTimer` is defined in `GameGlobals.h` as follows:

```
enum EEnemySpeedTimer
{
  E_SLOW = 5,
  E_MEDIUM = 10,
  E_FAST = 15,
  E_SUPER_FAST = 25,
};
```

We now have a player and an enemy that follows the player at increasing speeds. But the player still has no way to defend himself or to defeat the enemies. So let's define the last set of elements, the power-ups.

The PowerUp class

The power-ups in this game constitute a bomb, a missile launcher, and a shield. All three of these power-ups have some behavior in common. They all have icons with which the player must collide to activate them, they all stay on screen for a specific time after which they must disappear, and they can all be activated or deactivated. We separate these behaviors in a parent class named `PowerUp` as follows:

```
#ifndef POWERUP_H_
#define POWERUP_H_

#include "GameGlobals.h"

class GameWorld;

class PowerUp : public CCDrawNode
{
public:
  PowerUp() : time_left_(0), speed_(CCPointZero), is_active_(false),
must_be_removed_(false), game_world_(NULL){}
  ~PowerUp(){};

  virtual bool init(GameWorld* instance);

  virtual void Update();
  virtual void Tick();
  virtual void Spawn();
  virtual void Activate();
  virtual void Deactivate();

  CC_SYNTHESIZE(int, time_left_, TimeLeft);
  CC_SYNTHESIZE(CCPoint, speed_, Speed);
  CC_SYNTHESIZE(bool, is_active_, IsActive);
  CC_SYNTHESIZE(bool, must_be_removed_, MustBeRemoved);

protected:
  GameWorld* game_world_;
};

#endif // POWERUP_H_
```

The PowerUp class will extend the CCDrawNode class, since all the power-ups will need primitive drawing functionality. This class also defines a few variables to keep track of the time on screen, the movement speed, whether the power-up is active, and finally whether it should be removed by GameWorld. The main lifecycle functions are declared here and marked as virtual so the child classes can override them to implement their own respective behaviors. Let's now take a look at some of these functions defined in PowerUp.cpp:

```
bool PowerUp::init(GameWorld* instance)
{
  if(!CCDrawNode::init())
    return false;

  game_world_ = instance;
  // calculate how much time the power-up should wait on screen before
     activation
  time_left_ = MAX_POWERUP_WAIT_ON_SCREEN / 2 +
    CCRANDOM_0_1() * MAX_POWERUP_WAIT_ON_SCREEN / 2;
  // calculate speed
  speed_ = CCPoint(CCRANDOM_MINUS1_1() * 2,
    CCRANDOM_MINUS1_1() * 2);

  // draw the brown coloured ring
  drawDot(CCPointZero, POWERUP_ICON_OUTER_RADIUS,
    ccc4f(0.73725f, 0.5451f, 0, 1));
  drawDot(CCPointZero, POWERUP_ICON_OUTER_RADIUS - 3,
    ccc4f(0, 0, 0, 1));
  setScale(0.0f);

  return true;
}
```

The init function basically takes care of maintaining a reference to GameWorld for ease of access and initializing a few variables. Each power-up comes to life with its respective icon, but all those icons have their outer ring in common with each other, so we define that here in the parent class. We also set the scale initially to 0 since we will be animating the birth of each power-up in the Spawn function. We now look at the Update function that will be called at every tick by GameWorld:

```
void PowerUp::Update()
{
  // bounce within the boundary
  if(!RECT_CONTAINS_CIRCLE(game_world_->boundary_rect_, m_obPosition,
    POWERUP_ICON_OUTER_RADIUS))
  {
```

```
        // bounce off the left & right edge
        if( (m_obPosition.x - POWERUP_ICON_OUTER_RADIUS) <
          game_world_->boundary_rect_.origin.x ||
          (m_obPosition.x + POWERUP_ICON_OUTER_RADIUS) > (
            game_world_->boundary_rect_.origin.x +
            game_world_->boundary_rect_.size.width) )
          speed_.x *= -1;
        // bounce off the top & bottom edge
        if( (m_obPosition.y + POWERUP_ICON_OUTER_RADIUS) > (
          game_world_->boundary_rect_.origin.y +
            game_world_->boundary_rect_.size.height) ||
          (m_obPosition.y - POWERUP_ICON_OUTER_RADIUS) <
            game_world_->boundary_rect_.origin.y )
          speed_.y *= -1;
      }

      setPosition(m_obPosition.x + speed_.x, m_obPosition.y + speed_.y);
    }
```

This function basically takes care of moving the power-up within the boundary defined in `GameWorld` (similar to the `Enemy` class) by using the `RECT_CONTAINS_CIRCLE` function.

Let's take a look at the following code:

```
void PowerUp::Tick()
{
  -- time_left_;

  // remove this power-up in the next iteration when it's on-screen
    time is over
  if(time_left_ < 0)
  {
    must_be_removed_ = true;
    runAction(CCSequence::createWithTwoActions(CCEaseBackIn::create(
      CCScaleTo::create(0.25f, 0.0f)), CCRemoveSelf::create(true)));
  }
}
```

Each power-up must also have a life time after which it should be removed. This happens in the `Tick` function that is called by `GameWorld` once every second.

Let's take a look at the following code:

```
void PowerUp::Activate()
{
  // clear the geometry and stop all actions
  // now the child classes can add their own behaviour
  is_active_ = true;
  clear();
  stopAllActions();
}

void PowerUp::Deactivate()
{
  // remove this power-up in the next iteration
  runAction(CCSequence::createWithTwoActions(
    CCDelayTime::create(0.01f), CCRemoveSelf::create(true)));
  must_be_removed_ = true;
}
```

Finally, we have the `Activate` and `Deactivate` functions that set the appropriate flags and prepare the power-up for whatever behaviour the child class may define. Notice how the `clear` function is called in the `Activate` method. This happens because the power-up is initially nothing but an icon and must turn into its respective manifestation now that it has been triggered or activated. Hence, we call the `clear` function of parent class `CCDrawNode`, which basically clears all the geometry drawn inside the node so far. Now that we have the parent class defined, we can take the time to define each power-up separately starting with the `Bomb` class, followed by the `MissileLauncher` class and `Shield` class.

The Bomb class

The behavior of the `Bomb` class is quite simple: when triggered, this power-up creates a big explosion that stays on screen for a couple of seconds. All enemies that come in contact with this explosion die a miserable, fiery death. Let's begin by defining the `init` function of this power-up:

```
bool Bomb::init(GameWorld* instance)
{
  if(!PowerUp::init(instance))
    return false;
```

```
    // get vertices for a triangle
    vector<CCPoint> vertices;
    GameGlobals::GetRegularPolygonVertices(vertices, 3,
      POWERUP_ICON_INNER_RADIUS);
    // draw a triangle with a green border
    drawPolygon(&vertices[0], 3, ccc4f(0, 0, 0, 0), 3, ccc4f(0, 1, 0,
  1));

    return true;
  }
```

Right at the beginning, we must invoke the `init` function of the parent class and pass in the reference to `GameWorld`. Once that is done, we can generate the individual icon for this power-up, which in this case is nothing but a green coloured triangle. Let's wrap up the `Bomb` by overriding the `Activate` function:

```
void Bomb::Activate()
{
  // must activate only once
  if(is_active_)
    return;

  // first call parent function
  PowerUp::Activate();

  // create a blast 8 times the size of the player that should last
for
    2 seconds
  Blast* blast = Blast::createWithRadiusAndDuration(
    PLAYER_RADIUS * 8, 2.0f);
  // position blast over bomb
  blast->setPosition(m_obPosition);
  game_world_->AddBlast(blast);
  SOUND_ENGINE->playEffect("big_blast.wav");

  PowerUp::Deactivate();
}
```

This function must only be called once, hence the return statement at the beginning. We then immediately call the `Activate` function of the parent class, since we want the geometry cleared. Now comes the interesting part. This is where we actually create the explosion. This is taken care of by another class: `Blast`. Why couldn't we just create an explosion within this perfectly capable `Bomb` class itself? The reason will become abundantly clear when we define the behaviour of the missiles. For now, all I can tell you is that just like bombs, missiles also explode and hence that functionality is shared by the two and separated out. We then set the position of this blast over the bomb and finally hand it over to `GameWorld`. We also play a sound effect before deactivating the bomb. Let's now glance at the behaviour of the `Blast` class.

The Blast class

A blast represents nothing but an explosion that obliterates all enemies that it comes in contact with. The `Blast` class will inherit from `CCDrawNode` and will use a set of circles to draw an explosion in the `initWithRadiusAndDuration` function:

```
bool Blast::initWithRadiusAndDuration(float radius, float duration)
{
  if(!CCDrawNode::init())
  {
    return false;
  }

  radius_ = radius;
  duration_ = duration;

  // initially scale down completely
  setScale(0.0f);
  drawDot(CCPointZero, radius_, ccc4f(1, 0.34118f, 0, 1));
  drawDot(CCPointZero, radius_ * 0.8f, ccc4f(1, 0.68235f, 0, 0.25f));
  drawDot(CCPointZero, radius_ * 0.75f, ccc4f(1, 0.68235f, 0, 0.5f));
  drawDot(CCPointZero, radius_ * 0.7f, ccc4f(1, 0.68235f, 0, 0.5f));
  drawDot(CCPointZero, radius_ * 0.6f, ccc4f(1, 0.83529f, 0.40392f,
    0.25f));
  drawDot(CCPointZero, radius_ * 0.55f, ccc4f(1, 0.83529f, 0.40392f,
    0.5f));
  drawDot(CCPointZero, radius_ * 0.5f, ccc4f(1, 0.83529f, 0.40392f,
    0.5));
  drawDot(CCPointZero, radius_ * 0.4f, ccc4f(1, 1, 1, 0.25f));
  drawDot(CCPointZero, radius_ * 0.35f, ccc4f(1, 1, 1, 0.75f));
  drawDot(CCPointZero, radius_ * 0.3f, ccc4f(1, 1, 1, 1));
```

```
    // scale-up, then wait for 'duration_' amount of seconds
      before cooling down
    runAction(CCSequence::create(CCEaseSineOut::create(
      CCScaleTo::create(0.25f, 1.0f)), CCDelayTime::create(duration_),
      CCCallFunc::create(this, callfunc_selector(Blast::Cooldown)),
  NULL));

    return true;
  }
```

The `initWithRadiusAndDuration` function saves the blast radius that `GameWorld` will use for collision detection and also the duration after which this blast should cool down. We then draw circles of different colors to represent our vibrant explosion. We animate its entry and use the `CCDelayTime` to keep the explosion active for the time specified by `duration_` before finally telling it to cool down.

Let's take a look at the following code:

```
void Blast::Cooldown()
{
  // remove this blast in the next iteration
  must_be_removed_ = true;
  // animate exit then remove with cleanup
  runAction(CCSequence::createWithTwoActions(CCEaseSineOut::create(
    CCScaleTo::create(0.5f, 0.0f)), CCRemoveSelf::create(true)));
}
```

The cool down involves an exit animation and enabling the `must_be_removed_` flag so that `GameWorld` will remove this `Blast` in the next iteration.

The MissileLauncher class

The behavior of the `MissileLauncher` class is to spawn five missiles upon activation by the player. This class should also assign a target for each missile to hit and hand them over to `GameWorld`. This is how its `init` function looks inside `MissileLauncher.cpp`:

```
bool MissileLauncher::init(GameWorld* instance)
{
  if(!PowerUp::init(instance))
    return false;

  vector<CCPoint> vertices1;
  vector<CCPoint> vertices2;
```

```
    vector<CCPoint> vertices;

    // get two regular pentagons, one smaller than the other and with a
      slightly advance rotation
    GameGlobals::GetRegularPolygonVertices(vertices1, 5,
      POWERUP_ICON_INNER_RADIUS - 6, M_PI * -2/20);
    GameGlobals::GetRegularPolygonVertices(vertices2, 5,
      POWERUP_ICON_INNER_RADIUS, M_PI * 2/20);

    // run a loop to splice the pentagons together to form a star
    for(int i = 0; i < 5; ++i)
    {
      vertices.push_back(vertices1[i]);
      vertices.push_back(vertices2[i]);
    }

    // draw the star shaped polygon with yellow border
    drawPolygon(&vertices[0], 10, ccc4f(0, 0, 0, 0), 2,
      ccc4f(0.88235, 0.96078, 0, 1));

    return true;
  }
```

The `init` method for all power-ups takes care of creating the icon, so we begin by generating the vertices for this particular power-up's icon. Notice how we fetch vertices for two regular pentagons here and then splice them together into another `vector`. We then pass that vector to the `drawPolygon` function to get the yellow star with a border of 2 pixels. If you're confused, the following images will clear things up:

Inner Pentagon (vertices1)	**Outer Pentagon (vertices2)**	**Inner and Outer Pentagon (vertices)**
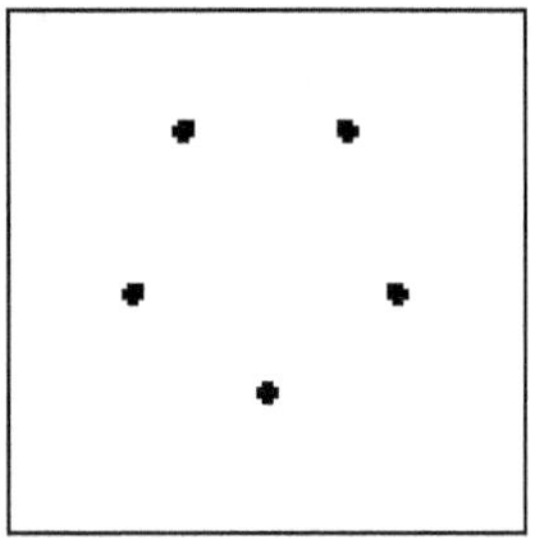	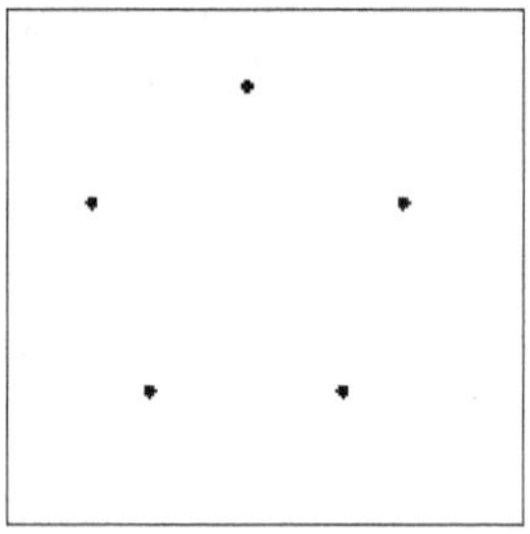	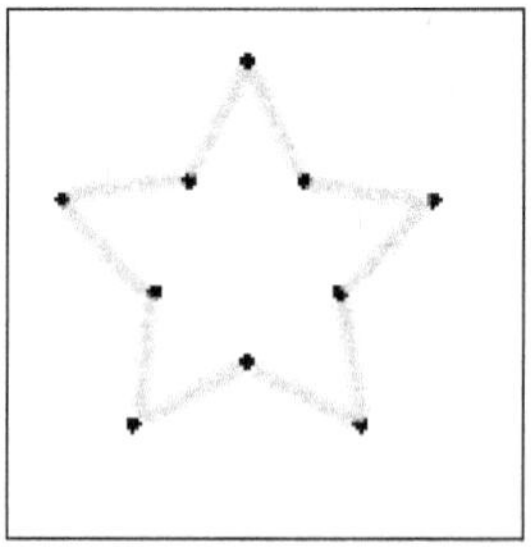

Now, let's define what happens when the missile launcher has been activated in the `Activate` function:

```
void MissileLauncher::Activate()
{
  if(is_active_)
    return;

  PowerUp::Activate();

  // generate a target for each missile
  vector<CCPoint> target = GenerateTargets();
  // generate an initial direction vertor for each missile
  vector<CCPoint> initial_direction;
  GameGlobals::GetRegularPolygonVertices(initial_direction, 5,
    SCREEN_SIZE.width/4, M_PI * 2/20);

  for(int i = 0; i < 5; ++i)
  {
    // create a missile with a target, initial direction & speed
    Missile* missile = Missile::createWithTarget(game_world_,
target[i],
      ccpMult(initial_direction[i].normalize(), MISSILE_SPEED));
    // position the missile over the launcher
    missile->setPosition(m_obPosition);
    game_world_->AddMissile(missile);
  }

  SOUND_ENGINE->playEffect("missile.wav");

  PowerUp::Deactivate();
}
```

The `MissileLauncher` class is supposed to spawn five missiles that fly towards enemies and explode on contact. Thus, the first thing we need to do is generate targets and initial directions for each missile. We then run a loop to create five `Missile` objects and pass in a reference to `GameWorld`, the target position, and the initial speed. The initial speed is a scalar multiplication of `initial_direction` with a constant called `MISSILE_SPEED`.

We set the position for each missile and hand them over to `GameWorld`. We wind up this missile launcher by playing a sound effect and finally deactivate this power-up since its job is done. Before we move to the `Missile` class, let's take a look at the `GenerateTargets` function:

```
vector<CCPoint> MissileLauncher::GenerateTargets()
{
  vector<CCPoint> target_points;
  target_points.clear();

  int targets_found = 0;

  int num_enemies = game_world_->enemies_->count();
  // loop through the first 5 enemies within GameWorld &
    save their positions
  for(int i = 0; i < num_enemies && targets_found < 5; ++i)
  {
    Enemy* enemy = (Enemy*)game_world_->enemies_->objectAtIndex(i);
    target_points.push_back(enemy->getPosition());
    ++ targets_found;
  }

  // if less than 5 enemies were found, fill up with random positions
    within the boundary
  while(targets_found < 5)
  {
    target_points.push_back(CCPoint(CCRANDOM_0_1() * (
      game_world_->boundary_rect_.origin.x +
      game_world_->boundary_rect_.size.width) , CCRANDOM_0_1() * (
      game_world_->boundary_rect_.origin.y +
      game_world_->boundary_rect_.size.height)));
    ++ targets_found;
  }

  return target_points;
}
```

This function returns a vector of `CCPoint`, which will represent the target for a given missile. So, we loop over the enemies currently held by `GameWorld` and save the position of the first five enemies we find. However, if we don't have enough targets after this loop, the missile still must fire to somewhere. Thus, we send that missile to any random point within the boundary of the game. So, we have launched five missiles with a target to hunt down and kill. Let's now take a look at the behaviour of a missile by defining the `Missile` class.

The Missile class

The behaviour of the missiles is to fly towards their assigned target points and explode. However, we want it to look cool so we define the behaviour of these missiles such that they follow a smooth curved path towards their targets. Now, let's define their creation in the `initWithTarget` function:

```
bool Missile::initWithTarget(GameWorld* instance,
  CCPoint target, CCPoint speed)
{
  if(!CCDrawNode::init())
  {
    return false;
  }

  game_world_ = instance;
  target_ = target;
  speed_ = speed;

  // generate vertices for the missile
  CCPoint vertices[] = {CCPoint(MISSILE_RADIUS * 1.75f, 0),
    CCPoint(MISSILE_RADIUS * -0.875f, MISSILE_RADIUS),
    CCPoint(MISSILE_RADIUS * -1.75f, 0),
    CCPoint(MISSILE_RADIUS * -0.875f, MISSILE_RADIUS * -1)};
  // draw a yellow coloured missile
  drawPolygon(vertices, 4, ccc4f(0.91765f, 1, 0.14118f, 1), 0,
    ccc4f(0, 0, 0, 0));

  // schedule to explode after 5 seconds
  scheduleOnce(schedule_selector(Missile::Explode), 5.0f);
  scheduleUpdate();

  return true;
}
```

The `Missile` class will also inherit `CCDrawNode`, which means we must call the parent class' `init` function. We save a reference to `GameWorld`, the target point, and the initial speed that this missile should move at. We then define the missile's visual representation by creating an array of vertices and passing them to the `drawPoly` function. This results in a yellow color-filled missile that is similar in shape to the `Player` entity. Finally, we schedule the `Explode` function to be called after 5.0f seconds. This is because we want this missile to automatically explode after sometime if it hasn't collided with any enemies.

We wind up this function by scheduling the `update` function, which we will define as follows:

```
void Missile::update(float dt)
{
  // find a vector pointing to the target
  CCPoint direction = ccpSub(target_, m_obPosition).normalize();
  // add the direction to the speed for smooth curved movement
  speed_.x += direction.x;
  speed_.y += direction.y;
  // normalize the speed & multiply with a constant
  speed_ = ccpMult(speed_.normalize(), MISSILE_SPEED);

  setPosition(m_obPosition.x + speed_.x, m_obPosition.y + speed_.y);

  // update the rotation of the missile
  float angle = ccpToAngle(ccpSub(m_obPosition, previous_position_));
  setRotation(CC_RADIANS_TO_DEGREES(angle * -1));
  previous_position_ = m_obPosition;

  // explode the missile if it has roughly reached the target
  if(m_obPosition.fuzzyEquals(target_, ENEMY_RADIUS * 1.5f))
  {
    Explode();
  }
}
```

The `update` function is responsible for updating the position and rotation of the missile. Thus, we calculate the difference between the target and the missile's current position. Normalizing this `CCPoint` will give us the direction in which this missile must move in order to hit its target. We then add this direction to `speed_` because we want the missile to move in a smooth curve towards its target. Finally, we normalize `speed_` and multiply it with a constant, `MISSILE_SPEED`. If we don't do this last step, the missile's speed will keep increasing and it will never reach its target.

We also set the rotation of this missile using the useful `ccpToAngle` function, passing in the current and previous positions. To wrap up the `update` function, we check whether the missile has reached its target by using the `fuzzyEquals` function of the `CCPoint` class. This function basically adds some tolerance to the equality checking of two points. In this case, this tolerance is the outer radius of an enemy. If a collision is detected, we order this missile to explode in the `Explode` function, which we will define as follows:

```
void Missile::Explode(float dt)
{
  // can't expode more than once
  if(has_exploded_)
    return;

  has_exploded_ = true;
  // create three blasts on explosion
  for(int i = 0; i < 3; ++i)
  {
    // create a blast twice the size of the player that should last
for
      quarter of a second
    Blast* blast = Blast::createWithRadiusAndDuration(
      PLAYER_RADIUS * 2, 0.25f);
    // position it randomly around the missile
    blast->setPosition(ccpAdd(m_obPosition,
      CCPoint(CCRANDOM_0_1() * PLAYER_RADIUS * 2 * i,
      CCRANDOM_0_1() * PLAYER_RADIUS * 2 * i)));
    game_world_->AddBlast(blast);
  }
  // remove this missile in the next iteration
  must_be_removed_ = true;
  runAction(CCSequence::createWithTwoActions(
    CCDelayTime::create(0.01f), CCRemoveSelf::create(true)));
  SOUND_ENGINE->playEffect("small_blast.wav");
}
```

A missile might explode on three different occasions; when it has run out of time, when it has reached its target, or when it has collided with an enemy on the way to its target. We must ensure that a missile must explode only once and hence we enable the `has_exploded_` flag to prevent further explosions. Each missile explodes and results in three blasts. In a loop, we create three `Blast` objects, position them, and hand them over to `GameWorld`. Notice that these blasts are smaller and stay for much lesser time than the blast created by the `Bomb`. We finally finish the `Explode` function by enabling the `must_be_removed_` flag, running a `CCRemoveSelf` action, and playing a sound effect. That wraps up our `Missile` class and it is time to define our last power-up, and my personal favorite, the `Shield` class.

The Shield class

The shield is without a doubt the most powerful of all the power-ups. That's because this shield not only protects the player from contact with the enemies, but also kills all enemies that come in contact with it. Now, the enemies know this and start moving away from the player the moment the shield is activated. Don't tell me you still like the `MissileLauncher` the most. The shield lasts for a whole of 10 seconds before it disables. The `Shield` class will override the `Tick` function in addition to the `Update`, `Activate`, and `Deactivate` functions from the `PowerUp` parent class.

The `init` function for the `Shield` class simply creates a cyan hexagon as the icon, and hence we will skip straight to the `Update` function that is called at every tick from `GameWorld`:

```
void Shield::Update()
{
  if(!is_active_)
  {
    PowerUp::Update();
  }
  else
  {
    // after activation, shield will follow the player
    setPosition(game_world_->player_->getPosition());
    setRotation(game_world_->player_->getRotation());
  }
}
```

The behavior of this power-up is different before and after activation. Before activation, the shield is like every other power-up: it just floats around the screen. After activation, however, the shield must stick to the player and rotate along with the player. Next up is the `Tick` function that is called by `GameWorld` once every second:

```
void Shield::Tick()
{
  if(is_active_)
  {
    -- shield_time_left_;

    // deactivate the shield when it's time is over
    if(shield_time_left_ <= 0)
    {
```

```
        Deactivate();
      }
      // start blinking the shield when there are just two seconds left
      else if(shield_time_left_ == 2)
      {
        CCActionInterval* blink = CCBlink::create(2.0f, 8);
        blink->setTag(SHIELD_BLINK_TAG);
        runAction(blink);
      }
    }
    else
    {
      PowerUp::Tick();
    }
  }
```

Before activation, the shield is dormant just like the other power-ups so we call the `Tick` function of the parent class. But after activation, we monitor how much time the shield has left till it must be disabled by the updating variable `shield_time_left_`. Initially, `shield_time_left_` is set to `10` and is decremented every `Tick`. When the value hits `0`, we `Deactivate` the shield. When the value hits `2`, we start blinking the shield so the user knows that shield is about to be disabled and that there are just 2 seconds of carnage left. We set a tag for the blinking action that will come in handy later.

Let's take a look at the following code:

```
void Shield::Activate()
{
  if(is_active_)
    return;

  // if a shield already exists on the player,
  if(game_world_->player_->GetShield())
  {
    // reset the existing shield
    game_world_->player_->GetShield()->Reset();
    // deactivate self
    Deactivate();
    removeFromParentAndCleanup(true);
  }
```

We first check if the player has a shield already enabled. Why should we do that? This is because we can't have two shields active at the same time—that would look silly! Instead, we reset the first shield and discard the second one.

Thus, if a shield is already active on the player, we disable this shield by calling the `Deactivate` method and call `removeFromParentAndCleanup`. Also, we call the `Reset` function of the shield currently active on the player, which looks like this:

```
void Shield::Reset()
{
  // reset the shield duration
  shield_time_left_ = SHIELD_DURATION;
  // stop any blinking action & show the shield if it was hidden due
to the blink
  stopActionByTag(SHIELD_BLINK_TAG);
  setVisible(true);
}
```

As you can see, we simply reset the duration of the shield and stop any blinking action. That last `setVisible` is there to undo any invisibility due to the blinking. Now, let's move back to the `Activate` function:

```
// else if shield doesn't exist on the player
 else
 {
  PowerUp::Activate();

  // set the shield duration
  shield_time_left_ = SHIELD_DURATION;
  setScale(0);

  // generate & draw a bigger cyan hexagon
  vector<CCPoint> vertices;
  GameGlobals::GetRegularPolygonVertices(vertices, 6,
    PLAYER_RADIUS * 2.5f);
  drawPolygon(&vertices[0], 6, ccc4f(0, 0, 0, 0), 4,
    ccc4f(0, 0.96862f, 1, 1));

  // animate the activation & life of the shield
  runAction(CCEaseBounceOut::create(CCScaleTo::create(0.25f, 1.0f)));
  runAction(CCRepeatForever::create(CCSequence::createWithTwoActions(
    CCEaseSineOut::create(CCScaleTo::create(0.25f, 1.15f)),
    CCEaseSineOut::create(CCScaleTo::create(0.25f, 1.0f)))));
```

```
    // inform the player that it now has a shield around it
    game_world_->player_->SetShield(this);
  }

  SOUND_ENGINE->playEffect("shield.wav");
}
```

If there is no shield active on the player, we call the `Activate` function of the parent class and initialize the shield's duration again. We also set the scale to `0`, since we want to animate the activation of the shield. Since `PowerUp::Activate` clears the node's geometry, we generate vertices for a hexagon that's big enough to cover the player. We then repeat a simple scale-up or scale-down animation and finally inform the player that it has a shield around it. Outside the `if-else` block, we play a sound effect marking the activation of the shield and finish off the `Activate` function.

In the `Deactivate` function (not shown in the code), we simply inform the player that it doesn't have the shield around it any more. With that, we wrap up our power-ups and can now move on to the game world.

Creating the game

Let's define the `CreateGame` function, which is called from the `init` function when `GameWorld` is created:

```
void GameWorld::CreateGame()
{
  // initialise counters & flags
  seconds_ = 0;
  enemies_killed_total_ = 0;
  enemies_killed_combo_ = 0;
  combo_timer_ = 0;
  score_ = 0;
  is_popup_active_ = false;

  // add the stars
  background_ = BackgroundManager::create();
  addChild(background_, E_LAYER_BACKGROUND);

  CreateBoundary();
  CreatePlayer();
  CreateContainers();
  CreateHUD();
```

```
    // initially add some enemies & a powerup
    AddEnemyFormation();
    AddPowerUp();

    // schedule the update and the tick
    scheduleUpdate();
    schedule(schedule_selector(GameWorld::Tick), 1.0f);
}
```

We start this function by initializing the following variables:

Variable	Description
seconds_	This is the amount of time the game has been active.
enemies_killed_total_	This is the total number of enemies killed.
enemies_killed_combo_	This is the number of enemies killed in the last 3 seconds.
combo_timer_	This counts down from 3 seconds every time an enemy is killed.
score_	This is the score earned by killing enemies and from combos.
is_popup_active_	This is the flag that is used to pause/start when a popup is activated/deactivated.

The function then proceeds to create and add the `BackgroundManager`. We will not discuss the `BackgroundManager` class, but it basically creates a `CCDrawNode` that draws a number of white circles with varying opacities to serve as a starry space background for the game.

The function then calls `CreateBoundary`, which creates a `CCDrawNode` with a semi-transparent white rectangle drawn inside it to represent the bounds of the play area. The `CreatePlayer` functions simply creates an object of the `Player` class and positions it in the center of the play area before adding it to `GameWorld`. The `CreateContainers` function creates and retains four `arrays`: `enemies_`, `powerups_`, `blasts_`, and `missiles_` to hold the `Enemy`, `PowerUp`, `Blast`, and `Missile` objects, respectively. The `CreateHUD` function simply creates and adds a `CCLabelBMFont` to display the score.

We also add a formation of enemies along with a power-up to get the user started. Finally, we schedule the `update` function and the `Tick` function to be called once every second.

The update loop

The `update` function for Inverse Universe will be similar to most other games where we update all the game elements and check for collisions. The code looks like this:

```
void GameWorld::update(float dt)
{
  // don't process if player is dying
  if(player_->is_dying_)
    return;

  // update each enemy
  CCObject* object = NULL;
  CCARRAY_FOREACH(enemies_, object)
  {
    Enemy* enemy = (Enemy*)object;
    if(enemy)
    {
      enemy->Update(player_->getPosition(), player_->GetShield() ==
NULL);
    }
  }

  // update each power-up
  object = NULL;
  CCARRAY_FOREACH(powerups_, object)
  {
    PowerUp* powerup = (PowerUp*)object;
    if(powerup)
    {
      powerup->Update();
    }
  }

  CheckCollisions();
  CheckRemovals();
}
```

We skip processing anything if the player's death animation is playing. We then iterate over the `enemies_` and `powerups_ arrays` and update each object they contain. Finally, we check for collisions and for objects that must be removed. We will skip discussing the `CheckRemovals` function but to give you a gist, it basically checks the state of the `must_be_removed_` flag for `Enemy`, `PowerUp`, `Blast`, and `Missile` and removes them if the flag is enabled.

Let's now look at the `CheckCollisions` function. This function will basically use circular collision detection by using the `CIRCLE_INTERSECTS_CIRCLE` function defined in `GameGlobals.h`. All you need to do is provide the center and radius of the two circles and the function returns `true` if a collision is found.

Let's take a look at the following code:

```
void GameWorld::CheckCollisions()
{
  // save player position & radius
  CCPoint player_position = player_->getPosition();
  float player_radius = player_->getRadius();

  // iterate through all enemies
  CCObject* object = NULL;
  CCARRAY_FOREACH(enemies_, object)
  {
    Enemy* enemy = (Enemy*)object;
    if(enemy)
    {
      CCPoint enemy_position = enemy->getPosition();

      // check with Player
      if(CIRCLE_INTERSECTS_CIRCLE(player_position, player_radius,
        enemy_position, ENEMY_RADIUS))
      {
        // if shield is enabled, kill enemy
        if(player_->GetShield())
        {
          enemy->Die();
          EnemyKilled();
        }
        // else kill player...but only if enemy has finished spawning
        else if(!enemy->getIsSpawning())
          player_->Die();
      }
```

A lot of the collision detection revolves around the enemies. So, we first check for collisions of each enemy with the player. If a collision is found, we either kill the player or the enemy based on the shield being enabled or disabled. Another thing to consider is how we check whether the enemy is spawning and skip killing the player. We do this on purpose, or else the player will die before the enemy's spawning is complete—thereby leaving the user bewildered about the player's death.

Let's take a look at the following code:

```
// check with all blasts
      CCObject* object2 = NULL;
      CCARRAY_FOREACH(blasts_, object2)
      {
        Blast* blast = (Blast*)object2;
        if(blast)
        {
          if(CIRCLE_INTERSECTS_CIRCLE(blast->getPosition(),
            blast->getRadius(), enemy_position, ENEMY_RADIUS*1.5f))
          {
            enemy->Die();
            EnemyKilled();
          }
        }
      }

      // check with all missiles
      object2 = NULL;
      CCARRAY_FOREACH(missiles_, object2)
      {
        Missile* missile = (Missile*)object2;
        if(missile)
        {
          if(CIRCLE_INTERSECTS_CIRCLE(missile->getPosition(),
            MISSILE_RADIUS, enemy_position, ENEMY_RADIUS*1.5f))
          {
            missile->Explode();
          }
        }
      }
    }
  }
```

We then proceed to check collisions of the enemy with the blasts and kill any enemy coming in contact with the blast. We also explode any missile that has come in contact with any enemy.

Let's take a look at the following code:

```
// check if player collides with any of the power-ups
  // activate the power-up if collision is found
  object = NULL;
  CCARRAY_FOREACH(powerups_, object)
  {
    PowerUp* powerup = (PowerUp*)object;
    if(powerup && !powerup->getIsActive())
    {
      if(CIRCLE_INTERSECTS_CIRCLE(player_position, player_radius,
powerup->getPosition(), POWERUP_ICON_OUTER_RADIUS))
      {
        powerup->Activate();
      }
    }
  }
}
```

Finally, we check for collisions between the player and the power-ups and activate the power-up on contact with the player. That wraps up the `CheckCollisions` function but before we move to the `Tick` function, let's take a look at the `EnemyKilled` function:

```
void GameWorld::EnemyKilled()
{
  // increment counters
  ++ enemies_killed_total_;
  ++ enemies_killed_combo_;
  // reset combo time
  combo_timer_ = COMBO_TIME;

  // add score & update the label
  score_ += 7;
  char buf[16] = {0};
  sprintf(buf, "Score: %d", score_);
  score_label_->setString(buf);
}
```

Quite simply, we increment the total number of enemies killed as well as the number of enemies killed in the current combo. We can then use the number of enemies killed in the current combo to reward the player with some extra points when the combo timer elapses. We also reset the combo timer, increment the score, and update the HUD. Next up is the `Tick` function:

```
void GameWorld::Tick(float dt)
{
  // don't tick if player is dying
  if(player_->is_dying_)
    return;

  ++ seconds_;

  -- combo_timer_;
  // show the combo achieved if time is up
  if(combo_timer_ < 0)
    combo_timer_ = 0;
  else if(combo_timer_ == 0)
    ComboTimeUp();

  // Tick each enemy
  CCObject* object = NULL;
  CCARRAY_FOREACH(enemies_, object)
  {
    Enemy* enemy = (Enemy*)object;
    if(enemy)
    {
      enemy->Tick();
    }
  }

  // Tick each power-up
  object = NULL;
  CCARRAY_FOREACH(powerups_, object)
  {
    PowerUp* powerup = (PowerUp*)object;
    if(powerup)
    {
      powerup->Tick();
    }
  }
```

```
    // add an enemy formation every 5 seconds
    if(seconds_ % 5 == 0)
      AddEnemyFormation();
    // add a powerup formation every 4 seconds
    if(seconds_ % 4 == 0)
      AddPowerUp();
  }
```

The first thing to do is to increment the `seconds_` counter. The use of this variable will become clear in the last section when we use it to make the game progressively more difficult. Next, we decrement the `combo_timer_` and call the `ComboTimeUp` function that displays the number of enemies killed by the player in the last 3 seconds.

Then, we call the `Tick` function for the `Enemy` and `PowerUp` objects. Finally, we add a new formation of enemies every 5 seconds and a new power-up every 4 seconds.

Adding tilt controls

Tilt controls, also referred to as the accelerometer, can be added to any `layer` in the same way touch controls are added. It is as simple as calling the `setAccelerometerEnabled(true)` function in the `init` function of `GameWorld` and then overriding the `virtual` function `didAccelerate`. Let's take a look at the `didAccelerate` function:

```
void GameWorld::didAccelerate(CCAcceleration* acceleration_value)
{
  HandleInput(ccp(acceleration_value->x, acceleration_value->y));
}
```

The `didAccelerate` function gets a parameter of type `CCAcceleration*`, which contains three values: `x`, `y`, and `z`. These three values signify how much the device has tilted in the *x*, *y*, and *z* directions. Take a look at the following table to understand the values Cocos2d-x passes into the `didAccelerate` function:

Tilt direction	**X**	**Y**
Extreme left	-0.9f to -1.1f	0.0f
Extreme right	0.9f to 1.1f	0.0f
Extreme forward	0.0f	0.9f to 1.1f
Extreme backward	0.0f	-0.9f to -1.1f

The preceding values are approximate and will differ a bit from device to device.

For the purpose of our game, we will need just horizontal and vertical movement, so we only use the `x` and `y` members of `acceleration_value`.

I'm sure you were expecting more, but the reason for separating the logic into the `HandleInput` function is because this game was first built on **win32** and the tilt controls were tested on an Android device later. So, I needed to put in touch controls for the win32 build. Anyway, the `HandleInput` function looks like this:

```
void GameWorld::HandleInput(CCPoint input)
{
  /// don't accept input if popup is active or if player is dead
  if(is_popup_active_ || player_->is_dying_)
    return;

  CCPoint input_abs = CCPoint(fabs(input.x), fabs(input.y));

  // calculate player speed based on how much device has tilted
  // greater speed multipliers for greater tilt values
  player_->speed_.x = input.x * ( (input_abs.x > 0.3f) ? 36 : (
    (input_abs.x > 0.2f) ? 28 : 20 ) );
  player_->speed_.y = input.y * ( (input_abs.y > 0.3f) ? 36 : (
    (input_abs.y > 0.2f) ? 28 : 20 ) );

  // update the background
  background_->setPosition(ccp(input.x * -30, input.y * -30));
}
```

We return from this function when there is a popup active or when the player is dying. That next bit of calculation is necessary to offer a more sensitive controlling experience. Basically, the user doesn't have to tilt his device all the way to the left if he wants the player to move to the left at full speed. Thus, we multiply larger values for larger readings and smaller values for smaller readings. We finally set the player's speed to the resultant calculation. One of the cool features of an accelerometer based game is to allow the users to calibrate the accelerometer. That is left to you, my intelligent reader, as an exercise. Now that we have recorded the user's input, let's add the movement logic into the `Player` class.

Moving the player

We had called the `scheduleUpdate` function in the `init` function of the `Player` class. Thus, we define the `update` function to handle the movement and rotation of the player:

```
void Player::update(float dt)
{
  CCDrawNode::update(dt);
  CCPoint previous_position = m_obPosition;
  UpdatePosition();
  UpdateRotation(previous_position);
}
```

We first save the previous position of the player because we need it while setting the rotation. The `UpdateRotation` function will just use `ccpToAngle` function to set the rotation of the player with a bit of easing, so we will skip it and discuss only the `UpdatePosition` function as follows:

```
void Player::UpdatePosition()
{
  // don't move if speed is too low
  if(ccpLength(speed_) > 0.75f)
  {
    // add speed but limit movement within the boundary
    CCPoint next_position = ccpAdd(m_obPosition, speed_);
    if(RECT_CONTAINS_CIRCLE(game_world_->boundary_rect_,
      next_position, PLAYER_RADIUS))
    {
      setPosition(next_position);
    }
    else
    {
      if(RECT_CONTAINS_CIRCLE(game_world_->boundary_rect_, CCPoint(
        next_position.x - speed_.x, next_position.y), PLAYER_RADIUS))
      {
        setPosition(ccp(next_position.x - speed_.x, next_position.y));
      }
      else if(RECT_CONTAINS_CIRCLE(game_world_->boundary_rect_,
CCPoint(
        next_position.x, next_position.y - speed_.y), PLAYER_RADIUS))
      {
        setPosition(ccp(next_position.x, next_position.y - speed_.y));
      }
    }
  }
}
```

We ignore the values that are less than a certain threshold; otherwise, the player will constantly be jerking around the screen owing to the accelerometer readings constantly fluctuating by minor values. The logic is to calculate the next position by adding up the speed and finally limiting the player within the boundary defined by `GameWorld`.

Adding progression and difficulty levels

By now, we have a fully functioning game but we still haven't ensured the game is challenging and addictive for the user. We must engage the player by increasing the intensity and difficulty of the game progressively. In our previous game, we had the option of designing levels that get more difficult, but this game isn't level based and is different every time.

With that in mind, a bit of spice is added by creating a variety of formations in which the enemies will spawn on screen. These formations will be increasingly difficult with the difficulty completely based on how long the user has managed to survive. We define a few enums and constants in `GameGlobals.h` before writing the functions that will add progression to our game:

```
enum ESkillTimer
{
  E_SKILL1 = 10,
  E_SKILL2 = 30,
  E_SKILL3 = 45,
  E_SKILL4 = 60,
  E_SKILL5 = 90,
  E_SKILL6 = 120,
};
```

First up, we have an enum called `ESkillTimer` that represents the skill level in terms of the number of seconds the user has survived the game. Next, we have enum `EEnemyFormation` defined as follows:

```
enum EEnemyFormation
{
  E_FORMATION_RANDOM_EASY = 0,
  E_FORMATION_VERTICAL_EASY,
  E_FORMATION_HORIZONTAL_EASY,
  E_FORMATION_POLYGON_EASY,
  E_FORMATION_RANDOM_MEDIUM,
  E_FORMATION_VERTICAL_MEDIUM,
  E_FORMATION_HORIZONTAL_MEDIUM,
  E_FORMATION_POLYGON_MEDIUM,
  E_FORMATION_RANDOM_HARD,
```

```
    E_FORMATION_VERTICAL_HARD,
    E_FORMATION_HORIZONTAL_HARD,
    E_FORMATION_POLYGON_HARD,
    E_FORMATION_MAX  //12
};
```

EEnemyFormation is an enum representing the various types of formations the enemies will be positioned in when they are added to the GameWorld. Next, we have a few arrays pre-defined as follows:

```
const int GameGlobals::skill1_formations[] = {0, 4};
const int GameGlobals::skill2_formations[] = {4, 4,
  4, 4, 1, 1, 1, 2, 2, 2};
const int GameGlobals::skill3_formations[] = {4, 4,
  4, 8, 8, 1, 1, 2, 2, 5, 5, 5, 6, 6, 6, 3, 3};
const int GameGlobals::skill4_formations[] = {4, 4,
  8, 8, 8, 5, 5, 5, 6, 6, 6, 3, 3, 3, 7, 7, 7};
const int GameGlobals::skill5_formations[] = {8, 8,
  8, 3, 3, 3, 5, 5, 6, 6, 9, 9, 10, 10, 7, 7, 7};
const int GameGlobals::skill6_formations[] = {8, 8,
  8, 5, 5, 6, 6, 9, 9, 10, 10, 7, 7, 7, 11, 11, 11};
```

We also have arrays that specify the frequency of the various formations for a specific skill level. We will stitch these different bits of information together in the GetEnemyFormationType function:

```
EEnemyFormation GameWorld::GetEnemyFormationType()
{
  // return a formation type from a list of formation types, based on
time user has been playing
  // the longer the user has survived, the more difficult the
formations will be
  if(seconds_ > E_SKILL6)
  {
    int random_index = CCRANDOM_0_1() * GameGlobals::skill6_
formations_size;
    return (EEnemyFormation)(GameGlobals::skill6_formations[random_
index]);
  }
  else if(seconds_ > E_SKILL5)
  {
    int random_index = CCRANDOM_0_1() * GameGlobals::skill5_
formations_size;
    return (EEnemyFormation)(GameGlobals::skill5_formations[random_
index]);
  }
```

```
    else if(seconds_ > E_SKILL4)
    {
      int random_index = CCRANDOM_0_1() * GameGlobals::skill4_
  formations_size;
      return (EEnemyFormation)(GameGlobals::skill4_formations[random_
  index]);
    }
    else if(seconds_ > E_SKILL3)
    {
      int random_index = CCRANDOM_0_1() * GameGlobals::skill3_
  formations_size;
      return (EEnemyFormation)(GameGlobals::skill3_formations[random_
  index]);
    }
    else if(seconds_ > E_SKILL2)
    {
      int random_index = CCRANDOM_0_1() * GameGlobals::skill2_
  formations_size;
      return (EEnemyFormation)(GameGlobals::skill2_formations[random_
  index]);
    }
    else if(seconds_ > E_SKILL1)
    {
      int random_index = CCRANDOM_0_1() * GameGlobals::skill1_
  formations_size;
      return (EEnemyFormation)(GameGlobals::skill1_formations[random_
  index]);
    }
    else
    {
      return E_FORMATION_RANDOM_EASY;
    }
  }
```

This function first checks up to which skill level the user has managed to survive and then returns an appropriate formation for the respective skill level. Even though the formations are chosen randomly, we still have control over how often a given formation can pop up for a given difficulty level. All we need to do is increase or decrease the number of occurrences of a formation type within the array for a skill level.

Now that we have the type of formation based on difficulty, we can proceed by actually adding the enemies to the game in the `AddEnemyFormation` function:

```
void GameWorld::AddEnemyFormation()
{
  // fetch an enemy formation
  EEnemyFormation type = GetEnemyFormationType();
  // fetch a list of positions for the given formation
  vector<CCPoint> formation = GameGlobals::GetEnemyFormation(
    type, boundary_rect_, player_->getPosition());
  int num_enemies_to_create = formation.size();
  int num_enemies_on_screen = enemies_->count();
  // limit the total number of enemies to MAX_ENEMIES
  if(num_enemies_on_screen + num_enemies_to_create >= MAX_ENEMIES)
  {
    num_enemies_to_create = MAX_ENEMIES - num_enemies_on_screen;
  }
  // create, add & position enemies based on the formation
  for(int i = 0; i < num_enemies_to_create; ++i)
  {
    Enemy* enemy = Enemy::create(this);
    enemy->setPosition(formation[i]);
    enemy->Spawn(i * ENEMY_SPAWN_DELAY);
    addChild(enemy, E_LAYER_ENEMIES);
    enemies_->addObject(enemy);
  }
}
```

This function begins by fetching the type of formation to create and passes it into the `GetEnemyFormation` function of the `GameGlobals` class. The `GetEnemyFormation` function will return a vector of `CCPoint` that we will use to position the enemies. At any given point, the total number of enemies on screen should not exceed 250, which in this case is held by constant `MAX_ENEMIES` defined in `GameGlobals.h`. We ensure the preceding condition is met and then run a loop where we create an `Enemy` object, set its position, call its `Spawn` function, and finally add it to the screen as well as the `enemies_ CCARRAY`.

By adding progression to Inverse Universe, we complete our fourth game. I have skipped discussing some of the functionality in the chapter, such as the `BackgroundManager` class, the way enemy formations are created and some of the helper functions. You will find the code for such features and more in the source bundle. Rest assured the comments will be enough to explain what's happening.

Summary

With Inverse Universe, we went back to the drawing board and came out with flying colors! You learned the difference between `CCDrawingPrimitives` and `CCDrawNode`. We also extended the `CCDrawNode` class to create each and every one of our game's elements. We implemented circle-to-circle collision detection and finally understood how tilt controls or the accelerometer work in Cocos2d-x. As a good game design principle, you also learned how to add progression to a game that is not level-based, while still keeping it open-ended.

In our next chapter, we'll get acquainted with an extremely lively friend, a friend that you can keep applying forces to, and a friend that can take any shape and size that you'd like—yes it's none other than our great friend Box2D!

5
Let's Get Physical!

For our fifth game, we will get down to the physics of things. Cocos2d-x comes bundled with two wonderful physics engines: Box2D and Chipmunk. In this chapter, we will make use of the versatile and robust Box2D physics engine to add some realism to our game.

In this chapter, you'll learn about the following:

- Box2D basics
- Setting up Box2D world and debug draw
- Creating Box2D bodies, fixtures, and shapes
- Manipulating simple physics at runtime
- Maintaining a state machine
- Listening for collisions
- Creating pools for reusable objects

An overview of Jumpy Clown

Our first physics game stars a clown that has a dream to reach the sky. Naturally, gravity pulls him down each time he jumps and so he needs our help. We need to build trampolines for him as he begins to fall, enabling to him reach as high as possible. We can build him a trampoline simply by sliding our finger across the screen. Every now and then, our clown runs into a bottle rocket that shoots him further upwards and a balloon which takes him steadily higher.

This is what we will achieve by the end of this chapter:

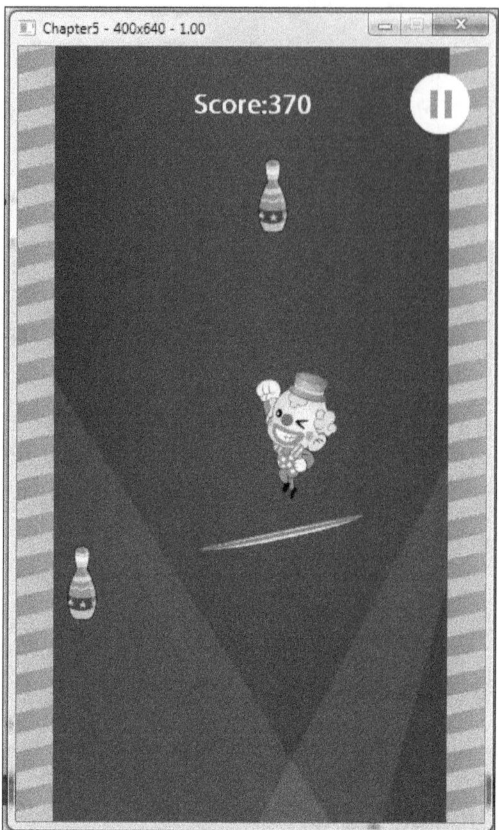

The basics of Box2D

The Box2D manual, found at `http://www.box2d.org/manual.html`, summarizes Box2D as a 2D rigid-body simulation library for games. Now what exactly do they mean by rigid body? A quick search on Google and you will know that a rigid body is one that does not deform regardless of the external forces exerted on it. Thus, Box2D is built to simulate hard objects such as rocks, walls, and bowling balls rather than soft bodies such as cotton, toothpaste, and mom's pudding!

In this section, you will get a brief overview of the various components of Box2D that we will interact with in the due course of time. However, I must insist you to read the manual provided at the preceding URL for a deeper understanding of what happens under the hood of this amazing physics engine.

The first object of the engine you will create is of type `b2World`. This is the object that manages the entire physics simulation. It provides factory methods to create bodies and joints, and even manages their memory for you.

The object of the engine you will interact with the most belongs to type `b2Body`. This class represents a single rigid body in the physics world. A body has a position and a velocity and reacts to forces. However, bodies have absolutely no idea of their *appearance*. Bodies might be static (don't react to forces), kinematic (don't react to forces but can have velocity), or dynamic (love to be thrown around and react to forces).

To define the geometry of a body, we make use of the `b2Shape` class. Box2D provides us with a number of shapes such as the circle, polygon, and edge shapes to name a few. Shapes are most importantly used by the engine in collision checking.

We have bodies and shapes, but they don't know each other. So, we need fixtures to bring them together. A fixture can hold a single shape and a body can hold any number of fixtures. However, a fixture is much more than just glue between a body and a shape. It describes a few essential properties of the body it is bound to, such as density, friction, and restitution (amount of bounce). It also describes collision filtering and the sensor properties for its body.

Box2D also provides constraints to restrict the movement of bodies known simply as joints. In addition to controlling movement, some joints provide motors that can drive the associated bodies.

Finally, there is the `b2Contact` class that provides information on two fixtures that collide. We receive this contact information by implementing the `b2ContactListener` class. This class provides various useful events that we will discuss in the course of this chapter.

One last detail before we are done with the basics. Box2D uses the MKS system of units and thus positions for each body you will ever create are in meters. I'm sure you're wondering how we could possibly represent an object that moves from 1.25 meters to 6.05 meters on screen. Also, Box2D being optimized to work with objects sized from 0.1 meters to 10 meters makes this even more confusing.

Essentially, whenever you're taking the position of a body and assigning it to your sprite, you need to convert the position from meters to pixels. Since the range of movement in meters is so small, we multiply the position value of the body by a constant and assign the product to the position of the sprite. Similarly, when you want to place your bodies and have screen coordinates that may be too large for Box2D to process efficiently, you divide the position value by the same constant and place your bodies accordingly.

This constant has come to be known as `PTM_RATIO` or the pixel-to-meter ratio. Since the base resolution for this game is 1280 x 800, we will define the pixel to meter ratio to be 128. Thus, when a body moves from 0.0f to 10.0f in the physics world, the corresponding sprite will move from 0.0f to 1280.0f on the screen. Now isn't that convenient?

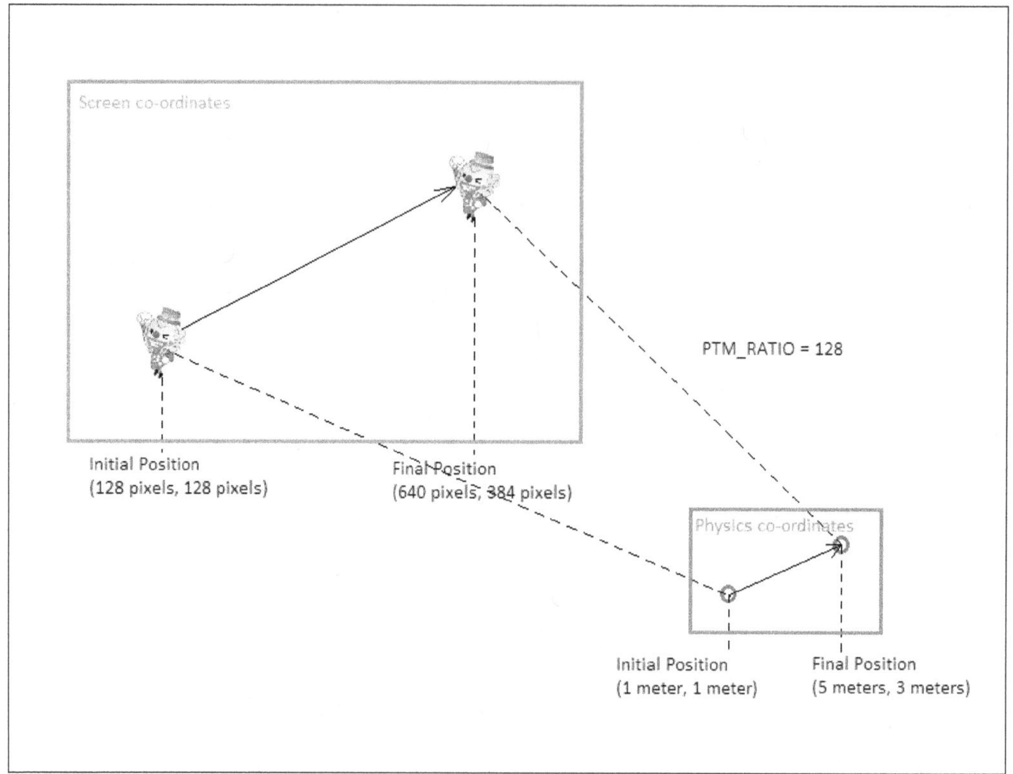

Creating the world

The first object of Box2D that you will create is the world that holds the simulation itself. In addition to the world, you will also create a few other things in the `CreateWorld` function from the `GameWorld.cpp` file:

```
void GameWorld::CreateWorld()
{
  // create world
  b2Vec2 gravity;
  gravity.Set(0, -10.0f);
```

```
    world_ = new b2World(gravity);
    // tell world we want to listen for collisions
    world_->SetContactListener(this);

    // create the moving container that will hold all the game elements
    game_object_layer_ = CCNode::create();
    addChild(game_object_layer_, E_LAYER_FOREGROUND);

  #ifdef ENABLE_DEBUG_DRAW
    debug_draw_ = new GLESDebugDraw(PTM_RATIO);
    world_->SetDebugDraw(debug_draw_);
    uint32 flags = 0;
    flags += b2Draw::e_shapeBit;
    //   flags += b2Draw::e_jointBit;
    //    flags += b2Draw::e_aabbBit;
    //    flags += b2Draw::e_pairBit;
    //    flags += b2Draw::e_centerOfMassBit;
    debug_draw_->SetFlags(flags);
  #endif
  }
```

We begin by creating a variable `gravity` of type `b2Vec2` and set its value. The `b2Vec2` object is Box2D's structure to represent a two dimensional vector. It is similar to the `CCPoint` object that we use in Cocos2d-x. We then create a new object of `b2World`, passing in the `gravity` variable. We also inform the world that we want to listen to collision-related events by calling the `SetContactListener` function and passing in a reference to `GameWorld`. We will discuss the outcome of this in the *Listening for collisions* section of this chapter.

The last object we will create is a `CCNode` object with the name `game_object_layer_`. We will add all our game elements' sprites to `game_object_layer_`. This includes the clown, the collectibles, and the power-ups.

Now when our clown rises higher and higher above the ground, we will simply move this `game_object_layer_` object so that the clown is always in the center of the screen. Thus, we can create an illusion of a camera that follows the main character.

We then proceed to create a new object of type `GLESDebugDraw`. You can find this class in the Box2D test bed provided with the Cocos2d-x C++ tests or more specifically at the path `cocos2d-x-2.2.5\samples\Cpp\TestCpp\Classes\Box2DTestBed\GLES-Render.cpp`. The `GLESDebugDraw` class takes care of rendering primitives based on the various objects contained within the world. What this means is that your bodies and joints will be represented on the screen by tiny colored shapes. For example, all dynamic bodies are colored red while all static ones are colored green!

Using debug draw

While creating an object of the `GLESDebugDraw` class, we need only pass in the pixel-to-meter ratio so the class knows exactly how much to scale the rendering of our physics objects. This class also gives us the option of choosing the elements we want to be drawn on to the screen. For this game, we only want our bodies' shapes to be drawn so all other flags are commented. Doing this will not render the shapes on the screen and we must add the following code to our layer's draw function:

```
#ifdef ENABLE_DEBUG_DRAW
void GameWorld::draw()
{
  CCLayer::draw();
  ccGLEnableVertexAttribs( kCCVertexAttribFlag_Position );
  kmGLPushMatrix();
  world_->DrawDebugData();
  kmGLPopMatrix();
}
#endif
```

An important thing to remember is that the `GLESDebugDraw` class is intended for debugging purposes only and should be turned off unless absolutely required. This is why the preceding code is wrapped inside a pre-processor conditional. You might use this class the most in the initial stages of developing a game when you're still creating the world and all its bodies, fixtures, and joints. So when you're done figuring out the sizes of the various shapes, be sure to comment the definition of this pre-processor directive in `GameGlobals.h`.

The following screenshot has been taken mid-game to show you the output of calling the `DrawDebugData` function of the `b2World` class. The red rectangle is the dynamic body of the clown, the green rectangles are the static bodies of the collectibles, and the green segment is the trampoline/platform over which the clown will bounce:

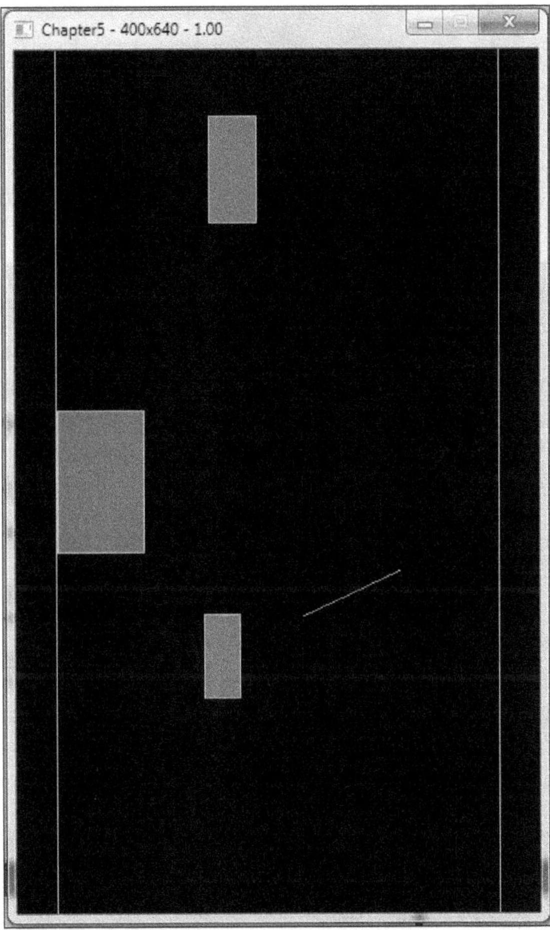

Stepping into the world

Once the world has been created, the simulation must actually be run. You can do this by calling the `Step` function of the `b2World` class, usually in the `update` function of your game, as follows:

```
world_->Step(dt, 8, 3);
```

The three parameters passed to the `Step` function are the time-step, the number of velocity iterations, and the number of position iterations, respectively. The variable `dt` passed into the `Step` function is passed to us from the `update` function of our `GameWorld` class, and the value held by `dt` is that of a variable time-step. We use the term variable to describe this value because the amount of time the Cocos2d-x engine will take to finish one single tick might vary continuously.

One drawback of using a variable time-step is that it makes the entire simulation hardware dependent. Thus the simulation might run faster on a machine having a powerful configuration, while it might run significantly slower on a machine having a poor configuration. Considering that this game is not too heavy graphically, we can assume that we will get a steady 60 FPS and thus we shall stick with the variable time-step.

The second argument, that is, velocity iterations, basically describes the number of times the simulation will process velocity for all moving bodies within a single time-step. The same goes for the third argument, that is, position iterations, which is the number of times the simulation will process position values within a single time-step. The values for velocity and position iterations suggested in the Box2D manual have been used for our game but you can tweak these values. It should suffice to keep in mind that there is a trade-off between speed and accuracy involved. Larger values for iterations assure a more accurate simulation but incur a performance cut.

Now that we have understood how to create and run the simulation, let's create and add some of our game's bodies and see some action.

Creating the GameObject class

Our game's elements are all physics bodies and will have sprites to represent them visually. It is a common practice to club these two entities together. Cocos2d-x has an inbuilt class to handle this known as `PhysicsSprite`, but since this is our first physics game, we shall create our own class called `GameObject` to do the job:

```
class GameObject : public CCSprite
{
public:
```

```
  GameObject() : game_world_(NULL), body_(NULL),
    type_(E_GAME_OBJECT_NONE) {}
  virtual ~GameObject();

  // returns an autorelease GameObject
  static GameObject* create(GameWorld* game_world,
    const char* frame_name);

  // accessors & mutators
  inline b2Body* GetBody() { return body_; }

  inline EGameObjectType GetType() { return type_; }
  inline void SetType(EGameObjectType type) { type_ = type; }

  virtual void Update()
  {
    // update position of sprite based on position of body
    if(body_)
    {
      setPosition(ccp(WORLD_TO_SCREEN(body_->GetPosition().x),
        WORLD_TO_SCREEN(body_->GetPosition().y)));
    }
  }

  virtual void SetBody(b2Body* body)
  {
    // save reference of self into b2Body
    if(body_)
    {
      body_->SetUserData(NULL);
      body_ = NULL;
    }
    if(body)
    {
      body->SetUserData(this);
      body_ = body;
    }
  }

protected:
  GameWorld* game_world_;
  b2Body* body_;
  EGameObjectType type_;
};
```

Our GameObject class will inherit from CCSprite and will have a type_ property to identify the various forms its children may take. We will also maintain reference to the b2Body object and provide setters and getters for the same. Our GameObject class will possess an update function that will set its appropriate position based on the position of its body, thereby handling the conversion from meters to pixels by virtue of the helper functions you can find in GameGlobals.h:

```
#define SCREEN_TO_WORLD(value)  (float)(value)/PTM_RATIO
#define WORLD_TO_SCREEN(value)  (float)(value)*PTM_RATIO
```

In the SetBody function, we store a reference to our GameObject class into the body object using the userData property of b2Body. The userData property is of type void* so we can store absolutely anything in it. This is extremely convenient because the body and the sprite will always be linked to each other if we do this.

Creating the walls

The first physics body we create is the body to represent the walls in our game. As you saw in the screenshot, the clown is restricted on both sides by walls. So let's create these walls in the CreateWall function in GameWorld.cpp:

```
void GameWorld::CreateWall()
{
  // wall will be a static body placed at the origin
  b2BodyDef wall_def;
  wall_def.position.Set(0, 0);
  wall_ = world_->CreateBody(&wall_def);

  // get variables for the wall edges
  float left_wall = SCREEN_TO_WORLD(WALL_WIDTH);
  float right_wall = SCREEN_TO_WORLD(SCREEN_SIZE.width - WALL_WIDTH);
  float top = SCREEN_TO_WORLD(SCREEN_SIZE.height);

  // create and add two fixtures using two edge shapes
  b2EdgeShape wall_shape;
  wall_shape.Set(b2Vec2(left_wall, 0), b2Vec2(left_wall, top));
  wall_->CreateFixture(&wall_shape, 0);
  wall_shape.Set(b2Vec2(right_wall, 0), b2Vec2(right_wall, top));
  wall_->CreateFixture(&wall_shape, 0);
}
```

We start by creating a `b2BodyDef` class, which basically is the body definition of the body we wish to create. We need this information because we must pass it into the `CreateBody` function, which will then return a new `b2Body` object.

At this moment, the body is a shapeless mass and it feels quite awkward. So we define a few variables that basically represent the left and right faces of the wall and its height. We then create two `b2EdgeShape` objects that will represent the left and right wall, respectively. We call the `Set` function and pass in the two end points for both the edge shapes. We then ask the wall body to create a fixture with each of these shapes. The second parameter we pass into `CreateFixture` is the density of the resultant fixture.

Creating the base

Now that we have walls, let's create our first `GameObject` class that will represent the base platform. When I say base platform, I mean the trampoline the clown will be trying relentlessly to jump off at the start of the game. We define the `CreateBasePlatform` function in `GameWorld.cpp`:

```
void GameWorld::CreateBasePlatform()
{
  // base platform will be a static body
  b2BodyDef platform_def;
  platform_def.position.Set(SCREEN_TO_WORLD(416),
    SCREEN_TO_WORLD(172));
  b2Body* base_platform_body = world_->CreateBody(&platform_def);

  // create an edge slightly above the bottom of the screen
  b2EdgeShape base_platform_shape;
  base_platform_shape.Set(b2Vec2(SCREEN_TO_WORLD(-SCREEN_SIZE.width),
    0.45f), b2Vec2(SCREEN_TO_WORLD(SCREEN_SIZE.width), 0.45f));
  b2FixtureDef base_platform_fixture_def;
  base_platform_fixture_def.shape = &base_platform_shape;
  // give the base platform perfectly elastic collision response
  base_platform_fixture_def.restitution = 1.0f;
  base_platform_body->CreateFixture(&base_platform_fixture_def);

  // create base platform, set physics body & add to batch node
  base_platform_ = GameObject::create(this, "cjtrapm01.png");
  base_platform_->SetBody(base_platform_body);
  base_platform_->SetType(E_GAME_OBJECT_PLATFORM);
  sprite_batch_node_->addChild(base_platform_, E_LAYER_CLOWN - 1);
}
```

As you can see, a lot of the code is similar to the code used in creating the walls, except for one minor detail. Here, we actually create a `b2FixtureDef` object instead of using the shape to create the fixture. We do so because we want to set the value for the restitution of the base platform's fixture. We set the restitution to 1.0f because that is what every clown's dream trampoline should be like—perfectly elastic—and also because we want the clown to keep jumping till the user makes the move.

We then proceed to call the `create` function of `GameObject`, passing in a reference to `GameWorld` and specifying the sprite's frame name. This will return an auto-release `GameObject`. All that's left is to set its physics body and type before finally adding it to the game's batch node.

Box2D copies the data out of body definitions and fixture definitions when you pass them into the `CreateBody` and `CreateFixture` functions, respectively. This means you can use the same `b2BodyDef` to create multiple `b2Body` objects.

Creating the clown

Now that we have built the boundary within which we will restrict the clown's movements, and a perfectly bouncy trampoline, it is time to actually create the clown. We will create a class to handle the daredevil personality of our clown and will very intelligently name the class `Clown`.

Our `Clown` class will inherit from `GameObject`, so we need not worry about updating the position of the clown with respect to his body. However, we will define the clown's state machine in this class. For now, let's look at the `CreateClown` function in the `GameWorld.cpp` file:

```
void GameWorld::CreateClown()
{
  // clown will be a dynamic body
  b2BodyDef clown_def;
  clown_def.type = b2_dynamicBody;
  // clown will start off at the centre of the screen
  clown_def.position.Set(SCREEN_TO_WORLD(SCREEN_SIZE.width/2),
    SCREEN_TO_WORLD(SCREEN_SIZE.height/2.75));
  b2Body* clown_body = world_->CreateBody(&clown_def);

  // create clown, set physics body & add to batch node
  clown_ = Clown::create(this);
```

```
    clown_->SetBody(clown_body);
    sprite_batch_node_->addChild(clown_, E_LAYER_CLOWN);
}
```

We begin by creating the body definition for the clown's body, marking it as dynamic and setting the initial position before using it to fetch a new body from the world. We then create an auto-release `Clown` object and pass the newly created `b2Body` into its `SetBody` function before adding the clown to the game's batch node. We haven't specified anything about the clown's appearance. Well, look no further than the `SetBody` function that you will find in `Clown.cpp`:

```
void Clown::SetBody(b2Body* body)
{
  // create a box shape
  b2PolygonShape clown_shape;
  clown_shape.SetAsBox(SCREEN_TO_WORLD(m_obContentSize.width * 0.5),
    SCREEN_TO_WORLD(m_obContentSize.height * 0.5f));

  // create a fixture def with the box shape and high restitution
  b2FixtureDef clown_fixture_def;
  clown_fixture_def.shape = &clown_shape;
  clown_fixture_def.restitution = 0.5f;
  body->CreateFixture(&clown_fixture_def);
  // don't let the clown rotate
  body->SetFixedRotation(true);

  // call parent class' function
  GameObject::SetBody(body);
}
```

We override the `SetBody` function from `GameObject` and as you can see, this function accepts a `b2Body` object as an argument. This is because every `GameObject` object will be provided a body by `GameWorld` and must simply add its respective fixtures—and that is exactly what we do by first defining a shape for the clown.

We make use of the `b2PolygonShape` class and call its convenient `SetAsBox` function, passing in half the width and half the height for the desired box. Notice how we create the box for the clown based on his content size while converting from screen to world dimensions.

We then create a fixture definition for the clown body's fixture, set the shape created previously, and give it a restitution coefficient of 0.5f. We then pass the newly created fixture definition to the body's `CreateFixture` function.

We finally call the `SetFixedRotation` function for the body, passing in `true`. This ensures that the body will not rotate under the influence of forces. In essence, the angular velocity for this body will always remain zero. We wind up this function by calling the `SetBody` function of the parent class. Now that we have defined what the clown will be made up of, let's take the time to define the various states that make him the star of the circus.

Defining the clown's state machine

A **Finite State Machine** (**FSM**) is nothing but a system to manage the various states that a particular machine (the clown in our case) can be in. You can create an FSM to describe the various stages of an entity's lifecycle. The term entity could be anything from the main character in a game where the states would be walking, running, jumping, shooting, dying, and so on. Similarly, an entity could be the game itself where the states would be: game world creation, game world update, collision detection, level completion, game over, and so on.

A common way to represent the states within an FSM is to enumerate them, which in the case of our clown's states is the following enum that you will find in the `GameGlobals.h` file:

```
enum EClownState
{
  E_CLOWN_NONE = 0,
  E_CLOWN_UP,
  E_CLOWN_DOWN,
  E_CLOWN_BOUNCE,
  E_CLOWN_ROCKET,
  E_CLOWN_BALLOON,
};
```

For this simple game, we have just five states the clown can be in, excluding the `E_CLOWN_NONE` state of course. The `Clown` class will have a `state_` property of the type `EClownState`. We will now look at the `SetState` function of the `Clown` class:

```
void Clown::SetState(EClownState state)
{
  // only accept a change in state
  if(state_ == state)
```

```
    return;

  state_ = state;

  // call respective state based action
  switch(state_)
  {
  case E_CLOWN_UP:
    StartGoingUp();
    break;
  case E_CLOWN_DOWN:
    StartComingDown();
    break;
  case E_CLOWN_BOUNCE:
    StartBounce();
    break;
  case E_CLOWN_ROCKET:
    StartRocket();
    break;
  case E_CLOWN_BALLOON:
    StartBalloon();
    break;
  }
}
```

We keep the `SetState` function straightforward. We perform processing only if there is a change in state. Why is this of importance you wonder? Well, consider that you create a new `CCAnimate` object to play a walking animation, as the character enters into the walking state every time the player presses the right arrow key. This way, you will be repeatedly creating a new `CCAnimate` object every time the right arrow key's event is fired!

Next, we write a switch case structure that handles each state and calls the respective function. The `StartGoingUp`, `StartComingDown`, and `StartBounce` functions change the current display frame for the clown, so we'll skip straight to the `StartRocket` function:

```
void Clown::StartRocket()
{
  setDisplayFrame(CCSpriteFrameCache::sharedSpriteFrameCache()->
    spriteFrameByName("cjroket.png"));
  // unschedule any previously scheduled selectors...possibly
    by another rocket/balloon
  unschedule(schedule_selector(Clown::FinishRocketBalloon));
  // stay in this state for some time
```

```
    scheduleOnce(schedule_selector(Clown::FinishRocketBalloon),
      ROCKET_DURATION);

    // no gravity while aboard a bottle rocket
    body_->SetGravityScale(0.0f);
    // decently high velocity while aboard a bottle rocket
    body_->SetLinearVelocity(b2Vec2(0.0f, 30.0f));

    // create neat jet stream for the rocket
    rocket_trail_ = CCParticleSystemQuad::create("explosion.plist");
    rocket_trail_->setDuration(-1);
    rocket_trail_->setPositionType(kCCPositionTypeRelative);
    game_world_->game_object_layer_->addChild(rocket_trail_);

    SOUND_ENGINE->playEffect("bottle_rocket.wav");
}
```

We begin by changing the current display frame. We then unschedule any previously scheduled selector and schedule a new one with the respective duration.

The next part is interesting, since we alter the physics of the clown's body. When the clown enters in to this state, we want him to shoot upwards at a constant velocity unaffected by gravity, so we do just that. We set the gravity scale to 0.0f, which means that the clown's body will not be influenced by the force of gravity and then set a decently high linear velocity pointing straight up.

That last bit of code will simply add a particle system to represent the jet stream of the rocket. I wonder how that clown holds on to such a powerful rocket without burning himself! The code for the `StartBalloon` function is similar to the `StartRocket` function, but the linear velocity we set is much lesser because a balloon tends to be slower than a rocket. Also, it doesn't have a jet stream so we don't add a particle system either.

However, unlike the rocket, the user can control the clown's horizontal movement via the accelerometer of course! You can find the relevant logic in the `didAccelerate` function inside `GameWorld.cpp`. So, let's discuss the callback that both these functions have scheduled, the `FinishRocketBalloon` function:

```
void Clown::FinishRocketBalloon(float dt)
{
    // after rocket/balloon, clown will be moving upwards
    SetState(E_CLOWN_UP);
    // resume normal gravity
    body_->SetGravityScale(1.0f);
```

```
    // remove any rocket jet stream if it exists
    if(rocket_trail_)
    {
      rocket_trail_->removeFromParentAndCleanup(true);
      rocket_trail_ = NULL;
    }
  }
```

Once both the states have finished, we set the clown's state to be moving upwards and resume normal gravity scale. We also remove any glorious particle systems that we may have added. Voila, you've implemented a simple yet elegant FSM.

Creating the platform

At this point in the game, we have a well-defined clown but he's still stuck endlessly bouncing on the base platform. We now need to write code to add the platforms that will help take the clown higher up in the world. We will create and use a single object of the `GameObject` class to represent the platform. Let's go over the `CreatePlatform` function from `GameWorld.cpp`:

```
void GameWorld::CreatePlatform()
{
  // platform will be a static body
  b2BodyDef platform_def;
  platform_def.position.Set(0, 0);
  b2Body* platform_body = world_->CreateBody(&platform_def);

  // create platform, set physics body & add to batch node
  platform_ = GameObject::create(this, "cjump01.png");
  platform_->setAnchorPoint(ccp(0, 0.25f));
  platform_->setVisible(false);
  platform_->SetBody(platform_body);
  platform_->SetType(E_GAME_OBJECT_PLATFORM);
  sprite_batch_node_->addChild(platform_, E_LAYER_PLATFORM);
}
```

We begin by creating a static body positioned at the origin and then create a new `GameObject` for the platform. We set the appropriate anchor point and hide `platform_`. We pass the newly created `b2Body` object into the `platform_` object and set its type to `E_GAME_OBJECT_PLATFORM` before adding it to the game's batch node.

I'm sure you noticed how we skipped adding any fixtures to the platform's body. This is because the shape of the platform depends completely on what points the user drags on the screen. Thus, we will add a fixture to the platform's body in the `AddPlatform` function when the user has finished touching the screen.

Adding and removing platforms

The user can drag across the screen any number of times but we will always use just one platform, ignoring the previously drawn platform. For this, we define the `AddPlatform` function in `GameWorld.cpp`:

```
void GameWorld::AddPlatform(CCPoint start, CCPoint end)
{
  // ensure the platform has only one edge shaped fixture
  if(platform_->GetBody()->GetFixtureList())
    return;

  // create and add a new fixture based on the user input
  b2EdgeShape platform_shape;
  platform_shape.Set(b2Vec2(SCREEN_TO_WORLD(start.x),
    SCREEN_TO_WORLD(start.y)), b2Vec2(SCREEN_TO_WORLD(
    end.x), SCREEN_TO_WORLD(end.y)));
  platform_->GetBody()->CreateFixture(&platform_shape, 0);
}
```

The first statement calls the `GetFixtureList` function of the `b2Body` class, which returns a pointer to the first `b2Fixture` object in the array of fixtures the body has applied to it. This `if` condition will ensure that the platform body never gets more than one fixture.

Then, we proceed to actually create the fixture by first creating an edge shape with the Box2D coordinates of the start and end points passed to this function. Now, we have a fixture for the platform's body drawn by the user. Since we will be using this single platform object throughout the game, it will have to be added and removed time and again.

We write the removing logic in the `RemovePlatform` function in `GameWorld.cpp`:

```
void GameWorld::RemovePlatform()
{
  // remove the existing fixture
  if(platform_->GetBody()->GetFixtureList())
  {
    platform_->GetBody()->DestroyFixture(
      platform_->GetBody()->GetFixtureList());
  }
}
```

As simple as that looks, we check whether the platform body has any fixtures on it and simply call the `DestroyFixture` function, passing in the pointer to the first fixture. That is all the code you will have to write to destroy the fixture's object, as Box2D handles everything else for you. You will find there are similar functions to destroy bodies and joints as well.

Adding the controls

We have the code in place to add and remove platforms based on the user's touch. So it's time to code the touch controls for the game. Let's look at the `ccTouchesBegan` function in `GameWorld.cpp`:

```
void GameWorld::ccTouchesBegan(CCSet* set, CCEvent* event)
{
  // don't accept touch when clown is in these states
  if(clown_->GetState() == E_CLOWN_ROCKET ||
    clown_->GetState() == E_CLOWN_BALLOON ||
    clown_->GetState() == E_CLOWN_UP)
    return;

  CCTouch* touch = (CCTouch*)(*set->begin());
  CCPoint touch_point = touch->getLocationInView();
  touch_start_ = CCDirector::sharedDirector()->
    convertToGL(touch_point);

  // remove any previously added platforms
  RemovePlatform();
  // convert touch coordinates with respect to game_object_layer_
    and position the platform there
```

```
    platform_->setPosition(game_object_layer_->
      convertToNodeSpace(touch_start_));
    platform_->setVisible(true);
    platform_->setScaleX(0);
  }
```

We start by storing the touch received into a variable called `touch_start_`. We then remove any previously added platforms. Since this is the first touch, we position the platform at the touch location, set it's visibility to true, and scale it down to `0`. Notice how we call the `convertToNodeSpace` function on `game_object_layer_`. This converts a point in the world coordinates to coordinates local to a given node. We must do this because the touch coordinates will be with respect to the `GameWorld` layer, whereas `platform_` has been added to the `game_object_layer_`. So when the `game_object_layer_` moves, the touch coordinates will have to be offset appropriately.

We must resize and rotate the platform based on the movement of the user's finger, which we'll do in the `ccTouchesMoved` function as follows:

```
void GameWorld::ccTouchesMoved(CCSet* set, CCEvent* event)
{
  // don't accept touch when clown is in these states
  if(clown_->GetState() == E_CLOWN_ROCKET ||
    clown_->GetState() == E_CLOWN_BALLOON ||
    clown_->GetState() == E_CLOWN_UP)
    return;

  CCTouch* touch = (CCTouch*)(*set->begin());
  CCPoint touch_point = touch->getLocationInView();
  touch_end_ = CCDirector::sharedDirector()->convertToGL(touch_point);

  // manipulate anchor point so the platform is correctly oriented
  platform_->setAnchorPoint( touch_end_.x >=
    touch_start_.x ? ccp(0, 0.5f) : ccp(1, 0.5f) );
  float length = ccpDistance(touch_end_, touch_start_);
  // scale the platform according to user input
  platform_->setScaleX(length / platform_->getContentSize().width);
  // manipulate rotation so that platform doesn't appear upside down
  float angle = CC_RADIANS_TO_DEGREES(-1 * ccpToAngle(ccpSub(
    touch_end_, touch_start_)));
  platform_->setRotation( touch_end_.x >=
    touch_start_.x ? angle : angle + 180 );
}
```

We begin by updating the `touch_end_` variable, which will track the last location of the user's finger on screen. Then, based on whether the finger has moved to the left or right of its initial position, we reset the anchor point. This is followed by setting the appropriate scale and rotation. If you're wondering why we're manipulating the anchor point and the rotation values, this table should clear things up:

Start point	End point	Platform without manipulation	Platform with manipulation
S = (0, 0)	E = (100, 100)	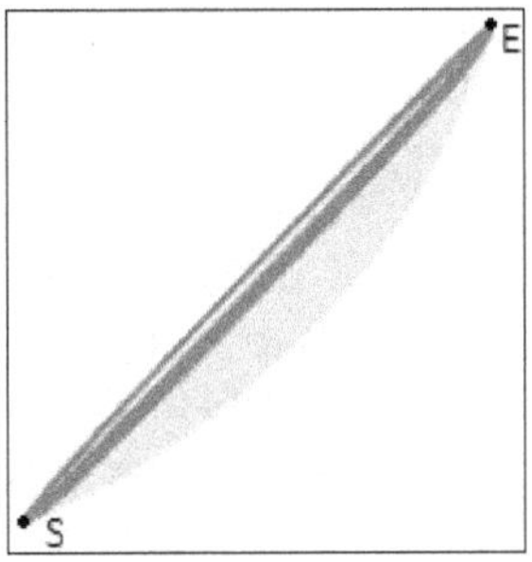 E S	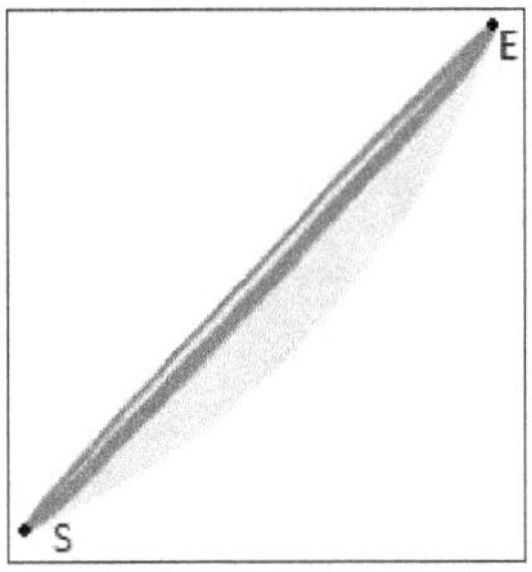 E S
S = (100, 100)	E = (0, 0)	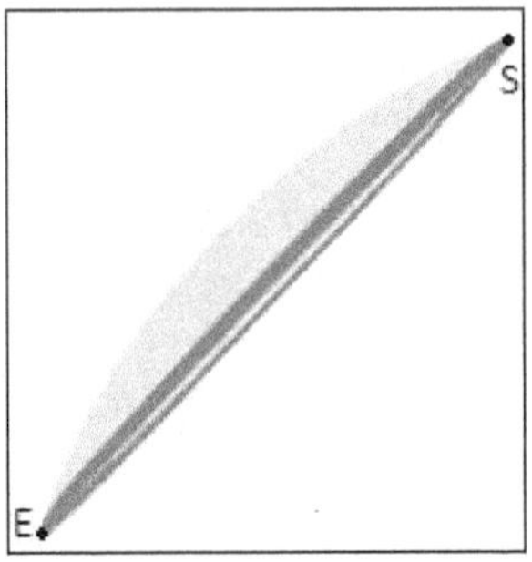 S E	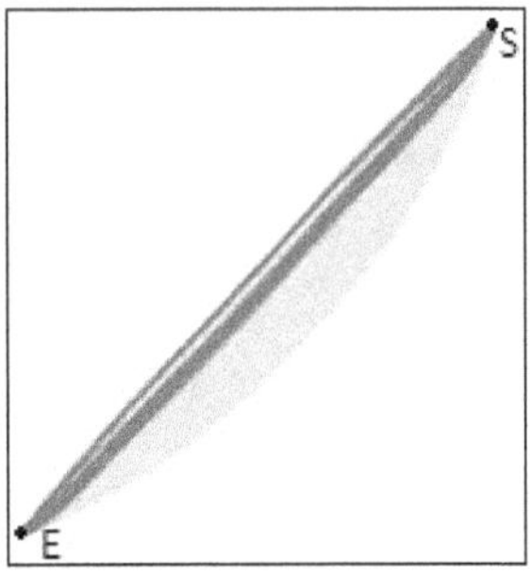 S E

Adjusting the anchor points basically orients the platform with respect to the player's touch points. If the player drags from left to right, the platform should be shown expanding from left to right. The only way we can achieve that is by setting the *x* coordinate of the anchor-point to `0`. The exact opposite is valid when the player drags from right to left.

In the `ccTouchesEnded` function, which is not discussed, we simply take the value of `touch_start_` and `touch_end_` and pass them to the `AddPlatform` function before resetting their values to `CCPointZero`.

So, we have written code to set the stage for the clown as well as to create the clown. We also wrote a couple of functions that create platforms for the clown to jump on, based on the user's touch. In its current state, the clown's body will simply bounce off the platform owing to the clown fixture's restitution value of 0.5f.

But we don't want that, do we? The length of the platform drawn by the user plays an important role to the amount the clown will jump. Shorter platforms must throw the clown with greater force than larger platforms. We do this in our next section where we listen for collisions.

Listening for collisions

If you remember, right after we created the world, we called its `SetContactListener` function and passed in a reference to `GameWorld`. We could do this because our `GameWorld` class inherits not only from `CCLayer`, but also from `b2ContactListener`. As a result of this, `GameWorld` can receive information about any and all pairs of fixtures colliding by implementing the `BeginContact` function as follows:

```
void GameWorld::BeginContact(b2Contact *contact)
{
  b2Body* body_a = contact->GetFixtureA()->GetBody();
  b2Body* body_b = contact->GetFixtureB()->GetBody();

  // only need to observe collisions that involve GameObjects
  if(body_a->GetUserData() == NULL || body_b->GetUserData() == NULL)
  {
    return;
  }

  // identify type of the objects involved in the collision
  EGameObjectType game_object_a_type =
    ((GameObject*)body_a->GetUserData())->GetType();
  EGameObjectType game_object_b_type =
    ((GameObject*)body_b->GetUserData())->GetType();

  // if a collision did not involve the clown, it will be ignored
  if(game_object_a_type != E_GAME_OBJECT_CLOWN && game_object_b_type
!=
    E_GAME_OBJECT_CLOWN)
    return;
```

```
    // separate the clown and the other object
    GameObject* other_object = (game_object_a_type !=
      E_GAME_OBJECT_CLOWN) ? (GameObject*)body_a->GetUserData() : (
      GameObject*)body_b->GetUserData();

    // based on type, call appropriate collision response function
    switch(other_object->GetType())
    {
    case E_GAME_OBJECT_PLATFORM:
      if(other_object == base_platform_)
      {
        DoBasePlatformCollision();
      }
      else
      {
        OnCollision(contact->GetManifold()->localNormal);
      }
      break;
    case E_GAME_OBJECT_COLLECTIBLE:
    case E_GAME_OBJECT_ROCKET:
    case E_GAME_OBJECT_BALLOON:
      ((Collectible*)other_object)->OnCollision();
      break;
    }
  }
```

The `BeginContact` function is passed a `b2Contact` object as an argument. The `b2Contact` class contains information relevant to the collision between two fixtures, such as the contact point, contact normal, and impulse among others.

We fetch the two fixtures involved in a collision and then get references to their respective bodies. Next, we must check whether the bodies have any user data, since we are interested in observing collisions involving the clown and other game objects.

We then fetch the game object type from the respective bodies so that we can return if this collision did not involve the clown. Once we are sure that this collision involved the clown, we must find out which object did the clown collide with and separate it into the `other_object` variable. Based on value of variable type_ belonging to `other_object`, we call the respective collision handling functions.

So far, we have only defined the platforms among which we treat the base platform differently as compared to the regular platforms that the user draws. Since the object type for both the base platform and the user drawn platform is the same, we check for equality between `other_object` and `base_platform_`, and then call `DoBasePlatformCollision()`. Otherwise, `other_object` is the one that the user has drawn and we call the `OnCollision` method, passing in the normal of the collision.

The `switch` case also handles collisions with objects having types `E_GAME_OBJECT_COLLECTIBLE`, `E_GAME_OBJECT_ROCKET`, and `E_GAME_OBJECT_BALLOON`. These are the collectibles we will discuss in detail in our next section. For now, just remember that we call the `OnCollision` function of a collectible from the `BeginContact` function.

Let's come back to the platform collision handlers. We will skip discussing the `DoBasePlatformCollision` function, since we simply change the display frame of the `base_platform_` object and schedule a callback to reset it to the original frame after a short duration.

The `OnCollision` function does a bunch of things, so let's take a look at it:

```
void GameWorld::OnCollision(b2Vec2 contact_normal)
{
  // ignore collisions when the clown is in these states
  switch(clown_->GetState())
  {
  case E_CLOWN_UP:
  case E_CLOWN_ROCKET:
  case E_CLOWN_BALLOON:
    return;
  }

  // stop the clown's movement
  clown_->GetBody()->SetLinearVelocity(b2Vec2_zero);
  // update the clown's state
  clown_->SetState(E_CLOWN_BOUNCE);
  // save the normal at the point of contact
  contact_normal_ = contact_normal;
  // animate the platform
  platform_->runAction(CCSequence::createWithTwoActions(
    CCAnimate::create(CCAnimationCache::sharedAnimationCache()->
    animationByName("platform_animation")), CCHide::create()));
  // schedule the actual collision response after a short duration
```

```
    scheduleOnce(schedule_selector(GameWorld::DoCollisionResponse),
      0.15f);

    has_game_begun_ = true;

    SOUND_ENGINE->playEffect("platform.wav");
  }
```

In the preceding function, we are overriding Box2D's default collision response and impulse calculation. This is because we want different impulses applied to the clown based on the user's input. So, all we need is the direction of the impulse that will be applied to the clown.

The first thing we do is check the state of the clown and return unless the clown is in the state `E_CLOWN_DOWN`. We then stop the clown's movement and also set the clown's state so the appropriate frame is set to the sprite. Then, we store the normal vector at the point of contact, which is passed to this function from `BeginContact` into the `contact_normal_` variable. We will use this as the direction of the impulse applied to the clown.

We then run an animation on the `platform_` object and also schedule a callback to the `DoCollisionResponse` function, which looks like this:

```
void GameWorld::DoCollisionResponse(float dt)
{
  // safe checking if the platform's fixture is deleted before this
    function is called
  if(!platform_->GetBody()->GetFixtureList())
    return;

  // fetch the shape from the platform body's fixture
  b2EdgeShape* platform_shape = (b2EdgeShape*)platform_->GetBody()->
    GetFixtureList()->GetShape();
  // get the difference vector
  b2Vec2 diff = platform_shape->m_vertex2 - platform_shape->m_vertex1;

  // calculate magnitude of the impulse based on the length of
    the platform
  float distance = WORLD_TO_SCREEN(diff.Length()) / MAX_PLATFORM_
WIDTH;
  float magnitude = PLATFORM_IMPULSE * (1.5f - (distance >
    1.0f ? 1.0f : distance));
```

```
    // impulse wil be in the direction of the contact normal
    b2Vec2 impulse = contact_normal_;
    // ensure impulse throws the clown up not down
    impulse.y = impulse.y < 0 ? impulse.y * -1 : impulse.y;
    impulse *= magnitude;

    // apply a linear impulse to the center of the clown's body
    clown_->GetBody()->ApplyLinearImpulse(impulse, clown_->GetBody()->
      GetWorldCenter());

    // collision response finished, now remove the platform
    RemovePlatform();
}
```

We need to fetch the edge shape from the platform body's fixture since the impulse depends on it. Thus, we need to first check if the platform body has any fixtures applied to it before calling the `GetShape` function. The `GetShape` function will simply return the `b2Shape` object bound to the fixture, which we will need to type-cast into `b2EdgeShape`. Now that we have the edge, we can calculate the difference between the end points of the edge and store the resultant `b2Vec2` into the `diff` variable. We can use the length of this vector to calculate the magnitude of the impulse to be applied to the clown into the `magnitude` variable.

We initialize a `b2Vec2` object by the name `impulse` with the `contact_normal_` object we saved in the `OnCollision` function. Then, we ensure that the `impulse` vector points in the upward direction before multiplying it by `magnitude`.

We can now call the `ApplyLinearImpulse` function on the body of the clown and pass in the `impulse` vector and also the position on the body where we want to apply the impulse, which in our case is the center of the clown's body.

We wind up the collision response by calling the `RemovePlatform` function that deletes the platform body's fixture. However, it is important to note that if we had deleted the fixture in the `OnCollision` function, we would be in trouble. This is because the `OnCollision` function was called from the `BeginContact` function. Also, the `BeginContact` function is a callback that is called within Box2D's time-step. This means that Box2D is still in the process of evaluating all of its objects and deleting any object right now would lead to pointers being orphaned—and a whole lot of mess.

Be careful not to delete any `b2Body`, `b2Joint`, `b2Fixture`, or `b2Contact` objects from within the time-step of Box2D, for example, in the `BeginContact` or `EndContact` functions.

Luckily, we had to play an animation on the platform and even wanted the clown to stay in the `E_CLOWN_BOUNCE` state for a short duration, so we had no choice but to delete the fixture later. This may not be the case all the time. The safe way to delete any bodies or fixtures on collision would be after the time-step has finished. This can be implemented by adding the required bodies or fixtures to a list and deleting the contents of that list after calling the `Step` function.

In essence, we have a fully functional game where the user can draw platforms, which upon collision with the clown will launch the clown higher up. The shorter the platform drawn, the higher the clown jumps. All this is fine, but the game looks very plain and quite empty. So let's fill it up with collectibles and a couple of special power-ups.

The Collectible class

The collectibles for this game will be represented by the `Collectible` class that inherits from `GameObject` and will be used to represent all three types of collectibles: the simple collectible, the rocket, and the balloon. It will possess a score value and a flag that marks whether it has been collected. It will possess functions to manage life events that we will discuss in this section, starting with the `SetBody` function:

```
void Collectible::SetBody(b2Body* body)
{
  b2PolygonShape collectible_shape;

  // create different box shapes for different collectibles
  switch(type_)
  {
  case E_GAME_OBJECT_COLLECTIBLE:
    collectible_shape.SetAsBox(SCREEN_TO_WORLD(
      m_obContentSize.width/2), SCREEN_TO_WORLD(
      m_obContentSize.height/2));
    break;
  case E_GAME_OBJECT_ROCKET:
  case E_GAME_OBJECT_BALLOON:
```

```
    collectible_shape.SetAsBox(SCREEN_TO_WORLD(
      m_obContentSize.width/2), SCREEN_TO_WORLD(
      m_obContentSize.height/4), b2Vec2(0, SCREEN_TO_WORLD(
      m_obContentSize.height/4)), 0);
    break;
  }

  // mark the fixture as a sensor
  b2FixtureDef collectible_fixture_def;
  collectible_fixture_def.shape = &collectible_shape;
  collectible_fixture_def.isSensor = true;
  body->CreateFixture(&collectible_fixture_def);

  // call parent class' function
  GameObject::SetBody(body);
}
```

All three collectibles will have a box shape fed into their fixtures but will look different based the value of `type_` variable. One important thing to notice is that this time we set a new property of the `b2FixtureDef` class—the `isSensor` property. A sensor in Box2D, to quote the manual, is a fixture that detects a collision but does not produce a response.

This is exactly what we want in our game since it would look pretty awkward if the clown kept bouncing off every bowling pin, bottle rocket, and balloon. We wind up the function by creating the fixture and passing the body to the `SetBody` function of the parent class.

Now, let's define the `Init` and `Reset` functions, which will enable us to reuse this object throughout our game:

```
void Collectible::Init(b2Vec2 position)
{
  // initialise position and scale
  body_->SetTransform(position, 0);
  setScale(1.0f);
}

void Collectible::Reset()
{
  // reset position outside boundary of game
  body_->SetTransform(b2Vec2(SCREEN_TO_WORLD(-1 * WALL_WIDTH),
    SCREEN_TO_WORLD(-1 * WALL_WIDTH)), 0);
  removeFromParentAndCleanup(true);
  is_collected_ = false;
}
```

The `Init` function sets the position of the body to the input provided and also resets the scale factor. This function will be called when the collectible has been added on to the game world. The `Reset` function—on the other hand—places the body right out of the screen while also removing itself from its parent and setting the `is_collected_` flag to `false`. This function will be called when the collectible has been removed from the game world. That is all we need to do to make this collectible reusable. We will now define the behavior of the collectibles when they collide with the clown:

```
void Collectible::OnCollision()
{
  // can be collected only once
  if(is_collected_)
    return;

  is_collected_ = true;
  // add respective score
  game_world_->AddScore(score_);
  // scale down and exit
  runAction(CCSequence::createWithTwoActions(
  CCSequence::createWithTwoActions(CCScaleTo::create(0.01f, 1.2f),
  CCScaleTo::create(0.1f, 0.0f)), CCCallFunc::create(this,
  callfunc_selector(Collectible::AfterCollision))));

  // inform player of respective state change
  if(type_ == E_GAME_OBJECT_ROCKET)
  {
    game_world_->GetClown()->SetState(E_CLOWN_NONE);
    game_world_->GetClown()->SetState(E_CLOWN_ROCKET);
  }
  else if(type_ == E_GAME_OBJECT_BALLOON)
  {
    game_world_->GetClown()->SetState(E_CLOWN_NONE);
    game_world_->GetClown()->SetState(E_CLOWN_BALLOON);
  }

  ShowParticle();

  SOUND_ENGINE->playEffect("collectible.wav");
}
```

This function is called from the `BeginContact` function we saw in the previous section. A collectible can only be collected once and hence the return statement at the start of the function. Then we inform `GameWorld` to add the score for this collectible and also play a simple animation. Based on which type of collectible this is, we need to inform the clown that a change of state has occurred. While doing this, we first set the clown's state to none and then to either the rocket or balloon state. This is done to handle cases like when the clown is already in the rocket state and collides with another rocket. Since our clown's `SetState` function only responds to a state change, the preceding scenario won't show any effect. The last thing we do is show a small burst of some particles.

The `AfterCollision` function simply informs `GameWorld` that this collectible should now be removed. With these functions, we have more or less completed defining the behavior of the collectibles. However, we will need to write the code to implement the reusing and caching of these collectibles.

Creating and reusing collectibles

While creating games, sometimes you may come across some of your game elements repeating themselves over and over as the level progresses. Consider you have a side-scrolling platform where your character is supposed to collect things such as coins, stars, health packs, and so on. Now, you might want to create these elements just before they enter the screen and delete them when the character collects them or when they exit the screen. However, this may not be the most efficient approach.

So, I will show you a commonly used technique of pooling or caching your game's elements so that they can be reused. What this means is that you will create a predefined maximum number of elements and place them in a container when the game or level loads. When required, elements will be removed from this container and merely added to the game world. Conversely, after their task is finished, they will be removed from the game world and added back to the container. This way, you don't waste any time creating and deleting objects.

For our game, we will create two `CCArray` containers named `pool_collectibles_` and `active_collectibles_` to maintain references to the collectibles in the pool and the ones added to the `GameWorld` object, respectively. We will also maintain a counter named `num_collectibles_active_` to keep track of the collectibles currently added to `GameWorld`. Let's look at the `CreateCollectibles` function from `GameWorld.cpp`:

```
void void GameWorld::CreateCollectibles()
{
  // create the pool and active containers
```

```
    pool_collectibles_ = CCArray::createWithCapacity(MAX_COLLECTIBLES);
    pool_collectibles_->retain();
    active_collectibles_ = CCArray::createWithCapacity(MAX_
COLLECTIBLES);
    active_collectibles_->retain();

    // all collectibles will be static bodies
    b2BodyDef body_def;
    body_def.type = b2_staticBody;
    body_def.position.Set(SCREEN_TO_WORLD(-1 * WALL_WIDTH),
      SCREEN_TO_WORLD(-1 * WALL_WIDTH));

    for(int i = 0; i < MAX_COLLECTIBLES; ++i)
    {
      // ensure there is one balloon and one rocket
      EGameObjectType type = (i == 1) ? E_GAME_OBJECT_BALLOON : (
        (i == 0) ? E_GAME_OBJECT_ROCKET : E_GAME_OBJECT_COLLECTIBLE );
      // create collectible, set physics body & add to the pool
      Collectible* collectible = Collectible::create(this, type);
      collectible->SetBody(world_->CreateBody(&body_def));
      pool_collectibles_->addObject(collectible);
    }
  }
```

We start the function by creating two new `CCArray` objects with a predefined capacity and retain them. Then, we define a `b2BodyDef` class for the collectible bodies and position them outside the boundary of the game.

In a loop, we create new `Collectible` objects, set their type and body, and finally add them to the `pool_collectibles_` array. We also ensure that there is one rocket collectible and one balloon collectible in the array. Now that we have everything ready to add collectibles on to the screen whenever required, we can define the `AddCollectible` function from `GameWorld.cpp`:

```
void GameWorld::AddCollectible(bool special)
{
  // do not exceed the maximum
  if(num_collectibles_active_ >= MAX_COLLECTIBLES)
    return;

  // loop through the pool of collectibles
  Collectible* collectible = NULL;
  int num_pool_collectibles = pool_collectibles_->count();
  for(int i = 0; i < num_pool_collectibles; ++i)
  {
```

```
        // if a special collectible is required, return one if available
        collectible = (Collectible*)pool_collectibles_->objectAtIndex(i);
        if(special && (collectible->GetType() == E_GAME_OBJECT_ROCKET ||
          collectible->GetType() == E_GAME_OBJECT_BALLOON))
          break;
        else if(!special && collectible->GetType() != E_GAME_OBJECT_ROCKET
          && collectible->GetType() != E_GAME_OBJECT_BALLOON)
          break;
      }

      // add the collectible to the batch node
      sprite_batch_node_->addChild(collectible, E_LAYER_COLLECTIBLES);

      // remove the collectible from the pool and add it to the active
    list
      pool_collectibles_->removeObject(collectible);
      active_collectibles_->addObject(collectible);
      ++ num_collectibles_active_;

      // position the collectible & then initialise it
      b2Vec2 position;
      position.x = SCREEN_TO_WORLD(WALL_WIDTH * 1.5f) +
        CCRANDOM_0_1() * SCREEN_TO_WORLD(SCREEN_SIZE.width -
        WALL_WIDTH * 3);
      position.y = distance_travelled_ + SCREEN_TO_WORLD(
        SCREEN_SIZE.height * 2);
      collectible->Init(position);
    }
```

The first thing we do is check to see whether we've already added all the collectibles we have and return if so. We then loop through the `pool_collectibles_` container and pick out a `Collectible` object. While doing this, we use the special flag passed to this function to decide between a simple collectible and a rocket or balloon.

Once the required collectible is found, we add it to the game's batch node. We must now update the respective containers so we simply remove the object from `pool_collectibles_` and add it to `active_collectibles_`, incrementing the `num_collectibles_active_` counter along the way.

The last couple of things left to do are to appropriately position the collectible and inform it that it has been added to the game world. We can now define the other half of this feature with the `RemoveCollectible` function from `GameWorld.cpp`:

```
void GameWorld::RemoveCollectible(Collectible* collectible)
{
  if(num_collectibles_active_ <= 0)
    return;

  -- num_collectibles_active_;
  // remove the collectible from the active list and add it back to
     the pool
  active_collectibles_->removeObject(collectible);
  pool_collectibles_->addObject(collectible);
  // reset the collectible so it is ready for reuse
  collectible->Reset();
}
```

The `RemoveCollectible` function first checks to see if there are any collectibles to remove in the first place. Then, as you may have guessed, the collectible object is removed from the list of active collectibles and placed back into pool. The counter is decremented and the collectible's state is reset so that it is ready to be used again. Remember that this function is called by the `Collectible` class when it has been collected (in the `Collectible::AfterCollision` function) or when it has exited the screen (in the `Collectible::Update` function).

Congratulations, you have learned how to implement the simplest technique to reuse your game's elements. I urge you to try out this technique to pool the hundreds of enemies we created in the previous game, Inverse Universe. Resource pooling is ideal for a game like Inverse Universe. With most of the elements created in our current game, the most important task still remains: the `update` loop.

The update loop

We already saw a line from the `update` function where we step the Box2D simulation. Let's now go over the remaining objects that need to be updated:

```
void GameWorld::update(float dt)
{
  // update the world
  world_->Step(dt, 8, 3);

  // update all game objects
  clown_->Update();
```

```
    if(base_platform_)
    {
      base_platform_->Update();
    }

    for(int i = 0; i < num_collectibles_active_; ++i)
    {
      ((Collectible*)active_collectibles_->objectAtIndex(i))->Update();
    }

    // update platform if user is dragging one
    if(platform_->isVisible() && !touch_start_.equals(CCPointZero))
    {
      platform_->setPosition(game_object_layer_->
        convertToNodeSpace(touch_start_));
    }

    // walls must move along with clown
    wall_->SetTransform(b2Vec2(0, clown_->GetBody()->GetPosition().y -
      SCREEN_TO_WORLD(SCREEN_SIZE.height/2)), 0);
    // background must scroll with respect to clown
    background_manager_->Update( has_game_begun_ ? ((clown_->GetBody()->
      GetLinearVelocity().y) * -1) : 0 );

    // game_object_layer_ must move in opposite direction of clown
    // subtract SCREEN_SIZE.height/2 so that clown always stays in
  centre
      of the screen
    float position_y = -1 * (clown_->getPositionY() - SCREEN_SIZE.
  height/2);
    game_object_layer_->setPositionY( position_y > 0 ? 0 : position_y );

    UpdateCounters();
  }
```

The `update` function of `GameWorld` calls the `Update` function for all of its game objects. Then, based on whether or not the user is dragging to create a new platform, the `platform_` object's position must be updated. As the clown's body moves vertically throughout the game, so must the left and right walls, and the background environment. Last but not the least, we move our `game_object_layer_` object downward as the clown moves upward to ensure that the clown is always in the center of the screen. Basically, we move the camera to follow the clown.

Let's now define the `UpdateCounters` function from `GameWorld.cpp`:

```
void GameWorld::UpdateCounters()
{
  // check if clown has moved higher
  int new_distance_travelled = clown_->GetBody()->GetPosition().y -
    SCREEN_TO_WORLD(SCREEN_SIZE.height/2);
  if(new_distance_travelled > distance_travelled_)
  {
    // add score for every meter covered
    AddScore(5 * (new_distance_travelled - distance_travelled_));
    distance_travelled_ = new_distance_travelled;

    // add a collectible every 5 meters
    if(distance_travelled_ % 5 == 0)
    {
      // add a rocket or balloon every 100 meters
      AddCollectible(distance_travelled_ % 100 == 0);
    }
  }
}
```

This function tracks how much distance the clown has covered in meters. Based on this quantity, a distance based score is added. Also, a collectible is added every 5 meters with a special collectible every 100 meters. We are done with the `update` loop after discussing the clown's `Update` function from `Clown.cpp`:

```
void Clown::Update()
{
  // call parent class' update
  GameObject::Update();
  // store the clown's highest position yet
  highest_position_ = m_obPosition.y >
    highest_position_ ? m_obPosition.y : highest_position_;

  // if clown has moved two screens lower than highest point,
    its game over
  if(highest_position_ - m_obPosition.y > SCREEN_SIZE.height * 2)
  {
    game_world_->GameOver();
  }

  // update rocket jet stream if it exists
```

```
    if(rocket_trail_) rocket_trail_->setPosition(m_obPosition.x -
      m_obContentSize.width/3, m_obPosition.y);

    // do not update state based on velocity for the following states
    switch(state_)
    {
    case E_CLOWN_BOUNCE:
    case E_CLOWN_ROCKET:
    case E_CLOWN_BALLOON:
      return;
    }

    // udpate state based on vertical component of linear velocity
    b2Vec2 velocity = body_->GetLinearVelocity();
    if(velocity.y >= 5.0f)
      SetState(E_CLOWN_UP);
    else
      SetState(E_CLOWN_DOWN);
}
```

The clown's `Update` function tracks the highest point the clown has reached in terms of screen coordinates into the `highest_position_` variable. This value is used to check for the game over condition. Whenever the clown has fallen more than two times the screen height, the game over condition is triggered.

We update the rocket's jet stream particle system if it exists. Now, we must monitor the linear velocity of the clown so that we can set the appropriate state. Thus, if the velocity is above 5 meters per second, we set the state to `E_CLOWN_UP` and `E_CLOWN_DOWN` otherwise. However, these states should not be set when the clown is bouncing off the platform or when the clown is holding on to the rocket or balloon, and hence the `switch` case with `return` statement.

With that, we reached the end of our fifth game and the first one using Box2D. When you play the game I'm sure you will find something missing. The game in its current state lacks progression. Thus, a user can go on playing indefinitely with nothing to make life more difficult. I urge you to take matters into your own hands. Add some fire to the bottom of the screen! A fire that gets closer to the clown the higher he goes. Miss a single platform and the clown plummets to a fiery fall. That would add a nice bit of challenge to the game, wouldn't it?

Summary

With Jumpy Clown, we implemented our first physics game. We covered some basics of Box2D. We then went on to create the physics world and run the simulation. We created shapes, bound them to fixtures, and bound these fixtures to bodies. You also learned how to listen for collisions and manipulated some basic physics at runtime. We implemented two other interesting things with this game which were an FSM for the clown and a technique to reuse game elements with pools.

This was a simple game with some new things going on under the hood, but don't get lazy now. Our next game involves some really interesting graphics programming. I sure felt as artsy as a graphics designer while developing the game, and I'm sure you will too!

6
Creativity with Textures

In this chapter, we will take a leap into a new direction and take things to the next level. You will learn how to programmatically generate textures and bind them to shapes so that they can be used in the game. Cocos2d-x is so flexible that it allows us to run our own rendering commands and we will take advantage of this fact.

In this chapter, you'll learn:

- How to use the `CCRenderTexture` class to draw into a texture
- How to apply various graphical effects to a texture to add aesthetics
- How to create a curved Box2D terrain
- How to apply a texture to a curve

An introduction to Penguins Can Fly

In our sixth game, *Penguins Can Fly*, we lead a cute little penguin through a wide expanse of vibrant, colorful, and breath-taking hills. The controls are quite simple, but the game takes some time to master. The player must simply tap the screen. Tapping the screen pulls the penguin towards the hill. Thus, the game becomes a skill-based judgment game where the player must learn the right moment to release the tap.

Quite a bit of code in this chapter has been ported to Cocos2d-x from a wonderful demo project (`https://github.com/haqu/tiny-wings`) in Cocos2d-iphone written by Sergey Tikhonov (`http://haqu.net/`). This demonstrates how some of the challenging features of the game are implemented. A lot of this chapter's explanation on the above demo project is inspired from an excellent tutorial written by Ali Hafizji on `http://www.raywenderlich.com/`. Please head out to these links if you want to take a look at the original. The original needs some understanding of Objective-C:

- `http://www.raywenderlich.com/33266/how-to-create-dynamic-textures-with-ccrendertexture-in-cocos2d-2-x`
- `http://www.raywenderlich.com/32954/how-to-create-a-game-like-tiny-wings-with-cocos2d-2-x-part-1`
- `http://www.raywenderlich.com/32958/how-to-create-a-game-like-tiny-wings-with-cocos2d-2-x-part-2`

We will discuss the following entities in this chapter:

- The `Terrain` class
    - Drawing into a texture using `CCRenderTexture`
    - Rendering the stripes, gradient, highlights, and noise
    - Generating a set of vertices to represent a hill
    - Binding a Box2D body to the vertices of the hill
    - Rendering, scrolling, and scaling the hill
- The `Penguin` class
    - The diving mechanism
    - Detecting perfect slides and triggering fevers
    - Leaping from one hill to the next
- The `GameWorld` class
    - Bringing it all together
    - The main `update` loop
    - The `PreSolve` contact event

This is what we will achieve by the end of this chapter:

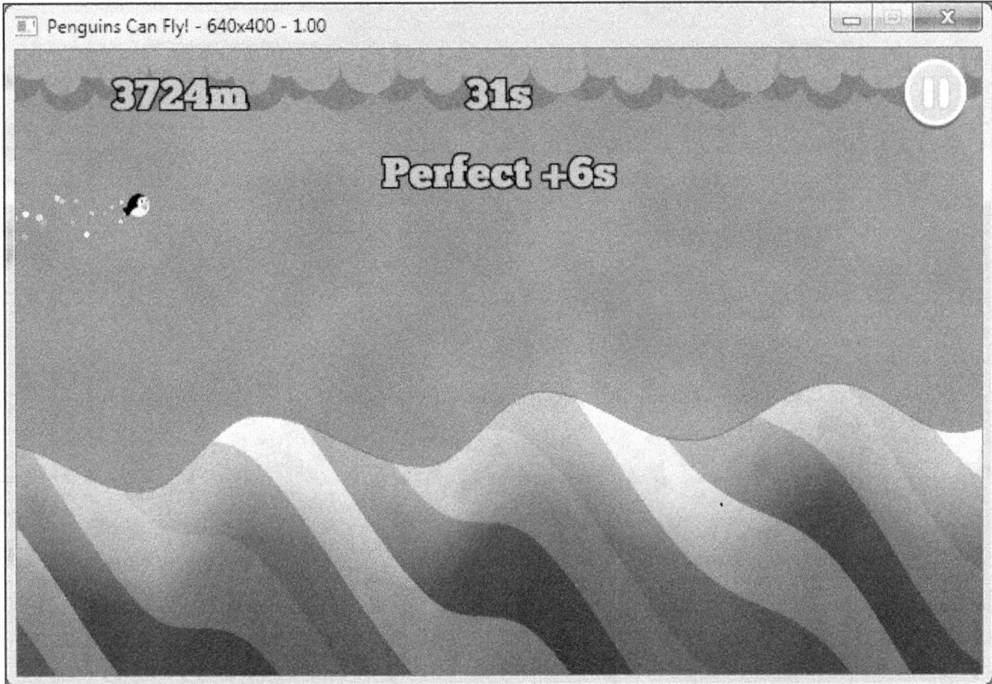

The Terrain class

The `Terrain` class is where we will do the most of our heavy lifting. This is the class that will create the hills in the game. When I say create, I mean give them that beautiful, colorful, materialistic appearance that you saw in the screenshot. In addition to that, this class will also generate the smooth curve of the hill and also create its physics body. Finally, it will be responsible for scrolling and scaling itself with respect to the penguin's position.

The `Terrain` class will inherit from `CCNode`. We will define this class in parts, starting with the most exciting part of all, the texture generation. We will then write code to generate the hills and the Box2D body. So, sharpen your pencils and smoothen your paintbrushes. Programmatic texture generation, here we come!

We will implement our `Terrain` class in the following steps:

- Generate a striped texture
    - Render the colored stripes
    - Render a gradient over the stripes
    - Render a highlight over the gradient
    - Render a thin border over the highlight
    - Finally apply a noise texture
- Generate the vertices for the hill
    - Generate key points for the hill
    - Generate vertices to represent the curved surface of the hill

Generating the striped texture

In *Chapter 4, Back to the Drawing Board*, we did some primitive drawing with Inverse Universe using the `CCDrawNode` class. However, that was much different in comparison to what we will be doing here. The highlight of this chapter will be using a few OpenGL commands to render some things on our own. It is imperative to have some basic knowledge of OpenGL to make the most of this chapter, so I strongly advise you to consult Google to cover the basics before diving into the code for this chapter. Alternatively, you could just use the OpenGL website as a starting point:

`https://www.opengl.org/sdk/docs/man4/`

If you were as curious as I was, you must have *Ctrl* and click or used *F12* on the `CCDrawNode` class to view what it actually does to draw primitives. If you didn't, it actually calculates the vertices for each shape and draws them each frame using OpenGL commands. That is exactly what we will do, but we will save all of that drawing into a texture. Confused? Well, everything will seem vibrant and colorful on the other side of the `GenerateStripedSprite` function (it's difficult to type *and* pronounce) from the `Terrain.cpp` file:

```
CCSprite* Terrain::GenerateStripedSprite(EStripeType stripe_type,
  int num_stripes)
{
  // create a texture that we can draw into
  CCRenderTexture* render_texture = CCRenderTexture::create(
    STRIPE_TEXTURE_SIZE, STRIPE_TEXTURE_SIZE);
```

```
    // begin with pure black
    render_texture->beginWithClear(0.0f, 0.0f, 0.0f, 0.0f);

    RenderStripes(stripe_type, num_stripes);
    RenderGradient();
    RenderHighlight();
    RenderTopBorder();
    RenderNoise();

    render_texture->end();
    // create a sprite out of the rendered texture & return it
    return CCSprite::createWithTexture(
      render_texture->getSprite()->getTexture());
}
```

Before we define this function with the tongue-twisting name, I want to show you the `CCSprite` that it returns to us:

The preceding image has a set of colored stripes, plus a gradient causing the image to be light at the top and dark at the bottom. That is then followed by a sort of yellow shine on the top of the image plus a very fine border across the top edge. Finally, a noise texture is applied to the image so it has a material appearance instead of looking completely flat.

Now, the first thing we do is create a new `CCRenderTexture` object, passing in the desired width and height of the resultant texture. We follow that up by calling the `beginWithClear` function on our new `render_texture` object. This sets up the renderer so that all subsequent OpenGL commands will draw into the texture instead of the frame buffer and consequently the screen. In addition to that, it also clears the texture and fills it with a color, as indicated by the parameters passed in.

After calling beginWithClear, every subsequent OpenGL command will affect the texture, and thus, we must call the end function of the CCRenderTexture class. This will stop the CCRenderTexture class from grabbing any further OpenGL commands. In essence, all that we want to draw into our custom texture will have to be drawn between these two functions: begin/beginWithClear and end. We will discuss each of the five functions you see in the following sections and I will show you the output after each step.

Drawing the stripes

In our texture, first we draw the stripes that will give our game its signature look. To do that, we define a function named RenderStripes that accepts the type of stripe and the number of stripes. The type of stripe is described by an enum named EStripeType, which you will find in the GameGlobals.cpp file. This is quite a large function with a lot of new things to learn. So, we'll discuss it part by part instead of all at once:

```
void Terrain::RenderStripes(EStripeType stripe_type, int num_stripes)
{
  // allocate memory for the position & colour arrays
  ccVertex2F* vertices = (ccVertex2F*)malloc(sizeof(ccVertex2F) * num_
stripes * 6);
  ccColor4F* colors = (ccColor4F*)malloc(sizeof(ccColor4F) * num_
stripes * 6);

  // initialise variables
  int num_vertices = 0;
  float x1 = 0.0f, x2 = 0.0f, y1 = 0.0f, y2 = 0.0f, dx = 0.0f, dy =
0.0f;

  // select between two colours or many colours
  bool two_colors = (CCRANDOM_MINUS1_1() > 0);
  ccColor4F color1 = GameGlobals::GetRandomColor();
  ccColor4F color2 = GameGlobals::GetRandomColor();
  ccColor4F c;
```

We begin by allocating memory for our two arrays, `vertices` and `colors`, which are of the type `ccVertex2F` and `ccColor4F`, respectively. These arrays will hold the position and color data at each vertex for each stripe. We then have a counter for the total number of vertices generated followed by variables to represent the coordinates of each vertex composing the stripe. The `EStripeType` enum that is passed as an argument to this function describes three types of stripes, that is, horizontal, diagonal (top-left to bottom-right), and diagonal (bottom-left to top-right). We will go over the code for each of them separately, starting with the horizontal stripes:

```
if(stripe_type == E_STRIPE_HORIZONTAL)
  {
    // initialise variables for the horizontal stripe
    dx = 0;
    dy = (float)STRIPE_TEXTURE_SIZE / (float)num_stripes;

    x1 = 0;
    y1 = 0;

    x2 = STRIPE_TEXTURE_SIZE;
    y2 = 0;

    // generate position & colour for each vertex of the stripe
    for (int i = 0; i < num_stripes; ++ i)
    {
      c = two_colors ? (i%2 ? color1 : color2) :
        GameGlobals::GetRandomColor();

      colors[num_vertices] = c;
      vertices[num_vertices ++] = vertex2(x1, y1);
      colors[num_vertices] = c;
      vertices[num_vertices ++] = vertex2(x2, y2);
      colors[num_vertices] = c;
      vertices[num_vertices ++] = vertex2(x1, y1 + dy);
      colors[num_vertices] = c;
      vertices[num_vertices ++] = vertices[num_vertices - 2];
      colors[num_vertices] = c;
      vertices[num_vertices ++] = vertices[num_vertices - 2];
      colors[num_vertices] = c;
      vertices[num_vertices ++] = vertex2(x2, y2 + dy);

      y1 += dy;
      y2 += dy;
    }
  }
```

Before we discuss the code, here is a visual representation of what this code block results in:

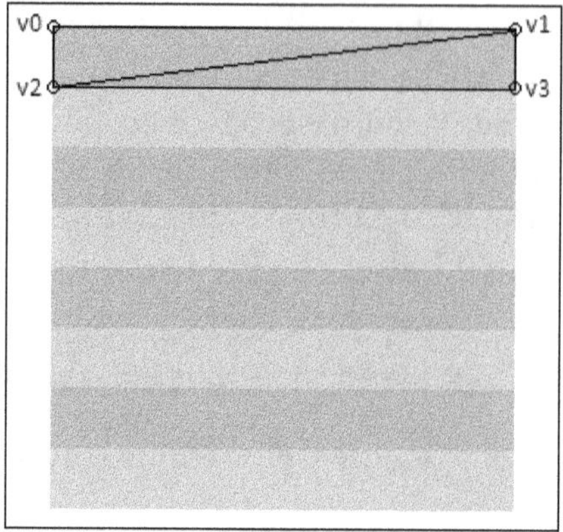

As you can see in the preceding figure, each stripe is nothing but a rectangle described by four vertices (**v0, v1, v2, v3**). However, we will draw this rectangle as two separate triangles. The two triangles will be described by vertices (**v0, v1, v2**) and (**v1, v2, v3**) respectively. That makes a total of six vertices for each stripe and that is why we multiply `num_stripes` by the number six while allocating memory to `vertices` and `colors`.

At the top of the block, we have defined the delta movement for both *x* and *y* coordinates into variables `dx` and `dy` respectively, followed by the initial values for the first stripe. We then write a loop that calculates six vertices for each stripe. In the loop, we either select from the two colors (as in the preceding figure) or we select a random color for each stripe. What follows is code to describe the six vertices (**v0, v1, v2**) and (**v1, v2, v3**) that will complete a single stripe. The loop terminates by incrementing `y1` and `y2` by `dy` to calculate vertices for the next stripe.

Now, let's look at code that generates vertices for the diagonal stripes:

```
else
{
  // initialise variables based on type of stripe
  dx = (float)STRIPE_TEXTURE_SIZE * 2 / (float)num_stripes;
  dy = 0;

  x1 = -STRIPE_TEXTURE_SIZE;
  y1 = (stripe_type == E_STRIPE_SLOPE_DOWN) ? 0 :
      STRIPE_TEXTURE_SIZE;

  x2 = 0;
  y2 = (stripe_type == E_STRIPE_SLOPE_DOWN) ?
    STRIPE_TEXTURE_SIZE : 0;
```

```
    // generate position & colours for two stripes at a time
    for (int i = 0; i < num_stripes / 2; ++ i)
    {
      c = two_colors ? (i%2 ? color1 : color2) :
        GameGlobals::GetRandomColor();

      for(int j = 0; j < 2; ++ j)
      {
        colors[num_vertices] = c;
        vertices[num_vertices ++] = vertex2(x1 + j *
          STRIPE_TEXTURE_SIZE, y1);
        colors[num_vertices] = c;
        vertices[num_vertices ++] = vertex2(x1 + j *
          STRIPE_TEXTURE_SIZE + dx, y1);
        colors[num_vertices] = c;
        vertices[num_vertices ++] = vertex2(x2 + j *
          STRIPE_TEXTURE_SIZE, y2);
        colors[num_vertices] = c;
        vertices[num_vertices ++] = vertices[num_vertices - 2];
        colors[num_vertices] = c;
        vertices[num_vertices ++] = vertices[num_vertices - 2];
        colors[num_vertices] = c;
        vertices[num_vertices ++] = vertex2(x2 + j *
          STRIPE_TEXTURE_SIZE + dx, y2);
      }

      x1 += dx;
      x2 += dx;
    }
  }
```

Before we discuss the code, here is a visual representation of what this code block results in when the stripe type is `E_STRIPE_SLOPE_DOWN`:

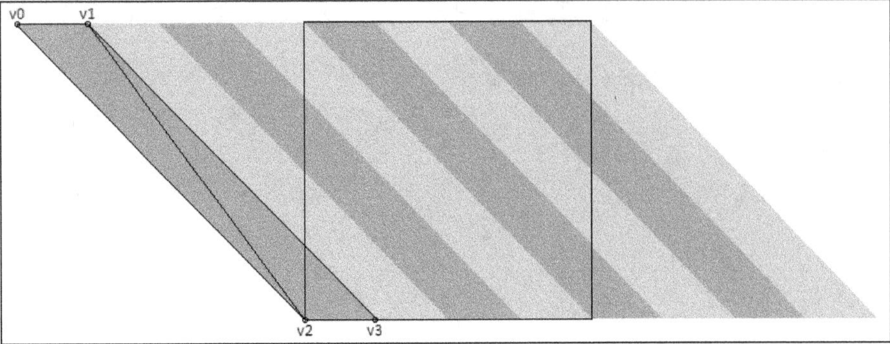

The logic we'll use to draw diagonal stripes will be quite different as compared to horizontal stripes. As you can see in the preceding figure, vertex **v0** of the first stripe starts far out to the left of the actual texture (indicated by the black outlined square in the center). Thus, we initialize `x1` with a value equal to `-STRIPE_TEXTURE_SIZE` and `x2` with `0`.

The variables `y1` and `y2` are defined based on whether our stripe will be top-left to bottom-right (`E_STRIPE_SLOPE_DOWN`) or bottom-left to top-right (`E_STRIPE_SLOPE_UP`). We then define a nested structure of loops that draws two stripes at a time. So, the vertices generated within the inner `for` loop will be for stripe-1 (green) and stripe-3 (green), then stripe-2 (yellow) and stripe-4 (yellow), and so on.

Now that we've calculated vertices for the various types of stripes, it is time to actually make the OpenGL calls that will do the rendering for us. So, let's take a look at the last part of the `RenderStripes` function:

```
// we're dealing with position & colour data here
setShaderProgram(CCShaderCache::sharedShaderCache()-
>programForKey(kCCShader_PositionColor));
CC_NODE_DRAW_SETUP();

// enable position & colour attributes
ccGLEnableVertexAttribs(kCCVertexAttribFlag_Position |
kCCVertexAttribFlag_Color);
// pass position & colour data
glVertexAttribPointer(kCCVertexAttrib_Position, 2, GL_FLOAT, GL_FALSE,
0, vertices);
glVertexAttribPointer(kCCVertexAttrib_Color, 4, GL_FLOAT, GL_TRUE, 0,
colors);
// set the blend function
glBlendFunc(GL_ONE, GL_ONE_MINUS_SRC_ALPHA);
// draw it...GL_TRIANGLES style!
glDrawArrays(GL_TRIANGLES, 0, (GLsizei)num_vertices);

// free what we allocated on top
free(vertices);
free(colors);
```

We kick off the rendering by setting the shader program for this node. Shaders are a huge aspect of graphics programming, but unfortunately they're way out of the scope of this book. For now, all you need to know is that shaders are simply programs that run on the GPU. Cocos2d-x comes with a bunch of default shaders that are loaded into the `CCShaderCache` class. You can also create and cache your own shaders into this class.

Here, we're rendering colored stripes and we're dealing only with the position and color for each stripe, which is why we select the `kCCShader_PositionColor` type of shader. You can find all the default shaders at the following path:

```
cocos2d-x-2.2.5\cocos2dx\shaders
```

We then use a convenience macro `CC_NODE_DRAW_SETUP()` that sets up the GL server state and links the shader program we set. We then call the `ccGLEnableVertexAttribs` function, passing in the flags `kCCVertexAttribFlag_Position` and `kCCVertexAttribFlag_Color`. This function informs OpenGL which attributes of the vertex will be used while rendering. The `ccGLEnableVertexAttribs` function has OpenGL function `glEnableVertexAttribArray` at its heart.

[You can find more information on `glEnableVertexAttribArray` at `https://www.khronos.org/opengles/sdk/docs/man/xhtml/glEnableVertexAttribArray.xml`.]

Next, we make two calls to the `glVertexAttribPointer` function, one each for the position and color attributes that we just enabled. This function basically tells OpenGL how to interpret the data that we're passing into this function via the arrays `vertices` and `colors`.

[You can find more information on `glVertexAttribPointer` at `https://www.khronos.org/opengles/sdk/docs/man/xhtml/glVertexAttribPointer.xml`.]

We must now set the blend mode by calling `glBlendFunc`, which basically specifies how the incoming values (the colored stripes we're about to render) will affect the existing values (so far, we have nothing, though). We pass in `GL_ONE` as the source factor, which means that all the existing values will be carried forward, and we pass in `GL_ONE_MINUS_SRC_ALPHA` as the destination factor, which means that the incoming values will be rendered wherever there is transparency in the existing values.

You can use this incredible visual tool to help you understand blend functions (`http://www.andersriggelsen.dk/glblendfunc.php`).

Finally, we call the `glDrawArrays` function that renders the vertex data that we just passed through `glVertexAttribPointer`.

The first parameter to `glDrawArrays`, `GL_TRIANGLES`, tells OpenGL that it should use all three vertices to draw a single triangle. The second parameter is the starting index from within the array where the vertices will be read. The last parameter is simply the number of vertices that we want rendered.

You can find more information on the `glDrawArrays` function at `https://www.khronos.org/opengles/sdk/docs/man/xhtml/glDrawArrays.xml`.

Now that we're done with the rendering, we must free the two arrays that we allocated memory to, at the start of the function. This winds up the `RenderStripe` function.

Adding a gradient

Now that we've drawn our stripes, we can go ahead and beautify the texture with a gradient. Remember that this texture will be applied to a landscape of mountains and we need to create an illusion of a shadow. Thus, our gradient will be light at the top and get darker towards the bottom. Let's take a look at the `RenderGradient` function from `Terrain.cpp`:

```
void Terrain::RenderGradient()
{
  // declare arrays for position & colour data
  ccVertex2F vertices[4];
  ccColor4F colors[4];
```

```
    // gradient will be light on top & dark at the bottom
    vertices[0] = vertex2(0, 0);
    vertices[1] = vertex2(STRIPE_TEXTURE_SIZE, 0);
    vertices[2] = vertex2(0, STRIPE_TEXTURE_SIZE);
    vertices[3] = vertex2(STRIPE_TEXTURE_SIZE, STRIPE_TEXTURE_SIZE);
    colors[0] = ccc4f(0.0f, 0.0f, 0.0f, 0.0f);
    colors[1] = ccc4f(0.0f, 0.0f, 0.0f, 0.0f);
    colors[2] = ccc4f(0.0f, 0.0f, 0.0f, 0.75f);
    colors[3] = ccc4f(0.0f, 0.0f, 0.0f, 0.75f);

    // we're dealing with position & colour data here
    setShaderProgram(CCShaderCache::sharedShaderCache()->programForKey(
      kCCShader_PositionColor));
    CC_NODE_DRAW_SETUP();

    // enable position & colour attributes
    ccGLEnableVertexAttribs(kCCVertexAttribFlag_Position |
      kCCVertexAttribFlag_Color);
    // pass position & colour data
    glVertexAttribPointer(kCCVertexAttrib_Position, 2,
      GL_FLOAT, GL_FALSE, 0, vertices);
    glVertexAttribPointer(kCCVertexAttrib_Color, 4,
      GL_FLOAT, GL_FALSE, 0, colors);
    // draw it...GL_TRIANGLE_STRIP style!
    glDrawArrays(GL_TRIANGLE_STRIP, 0, 4);
}
```

At the start of the function, we define two arrays to hold the position and color information for the gradient. We then fill in the positions as the top-left, top-right, bottom-left, and bottom-right corners into the vertices array. This is followed by filling in the color data, which is a completely transparent black color at the top with 75 percent opacity at the bottom.

Just by doing that, we have created a gradient, as OpenGL will automatically interpolate the alpha values between 0 and 75 percent when it runs the position-color shader. I am sure that you noticed how the arrays have only four elements instead of the six we had for the stripes. This is because we use a different drawing mode, named `GL_TRIANGLE_STRIP`, this time. `GL_TRIANGLE_STRIP` informs OpenGL that every triangle it draws will have the first two vertices same as the last two vertices of the previous triangle.

Thus, at the time of rendering, the gradient will be composed of two triangles having vertices {(`0`, `0`), (`STRIPE_TEXTURE_SIZE`, `0`), (`0`, `STRIPE_TEXTURE_SIZE`)} and {(`STRIPE_TEXTURE_SIZE`, `0`), (`0`, `STRIPE_TEXTURE_SIZE`), (`STRIPE_TEXTURE_SIZE`, `STRIPE_TEXTURE_SIZE`)}, respectively.

I'm sure you're wondering why we didn't use GL_TRIANGLE_STRIP while rendering the stripes given that we could have saved two vertices for each stripe. Since GL_TRIANGLE_STRIP causes triangles to share their vertices, all the triangles it draws must be connected or adjacent to each other. If you remember, while calculating vertices for the diagonal stripes, we were drawing two stripes that were apart from each other. That's the reason why we had to use GL_TRIANGLES. So far, this is what our texture looks like:

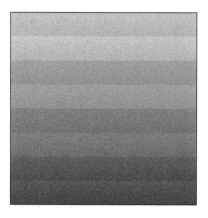

Adding some highlight

We will add some more realism to our texture by giving it some shine at the top to resemble sunlight falling on the surface of the hill. The RenderHighlight function from the Terrain.cpp file will do exactly that:

```
void Terrain::RenderHighlight()
{
  // declare arrays for position & colour data
  ccVertex2F vertices[4];
  ccColor4F colors[4];

  // highlight will be yellowish on top & nothing at the bottom
  vertices[0] = vertex2(0, 0);
  vertices[1] = vertex2(STRIPE_TEXTURE_SIZE, 0);
  vertices[2] = vertex2(0, STRIPE_TEXTURE_SIZE/3);
  vertices[3] = vertex2(STRIPE_TEXTURE_SIZE, STRIPE_TEXTURE_SIZE/3);
  colors[0] = ccc4f(1.0f, 1.0f, 0.5f, 0.4f);
  colors[1] = ccc4f(1.0f, 1.0f, 0.5f, 0.4f);
  colors[2] = ccc4f(1.0f, 1.0f, 0.5f, 0.0f);
```

```
    colors[3] = ccc4f(1.0f, 1.0f, 0.5f, 0.0f);

    // we're dealing with position & colour data here
    setShaderProgram(CCShaderCache::sharedShaderCache()->programForKey(
      kCCShader_PositionColor));
    CC_NODE_DRAW_SETUP();

    // enable position & colour attributes
    ccGLEnableVertexAttribs(kCCVertexAttribFlag_Position |
      kCCVertexAttribFlag_Color);
    // pass position & colour data
    glVertexAttribPointer(kCCVertexAttrib_Position, 2,
      GL_FLOAT, GL_FALSE, 0, vertices);
    glVertexAttribPointer(kCCVertexAttrib_Color, 4,
      GL_FLOAT, GL_FALSE, 0, colors);
    // set the blend function
    glBlendFunc(GL_SRC_ALPHA, GL_ONE_MINUS_SRC_ALPHA);
    // draw it...GL_TRIANGLE_STRIP style!
    glDrawArrays(GL_TRIANGLE_STRIP, 0, 4);
}
```

Much of the code here is similar to the function `RenderGradient`, except that the highlight will be applied only to the upper one-third of the texture and the color will be a shade of yellow. Another difference here is the presence of the function `glBlendFunc`. This is what our texture looks like with some highlight applied:

Drawing the border

We now add a thin border to the top of the texture, which when applied to the hills will provide an outline and represent the surface of the hill. The `RenderTopBorder` function from `Terrain.cpp` will take care of that. This function bears resemblance to the last two functions, so we shall skip discussing it in detail. The function simply renders a 3-pixel thick gray rectangle at the top of the texture. I'm sure you'll understand this function when you look at it in the source bundle.

Moving on, this is how the texture will look after this function has returned. I've taken the liberty of zooming in so that you can see the border clearly:

Adding some noise

We've added a lot of effects to the texture, but it still lacks a material feel and it appears flat. So, we'll add some noise to the texture in the `RenderNoise` function from the `Terrain.cpp` file:

```
void Terrain::RenderNoise()
{
  // create a sprite with readymade noise
  CCSprite* noise = CCSprite::create("noise1.png");
  // set the proper blend function
  ccBlendFunc blend_func;
  blend_func.src = GL_DST_COLOR;
  blend_func.dst = GL_ZERO;
  noise->setBlendFunc(blend_func);
```

```
    // position the sprite at the centre of the texture
    noise->setPosition(ccp(STRIPE_TEXTURE_SIZE/2,
      STRIPE_TEXTURE_SIZE/2));
    // call visit to render the sprite...twice gives added contrast
    noise->visit();
    noise->visit();
}
```

I'm sure you were expecting more than that! Well, every `CCSprite` class defines the similar set of OpenGL commands in its `draw` function like the ones we just wrote. So, all we really need to do here is create a `CCSprite` with a pre-rendered noise texture and call its `visit` function.

With the `RenderNoise` function, we complete the generation of a multicolor, realistic, striped texture. With the complicated rendering behind our back, we can now move forward to the creation of the hills. Before that, this is what the texture looks like after the `RenderNoise` function has returned:

Generating the hills

The shape of the hills in *Penguins Can Fly* won't be ultra-realistic, but they should be diverse enough to offer the player an engaging and exciting experience. We will split the algorithm to generate the structure of the hills into two parts: generation of key points and generation of smooth curves. The key points will basically be the peak and bottom points of the hill. After these points are generated, we will have a staircase structure with flat lines between the peak and bottom. We will then write code to interpolate a smooth curve between these key points.

Generating the hill key points

The hill key points will be nothing but the highest and lowest points on the surface of the hill. We must ensure that a peak is followed by a bottom, and vice versa, to ensure smooth continuity. Also, we would like to control the amount by which a peak rises and the amount a bottom falls. This would enable us to make the terrain easier or more difficult. Let's now take a look at the `GenerateHillKeyPoints` function from the `Terrain.cpp` file:

```
void Terrain::GenerateHillKeyPoints(float start_x)
{
  // initialise variables
  num_hill_key_points_ = 0;

  float x, y, dx, dy, ny;

  // first hill key point will be a bit outside the left edge of the
screen
  x = start_x - SCREEN_SIZE.width * 0.25f;
  y = 0;
  hill_key_points_[num_hill_key_points_ ++] = vertex2(x, y);

  // the first peak
  x = start_x;
  y = SCREEN_SIZE.height * 0.4f;
  hill_key_points_[num_hill_key_points_ ++] = vertex2(x, y);
```

We begin this function by initializing the number of hill key points and variables that will represent the *x* and *y* coordinates of each key point. We now initialize the first hill key point as being outside the left edge of the screen and right at the bottom. We then create the first peak at the *x* coordinate that is passed to this function and at a considerable height from the bottom of the screen. Continuing with the `GenerateHillKeyPoints` function from the `Terrain.cpp` file:

```
  // set the minimum & range quantities
  int min_dx = 160, range_dx = 80;
  int min_dy = 60,  range_dy = 60;
  // +1 - going up, -1 - going  down
  float sign = -1;
  // set the limits
  float max_height = SCREEN_SIZE.height * 0.5f;
  float min_height = SCREEN_SIZE.height * 0.25f;
```

Now that we've specified how the start of the hill will look, we can write a simple algorithm to generate the rest of the hill. First, we need to define a few parameters for the algorithm. The `min_dx` and `min_dy` variables will represent the minimum distance any two hill key points will have between each other, whereas the `range_dx` and `range_dy` variables will be used to select a random distance value that will be added to `min_dx` and `min_dy`. The sign variable will be toggled between `1` and `-1` so that the algorithm generates a peak followed by a bottom followed by a peak and so on. Finally, we define a couple of constraints that prevent the algorithm from generating key points that are too high or too low.

In the `GameGlobals.h` file, you will find `MAX_HILL_KEY_POINTS` defined as `100`. So, we have 50 peaks and 50 bottoms.

Let's look at the following code:

```
// first set of points
while (num_hill_key_points_ < MAX_HILL_KEY_POINTS - 15)
{
  dx = CCRANDOM_0_1() * range_dx + min_dx;
  x += dx;
  dy = CCRANDOM_0_1() * range_dy + min_dy;
  ny = y + dy * sign;
  if(ny > max_height) ny = max_height;
  if(ny < min_height) ny = min_height;
  y = ny;
  sign *= -1;
  hill_key_points_[num_hill_key_points_++] = vertex2(x, y);
}
```

In the preceding code, we define the majority of the hill key points. The reason we don't define them all in a single loop is because we want to create a kind of ramp at the end of the hill for the penguin to launch off. As you read earlier, we use `range_dx/dy` in combination with `min_dx/dy` to generate a delta into `dx` and `dy`. We then multiply the *y* coordinate with `sign` and restrict it within the appropriate constraints. Finally, we toggle `sign` by negating it and save the new hill point as a `ccVertex2F` object in the `hill_key_points_` array.

Let's now look at the last part of the function that takes care of generating the ramp-like structure towards the end of the hill. This loop will gradually lower the peak and bottom hill key points so that the last peak is high enough to act like a ramp for the penguin to take off.

Let's look at the following code:

```
// points that will go lower and lower
  min_height = SCREEN_SIZE.height * 0.1f;
  while (num_hill_key_points_ < MAX_HILL_KEY_POINTS - 2)
  {
    dx = CCRANDOM_0_1() * range_dx + min_dx;
    x += dx;
    dy = CCRANDOM_0_1() * range_dy + min_dy;
    ny = ( (y + dy * sign) < hill_key_points_[
      num_hill_key_points_ - 2].y ) ? (y + dy * sign) :
      (y + dy * sign * 0.5f);
    if(ny < min_height) ny = min_height;
    y = ny;
    sign *= -1;
    hill_key_points_[num_hill_key_points_++] = vertex2(x, y);
  }

  // finally a nice upward slope...the ramp to launch the penguin
  x += min_dx + range_dx * 3;
  y += min_dy + range_dy * 1.5f;
  hill_key_points_[num_hill_key_points_++] = vertex2(x, y);

  // last point will be way down below
  x += min_dx + range_dx * 1.5f;
  y = 0;
  hill_key_points_[num_hill_key_points_++] = vertex2(x, y);

  // initialise left most & right most key points
  from_key_point_ = 0;
  to_key_point_ = 0;
}
```

We start the loop by lowering `min_height` to `SCREEN_SIZE.height * 0.1f` from `SCREEN_SIZE.height * 0.25f`. This `while` loop is similar to the previous one except that it possesses a condition that ensures each peak is lower in elevation than the previous peak. The loop still doesn't create the ramp for us though. That is why we add the last two hill key points by ourselves.

Notice how the first hill key point that we add manually has the range multiplied so as to increase the distance between this key point and the previous, thereby creating a ramp. We then finish the hill structure off by creating the last key point at the bottom of the screen. We will discuss the `from_key_point_` and `to_key_point_` variables in a bit. For now, I have a screenshot of the hill key points that are generated by this function, so you know exactly what we have achieved:

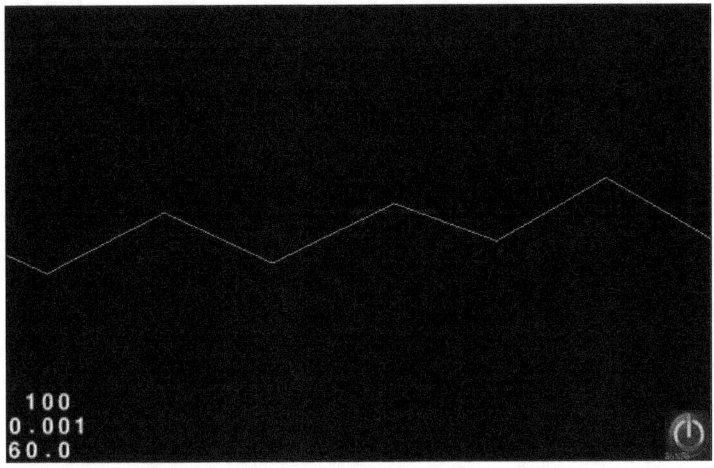

Generating the curve of the hill

In the preceding screenshot, you can tell that we have the key points correct. But this is not gameplay material. In order to make things realistic and fun, we will need to give the hills a smooth, curved surface over which the penguin can easily slide and take off too. We will make use of a simple cosine curve to achieve a neatly interpolated curve between two hill key points. If you're rusty on your trigonometry, this is what a cosine curve looks like:

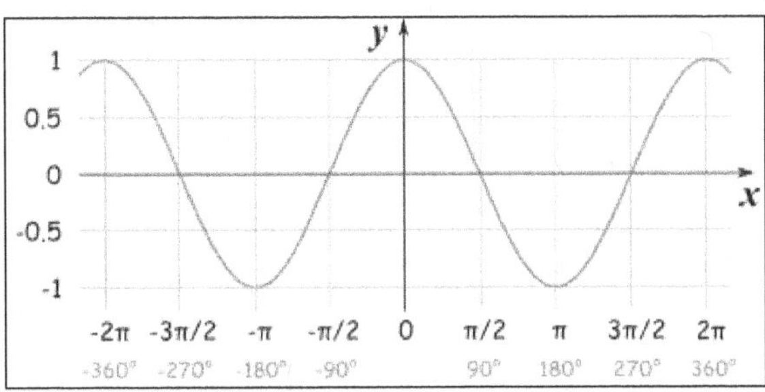

So, we want the *y* coordinates of the slope to be a factor of a cosine curve as it passes from 0 to pi. All this happens in the `GenerateBorderVertices` function of `Terrain.cpp`:

```
void Terrain::GenerateBorderVertices()
{
  // initialise variables
  num_border_vertices_ = 0;
```

```
    ccVertex2F p0, p1, pt0, pt1;
    p0 = hill_key_points_[0];

    for (int i = 1; i < num_hill_key_points_; ++ i)
    {
      p1 = hill_key_points_[i];

      // calculate the number of segments between adjacent key points
      int h_segments = floorf((p1.x - p0.x) / HILL_SEGMENT_WIDTH);
      // calculate delta x
      float dx = (p1.x - p0.x) / h_segments;
      // calculate delta theta
      float da = M_PI / h_segments;
      // calculate x-axis & amplitude for the cosine wave
      float ymid = (p0.y + p1.y) / 2;
      float ampl = (p0.y - p1.y) / 2;
      pt0 = p0;
      border_vertices_[num_border_vertices_++] = pt0;

      // for each segment, calculate x & y coordinate
      for (int j = 1; j < h_segments + 1; ++ j)
      {
        // x coordinate is last coordinate plus delta
        pt1.x = p0.x + j * dx;
        // y coordinate taken from the cosine wave
        pt1.y = ymid + ampl * cosf(da * j);
        border_vertices_[num_border_vertices_ ++] = pt1;
        pt0 = pt1;
      }

      p0 = p1;
    }
  }
```

At the start of the function, we initialize the various variables and counters.

> Remember that we will interpolate between two hill key points. These two key points will be represented by the variables `p0` and `p1` within the loop.

We initialize `p0` to point to the first key point in the `hill_key_points_` array and start the `for` loop from `1` instead of `0`.

Inside the loop, we initialize `p1` and calculate the number of segments between `p0` and `p1` based on the width of each segment (`HILL_SEGMENT_WIDTH` value as `15`). We must calculate the delta for the *x* coordinate and for the angle (theta). We then calculate the midpoint of the segment between `p0` and `p1` in terms of the *y* coordinate into the `ymid` variable. This will act as the *x* axis for our cosine curve. We also define an amplitude that we will multiply by the cosine curve; the larger the amplitude, the greater the distance between the peak and bottom of the cosine curve.

We then run a loop to interpolate from `p0` to `p1`, one segment at a time. Inside the loop, we calculate the vertices of the individual segment that will make up the curve. Notice how we use the `cosf` function to calculate the *y* coordinate of the curve. The following screenshot shows what happens when the points generated in the `border_vertices_` array are joined:

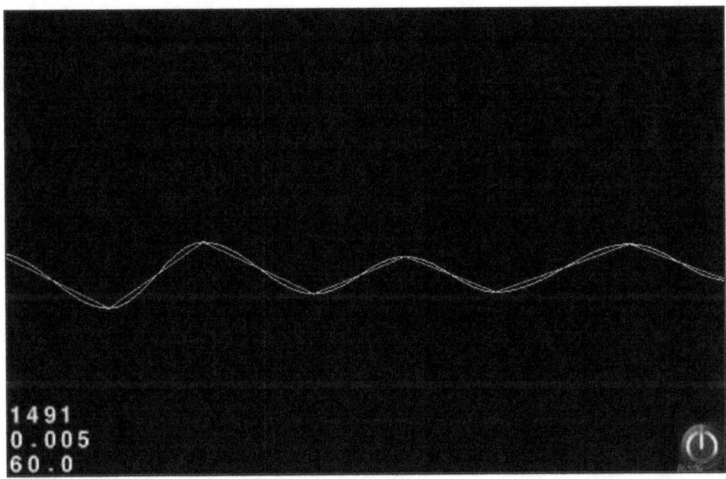

In this screenshot, you can see the hill key points and the smooth curve that is generated around them. At this point, we have a smoothly interpolated surface of the hill. We can now build a Box2D body with the vertices generated in the `GenerateBorderVertices` function.

Creating the Box2D body for the hill

The Box2D body of the hill will be static and its fixture will contain a chain shape. Let's take a look at what exactly happens in the `CreateBody` function of `Terrain.cpp`:

```
void Terrain::CreateBody()
{
  // create a body only the first time...after that only
    create fixture
```

```
    if(body_ == NULL)
    {
      b2BodyDef bd;
      bd.position.Set(0, 0);
      body_ = world_->CreateBody(&bd);
    }

    // create array for the vertices
    b2Vec2 vertices[MAX_BORDER_VERTICES];
    int num_vertices = 0;
    // loop through border_vertices_, convert screen
      coordinates to physics coordinates
    for (int i = 0; i < num_border_vertices_; ++ i)
    {
      vertices[num_vertices ++].Set(SCREEN_TO_WORLD(
        border_vertices_[i].x), SCREEN_TO_WORLD(border_vertices_[i].y));
    }

    // finish up the last two vertices to form a loop
    vertices[num_vertices ++].Set(SCREEN_TO_WORLD(border_vertices_[
      num_border_vertices_ - 1].x), 0);
    vertices[num_vertices ++].Set(SCREEN_TO_WORLD(
      border_vertices_[0].x), 0);

    // create the chain fixture with above vertices
    b2ChainShape shape;
    shape.CreateChain(vertices, num_vertices);
    body_->CreateFixture(&shape, 0);
  }
```

We begin by creating a static `b2Body` object into the member variable `body_` of class `Terrain`. We then declare an array of type `b2Vec2` named `vertices` before filling it up with the vertices we just calculated and fed into `border_vertices_`. Notice the helper macro `SCREEN_TO_WORLD` converting the coordinates from pixels to meters. Once this is done, we simply create a `b2ChainShape` object passing in the `vertices` array along with the number of vertices the chain should have. We wind up this function by creating a new fixture that will glue `body_` to the chain shape.

In our `Terrain` class, we have written code to generate a striped texture, generate vertices for a smooth curved hill, and even created a Box2D body. We still haven't rendered the hill though. We still need to bind the striped texture to the vertices of the curve and render the hill.

Rendering the hills

Before we write code to render the hills inside the `draw` function, we need to save the texture we generated by calling the `GenerateStripedSprite` function. So, let's take a look at a part of the `init` function from `Terrain.cpp`:

```
bool Terrain::init(b2World* world, float start_x)
{
  .
  .
  .
  // select between a type of stripe
  EStripeType stripe_type = (EStripeType)((int)(CCRANDOM_0_1() *
    (E_STRIPE_SLOPE_DOWN + 1)));
  // generate the stiped sprite
  sprite_ = GenerateStripedSprite(stripe_type , 8);
  // retain for use since we won't be adding it
  sprite_->retain();
  // setup the texture to repeat and stick to the edge
  ccTexParams tex_params;
  tex_params.minFilter = GL_LINEAR;
    tex_params.magFilter = GL_LINEAR;
  tex_params.wrapS = GL_REPEAT;
    tex_params.wrapT = GL_CLAMP_TO_EDGE;
  sprite_->getTexture()->setTexParameters(&tex_params);
  .
  .
  .
  .
}
```

Before we generate a texture, we must choose what type of stripes we want it to have. We then pass this stripe type into the `GenerateStripedSprite` function. If you remember, the `GenerateStripedSprite` function returns a pointer to a new `CCSprite`, which we now save into a member variable of class `Terrain` named `sprite_`. Since we won't really be adding the `sprite_` to the scene graph, we must retain it.

We also define the texture parameters for this sprite's texture, since we intend on repeating it along the vertices of the hill. Doing this will keep the sprite ready to be bound to the hill's vertices, but it won't actually render anything. So, we must define the `draw` function that class `Terrain` will override from `CCNode` as follows:

```
void Terrain::draw()
{
  // can't render without a sprite
```

```
    if(sprite_ == NULL)
    {
      return;
    }

    CC_NODE_DRAW_SETUP();

    // bind the texture for this node
    ccGLBindTexture2D(sprite_->getTexture()->getName());
    // enable position & colour attributes
    ccGLEnableVertexAttribs(kCCVertexAttribFlag_Position |
  kCCVertexAttribFlag_TexCoords);
    // pass position & colour data
    glVertexAttribPointer(kCCVertexAttrib_Position, 2, GL_FLOAT, GL_
  FALSE, 0, hill_vertices_);
    glVertexAttribPointer(kCCVertexAttrib_TexCoords, 2, GL_FLOAT, GL_
  FALSE, 0, hill_tex_coords_);
    // draw it...GL_TRIANGLE_STRIP style!
    glDrawArrays(GL_TRIANGLE_STRIP, 0, (GLsizei)num_hill_vertices_);
  }
```

We begin by checking whether the stripe texture sprite exists. You should be familiar with the code in this function by now, so I'll only highlight the differences. We call the `ccGLBindTexture2D` function here and pass in the name of the striped texture stored within `sprite_`. This is a method from Cocos2d-x that essentially calls the OpenGL command `glBindTexture`. The `glBindTexture` function simply binds a texture pointed to by the specified name to the active texture unit, which in this case is the node we're rendering.

> You can find more information on `glBindTexture` at `https://www.khronos.org/opengles/sdk/docs/man/xhtml/glBindTexture.xml`.

Another difference I'm sure you noticed is the flags we passed into `ccGLEnableVertexAttribs`. In this case, we're passing in the position and texture coordinates and not colors, so we enable the flags `kCCVertexAttribFlag_Position` and `kCCVertexAttribFlag_TexCoords` respectively. We then pass the position data stored inside `hill_vertices_` and the texture coordinate data stored inside `hill_tex_coords_` to OpenGL before calling `glDrawArrays` with the `GL_TRIANGLE_STRIP` draw mode.

But when did we create the arrays `hill_vertices_` and `hill_tex_coords_`? Well, we haven't yet. So, let's look at the `ResetVertices` function from `Terrain.cpp` and see how these arrays are filled up. This one is a slightly large function, so we will look at it in parts:

```
void Terrain::ResetVertices()
{
  // calculate the area of the hill that is currently visible plus a 
buffer of 
    0.125 * screen width
  float left_side = offset_x_ - SCREEN_SIZE.width * 
    0.125f / m_fScaleX;
  float right_side = offset_x_ + SCREEN_SIZE.width * 
    1.125f / m_fScaleX;

  // loop to calculate the left most key point
  while (hill_key_points_[from_key_point_ + 1].x < left_side)
  {
    from_key_point_ ++;
    if (from_key_point_ > num_hill_key_points_ - 1) {
      from_key_point_ = num_hill_key_points_ - 1;
      break;
    }
  }

  // loop to calculate the right most key point
  while (hill_key_points_[to_key_point_].x < right_side)
  {
    to_key_point_ ++;
    if (to_key_point_ > num_hill_key_points_ - 1) {
      to_key_point_ = num_hill_key_points_ - 1;
      break;
    }
  }
```

We begin this function by calculating the left and right limits of the hill. These limits are important because we will render only that area of the hill that is contained within these limits, as opposed to the entire hill. The `offset_x_` variable that is used in this calculation is nothing but the horizontal distance the hill has moved from its initial position. We must update `offset_x_` with respect to the position of the penguin to ensure that the hills scroll but more on that later.

Next, we have two while loops to identify the left-most and right-most hill key points based on `left_side` and `right_side`. We store these values into `from_key_point_` and `to_key_point_` respectively. If you remember, both these variables were initialized to 0 at the end of the `GenerateHillKeyPoints` function. We can use these two variables to govern how many hill key points will be used in rendering the hill, which is handled in the next part of the `ResetVertices` function:

```
// only loop if visible key points have changed
  if (prev_from_key_point_ != from_key_point_ ||
    prev_to_key_point_ != to_key_point_)
  {
    // initialise variables
    num_hill_vertices_ = 0;
    ccVertex2F p0, p1, pt0, pt1;
    p0 = hill_key_points_[from_key_point_];

    // calculate curve vertices from left most to right most key point
    for(int i = from_key_point_ + 1; i < to_key_point_ + 1; ++ i)
    {
      p1 = hill_key_points_[i];

      // calculate the number of segments between adjacent key points
      int h_segments = floorf((p1.x - p0.x) / HILL_SEGMENT_WIDTH);
      int v_segments = 1;
      // calculate delta x
      float dx = (p1.x - p0.x) / h_segments;
      // calculate delta theta
      float da = M_PI / h_segments;
      // calculate x-axis & amplitude for the cosine wave
      float ymid = (p0.y + p1.y) / 2;
      float ampl = (p0.y - p1.y) / 2;
      pt0 = p0;

      // calculate vertices for each segment
      for(int j = 1; j < h_segments + 1; ++ j)
      {
        pt1.x = p0.x + j * dx;
        pt1.y = ymid + ampl * cosf(da * j);

        // calculate vertices for two triangles...cuz we render
          using GL_TRIANGLE_STRIP
```

```
            for(int k = 0; k < v_segments + 1; ++ k)
            {
              hill_vertices_[num_hill_vertices_] = vertex2(pt0.x,
                pt0.y - (float)STRIPE_TEXTURE_SIZE / v_segments * k);
              hill_tex_coords_[num_hill_vertices_++] = vertex2(
                pt0.x /(float)STRIPE_TEXTURE_SIZE, (float)k / v_segments);
              hill_vertices_[num_hill_vertices_] = vertex2(pt1.x,
                pt1.y - (float)STRIPE_TEXTURE_SIZE / v_segments * k);
              hill_tex_coords_[num_hill_vertices_++] = vertex2(
                pt1.x / (float)STRIPE_TEXTURE_SIZE, (float)k / v_
segments);
            }
            pt0 = pt1;
          }

          p0 = p1;
        }

        // update previous left most & right most visible key points
        prev_from_key_point_ = from_key_point_;
        prev_to_key_point_ = to_key_point_;
      }
    }
```

We start with an `if` condition that checks if the new key points calculated are not the same as before. This optimizes our code a bit. Within the conditional, we initialize the number of hill vertices that we will generate in this code block. We also initialize a few variables that are too similar to the ones we saw in the `GenerateBorderVertices` function. In fact, if you look closely, you will realize that this function is similar to `GenerateBorderVertices`, which generates the curved surface of the hill.

However, there are a few differences that I will highlight. The first difference is the absence of `border_vertices_`, since the purpose of this function is to determine the vertices and texture coordinates required for rendering. Hence, we have the `hill_vertices_` and `hill_tex_coords_` arrays where we save the appropriate data.

There is also an additional variable, `v_segments`, which in turn spawns a new inner for loop. The inner for loop simply uses the variables `pt0` and `pt1` to calculate the vertices for two triangles (`GL_TRIANGLE_STRIP`) to render each horizontal segment. These vertices are stored in the `hill_vertices_` array. The following diagram will help you understand what the triangles' vertices will be:

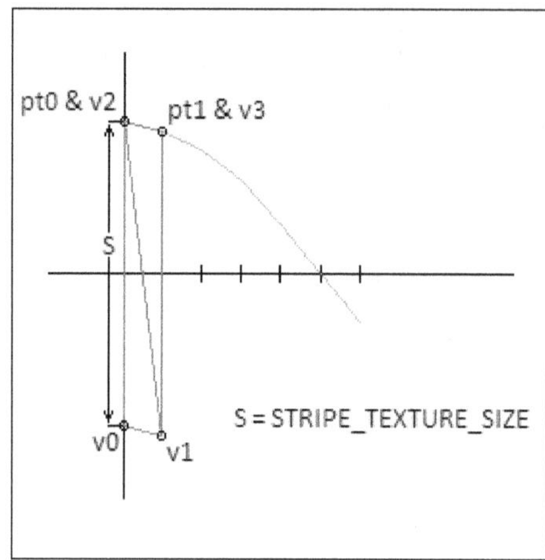

In the preceding figure, each horizontal segment (`pt0 -> pt1`) will be drawn by two triangles (**v0**, **v1**, **v2**) and (**v1**, **v2**, **v3**).

Along with the triangle vertices, the loop also calculates the texture coordinate for each of the vertices. Remember that texture coordinates usually go from `0` to `1`. So, for the *x* component of the texture coordinate, we will divide the *x* component of the particular vertex by the size of the texture. Since the texture parameters are set to repeat, we don't need to worry about anything else.

For the *y* coordinate, we will just set the bottom texture coordinate to `0` and the top texture coordinate to `1`. This way, the texture is fully distributed vertically. Finally, we update the `prev_from_key_point_` and `prev_to_key_point_` to `from_key_point_` and `to_key_point_`, respectively. In this way, we have calculated the vertices and texture coordinates that will be used in the `draw` function.

Updating the hill

The `Update` function of the `Terrain` class is called every tick from `GameWorld` with the penguin's position passed as an argument. The `Update` function takes care of two important tasks:

- It updates the position and scale of the hill based on the penguin's position

- It resets the current hill and generates a new one once the hill has left the screen

Let's see how this is done in the `Update` function of `Terrain.cpp`:

```
void Terrain::Update(CCPoint penguin_position)
{
  // determine current height & minimum height
  float height = penguin_position.y;
  const float min_height = SCREEN_SIZE.height * 0.6f;
  height = (height < min_height) ? min_height : height;

  // scale only if penguin is above SCREEN_SIZE.height * 0.6f
  float scale = min_height / height;
  setScale(scale * 1.25f);
  // update scrolling
  SetOffsetX(penguin_position.x);

  // check if terrain has left screen
  if(from_key_point_ >= MAX_HILL_KEY_POINTS - 1 && to_key_point_ >=
    MAX_HILL_KEY_POINTS - 1)
  {
    // reset the old data
    Reset();
    // create a new hill a couple of screens ahead of the penguin
    init(world_, penguin_position.x + SCREEN_SIZE.width * 2);
  }
}
```

We begin by storing the elevation of the penguin into the `height` variable. We also initialize another variable `min_height` with the value `SCREEN_SIZE.height * 0.6f`. We then use these variables to calculate the amount that the entire hill should be scaled into the `scale` variable. The calculation works in such a way that hill only scales down when the penguin's *y* coordinate has risen above 0.6 times the height of the screen. We also pass the *x* component of the penguin's position to the `SetOffsetX` function that we will discuss next.

The last part of the `Update` function checks to see whether the hill has scrolled out of the screen by comparing the values of the `from_key_point_` and `to_key_point_` variables. These variables specify the left-most and right-most key points of the visible area of the hill. Thus, if both variables are past the total number of key points, it is safe to say that the hill has left the screen.

In that case, we simply call the `Reset` function of `Terrain`, which makes sure that the striped sprite is released and the body's fixtures are destroyed while also resetting all the appropriate counters and variables. After `Reset`, we call the `init` function and pass in a reference to the physics world and the starting point for the next set of hills. We position the next set of hills a couple of screens ahead of the penguin, giving the players a second to catch their breath.

Let's now take a look at the `SetOffsetX` function that is responsible for scrolling the hills:

```
void Terrain::SetOffsetX(float offset_x)
{
  // update only if offset is different or if its a new game
  if (offset_x_ != offset_x || first_time_)
  {
    first_time_ = false;
    offset_x_ = offset_x;
    // leave some gap so the penguin is not stuck to the left
      of the screen
    setPositionX(SCREEN_SIZE.width / 8 - offset_x_ * m_fScaleX);

    // reset the drawable vertices of the hill
    ResetVertices();
  }
}
```

The `if` condition ensures that we proceed further only when the offset passed into this function is different from the existing offset or if this is the first time `SetOffsetX` is called. What follows next is code to set the position of the hill based on the offset and scale factor, while also allowing the player to stay 0.125 times the screen width ahead of the terrain. Finally, we call the `ResetVertices` function that will update the vertices and texture coordinates so the appropriate area of the hill is rendered.

At this point, our `Terrain` class is capable of generating a realistic yet beautiful striped texture, creating smooth and interpolated vertices for a hill. It also creates a physics body along those vertices, rendering itself and even scrolling and scaling itself. Now, it's time to look at the other main entity of the game: the `Penguin` class.

The Penguin class

The `Penguin` class publicly inherits from `CCSprite` and it is similar in terms of structure to the `GameObject` class you saw in the previous chapter. It possesses a `b2Body` object along with functions that update its position based on its body. The body of the penguin will have a circle-shaped fixture applied to it. We will skip all of that boilerplate code and discuss the behavior of the penguin.

Penguin behavior	Description
Awake	The penguin will be asleep at the start of the game. The player will have to touch the screen to wake him up.
Diving	This is true as long as the player is tapping the screen. A downward force is constantly applied to the penguin so long as he is diving.
Flying	This is true when the penguin is airborne and false when he is sliding on the surface of the hill.
Perfect slide	When the penguin launches off a slope above a certain velocity, it's a perfect slide.
Fever	The penguin enters into a trance like fever when he does three perfect slides in a row and leaves the fever mode when he has a bad landing.
Leaping	The penguin enters this state when he reaches the end of a particular hill. It leaves this state when it approaches the start of the next hill.

Let's now write the functions that define the behavior of the penguin based on the preceding states, starting with the `SetIsAwake` function from the `Penguin.cpp` file:

```
void Penguin::SetIsAwake(bool is_awake)
{
  // activate the body & apply impulse in the top-right direction
  if(is_awake)
  {
    is_awake_ = true;
    body_->SetActive(true);
    body_->ApplyLinearImpulse(b2Vec2(0.1f, 0.2f),
      body_->GetWorldCenter());
  }
  // deactivate the body
  else
  {
    is_awake_ = false;
    body_->SetActive(false);
  }
}
```

As you can read from the table, the penguin is initially asleep and hence the is_awake_ flag is initialized to `false`. However, when the player touches the screen for the first time, this function is called with a value of `true` passed in. In that case, we activate the physics body and apply an impulse such that the penguin is pushed in the upright direction. Bodies that are not active have no physics processing; so the `ApplyImpulse` function would have been without effect if we had not activated the penguin's body.

Conversely, when `SetIsAwake` is called with the false argument, we merely deactivate the physics body. Let's now look at the `SetIsDiving` function of `Penguin.cpp`:

```
void Penguin::SetIsDiving(bool is_diving)
{
  if(is_diving_ == is_diving)
    return;

  is_diving_ = is_diving;

  // set sprite for the respective state
  if(is_diving_)
  {
    initWithFile("penguin_3.png");
  }
  else
  {
    initWithFile("penguin_2.png");
  }
}
```

This function just toggles the `is_diving_` flag and resets the sprite for the penguin. However, the real magic happens in the update loop, but more on that later. For now, we'll proceed to the `SetIsFlying` function of `Penguin.cpp`:

```
void Penguin::SetIsFlying(bool is_flying)
{
  if(is_flying_ == is_flying)
    return;

  is_flying_ = is_flying;

  // if penguin has taken off, check for a perfect slide
  if(is_flying_ && !is_leaping_)
  {
    // if take off velocity is above certain threshold,
      its a perfect slide
    if(body_->GetLinearVelocity().Length() >=
      PERFECT_TAKE_OFF_VELOCITY)
    {
      OnPerfectSlide();
    }
  }
}
```

This function is called every tick and the parameter passed in, and it informs us whether the penguin is currently on the ground or airborne based on whether or not a contact exists between the penguin and the terrain.

The sole purpose of this function is to determine whether the penguin has managed to pull off a perfect slide. To do that, we simply check what the magnitude of the velocity vector is when the penguin enters the flying stage, that is, when it has just taken off. If this value is greater than a predetermined threshold (`PERFECT_TAKE_OFF_VELOCITY`), we can safely say that the slide was carried out with perfection.

Let's now define the way in which we can reward the player for a perfect slide in the `OnPerfectSlide` function of `Penguin.cpp`:

```
void Penguin::OnPerfectSlide()
{
  // increment counters
  ++ num_perfect_slides_;
  ++ total_perfect_slides_;

  // 3 slides in a row activate fever mode
  if(num_perfect_slides_ == 3)
  {
    StartFever();
  }

  // a perfect slide deserves some extra time
  int time = 3 * (is_feverish_ ? 2 : 1);
  game_world_->AddTime(time);

  // inform player of the perfect slide
  char buf[16] = {0};
  sprintf(buf, "Perfect +%ds", time);
  game_world_->ShowMessage(buf);
}
```

At the start of the function, we increment the `num_perfect_slides_` and `total_perfect_slides_` counters that stand for the number of consecutive perfect slides and the total number of perfect slides respectively. The next `if` condition simply turns the fever mode on. The fever mode is visually represented by a trail of particles behind the penguin.

The code after that deals with adding time to the gameplay. Where did this concept of time-keeping come from? In this game, players have a limited amount of time (in seconds) to get the penguin as far as they can. The only way to increase this playing time is to perform perfect slides and to leap off from one hill to the next. On a perfect slide, players are rewarded 3 seconds and on leaping off from one hill to the next, players are rewarded 5 seconds. The best thing about fever mode is that the player is awarded with double time as long as the penguin is in fever mode.

The last bit of code calls the `ShowMessage` function from the `GameWorld` class that accepts a char array as input and displays the text within the char array with some gratuitous animations for entry and exit. We're almost done with the behavior of our little penguin, except for leaping, which we will define in the `StartLeap` and `FinishLeap` functions of `Penguin.cpp`:

```
void Penguin::StartLeap()
{
  if(is_leaping_)
    return;

  // successfully conquered a hill...reward player with extra time
  is_leaping_ = true;
  game_world_->AddTime(5 * (is_feverish_ ? 2 : 1));
  // no gravity so the penguin can be transported weightlessly to the
next hill
  body_->SetGravityScale(0.0f);
}

void Penguin::FinishLeap()
{
  if(!is_leaping_)
    return;

  is_leaping_ = false;
  // next hill has arrived, turn gravity back on
  body_->SetGravityScale(1.0f);
  is_diving_ = false;
}
```

In the StartLeap function, we simply tell GameWorld to award the player 5 seconds of time and to double that if the penguin is feverish. Along with that, we also set the gravity scale on the penguin's body to 0. If you remember from the previous chapter, this simply means that the said physics body will not be affected by gravity. The reason why we're doing this here is so that we can effortlessly lift the penguin high up so that the player is ready to take on the next hill. You will see that code in action when we define the updating functions of the Penguin class. Conversely, in the FinishLeap function, we finish a leap when the penguin is close enough to the next set of hills. Hence, we set the gravity scale to its default value.

Updating the penguin

Now that we've defined most of the penguin's behavior, it's time to tie it all together with the update logic. We will split the update logic into two main methods: UpdatePhysics and UpdateNode. Here is the code for the UpdatePhysics function of Penguin.cpp:

```
void Penguin::UpdatePhysics()
{
  if(is_diving_)
  {
    // if penguin is asleep, awaken him and cancel the dive
    if(!is_awake_)
    {
      SetIsAwake(true);
      is_diving_ = false;
    }
    // else apply a downward force provided penguin isn't leaping
    else if(!is_leaping_)
    {
      body_->ApplyForceToCenter(b2Vec2(0.5f, -2.0f));
    }
  }

  // restrict velocity between minimum & maximum
  b2Vec2 vel = body_->GetLinearVelocity();
  vel.x = vel.x < MIN_PENGUIN_VELOCITY_X ? MIN_PENGUIN_VELOCITY_X :
    (vel.x > MAX_PENGUIN_VELOCITY_X ? MAX_PENGUIN_VELOCITY_X : vel.x);
  vel.y = vel.y < MIN_PENGUIN_VELOCITY_Y ? MIN_PENGUIN_VELOCITY_Y :
    (vel.y > MAX_PENGUIN_VELOCITY_Y ? MAX_PENGUIN_VELOCITY_Y : vel.y);
  body_->SetLinearVelocity(vel);

  UpdateLeap();
}
```

This function begins by checking if the player wants the penguin to dive. Remember that this flag is set in the `SetIsDiving` function when the player taps the screen. Within this condition, we must first check if the penguin is awake or not. At the start of the game, the penguin is asleep, so we wake him up and reset the `is_diving_` flag. In the `else if` condition, we check if the penguin is not currently leaping. Then, we apply a downward force causing the penguin to lunge towards the hill.

Outside the conditional, we ensure that the velocity of the penguin stays within the limits defined by the four variables, that is, `MIN_PENGUIN_VELOCITY_X`, `MIN_PENGUIN_VELOCITY_Y`, `MAX_PENGUIN_VELOCITY_X`, and `MAX_PENGUIN_VELOCITY_Y`. You can find these variables defined in `GameGlobals.h`.

To finish off this function, we make a call to the `UpdateLeap` function of `Penguin.cpp`:

```
void Penguin::UpdateLeap()
{
  if(!is_leaping_)
    return;

  b2Vec2 vel = body_->GetLinearVelocity();
  b2Vec2 new_vel = vel;
  // increase the velocity
  new_vel.x += (MAX_PENGUIN_VELOCITY_X - new_vel.x) / 15.0f;
  new_vel.y += (MAX_PENGUIN_VELOCITY_Y - new_vel.y) / 15.0f;
  // ensure velocity doesn't exceed maximum
  new_vel.x = (new_vel.x > MAX_PENGUIN_VELOCITY_X
    ) ? MAX_PENGUIN_VELOCITY_X : new_vel.x;
  new_vel.y = (new_vel.y > MAX_PENGUIN_VELOCITY_Y
    ) ? MAX_PENGUIN_VELOCITY_Y : new_vel.y;
  body_->SetLinearVelocity(new_vel);
}
```

The `UpdateLeap` function must ensure that the penguin moves from one hill to the next. To do this, we increase the x and y components of the penguin's linear velocity every time this function is called. We also ensure that we stay within the velocity limits. This will simply cause the penguin to soar high above the hills, thereby ensuring it doesn't fall off the cliff and into the terrible abyss. Why don't you see what's below the hills?

We will now discuss the `UpdateNode` function of `Penguin.cpp`:

```
void Penguin::UpdateNode()
{
  // set node position based on body
  CCPoint previous_position = m_obPosition;
  setPositionX(WORLD_TO_SCREEN(body_->GetPosition().x));
  setPositionY(WORLD_TO_SCREEN(body_->GetPosition().y));

  // set rotation based on body
  float angle = CC_RADIANS_TO_DEGREES(-1 * ccpToAngle(
    ccpSub(m_obPosition, previous_position)));
  setRotation(angle);

  // fetch list of contacts
  b2Contact* contact = game_world_->GetWorld()->GetContactList();
  // if contact exists, penguin has landed
  if(contact)
  {
    SetIsFlying(false);
  }
  // else penguin is airborne
  else
  {
    SetIsFlying(true);
  }

  // update the trail if penguin is feverish
  if(is_feverish_)
  {
    trail_->setPosition(m_obPosition);
  }
}
```

You must recognize the first steps within the function where we simply set the position and rotation for the penguin's node according to its body. What follows next is another way to check for collisions, where we simply iterate over the list of the contacts that the Box2D world has recorded. Since we have just one dynamic body (the penguin) and one static body (the hill), it is safe for us to assume that the penguin has landed on the hill whenever we find a contact in the list.

Now, I'm sure you're wondering what's wrong with using contact listeners like we did in the previous chapter. The `BeginContact` and `EndContact` callbacks are called very frequently, owing to the curved shape of the surface of the hill. To see exactly what I mean, you should implement the `BeginContact` and `EndContact` functions in `GameWorld.cpp`. Put in a call to the `CCLOG` function in both the callbacks to see just how often they're fired.

Once we've detected a collision, we react to it by calling the `SetIsFlying` function. The last bit of code there is to reset the position of the trail so long as the penguin is feverish. At this point, we have defined the two major entities of the game: the `Terrain` class and the `Penguin` class.

On to the game world

We'll start by looking at the `CreateGame` function that is called from the `init` function when `GameWorld` is created:

```
void GameWorld::CreateGame()
{
  // player starts off with 30 seconds
  time_left_ = 30;

  // create & add the first set of hills at 0
  terrain_ = Terrain::create(world_, 0);
  addChild(terrain_, E_LAYER_FOREGROUND);

  // create & add the sky
  sky_ = Sky::create();
  addChild(sky_, E_LAYER_BACKGROUND);

  // create & add the penguin to the hills
  penguin_ = Penguin::create(this, "penguin_1.png");
  terrain_->addChild(penguin_, E_LAYER_FOREGROUND);

  CreateHUD();

  // enable touch and schedule two selectors; the seconds
    ticker and the update
  setTouchEnabled(true);
  schedule(schedule_selector(GameWorld::Tick), 1.0f);
  scheduleUpdate();
}
```

We begin this function by initializing a variable called `time_left_` to `30`. This means that the player starts off with 30 seconds to take the penguin as far as possible. We then create the hills, sky, and penguin. Notice how the penguin is added to `terrain_` instead of `this` (`GameWorld`). By doing this, we only need to move and scale the `terrain_` object to simulate the movement of a camera following the penguin as he glides across the hill. The rest is boilerplate code that you've seen before. Let's look at the `update` function from `GameWorld`:

```
void GameWorld::update(float dt)
{
  // update penguin physics
  penguin_->UpdatePhysics();

  // update the world
  // slow it down...otherwise the game is too fast to enjoy!
  world_->Step(dt * 0.5f, 8, 3);

  // update penguin node
  penguin_->UpdateNode();

  // update the hills and sky
  terrain_->Update(penguin_->getPosition());
  sky_->Update(penguin_->getPosition(), terrain_->GetOffsetX(),
    terrain_->getScale());

  // if penguin has gone beyond the second last key point,
    its time to take a leap
  if(penguin_->getPositionX() > terrain_->GetCliffKeyPoint().x &&
    !penguin_->GetIsLeaping())
  {
    penguin_->StartLeap();
  }
  // check if the penguin is leaping first
  if(penguin_->GetIsLeaping())
  {
    // if the next hill's foot is close enough, its time to stop
      leaping & time to start falling
    if(terrain_->GetFootKeyPoint().x > penguin_->getPositionX() &&
      terrain_->GetFootKeyPoint().x - penguin_->getPositionX() <=
      SCREEN_SIZE.width * 1.75f)
    {
      penguin_->FinishLeap();
    }
  }
```

```
    // update the distance counter & label
    int new_distance_travelled = penguin_->getPositionX();
    if(new_distance_travelled > distance_travelled_)
    {
      char buf[16] = {0};
      sprintf(buf, "%dm", (int)(new_distance_travelled / 2));
      distance_label_->setString(buf);
      distance_travelled_ = new_distance_travelled;
    }
  }
```

We start this function off by calling the `UpdatePhysics` function on the penguin. Then, we step into the Box2D world and call the penguin's `UpdateNode` function, followed by the `Update` functions of the `Terrain` and `Sky` classes respectively. Notice how we've halved the delta time there. This is to slow down the game as it is just too fast to play. Try it and see for yourself.

The next bit of code is important since it is here that we toggle the penguin's leaping state. First we check if the penguin has surpassed the terrain's cliff by calling the `GetCliffKeyPoint` function on `terrain_`. Then, we check whether the penguin isn't already leaping. As its name suggests, this function `GetCliffKeyPoint` returns to us the key point of the cliff, which is nothing but the second last key point in the array `hill_key_points_` from the `Terrain` class.

Now that the penguin is leaping, we monitor the time when the leaping should be stopped. To know when to stop leaping, we need to know the location of the next foothill. That is exactly what `GetFootKeyPoint` of `Terrain` returns to us. Thus, our `if` condition basically checks if there is the appropriate distance between the penguin and the next foothill before calling the `FinishLeap` function of `Penguin`. The last bit of code you see there is similar to what we saw in the previous chapter, and it is used to update the HUD to track the distance the penguin has travelled thus far.

We'll now take a look at the `PreSolve` function, which is one of the callbacks `b2ContactListener` provides to us. The `PreSolve` function is called for a given contact before that contact goes into Box2D's solver. Here is the `PreSolve` function from `GameWorld.cpp`:

```
void GameWorld::PreSolve(b2Contact* contact, const b2Manifold*
oldManifold)
{
  // get the world manifold for this contact
  b2WorldManifold world_manifold;
  contact->GetWorldManifold(&world_manifold);
  // get velocity of the penguin
```

```
  b2Vec2 velocity = penguin_->GetBody()->GetLinearVelocity();

  // get angles for the velocity & normal vectors
  float velocity_angle = atan2f(velocity.y, velocity.x);
  float normal_angle = atan2f(world_manifold.normal.y, world_manifold.
normal.x);

  // it is a bad landing if the difference in angles is above a
certain threshold
  if (normal_angle - velocity_angle > BAD_LANDING_ANGLE_DIFF)
  {
    penguin_->OnBadLanding();
  }
}
```

First, we get the `b2WorldManifold` object for the current contact. The `b2WorldManifold` structure provides a normal for the collision and an array containing the points where two fixtures have collided. Next, we record the linear velocity of the penguin's body. We then calculate two angles: the angle of the penguin's velocity vector and the angle of the contact's normal vector. Then, we specify that if the difference between these two angles is greater than a predetermined threshold (`BAD_LANDING_ANGLE_DIFF`), the player has made a bad landing. `BAD_LANDING_ANGLE_DIFF` holds a value in radians and can be found in `GameGlobals.h`.

We're almost done with the gameplay. While defining the `Penguin` class, there was some talk of time being added for a perfect slide and a leap and we also initialized the variable `time_left_` in the `CreateGame` function. It means that we must keep track of the time somewhere. This is done by the `Tick` function of `GameWorld.cpp`:

```
void GameWorld::Tick(float dt)
{
  // tick only after the game has started till before it ends
  if(!has_game_begun_ || has_game_ended_)
    return;

  // decrement the time counter
  -- time_left_;

  // update the label
  char buf[16] = {0};
  sprintf(buf, "%ds", time_left_);
  time_label_->setString(buf);

  // no more time...game over
```

```
    if(time_left_ <= 0)
    {
      GameOver();
    }

    // when there 5 seconds or less, start animating the label &
      playing a sound
    if(time_left_ <= 5)
    {
      if(time_label_->numberOfRunningActions() <= 0)
      {
        CCActionInterval* scale_up_down =
          CCSequence::createWithTwoActions(
          CCScaleTo::create(0.2f, 1.2f),
          CCScaleTo::create(0.2f, 1.0f));
        time_label_->runAction(CCRepeatForever::create(scale_up_down));

        CCActionInterval* shake =
          CCSequence::createWithTwoActions(
          CCRotateBy::create(0.05f, 20.0f),
          CCRotateBy::create(0.05f, -20.0f));
        time_label_->setRotation(-10.0f);
        time_label_->runAction(CCRepeatForever::create(shake));
      }
    }
  }
```

We want this function to be processed only after the game has begun and before it has ended; hence, the `if` condition. We then decrement the `time_left_` variable, which keeps track of the amount of time the player has remaining. Then, we update the HUD to reflect the time left and call `GameOver` when the player has run out of time. Also, to alert the user, we animate the time label when time left is 5 seconds or less.

This winds up the `Tick` function and also completes our sixth and most challenging game yet. I have skipped discussing some things, including the `Sky` class and touch handling. I know that by now, these things shouldn't cause you to scratch your head in confusion. So, go have some fun and revel in the satisfaction of what you've accomplished in this chapter!

Summary

With *Penguins Can Fly*, we implemented yet another Box2D game, but we took a big bite with this one. We started by using the `CCRenderTexture` class to generate the sprite that we would use to create our picturesque landscape and then spent a decent amount of time rendering the stripes, gradients, and highlights into the texture. We wrote a neat little algorithm to generate the smooth curve of the hill and bound a Box2D body to that curve. We also discussed collisions in Box2D.

You learned so much in this chapter and did so much hard work. Let's keep it going with the next chapter, where you will learn how to use a tile-based editor and create a simple tile-based platform game with a reusable tile-based collision detection algorithm.

7

Old is Gold!

In this chapter, we will be heading back in time to an era where games were made the hard way, where memory constraints compelled game developers to pick their brains in order to incorporate various features into games without compromising on performance. Among the many techniques used in the good old days, tile-based engines were the most common and efficient ways of developing games that needed to have large detailed levels. To this day, many games still use the same underlying tile-based architecture because old is gold!

In this chapter, you'll learn:

- How a tile-based game works
- How to create a tile-based level using the Tiled Map Editor
- How to implement tile-based collision detection

An introduction to Iceman

Our seventh game will be called *Iceman* and it revolves around an elderly ice-digger who has fallen into a frozen land beneath. All this iceman has is his old trustworthy shovel. He must hammer his way back up to the surface while tackling mighty walruses along the way. Oh yes, this elderly fellow has quite a bit of life left within him.

This is what we will achieve by the end of this chapter:

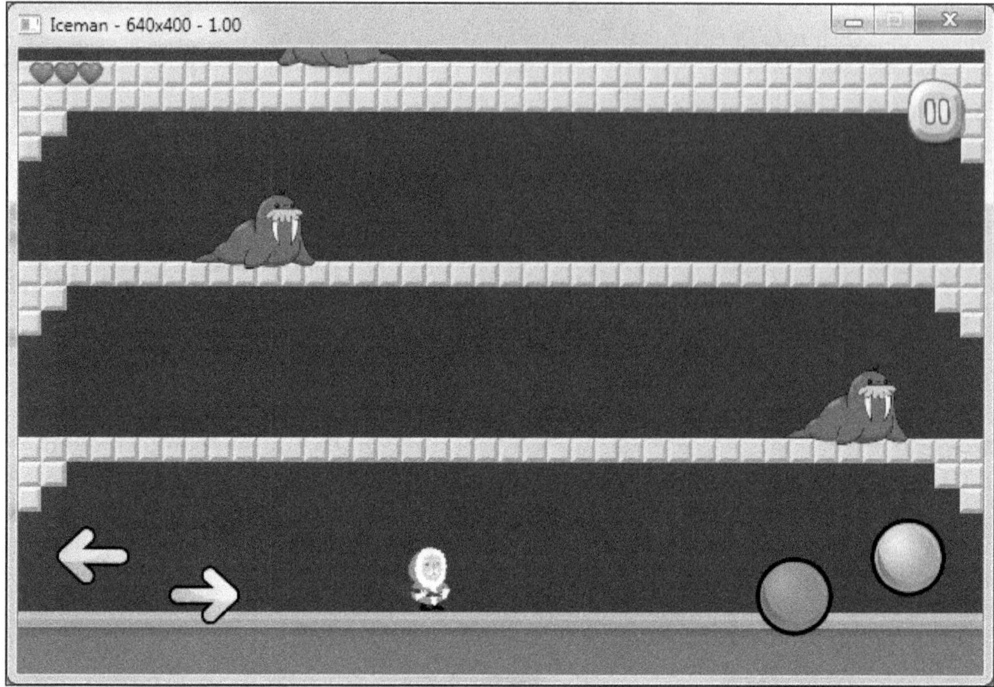

What is a tile-based game?

Let's answer this question by breaking it down to the bare minimum: the tile. A tile can be considered as a tiny piece of a big jigsaw puzzle. A tile is usually rectangular for orthogonal maps and diamond or hexagonal shaped for isometric maps. A tile contains graphical data and sometimes even level-specific data. A bunch of such tiles arranged together comprise a map. A map can be anything from a small section of a level or may be even an entire level itself, as we will see in this game. Thus, a tile-based game will use this logic of arranging tiles in various layouts to create a level.

One of the most obvious benefits of deciding to go with tile-based logic for a game is saving on images for the graphics of the levels. Since a level will contain multitudes of tiny tiles, all we will ever have to do is design a few tiles and reuse them throughout a given map or level. This has a huge performance gain, since these tiles can be batched together while rendering.

However, when you think of designing multiple levels for a game, you will need a capable editor—especially when a level can be limited only to the imagination of the level designer. Since tile-based games have been there for decades, there are many editors that will serve your purpose quite well. For this game, we will be using the Tiled Map Editor, as it is seamlessly integrated into Cocos2d-x.

What is the Tiled Map Editor?

The Tiled Map Editor (`http://www.mapeditor.org/`) is a free, flexible, general purpose tile map editor. This editor can be used to create levels for any kind of game—be it a full-scale RPG/RTS game, a Breakout clone, or a platformer (like in our case). At the time of writing this chapter, the latest version of Tiled is 0.10.2 and it is the Qt version of the same. You can choose to opt for the Java one and that works fine as well.

Creating a new tile map

Once you have visited the preceding link and downloaded the appropriate version for your development environment, start Tiled and you will see a window like this:

Looks pretty neat and simple, doesn't it? Tiled is extremely versatile and useful without being as intimidating as other editors. Well, what are you waiting for? Let's begin creating our first tile map. Select the **New** button from the toolbar or go to **File** | **New**. You will get a dialog box like this:

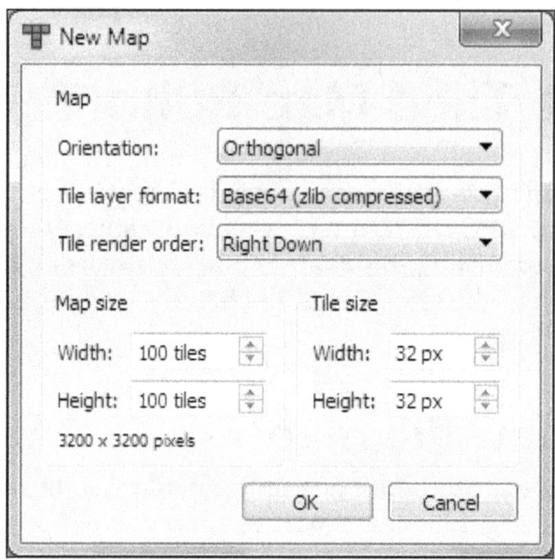

If you take a look at the different orientations supported, your options are: **Orthogonal**, **Isometric**, and **Isometric (staggered)**. If you're wondering what orthogonal maps will look like, *Mario* is an excellent example, and *SimCity* is an example of isometric maps. As you can judge from the screenshot of the game, *Iceman* will use orthogonal maps. So, you can leave the orientation as orthogonal.

The next options of significance are the **Map size** and **Tile size** options. The map size will describe the width and height of the map in terms of number of tiles horizontally and vertically respectively. The tile size will describe the width and height of a single tile in pixels. If you look at the screenshot of the preceding dialog box, the final size of the map in pixels is given as 3200 x 3200 pixels.

The tile size for Iceman will be set as 32 pixels. Now, the size of the tiles within a game has to be decided carefully at the start of development. This is something that you, as a developer, will have to discuss with your graphics designer, since it is the graphics designer who will create the tilesets for the game. For this game, we settled for a tile size of 32 pixels in width and height.

For Iceman, our hero will start at the bottom of the screen and jump his way up to the top. So, this is a vertically scrolling platformer. As such, we will adjust the width of the map so that it matches the width of our design resolution of 1280 pixels, that is, 40 tiles. Since each level might get larger and larger in terms of height, let's just start off with 75 tiles. This will give you a map of size 1280 x 2400 pixels. That's it, hit **OK** and you're ready to go.

Adding a tileset

You will see that an empty layer has already been created for you under the **Layers** view. You are free to have any number of layers within a given map. The important thing to remember is that a layer can have only one tileset. Now, what exactly is this tile set you wonder? This is what the tile set for Iceman looks like:

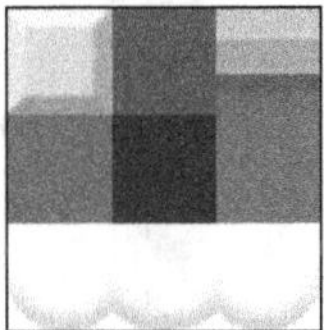

You're smart enough to realize that the preceding image describes the various tiles that comprise a level. An image tells Tiled about the different kinds of tiles we would like to use for a given layer.

So, let's add the preceding tile set to the layer. Click on the **New Tileset** button from the **Tilesets** view or go to **Map** | **New Tileset**. You will now see a dialog box that looks like this:

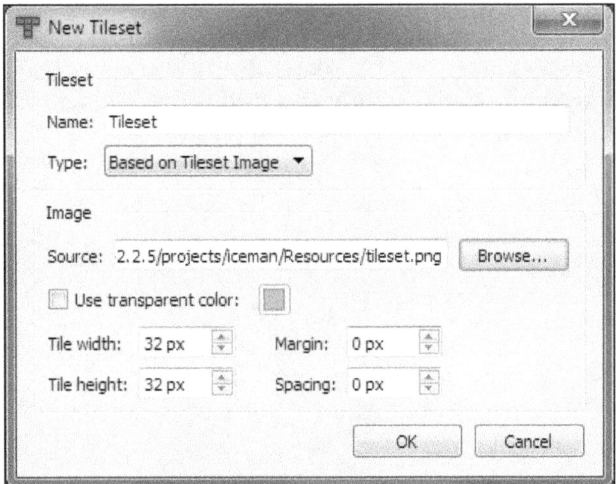

You can name this tileset whatever you like and select `tileset.png` as the image for this tileset from the `Resources` folder inside this chapter's source code bundle. You can leave the tile width and height as **32** pixels and hit the **OK** button. At this point, Tiled should look like this:

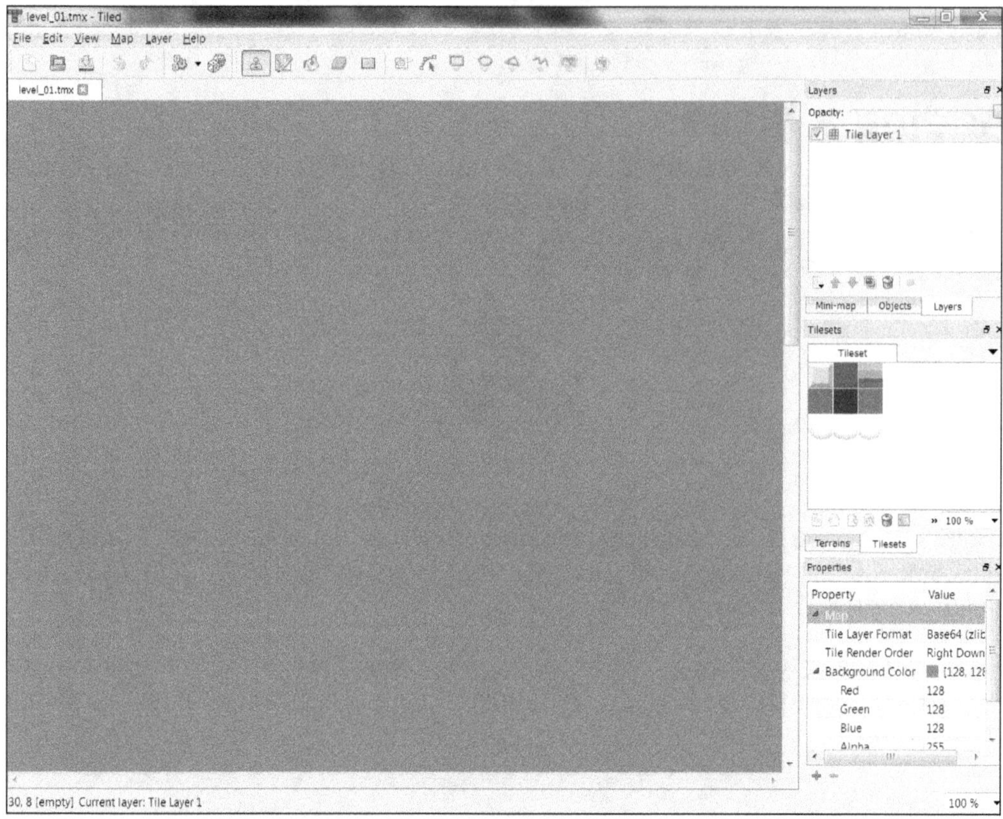

Notice how the image you selected shows up under the **Tilesets** view. We can now start adding some tiles to the layer.

Adding a tile layer

Before you add any tiles to the layer, rename the layer named `Tile Layer 1` as `Bricks`. When we write the code to create the tile map in our game world, we will fetch this layer by the name `Bricks`. Now, select the first tile in the tileset by clicking on it. As you move the cursor to the large vacant gray area, you can see the tile you just selected jumps around behind the cursor. It does so because it is actually snapping to the grid within the layer. At the bottom-left corner in the status bar, you will notice the details of the current column and row you are currently hovering over.

To place the tile, simply click anywhere on the grid. You can place multiple tiles at a time by clicking and dragging over an area, just like painting. If you glance at the toolbar, there are many tools using which you can fill single tiles, select a rectangular portion of the grid and bucket fill it with tiles, and even erase tiles. You can find a best practices guide complete with a handy set of keyboard shortcuts at `https://github.com/bjorn/tiled/wiki`.

This is what the first level looks like with all the tiles in place:

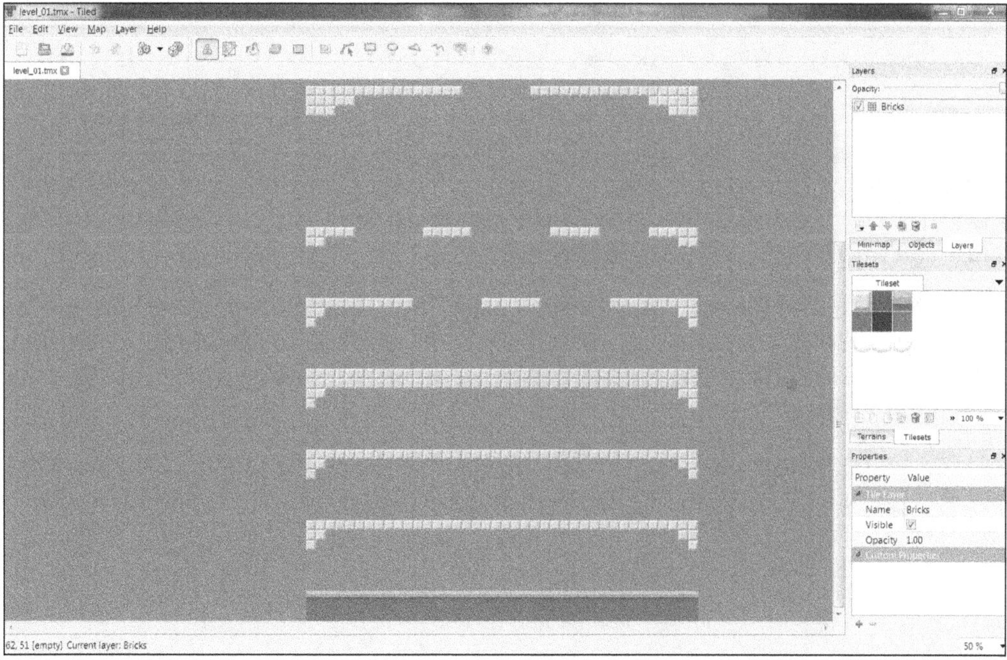

In this way, you can simply create a tile map and fill it with different tiles.
Do remember to keep saving though.

We shall now take a break from Tiled to see how we can create and add this layer in Cocos2d-x. Take a look at the following code snippet:

```
CCTMXTiledMap* tiled_map = CCTMXTiledMap::create(
  "level_01.tmx");
addChild(tiled_map);
```

This is all the code you need to write to have your tile map and all of its tiles appear on screen. The classes at `"cocos2d-x-2.2.5\cocos2dx\tilemap_parallax_nodes"` take care of parsing the TMX file and getting everything in place.

We can fetch our `Bricks` tile layer with the following code, which returns a pointer to a `CCTMXLayer` object:

```
CCTMXLayer* bricks_layer_ = tiled_map_->layerNamed("Bricks");
```

We can then fetch the value of any tile within the layer with the following command, which returns an integer value that describes the GID at a particular tile:

```
bricks_layer_->tileGIDAt(ccp(column, row));
```

The GID is an efficient way to decide what type of tile exists at a particular position or whether it is empty. To know what a particular tile's GID will be, click on any one of the tiles in the **Tilesets** view. Now, glance at the **ID** parameter in the **Properties** view below the **Tilesets** view. This ID is incremented by 1 and returned as the GID when you query the `tileGIDAt` function.

Tiles within a tileset are given IDs incrementally. If you click the tile at the bottom-right corner of the tileset, you will notice that it has an ID of 8. For an empty tile, `tileGIDAt` will return 0. We will use this function when we write the collision detection algorithm later in the chapter.

Of course, filling tiles into the tile layer is just the beginning; we still need to figure out a way to position the iceman, the enemies, and the platforms. We will do this in our next section.

Adding an objects layer

Along with adding tiles, providing IDs to individual tiles and providing an API to access the GID of any tile in the grid, Tiled also provides another type of layer called the objects layer. An objects layer lets you draw portions of the map and identify them as areas of significance. These portions or objects can be used to mark areas on the map where characters can spawn, where collectibles and power-ups can appear, or where hidden portals may lie.

For Iceman, we will use the objects layer to hold the following information:

- The hero's spawn point (`HeroSpawnPoint`)
- The enemies' spawn points (`EnemySpawnPoint`)
- The platforms' spawn points (`PlatformSpawnPoint`)
- The level completion point (`LevelCompletePoint`)

Click on the **New Layer** button and select **Add Object Layer** or go to **Layer** | **Add Object Layer**. A new layer with a different icon will show up in the **Layers** view; name this layer `Objects`. Notice how the toolbar buttons change when you select the objects layer. We can now start adding the various points of significance that we had discussed previously.

We will only use simple rectangular areas to indicate the various points that we need so select the **Insert Rectangle** button from the toolbar and click anywhere on the map. Notice how a small square appears on the area you clicked. To reposition or resize this object, select the **Select Objects** button from the toolbar. You can also insert objects of other shapes and sizes by using the respective tools.

Now, select the rectangular object you just added and shift your attention to the **Properties** view at the bottom-right corner of Tiled to observe the various parameters for each object. We shall start by giving this object its name, that is, `HeroSpawnPoint`. We don't need anything else from this object other than its position, so we can move on to adding an object for an enemy spawning point.

Add an object at any location of your choice on the map and name the object `EnemySpawnPoint`. Along with providing so many options, Tiled also gives us the luxury of adding arbitrary properties to each object—be it Tile layers, object layers, tilesets, or objects. We can define custom properties for any of the preceding objects and access them through code.

Why is it so awesome to be able to add custom properties to everything? Imagine designing multiple levels where each level must be finished within a specific time limit. Simply add a custom property to the tile layer named `TimeLimit` and assign different values for different levels. Another scenario would be defining unique parameters for different objects. Like in our case, we want to be able to define a different speed for each enemy and moving platform to ensure our levels get progressively more difficult.

So, go ahead and add your first custom property to the `EnemySpawnPoint` object that you just created. To do so, click on the dark blue **+** sign below the **Properties** view. This will bring up a tiny box where you need to input the name of this custom property. Let's call it `speed_x`. Obviously, this will stand for the horizontal speed at which an enemy will move in the game. So, add another property `speed_y` to this object to represent the vertical speed.

After adding all the objects, this is what the tile map will look like:

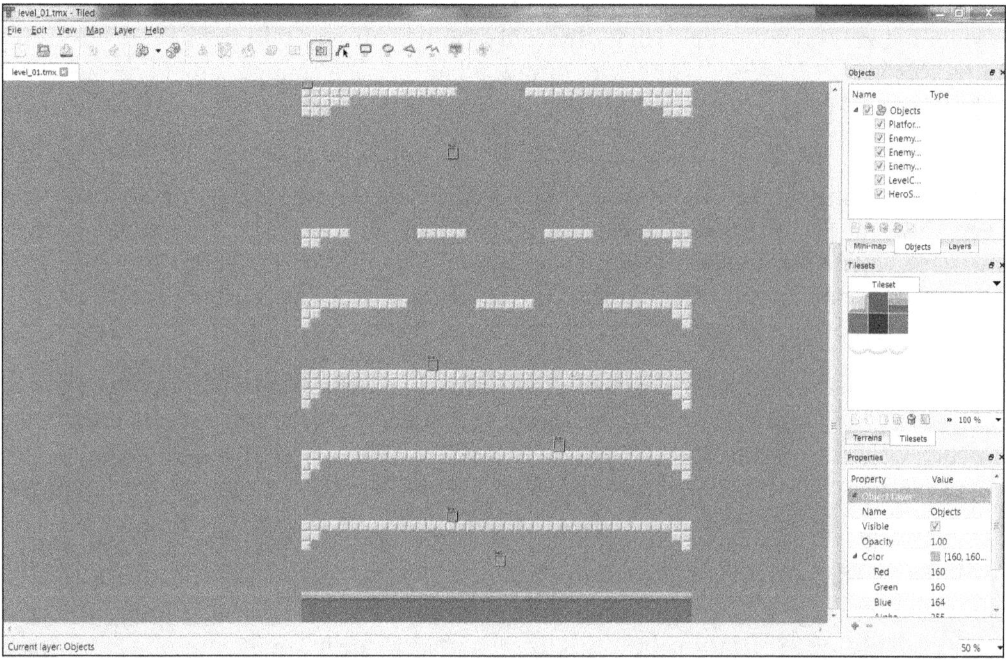

Take a look at the list of objects in the view on the top-right of Tiled and you'll see the various objects added. Open up any of the TMX files for the levels from the `Resources` folder and check them out. For now, you need to learn how to access these objects and their custom properties in code. So, let's take a look at the `CreateTiledMap` function from the `GameWorld.cpp` file:

```
void GameWorld::CreateTiledMap()
{
  // generate level filename
  char buf[128] = {0};
  sprintf(buf, "level_%02d.tmx", GameGlobals::level_number_);
  // create & add the tiled map
  tiled_map_ = CCTMXTiledMap::create(buf);
  addChild(tiled_map_);

  // get the size of the tiled map
  columns_ = (int)tiled_map_->getMapSize().width;
  rows_ = (int)tiled_map_->getMapSize().height;

  // save a reference to the layer containing all the bricks
  bricks_layer_ = tiled_map_->layerNamed("Bricks");

  // parse the list of objects
  CCTMXObjectGroup* object_group =
    tiled_map_->objectGroupNamed("Objects");
  CCArray* objects = object_group->getObjects();
  int num_objects = objects->count();

  for(int i = 0; i < num_objects; ++i)
  {
    CCDictionary* object = (CCDictionary*)(
      objects->objectAtIndex(i));

    // create the Hero at this spawning point
    if(strcmp(object->valueForKey("name")->getCString(),
      "HeroSpawnPoint") == 0)
    {
      CreateHero(ccp(object->valueForKey("x")->floatValue(),
        object->valueForKey("y")->floatValue()));
    }
    // create an Enemy at this spawning point
    else if(strcmp(object->valueForKey("name")->getCString(),
      "EnemySpawnPoint") == 0)
    {
```

```
            CCPoint position = ccp(object->valueForKey("x")->floatValue(),
              object->valueForKey("y")->floatValue());
            CCPoint speed = ccp(object->valueForKey(
              "speed_x")->floatValue(), object->valueForKey(
              "speed_y")->floatValue());
            CreateEnemy(position, speed);
          }
          // create a Platform at this spawning point
          else if(strcmp(object->valueForKey("name")->getCString(),
            "PlatformSpawnPoint") == 0)
          {
            CCPoint position = ccp(object->valueForKey("x")->
              floatValue(), object->valueForKey("y")->floatValue());
            CCPoint speed = ccp(object->valueForKey(
              "speed_x")->floatValue(), object->valueForKey(
              "speed_y")->floatValue());
            CreatePlatform(position, speed);
          }
          // save the point where the level should complete
          else if(strcmp(object->valueForKey("name")->getCString(),
            "LevelCompletePoint") == 0)
          {
            level_complete_height_ = object->valueForKey(
              "y")->floatValue();
          }
        }
    }
```

We start off by generating the path for the level, creating a new `CCTMXTiledMap` object with the given file as input, and adding it to the game world. We also store the size of the map and maintain a reference to the `Bricks` layer. Next, we call the `objectGroupNamed` function of the `CCTMXTiledMap` class that will return a pointer to an object of the `CCTMXObjectGroup` class. `CCTMXObjectGroup` will contain all the objects within a given objects layer. We can get these objects by calling the `getObjects` function, which will return a `CCArray` class containing the objects. The function then loops through each of the objects and accesses each of them. An object from the objects layer is represented as a `CCDictionary` object. I encourage you to print out all the keys for this dictionary and see for yourself how many properties of the object we can access.

For Iceman, we will only extract the information that we require, as you can see for yourself. The moment we find an object named `HeroSpawnPoint`, we create a hero and subsequently the enemies and platforms as well. We also save the *y* component of the `LevelCompletePoint` object into the `level_complete_height_` variable. So, remember not to add two `HeroSpawnPoint` to your tile maps. That would have two icemen in the game world and one would simply stare back at you throughout the game (dangling pointers to elderly icemen are the worst!).

Just like that, we are all set to begin coding the gameplay. Tiled being so easy to use, anyone with zero programming knowledge can create a multitude of levels in no time and you can access it in code rather effortlessly, like we've seen in the past two sections. Next up, we'll write a collision detection algorithm that works well with our tiles.

Tile-based collision detection

Tile-based games having been there for so long, there are a whole bunch of different techniques developers have used to implement collision detection in their games. While learning the subject myself, I came across this brilliant article written by a programmer named Rodrigo Monteiro (`http://higherorderfun.com/blog/`). He has described a few of the techniques used for tile-based collision detection and cataloged a lot of information on them in the article, which you can find here: `http://higherorderfun.com/blog/2012/05/20/the-guide-to-implementing-2d-platformers/`.

The algorithm we will be using is based on the pseudo code that Rodrigo describes in the article. The reason we are discussing collision detection before any of the other gameplay is because this algorithm is flexible in nature and can be plugged in to any other tile-based game with little or no modifications necessary. It can be used even in games that are not made with Tiled. I can vouch for this, having used this very algorithm in three of my own games.

The algorithm is divided into two parts: vertical and horizontal collision detection. This has been done so that you can understand it easily, and I strongly advise you to combine both the vertical and horizontal algorithms into one as they are quite similar. For the purpose of collision detection, each character will be represented by an axis aligned bounding box (AABB). AABBs are nothing but rectangles that do not rotate.

The algorithm will check for conditions of intersection between such AABBs and tiles that qualify for collisions. Before we dive into the code, let's take a look at the process for vertical collision detection:

1. Find the row that the forward facing edge of the AABB occupies. In case of upward movement, the forward-facing edge would be the top edge, and it would be the bottom edge of the AABB for downward movement. The following screenshot should help to visualize what happens in this step:

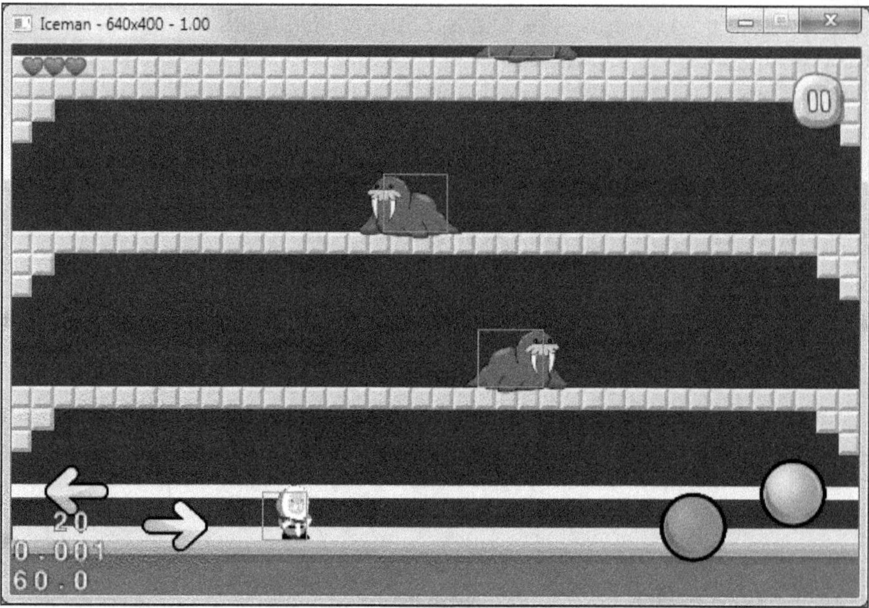

2. For upward movement, the row in question will be the one colored yellow, and for downward movement, the green one.

3. Find the columns that are occupied by the left and right edge of the AABB, which in this case are the green and yellow columns respectively, in the following screenshot:

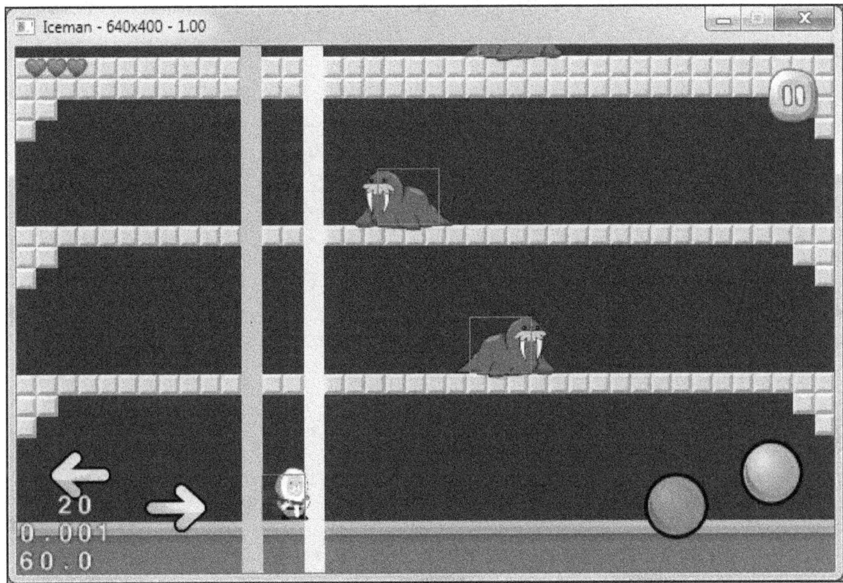

4. For each column from left to right, check each tile of each row in the direction of movement until a collision is found.

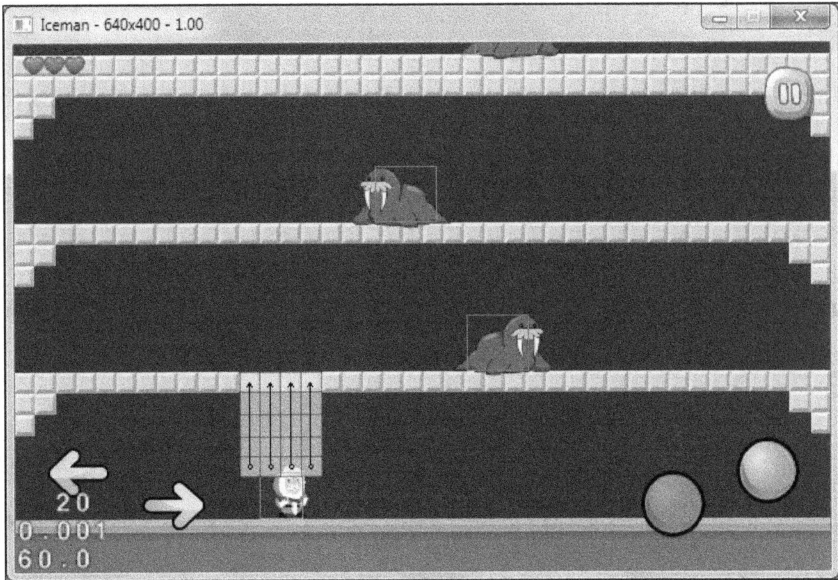

5. In the figure, the yellow tiles are the ones that are scanned for upward movement, as indicated by the arrows.
6. If a collision tile has been found in the preceding step, check to see whether the AABB intersects with that particular tile. If an intersection exists, it is a collision.

This pseudo code is given full form in the `CheckVerticalCollisions` function of `GameWorld.cpp`. We will discuss the implementation in steps like the preceding pseudo code:

```
bool GameWorld::CheckVerticalCollisions(GameObject* game_object)
{
  int visible_rows = (int)tiled_map_->getMapSize().height;
  int visible_cols = (int)tiled_map_->getMapSize().width;

  CCRect aabb = game_object->GetAABB();
  CCPoint speed = game_object->GetSpeed();

  // since we're checking vertically, save the row occupied by the
aabb
  int aabb_row = GET_ROW_FOR_Y(aabb.origin.y, visible_rows);
  if(speed.y > 0)
  {
    // if we're going up, save the row occupied by the top edge of the
aabb
    aabb_row = GET_ROW_FOR_Y(aabb.origin.y +
      aabb.size.height, visible_rows);
  }
```

We begin the function by storing the size of the map and also the AABB for the `GameObject` class passed in as parameter. This algorithm simply needs an AABB. However, we have passed it a reference to the `GameObject` class so it can call the collision response function. In the first step, we check the `speed_` variable to determine whether we are moving upwards or downwards and calculate the row occupied by the forward edge of the AABB, storing it into variable `aabb_row`.

The `GET_ROW_FOR_Y` function is a helper macro that returns the row at a given point. You can find this macro and a few more in `GameGlobals.h`.

Let's take a look at the following code:

```
  // also save the columns occupied by the left & right edges of the
aabb
  int aabb_start_col = GET_COL_FOR_X(aabb.origin.x);
```

```
    int aabb_end_col = GET_COL_FOR_X(aabb.origin.x + aabb.size.width);

    // bounds checking
    if(aabb_row < 0 || aabb_row >= visible_rows ||
        aabb_start_col < 0 || aabb_start_col >= visible_cols ||
        aabb_end_col < 0 || aabb_end_col >= visible_cols)
      return false;

    // initialise flags & counters
    bool found_collidable = false;
    int current_col = aabb_start_col;
    int current_row = aabb_row;
```

In the second step, we call another macro by the name `GET_COL_FOR_X` and pass in the left and right end points of the AABB to get the left and right columns. These are stored into the variables `aabb_start_col` and `aabb_end_col` respectively.

We then ensure that we're not checking outside the tile map, because querying the tile map for tiles that are beyond its bounds will result in an assert. We also initialize a few flags and counters.

Let's take a look at the following code:

```
  while(current_row >= 0 && current_row < visible_rows)
  {
    // check for every column that the aabb occupies
    for(current_col = aabb_start_col; current_col <= aabb_end_col;
  ++current_col)
    {
      // check if a brick exists at the given row & column
      if(bricks_layer_->tileGIDAt(ccp(current_col, current_row)))
      {
        found_collidable = true;
        break;
      }
    }

    // from current tile, keep moving in same direction till a brick is
  found
    if(found_collidable == false)
    {
      current_row = (speed.y < 0) ? (current_row + 1):(current_row - 1);
    }
```

As you read in the pseudo code, we must scan from the left column to the right column for each row in the direction of movement. Thus, we start a `while` loop that will iterate through each row within the bounds of the map, starting from `current_row`. Inside this loop, we add a `for` loop that checks from each tile from the left column to the right column for this particular row. We can now use the values contained within `current_col` and `current_row` to check if a brick exists at that particular tile by calling the `tileGIDAt` function on the `bricks_layer_` object. If a tile has been found, then we break out of this `for` loop.

Outside the `for` loop, the variable `found_collidable` is checked to determine whether we need to keep scanning for collision tiles or should we move ahead to the collision response. Thus, if `found_collidable` is `false`, we decrement or increment `current_row`, depending on whether this particular `GameObject` class wants to move up or down respectively. Read that again! We decrement the row if we want to move up and increment to move down. That is because Tiled treats the top-left corner as the origin while placing its tiles.

That winds up the third step, and at this point, the `found_collidable` variable tells us whether a collision tile has been found. If a collision tile has indeed been found, then the variables `current_col` and `current_row` can be used to identify it. Let's now move to the next step, which will wrap up the vertical collision checking function:

```
if(found_collidable)
{
  // going down
  if(speed.y < 0)
  {
    // if the bottom edge of aabb is lower than the top edge of
     the collidable row
    if(aabb.origin.y <= GET_Y_FOR_ROW(current_row, visible_rows))
    {
      // its a collision, do something
      game_object->CollisionResponse(current_col, current_row,
        E_COLLISION_BOTTOM);
    }
    else
    {
      // not a collision
      found_collidable = false;
    }
```

```
      }
      // going up
      else
      {
        // if the top edge of aabb is higher than the bottom edge of
         the collidable row
        if((aabb.origin.y + aabb.size.height) >= GET_Y_FOR_ROW(
          current_row + 1, visible_rows))
        {
          // its a collision, do something
          game_object->CollisionResponse(current_col, current_row,
            E_COLLISION_TOP);
        }
        else
        {
          // not a collision
          found_collidable = false;
        }
      }
    }

    return found_collidable;
```

This block of code executes only if a collision tile has been found. In that case, based on whether we're going up or down, the *y* component of the respective AABB edge is compared with the *y* component of the respective upper or lower row. If the values indicate an overlap or intersection, we have found a collision and we call the respective collision response function, passing in the column and row of the collision tile while also specifying whether the collision occurred above or below AABB.

Inside `GameWorld.cpp`, you will find a similar function by the name `CheckHorizontalCollisions`. Just like its name, even the definition of this function is similar to the `CheckVerticalCollisions` function. As such, I will only highlight the differences in the next paragraph. So make sure you read through the function from the source bundle for this chapter before moving ahead.

Since we're checking horizontally instead of vertically, we find the column instead of the row occupied by the forward-facing edge of AABB. Similarly, we find the start and end rows indicated by the top and bottom edges of AABB, respectively.

Throughout the function, we simply swap the rows with columns and it performs horizontal collision detection. The final difference between vertical and horizontal collision detection functions is the type of collision that we pass into the `CollisionResponse` function.

With these two functions, we have written a simple and reusable tile-based collision detection algorithm. If you want to see the algorithm in action, you should run the game in debug mode. You can do that by uncommenting the following line in `GameGlobals.h`:

```
#define ICEMAN_DEBUG_MODE
```

A few important lines of code elude us for the moment, that is, the collision response logic that we will get to when we define the hero's class, which we are just about to. But before that, we need to define a base class for the hero, enemy, and platform to inherit from.

The GameObject class

All the gameplay entities in this game share a few things in common. They all need an axis aligned bounding box for collision detection, they all also possess some speed, and they also possess a type attribute. Thus, their parent class `GameObject` is defined as follows in `GameObject.h`:

```
class GameObject : public CCSprite
{
public:
  GameObject() : game_world_(NULL),
    type_(E_GAME_OBJECT_NONE),
    aabb_(CCRectZero),

#ifdef ICEMAN_DEBUG_MODE
    aabb_node_(NULL),
#endif

    speed_(CCPointZero) {}

  virtual ~GameObject()
  {}

  virtual void SetAABB(CCRect aabb)
```

```
  {
    aabb_ = aabb;

#ifdef ICEMAN_DEBUG_MODE
    // draw the AABB in debug mode only
    CCPoint vertices[4];
    vertices[0] = CCPointZero;
    vertices[1] = ccp(0, aabb_.size.height);
    vertices[2] = ccp(aabb_.size.width, aabb_.size.height);
    vertices[3] = ccp(aabb_.size.width, 0);

    aabb_node_ = CCDrawNode::create();
    aabb_node_->drawPolygon(vertices, 4, ccc4f(0, 0, 0, 0), 1,
      ccc4f(1, 0, 0, 1));
    aabb_node_->setPosition(aabb_.origin);
    game_world_->addChild(aabb_node_);
#endif
  }

  inline CCRect GetAABB() { return aabb_; }
  virtual void SetSpeed(CCPoint speed) { speed_ = speed; }
  inline CCPoint GetSpeed() { return speed_; }

  virtual void Update()
  {
    aabb_.origin.x += speed_.x;
    aabb_.origin.y += speed_.y;

#ifdef ICEMAN_DEBUG_MODE
    aabb_node_->setPosition(getParent()->convertToWorldSpace(aabb_.
origin));
#endif
  }
  virtual void CollisionResponse(int tile_col, int tile_row,
    ECollisionType collision_type) {}

protected:
  GameWorld* game_world_;
  EGameObjectType type_;
  CCRect aabb_;
```

```
  CCPoint speed_;

#ifdef ICEMAN_DEBUG_MODE
public:
  CCDrawNode* aabb_node_;
#endif
};
```

The `GameObject` class inherits from `CCSprite`. It possesses a `CCRect` object to represent the AABB, a `CCPoint` object to represent the speed, and an attribute of the type `EGameObjectType`, which is defined in `GameGlobals.h`.

The `GameObject` class also contains a `virtual Update` function that merely adds `speed_` to `aabb_`. This function will be called from the respective child classes right before the collision checking functions are called. Aside from these member variables and functions, the `GameObject` class also possesses a `CCDrawNode` to visually represent and update the AABB while in debug mode. Now that we have this base class defined, let's begin coding in the individual entities of the game starting with the lead character: the hero.

The Hero class

The `Hero` class will inherit from `GameObject` and will be responsible for handling the state machine of the hero and collision response, among a few other things. The constructor for the `Hero` class looks something like this:

```
Hero::Hero()
{
  type_ = E_GAME_OBJECT_HERO;
  state_ = E_HERO_STATE_NONE;
  is_on_ground_ = false;
  current_ground_height_ = 0.0f;
  platform_below_ = NULL;
}
```

We start off by setting the `type_` of this object to `E_GAME_OBJECT_HERO`. We then initialize the member variables. The `state_` variable (like you saw in *Chapter 5, Let's Get Physical!*) is the key to maintaining the state machine for the hero's behavior. We also have an `is_on_ground_` flag that indicates when the hero is standing on a surface, which could be either a brick or a moving platform. So, we can set the appropriate state accordingly. We also have a `current_ground_height_` variable that measures the height the hero has managed to reach and is at currently. This increases as the hero moves higher from one platform to another and reduces when he falls down. Lastly, we maintain a reference to a `Platform` object.

The various states that the player can have are enumerated by enum `EHeroState` in `GameGlobals.h` as follows:

```
enum EHeroState
{
 E_HERO_STATE_NONE = 0,
 E_HERO_STATE_IDLE,
 E_HERO_STATE_WALKING,
 E_HERO_STATE_JUMPING,
 E_HERO_STATE_SWINGING,
 E_HERO_STATE_DYING,
 E_HERO_STATE_WINNING,
};
```

The state machine in this class is identical to the `Clown` class you saw in *Chapter 5, Let's Get Physical!*. So, I will skip going over the details of the `SetState` function and each subsequent state function. We saw how the collision detection works in the previous sections and left the collision response for later. Now, it is time to define how the hero will respond to collisions. So, let's define the `CollisionResponse` function in `Hero.cpp`:

```
void Hero::CollisionResponse(int tile_col, int tile_row,
  ECollisionType collision_type)
{
 switch(collision_type)
 {
 case E_COLLISION_TOP:
  // stop moving
  speed_.y = 0;
  // collision occured above AABB...reposition the AABB
    one pixel below the collided tile
  aabb_.origin.y = GET_Y_FOR_ROW(tile_row + 1,
    game_world_->GetRows()) - aabb_.size.height - 1;
  // tell the game world to remove this brick
  game_world_->RemoveBrick(tile_col, tile_row);
  break;
 case E_COLLISION_BOTTOM:
  // stop moving
  speed_.y = 0;
  // collision occured below AABB...reposition the
    AABB one pixel above the collided tile
  aabb_.origin.y = GET_Y_FOR_ROW(
    tile_row, game_world_->GetRows()) + 1;
  // hero has landed on a brick
  SetIsOnGround(true);
```

```
      break;
    case E_COLLISION_LEFT:
      // stop moving
      speed_.x = 0;
      // collision occured to the left AABB...reposition
        the AABB one pixel after the collided tile
      aabb_.origin.x = GET_X_FOR_COL(tile_col + 1) + 1;
      break;
    case E_COLLISION_RIGHT:
      // stop moving
      speed_.x = 0;
      // collision occured to the right AABB...reposition
        the AABB one pixel before the collided tile
      aabb_.origin.x = GET_X_FOR_COL(tile_col) -
        aabb_.size.width - 1;
      break;
    }
  }
```

As you read earlier, the collision detection passes in the column and row of the collision tile, and also the type of collision that was detected. Based on this collision type, we have a little switch case that quite simply handles each type of collision separately. This comes in handy when you'd want to have different animations for when your character hits his head against the ceiling (`E_COLLISION_TOP`) and when it hits the chest against the wall (`E_COLLISION_RIGHT`).

For each type of collision, the first thing to do is to prevent the hero from continuing in the same state of motion, and that is why we set the speed in the respective direction to `0`. We then proceed to correct the position of the AABB so that it is just one pixel away from the collision tile. This is done irrespective of the type of collision, because we would never want the hero to overlap any of the bricks.

An interesting thing is done for collisions that occur above the hero. We tell `GameWorld` to remove the brick at the given column and row. For collisions below the player, we call the `SetIsOnGround` function with `true` as the parameter.

The hero in Iceman seems like an elderly chap, but don't be fooled because he still has a lot of speed. Let's see how he works so energetically in the `UpdateSpeed` function of `Hero.cpp`:

```
void Hero::UpdateSpeed(bool must_go_left,
  bool must_go_right, bool must_jump)
{
  // add gravity & clamp vertical velocity
  speed_.y += GRAVITY;
```

```
speed_.y = (speed_.y < MAX_VELOCITY_Y) ?
  MAX_VELOCITY_Y : speed_.y;

// is the hero above a platform
if(platform_below_)
{
 // stop falling due to gravity
 speed_.y = 0;
 // move the hero along with the platform he's standing on
 aabb_.origin.x += platform_below_->GetSpeed().x;
 aabb_.origin.y = platform_below_->GetAABB().getMaxY();
}

// set speed accordingly if the hero must jump
if(must_jump && is_on_ground_)
{
 speed_.y = TILE_SIZE * 0.75f;
}

// increase/decrease the horizontal speed based on the
  button pressed
if(must_go_left)
{
 speed_.x -= HERO_MOVEMENT_FORCE;
 speed_.x = (speed_.x < -MAX_VELOCITY_X) ?
   -MAX_VELOCITY_X : speed_.x;
 setFlipX(true);
}
if(must_go_right)
{
 speed_.x += HERO_MOVEMENT_FORCE;
 speed_.x = (speed_.x > MAX_VELOCITY_X) ?
   MAX_VELOCITY_X : speed_.x;
 setFlipX(false);
}

// gradually come to a halt if no button is pressed
if(!must_go_left && !must_go_right)
{
 speed_.x -= speed_.x / 5;
}

// change from idle to walking & vice versa based on
  horizontal velocity
```

```
    if(fabs(speed_.x) > 0.5f)
    {
      SetState(E_HERO_STATE_WALKING);
    }
    else if(state_ == E_HERO_STATE_WALKING)
    {
      SetState(E_HERO_STATE_IDLE);
    }
  }
```

This function is called from the `Update` function of the same class and is passed the flags that indicate whether the player has pressed the left, right, or jump buttons on the screen. We begin this function by first adding the force of gravity to the *y* component of `speed_` and clamp it to a maximum value.

Before we react to the user input flags, we must first check to see whether the hero is standing above a platform. If he is, then most certainly he shouldn't be falling. Also, he should now move with the platform beneath him so we add the platform's horizontal speed to `aabb_`. We also set the *y* component of the `aabb_` to be right above the platform.

With that out of the way, we can react to the respective user input flags. If jump is pressed, we simply add a predefined value to the *y* component of `speed_`, which will send the hero shooting upwards. Similarly, if the left or right buttons are pressed, we subtract or add a predefined force to the *x* component of `speed_`. Finally, we flip the hero so that he is facing the same direction as he is moving towards.

We also have a condition when the player releases the buttons. The hero must now come to a stop and that is exactly what the next condition does. Notice how the *x* component is gradually reduced; this is to avoid the hero coming to a sudden halt. The last condition checks the *x* component of `speed_` to set the appropriate walking or idle state.

Let's now focus our attention on the `Update` function of the `Hero.cpp` file:

```
void Hero::Update(bool must_go_left, bool must_go_right,
  bool must_jump, bool must_swing)
{
  // let the hero die in peace
  if(state_ == E_HERO_STATE_DYING)
    return;

  // update speed based on user input
```

```
UpdateSpeed(must_go_left, must_go_right, must_jump);

// this enables the hero to leave from the left edge and
  reappear from the right edge
if(aabb_.origin.x < TILE_SIZE)
{
 aabb_.origin.x = SCREEN_SIZE.width -
   TILE_SIZE - aabb_.size.width;
}
if(aabb_.origin.x + aabb_.size.width >
  SCREEN_SIZE.width - TILE_SIZE)
{
 aabb_.origin.x = TILE_SIZE;
}

// update the AABB
GameObject::Update();
// check for collisions
game_world_->CheckCollisions(this);
game_world_->CheckHeroEnemyCollisions();
game_world_->CheckHeroPlatformCollisions();

setPosition(ccp(aabb_.origin.x + aabb_.size.width * 0.5f,
  aabb_.origin.y + m_obContentSize.height * 0.5f));

// check if the hero should swing
if(must_swing)
{
 SetState(E_HERO_STATE_SWINGING);
}
else if(state_ == E_HERO_STATE_SWINGING)
{
 SetState(E_HERO_STATE_IDLE);
}

// check if the hero could be falling
if(fabs(speed_.y) > 0.1f)
{
 SetIsOnGround(false);
}
}
```

The hero's `Update` function is called from the main `Update` loop of `GameWorld` and is passed four flags that basically indicate which onscreen buttons the player has currently pressed. We begin this function by checking whether the hero is in the dying state and quietly return from there if this condition is met. We then call the `UpdateSpeed` function, followed by a conditional that ensures the hero reappears at one end of the screen on exiting from the other end.

We now call the `Update` function of `GameObject`, which simply updates the `aabb_` with the `speed_`. With this updated `aabb_`, we now call the `CheckCollisions` function from `GameWorld`, which internally calls the `CheckVerticalCollisions` and `CheckHorizontalCollisions` functions that you saw earlier. In addition to this, we also ask `GameWorld` to check for collisions with the hero and the enemies and the platforms.

Once the collision detection and response has completed, we set the corrected position of the hero. Now, if the user has pressed the swing button, we set the appropriate swinging state. Finally, we check to see if the vertical speed is greater than a minimum value. This indicates that the player is airborne so we call the `SetIsOnGround` function, passing in `false` as the parameter.

Now that we have the collision response and the `Update` functions out of the way, all we have left is the `SetIsOnGround` function and we're done coding our zesty old chap.

Let's look at the following code:

```
void Hero::SetIsOnGround(bool is_on_ground)
{
 /// only accept a change
 if(is_on_ground_ == is_on_ground)
  return;

 is_on_ground_ = is_on_ground;

 if(is_on_ground_)
 {
  // save the height the hero is at currently
  current_ground_height_ = aabb_.origin.y;
  SetState(E_HERO_STATE_IDLE);
 }
 else
```

```
    {
      // going up means jumping...for now
      if(speed_.y > 0)
      {
        SetState(E_HERO_STATE_JUMPING);
      }
    }
  }
```

In the `SetIsOnGround` function, we proceed only if there is a change in this information. If the hero has indeed landed on ground, we update the `current_ground_height_` variable to whatever height the bottom edge of AABB is at currently before setting the hero to idle. However, if the hero is not on the ground and the *y* component of `speed_` is positive, it means that the hero is jumping and we must set the appropriate state. With that, we are done with class `Hero`. Let's now quickly define the `Enemy` class.

The Enemy class

The enemies in Iceman are represented by charming chocolate colored walruses. The one annoying attribute to these chubby creatures is that they rebuild any bricks the hero might have painstakingly broken. Other than that, these creatures are fairly harmless and one knock of the hero's shovel and they're dead meat.

The `Enemy` class, like the `Hero` class, will inherit from `GameObject`. The constructor for the `Enemy` class from the `Enemy.cpp` file looks like this:

```
Enemy::Enemy()
{
  type_ = E_GAME_OBJECT_ENEMY;
  state_ = E_ENEMY_STATE_NONE;
  tile_col_to_build_ = -1;
  tile_row_to_build_ = -1;
  must_be_removed_ = false;
}
```

We begin by defining the type as `E_GAME_OBJECT_ENEMY` and initialize the `state_`, column and row variables. These column and row variables will be used to identify which vacant areas of the map this enemy will reinforce. Finally, we have the `must_be_removed_` flag that you have seen before in previous chapters. The enemies in this game, like the ones in previous chapters, are maintained by `GameWorld` in a vector and must be removed after they've been whacked in the head with a rusty shovel.

The various states an enemy can be in are enumerated by enum `EEnemyState` in `GameGlobals.h` as follows:

```
enum EEnemyState
{
  E_ENEMY_STATE_NONE = 0,
  E_ENEMY_STATE_WALKING,
  E_ENEMY_STATE_DYING,
  E_ENEMY_STATE_BUILDING,
};
```

Yup, these lazy walruses can exist in only three states. The collision response for the enemies is identical to the hero, except that they don't need to know whether they're on the ground or not and they do not break any bricks. So, we will skip straight to the one thing that makes these creatures interesting: their ability to reinforce the holes in the ground. Let's take a look at the `CheckForHoles` function of `Enemy.cpp`:

```
void Enemy::CheckForHoles()
{
  // get the next tile column & row in the direction of movement
  int tile_col = GET_COL_FOR_X(aabb_.origin.x) + (speed_.x > 0 ? 1 :
0);
  int tile_row = GET_ROW_FOR_Y(aabb_.origin.y, game_world_->GetRows())
+ 1;

  // get the tile's GID
  int tile_GID = game_world_->GetBricksLayer()->tileGIDAt(ccp(tile_
col, tile_row));
  // check if there is an empty tile
  if(tile_GID == 0)
  {
   // save the column and row of this empty tile
   tile_col_to_build_ = tile_col;
   tile_row_to_build_ = tile_row;
   // start building
   SetState(E_ENEMY_STATE_BUILDING);
  }
}
```

In order to impart this simple intelligence to the enemy, we shall check for empty tiles right in front of the tile the enemy is currently resting on. Thus, we calculate the `tile_col` and `tile_row` variables to store the next column in the direction of movement and the row right below the enemy's `aabb_` respectively.

We now call the GetBricksLayer function from GameWorld and query the GID at the column and row we just calculated. If the GID is returned as 0, it means that there is a vacant tile right in front of this enemy. Then, we save this column and row into the appropriate variables and tell the enemy to start building. After the building animation has run in the FinishBuilding function, this enemy will simply tell GameWorld to add a brick at tile_col_to_build_ and tile_row_to_build_ by calling the AddBricks function.

Let's now define the Update function for the Enemy class:

```
void Enemy::Update()
{
 // reverse the direction of movement when this enemy reaches
   the left & right edge
 if(aabb_.origin.x + speed_.x <= TILE_SIZE || aabb_.origin.x +
   aabb_.size.width >= SCREEN_SIZE.width - TILE_SIZE)
 {
  SetSpeed(ccp(speed_.x * -1, speed_.y));
 }

 // check for holes in the ground when not already building
 if(state_ != E_ENEMY_STATE_BUILDING)
 {
  // update the AABB
  GameObject::Update();
  // check for collisions
  game_world_->CheckHorizontalCollisions(this);

  // check for any holes in the ground
  CheckForHoles();
 }

 // update position
 setPosition(ccp(aabb_.origin.x + aabb_.size.width * 0.5f,
   aabb_.origin.y + aabb_.size.height * 0.5f));
}
```

The first if condition in this function ensures that the enemies turn back and move in the opposite direction once they have reached either the left or right edge of the screen. If the enemy is not already in the building state, we call the Update function of GameObject, ask GameWorld to check for horizontal collisions, and check for holes. We wind up this function by updating the position of this mighty walrus.

We're almost done defining our entities with just one left: the moving platforms. Although I have defined a separate class called `Platform` to describe these moving platforms, I admit that it could have been avoided. The reason I say this is the only thing the `Platform` class does differently than the `GameObject` class is the update mechanism. Thus, we shall discuss only the `Update` function from the `Platform` class. This is what it looks like in the `Platform.cpp` file:

```
void Platform::Update()
{
  // update the AABB
  GameObject::Update();

  // reverse the direction of movement when this platform
    reaches the left & right edge
  if(aabb_.origin.x < TILE_SIZE || aabb_.origin.x +
    aabb_.size.width > SCREEN_SIZE.width - TILE_SIZE)
  {
    speed_.x *= -1;
  }

  setPosition(ccp(aabb_.origin.x + aabb_.size.width * 0.5f,
    aabb_.origin.y + aabb_.size.height * 0.5f));
}
```

The `Update` function from the `Platform` class begins by calling the parent class' `Update` function. The function then checks to see if this platform's AABB has reached either ends of the screen. In that case, the *x* component of the speed is simply reversed. That last line simply sets the updated position of the AABB to the sprite.

Now that we have defined how our platforms behave, let's go ahead and define the slightly more interesting section on detecting collisions between the hero, platforms, and enemies.

Collisions with moving platforms and enemies

If you think about implementing moving platforms, it might seem a bit tricky at first—considering how characters standing right on top of them are supposed to move along with them. We don't have a concept of friction here since there is no physics engine. Also, moving platforms cannot be represented simply by tiles since they have to move smoothly across the screen. If they were represented by tiles, they would jump from one column to the next while moving horizontally. Thus, we will represent a moving platform simply as an axis aligned bounding box.

One thing worth observing is in the `UpdateSpeed` function of class `Hero`. Right after we've added gravity, we check whether the hero is standing on a platform and act accordingly. It is imperative that this happens before we add any subsequent forces based on user input. Failing to do so will cause the hero to be stuck on the platform irrespective of user input as we are manually setting the AABB's position inside the preceding `if` conditional.

Now that we have understood how to treat moving platforms, let's look inside the `CheckHeroPlatformCollisions` function of `GameWorld.cpp`:

```
void GameWorld::CheckHeroPlatformCollisions()
{
  CCRect hero_aabb = hero_->GetAABB();

  // loop through the list of platforms
  for(int i = 0; i < num_platforms_; ++i)
  {
    CCRect platform_aabb = platforms_[i]->GetAABB();
    // check for collisions between the hero & platform aabbs
    if(hero_aabb.intersectsRect(platform_aabb))
    {
      // is the hero below or above the platform
      if(hero_aabb.getMidY() <= platform_aabb.getMidY())
      {
        // reposition the hero one pixel below the platform
        hero_aabb.origin.y = platform_aabb.origin.y -
          hero_aabb.size.height - 1;
        hero_->SetAABB(hero_aabb);
        // hero should start falling down
        hero_->SetSpeed(ccp(hero_->GetSpeed().x, GRAVITY));
      }
      else
      {
        // inform the hero that he has landed on a platform
        hero_->SetPlatformBelow(platforms_[i]);
      }
      return;
    }
  }

  // inform the hero that there is no platform below him
  hero_->SetPlatformBelow(NULL);
}
```

This function iterates through the vector of platforms filled up by `GameWorld` at the time of level creation. Within this loop, we perform simple rectangular collision detection between the AABBs of the hero and platform. If a collision is found, the first order of business is to determine whether the hero collided with the platform from above or below by comparing the *y* coordinate of the centers of both AABBs.

If the hero collided from above, we simply save the current platform into the hero. If the hero has collided from below, then we respond to the collision here itself because the hero's collision response function deals with tiles only. In response to the collision, we correct the position of the hero's AABB to be right below the platform's AABB. We also readjust the *y* component of the hero's speed sending him back down.

With that done, let's look at the `CheckHeroEnemyCollisions` function of `GameWorld.cpp`:

```
void GameWorld::CheckHeroEnemyCollisions()
{
  CCRect hero_aabb = hero_->GetAABB();

  // loop through the list of enemies
  for(int i = 0; i < num_enemies_; ++i)
  {
    // check for collisions between the hero & enemy aabbs
    if(hero_aabb.intersectsRect(enemies_[i]->GetAABB()))
    {
      // if the hero is swinging
      if(hero_->GetState() == E_HERO_STATE_SWINGING)
      {
        // enemy dies
        enemies_[i]->SetState(E_ENEMY_STATE_DYING);
      }
      else
      {
        // hero dies
        ReduceHeroLives();
        hero_->SetState(E_HERO_STATE_DYING);
      }
    }
  }
}
```

Just like we did in the previous function, we loop through the vector of enemies that GameWorld fills up at the time of level creation. We then perform simple rectangular collision detection between the AABBs. If a collision is found and the hero is in the swinging state, we tell the enemy to die. If the hero isn't swinging when a collision occurs, then he must die. We also call the ReduceHeroLives function, which decrements the hero's life, and either restarts the level or displays the game over popup based on how many lives the hero has left.

Let's now tie everything together by defining update function of GameWorld:

```
void GameWorld::update(float dt)
{
  // update the game's main elements
  UpdatePlatforms();
  UpdateEnemies();
  UpdateHero();

  // check for level completion
  if(hero_->GetCurrentGroundHeight() >= level_complete_height_)
  {
    hero_->SetState(E_HERO_STATE_WINNING);
  }

  // scroll the tiled map with some offset
  float curr_y = tiled_map_->getPositionY();
  float next_y = SCREEN_SIZE.height * 0.1f - hero_-
>GetCurrentGroundHeight();
  tiled_map_->setPositionY( curr_y + (next_y - curr_y) / 5 );

  // remove any dead enemies
  RemoveEnemies();
}
```

Since our collision detection functions handle most of the heavy-duty work, we simply call the Update functions of various game entities. In addition to that, we also check to see whether the hero has managed to reach the level completion height that we have defined while creating the level.

The next part of the update function of GameWorld deals with scrolling the tile map to follow the hero with an offset of SCREEN_SIZE.height * 0.1f. We also add some easing to this. Finally, we check if any enemies need to be removed and remove them from their vector as well as from the scene.

We shall also discuss two functions of `GameWorld` used by the `Hero` and `Enemy` classes: `RemoveBrick` and `AddBrick`.

Let's look at the following code:

```
void GameWorld::RemoveBrick(int tile_col, int tile_row)
{
  bricks_layer_->removeTileAt(ccp(tile_col, tile_row));
  SOUND_ENGINE->playEffect("brick.wav");
}
```

We can remove tiles from layers at runtime by calling the `removeTileAt` function and passing in a `CCPoint` object containing the column and row of the tile we want gone.

Let's look at the following code:

```
void GameWorld::AddBrick(int tile_col, int tile_row)
{
  // bounds checking
  if(tile_col < 0 || tile_row < 0 || tile_col >= columns_
    || tile_row >= rows_)
    return;

  // check if a brick already exists there
  if(bricks_layer_->tileAt(ccp(tile_col, tile_row)))
    return;

  // add a brick at the given column & row
  bricks_layer_->setTileGID(1, ccp(tile_col, tile_row));
}
```

The `AddBrick` function begins by checking for any violation of the bounds of the tile map and follows that up with a check to see whether the requested tile is indeed empty. In that case, the `setTileGID` function of the `CCTMXLayer` class is called, passing in the GID and a `CCPoint` class containing the column and row where we want to add the tile.

With that, we complete this chapter. I have skipped discussing a few things in this chapter, mainly the creating of the controls and the HUD and touch handling. But after reading the first six chapters, I trust that you can figure out all that boilerplate stuff for yourself.

Summary

While I started the chapter expressing that we'll be heading back in time, it doesn't seem quite so true. Many games today still rely on old-fashioned methods to accomplish simple things. In this chapter, we understood how a tile-based game works. We then spent a decent amount of time learning the Tiled Map Editor and explored the various ways we can use its features to design levels. Finally, we implemented a reusable tile-based collision detection algorithm.

In our next chapter, we will head back to Box2D and implement a physics game that involves some complex level design.

8
Box2D Meets RUBE

In this chapter, we will use Box2D to create yet another physics game. This time, we will make use of an amazing physics editor that goes by the name Really Useful Box2D Editor, more commonly referred to as RUBE. After you've read through this chapter, you will see why the creator of RUBE named it that way!

In this chapter, you'll learn:

- How to create a complete physics world using RUBE
- How to add level design parameters into a physics level using RUBE
- How to use Box2D's `PostSolve` function
- How to implement explosions in Box2D

An introduction to Angry Fish

I'm sure, just by reading that title, you know what to expect from this chapter and game. The player will have to use a catapult to hurl a series of extremely offended (haven't yet worked out why they're offended) fish towards an intricately constructed scaffolding, thereby bringing it down and destroying the cats that are housed within.

We shall go about this chapter in the following way:

- Creating a scene with some bodies and fixtures with RUBE
- Running the scene within RUBE
- Creating the game's bodies with RUBE
- Adding custom properties to a scene with RUBE
- Exporting the scene and generating a level in Cocos2d-x using `b2dJson`
- Defining the `Fish` class and its various subclasses
- Defining the `Cat` class and finishing up the game

This is what we will achieve by the end of this chapter:

A brief introduction to RUBE

When creating a physics game that has even the most minimal level of design involved, it is often feasible to use a physics editor. Getting a physics game to feel real is a challenge that is often more time consuming than it should be. This is especially the case if you're using a physics engine that you have not created by yourself.

Out of the many physics editors that I came across, I found RUBE to be the most versatile one. RUBE was created by Chris Campbell, also known as iforce2d. If you've ever searched for queries about Box2D, more often than not, you will see Chris' name (iforce2d) in forums answering the OP's questions. You can download a trial version of RUBE at: `https://www.iforce2d.net/rube/`. At the time of writing this chapter, the latest version of RUBE was 1.6.1.

The preceding website has all the information you need on the features and setting up of RUBE. It even has a complete set of video tutorials that will tell you exactly how to use it. Nevertheless, I will collate the necessary information to get us going in this chapter. Once you've downloaded the trial version and have run the executable, this is what it should like:

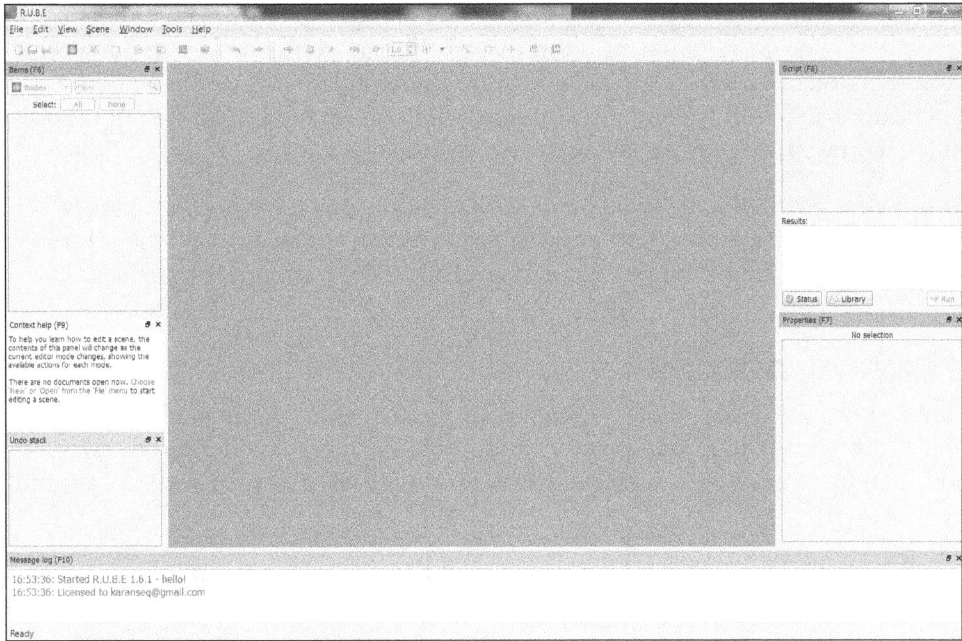

So, go ahead and select the **New** button from the toolbar, or go to **File** | **New scene**, and you should have something like this:

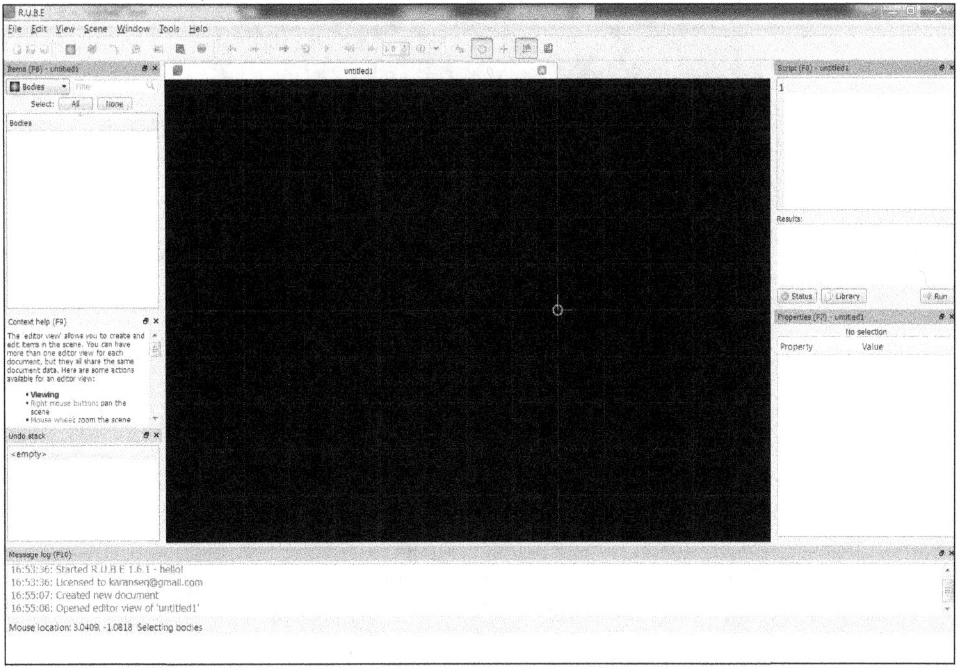

You now have an empty physics world in front of you, with the origin at the center of the editor. You can zoom in and out by scrolling the mouse and pan the world by dragging on it with the right mouse button pressed. On the toolbar, you have a set of buttons that will take you into a particular editing mode. You can edit bodies, fixtures, vertices, joints, images, samplers, and the world.

In the editor, you will notice a red and white circle around the origin that is RUBE's cursor. Most manipulations that you will do in any of the editing modes are all done with respect to the cursor. Enough reading, let's create a few bodies!

Creating bodies

To create your first body, hit the spacebar or go to **Scene** | **Actions** to see the **Actions** menu. Now go to **Add** | **Add body** and you will see the many default fixtures that a body can be created with. Go ahead and create one of each type and see what the editor looks like.

I added bodies in the order they were listed in the actions menu and this is what my editor looked like:

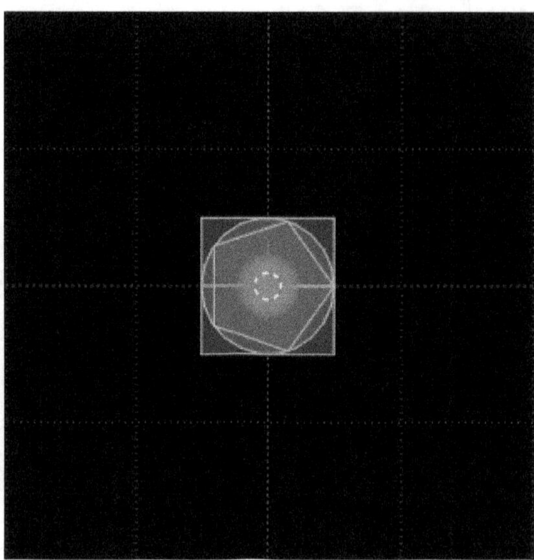

Notice how all the bodies are stacked one on top of each other. This is because when bodies are created they are placed wherever the cursor is. Since I didn't move my cursor, all the bodies I created are at the same place. Press **C** to move the cursor wherever you want and try adding the bodies away from each other this time. This is what my editor looks like now:

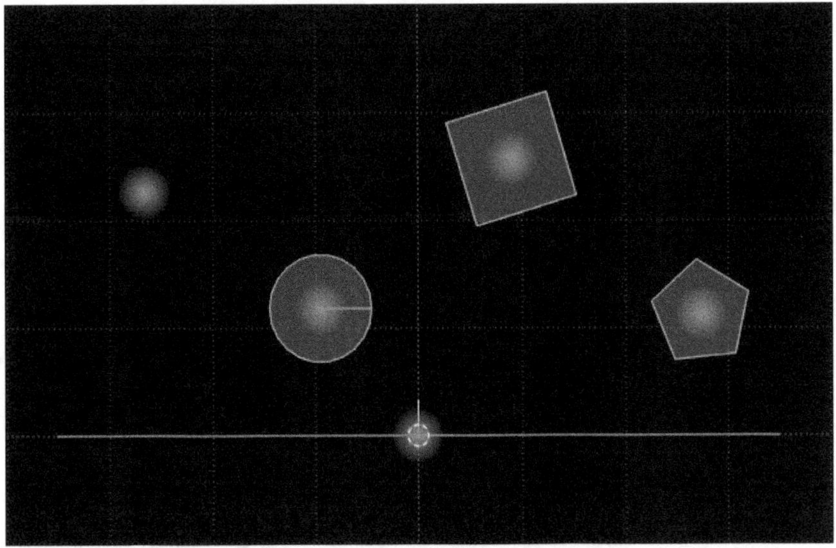

That awkward, shapeless, glowing thing on the left is how a body looks with no fixtures applied to it. I'm sure you're noticing how the edge body is much larger in the screenshot than the default edge created by RUBE, and how the square and the pentagon are rotated. That is because in the body editing mode I selected the edge body and scaled it up. Similarly, I selected the square body and the pentagon body, and rotated them.

While we're on the topic of selecting bodies, let's take a look at the properties of a body that we can set within the **Properties** window inside RUBE. This is what it looks like with the circle fixture selected:

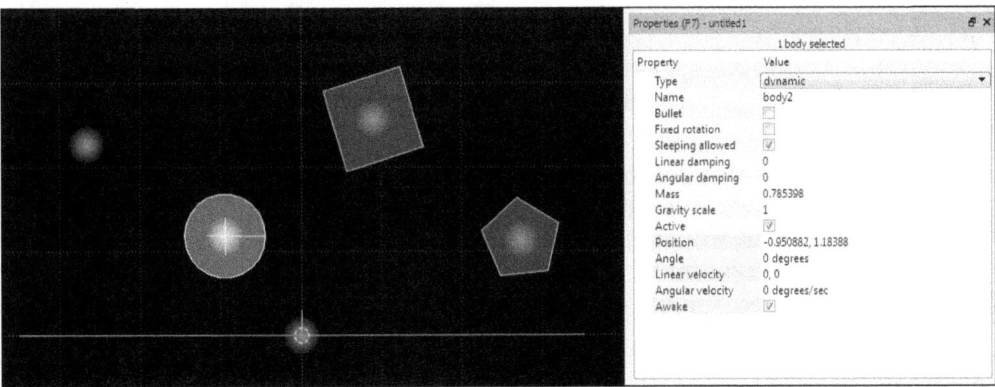

As you can see for yourself, these properties are the same as what we have seen in the `b2BodyDef` structure and `b2Body` class. The same applies for fixtures and joints as well. Well, it's now time to see the physics in action by running the scene.

Running the scene

To run the scene, you can either hit *Ctrl* + *R* or click the red colored arrow on the toolbar. This will open a player for the currently selected editor. This is what it should look like for our current scene:

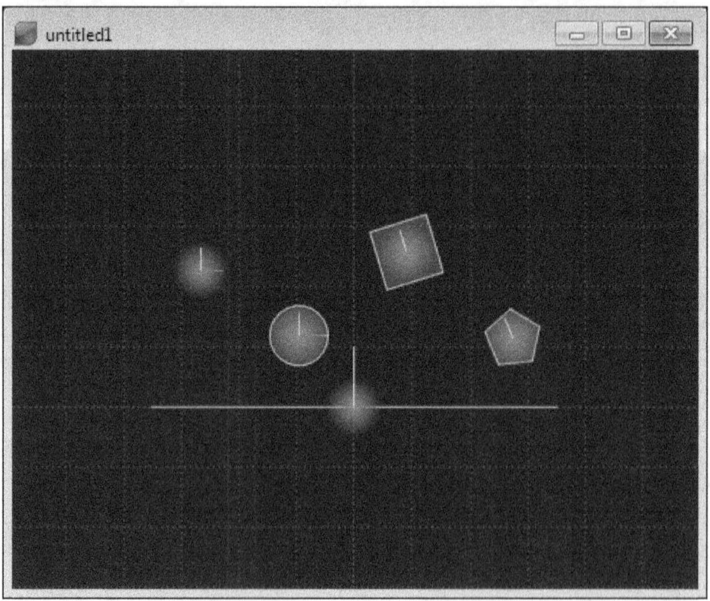

To run the simulation, hit the spacebar. You can now see the bodies fall under gravity into an infinite abyss. Why don't you change the type of that edge body to static and give it another go?

I'm sure you can appreciate what a great advantage it is to have a simulator within the editor itself. It immensely saves time that would be wasted in exporting the data and running it within the game. Of course, there is a limit to how much can be done within the simulator. You cannot apply forces or listen for contacts, but this simulator is powerful enough to tweak your level, and the many moving bodies and motors that it might have. The simulator also provides a mouse joint that you can use to fling bodies around, quite the same way that you would in a Box2D game.

In our next section, we will import images into the editor to help us shape our bodies more effectively. We will also create a basic template for a level of *Angry Fish*. That is quite a bit of work so why don't you take a break, build as many things as you like with RUBE, fling them around in the simulator, and come back when you've had enough. Make sure to read the descriptive **Context help** whenever you have a doubt.

Importing images

Many a times you may want your physics bodies to have shapes more like the characters or entities that they will be representing within the game. In such cases, an editor can be extremely beneficial in defining the shape for your physics body's fixture. RUBE allows us to import an image and trace the vertices for the fixture of the underlying physics body. In version 1.6, this process has been automated with the addition of samplers!

To import an image into RUBE, simply drag it into the editor. You can use the `cat.png` image from the `Resources` directory of the source bundle for this chapter. Once dragged into RUBE, go to image editing mode by clicking on the **Edit images** button in the toolbar or pressing *I* on your keyboard.

Now select the image of the cat that you just dragged into the editor, bring up the actions menu and select **Sampler | Create body + fixture from image**. Notice that if you don't have an image selected, the option will be disabled. In the prompts that followed, I left in the default values and this is what the editor looked like:

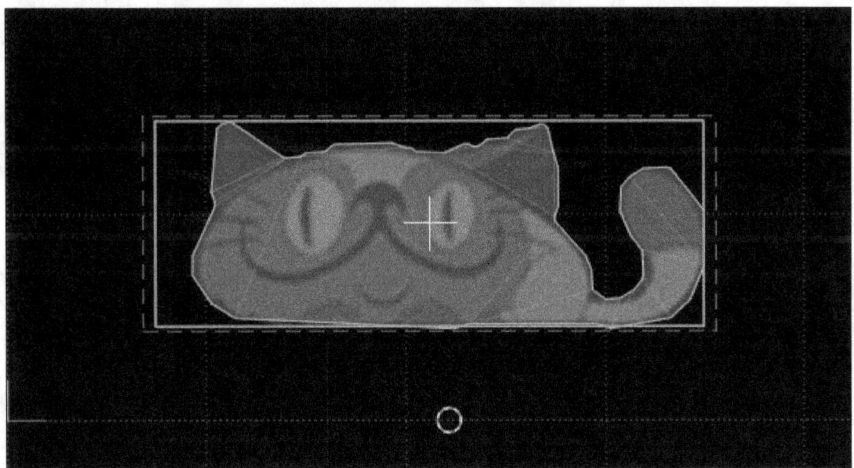

You can run the scene and play with the resultant physics body that is created. If you enter the vertices mode, you will notice that the fixture for the cat's body—although quite accurate—has way too many vertices. You can manually edit/remove the vertices or tweak the inputs to the sampler in the prompts that you faced to get fewer vertices for a more lightweight fixture.

In this way, you can use RUBE to effortlessly create bodies and fixtures for the various entities in your game. Next up, we will create a basic primer or template level for our game.

Creating a level with RUBE

Our template level needs a catapult to hurl the fish across the screen, a few bodies that will form the scaffolding, and the cats. For the catapult, we will create a simple rectangular body joined to the ground by a revolute joint. We will also customize the properties of the revolute joint to make the catapult as realistic as we can.

Since you already know how to create the bodies of various fixtures, I'm sure you can whip up the world within the following screenshot in no time. However, you can find the basic template file named `Level00.rube` in the `Resources` folder of the source bundle for this chapter. This is what the bodies within the template look like in the editor:

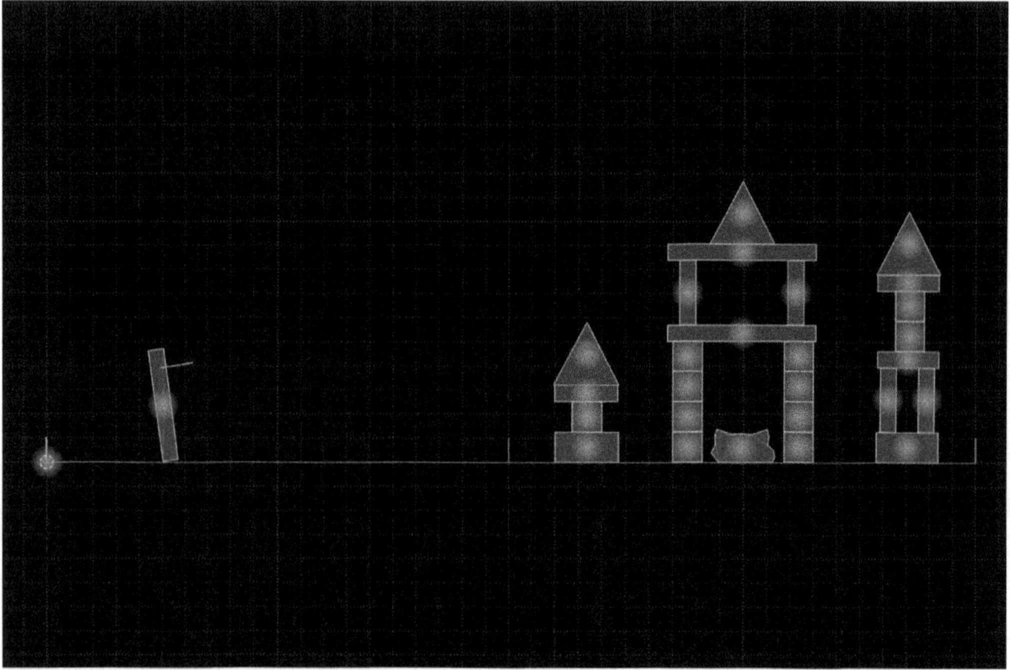

Open the `Level00.rube` file, run the simulation, drag the catapult on the left side of the screen, and release it. Rest assured, we will create the catapult in the next section and you will see how we achieved the behavior that you will see in the simulation. For now, add a circle fixture body near the catapult's ledge (refer to the following screenshot), then run the simulation again and have some fun!

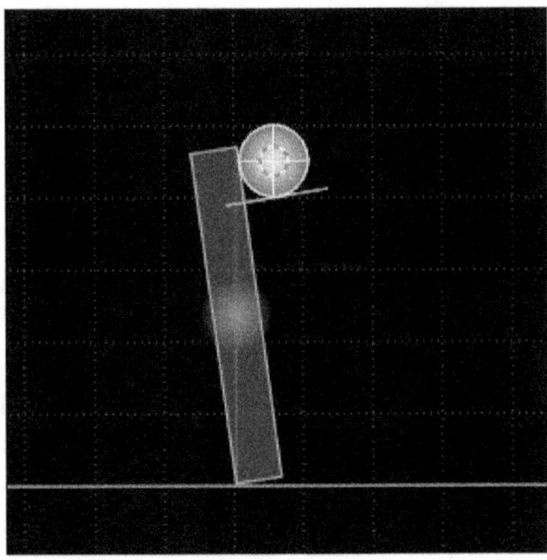

Creating the catapult

Before we actually create the catapult, we need to learn something about the revolute joint. To quote the Box2D manual:

> *A revolute joint forces two bodies to share a common anchor point, often called a hinge point. The revolute joint has a single degree of freedom: the relative rotation of the two bodies. This is called the joint angle.*

The revolute joint needs two bodies and an anchor point in the world space. In our case, the two bodies are the ground and the catapult, and the anchor point will be the point where the catapult touches the ground.

With `Level00.rube` open in the editor, and with the **Edit joints** mode selected, select the revolute joint named `catapult_joint` and delete it. Now go back to the **Edit bodies** mode and select the ground body as well as the catapult body (hold down the *Shift* key for multiple selections). Since RUBE will use the cursor as the location for the anchor point for the revolute joint, we need to move the cursor to the hinge point of our choice (once again, that is the point where the catapult touches the ground). Once you've done that, bring up the actions menu and go to **Add** | **Add joint** | **Revolute**. You can now run the simulation to see how the bodies behave with the joint constraining them.

Now that we have the default behavior of the revolute joint in place, we can add properties to achieve the behavior of a catapult. The first thing to implement is limits for the revolute joint. Limits force the joint angle to remain between a lower and upper bound. The limit will apply as much torque as needed to the constrained bodies to make this happen.

Select the joint that you just created and set the **Lower limit** and **Upper limit** values to `10` and `60`, respectively, within the **Properties** window. Also enable the **Enable limit** checkbox and run the simulation. The catapult's rotation is now restricted between two angles like we want, but it doesn't really move back to its original angle. For that, we need to enable the motor on this joint. A joint motor allows you to specify the joint speed and a maximum torque. The motor will move the joint with the specified speed unless the required torque exceeds the specified maximum torque.

Enable the **Enable motor** checkbox and fill in values `-250` and `2000` into **Motor speed** and **Max motor torque**, respectively. You can play around with these values to understand how the joint motor actually works. Run the simulation and you will see that dragging and releasing the catapult actually causes it to return to its original angle.

Now that we know how to create bodies and have created a functional catapult, we can move ahead to specify a few level design parameters using an invaluable feature of RUBE: custom properties.

Adding custom properties

Many a times, you might want your game's elements to have properties other than physics characteristics. RUBE takes care of this by virtue of custom properties that can be assigned to bodies, fixtures, joints, images, and even the world. You can name your custom property whatever you like and bind it to one of the preceding entities. A custom property can be an integer, float, string, vec2, bool, or color. Once a custom property is added to an entity, it can be assigned a value from within the **Properties** window—just like the physics properties.

For our game, we will need the bodies to have a couple of properties and the world to have a single property, as listed in the following table:

Custom property	**Entity**	**Description**
`SpriteName`	Body	This is the name of the image that will be used to represent this body in Cocos2d-x.
`IsCat`	Body	Whether this object is a cat or just a regular object.
`ListOfFish`	World	This is a sequence of numbers describing the order and type of fish that will be available to the player for a given level.

To add the preceding custom properties, go to **Scene** | **Scene settings**. This will launch a window that looks like this:

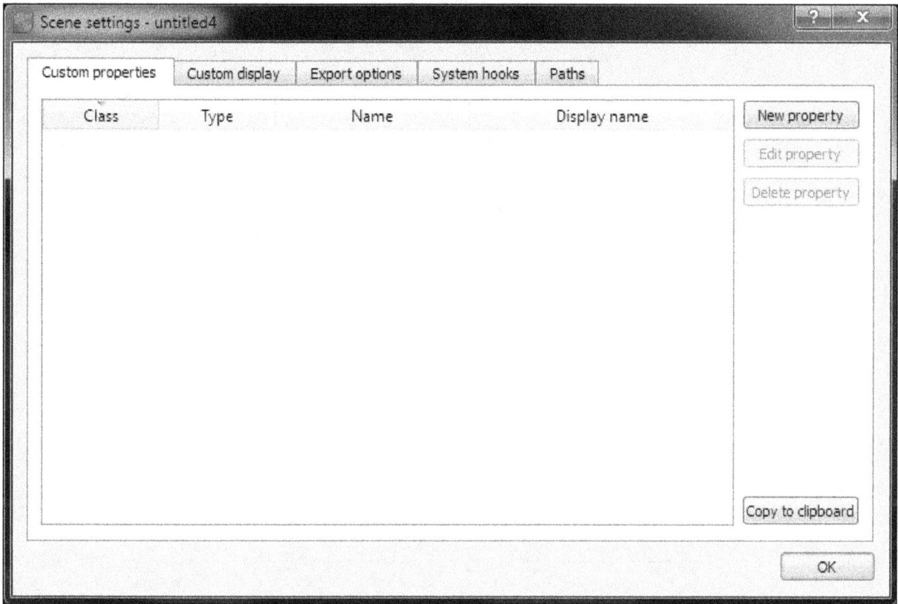

Now click on **New property**. In the window that opens, add the following entries to create the `SpriteName` custom property:

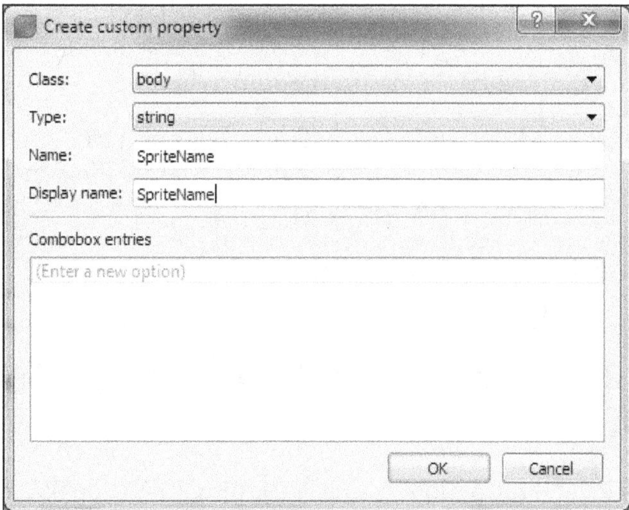

Similarly, add the other two custom properties. Now when you click on a body within the editor, the **Properties** window should look something like this:

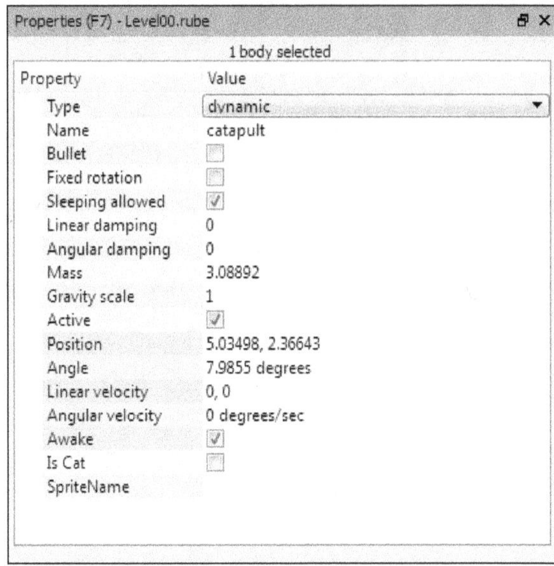

You can open the RUBE file for each level in the source bundle for this chapter and play around with it as much as you like. This is all that we will be doing with RUBE in this chapter, but one important thing remains to be done. We need to export the information within these RUBE files so we can access them back in the Cocos2d-x environment. Unfortunately, the trial version does not let you export the raw data within the RUBE files. However, I have exported the raw data for each of the five levels, and you can find the JSON files in the source bundle.

We have barely scratched the surface with the abilities of the editor, but we've implemented enough to save a lot of time with our *Angry Fish* game. We still have a lot of work to do. We need to parse the raw data exported from RUBE and use it to generate the physics level. We then need to code in the functionality for the various kinds of fish, and the cats, and wrap up the gameplay.

Generating a world using data exported from RUBE

RUBE exports its level information in a neat and tidy JSON file. We can create a complete physics world from this exported JSON file by using a JSON parser along with a class called `b2dJson`. You can find the required files in the RUBE download package as well as in the source bundle for this chapter.

Before we go ahead, let's discuss how our Box2D world will be created for this chapter. We will split the world creation into two main functions: `CreateWorld` and `CreateGameObjects`. In the `CreateWorld` function, we will use the `b2dJson` class to create a `b2World` object, based on data exported from RUBE. In the `CreateGameObjects` function, we will create sprites for all the physics bodies within the world.

Without further ado, let's begin with some code. This is the `CreateWorld` function from `GameWorld.cpp`:

```
void GameWorld::CreateWorld(b2dJson* json, int level)
{
  // get file data and parse it to get b2dJson
  char buf[32] = {0};
  sprintf(buf, "Level%02d.json", level);
  //sprintf(buf, "testing.json");
  unsigned long size;
  char* data_uc = (char*)CCFileUtils::sharedFileUtils()->
    getFileData(buf, "rb", &size);

  // error message
  std::string msg = "could not load file";

  world_ = json->readFromString(data_uc, msg);
  // tell world we want to listen for collisions
  world_->SetContactListener(this);

  // delete char buffer
  delete data_uc;

#ifdef ENABLE_DEBUG_DRAW
  debug_draw_ = new GLESDebugDraw(PTM_RATIO);
  world_->SetDebugDraw(debug_draw_);
  uint32 flags = 0;
  flags += b2Draw::e_shapeBit;
  flags += b2Draw::e_jointBit;
  debug_draw_->SetFlags(flags);
#endif
}
```

The `CreateWorld` function is called when `GameWorld` is created, and takes a pointer to a `b2dJson` object along with the level number. In this function, we generate the name for the respective level file and use the `getFileData` function from `CCFileUtils` to read the file's contents.

We then pass the file data into the `readFromString` function of class `b2dJson`, which will return a pointer to a newly created `b2World` object. This is how simple it is to generate a physics world using the data exported from RUBE. We wind up this function by setting `GameWorld` as the contact listener and setting up debug draw like you've seen in previous chapters.

The `b2dJson` class provides an extensive set of functions that can be used to query almost everything related to the physics world it created using the data exported from RUBE. We will use some of the functions to save references to a few relevant bodies and extract the custom properties we set in the editor.

Let's take a look at how this is done in the `CreateGameObjects` function from `GameWorld.cpp`:

```
void GameWorld::CreateGameObjects(b2dJson* json)
{
  // save references to a few important bodies
  boundary_body_ = json->getBodyByName(string("ground"));
  catapult_body_ = json->getBodyByName(string("catapult"));
  catapult_joint_ = (b2RevoluteJoint*)json->getJointByName(
    string("catapult_joint"));

  // extract the list of fish (comma separated string) for this level
  fish_list_ = json->getCustomString((void*)world_,
    "ListOfFish", "");

  // get all bodies from the world that have a sprite name
    i.e. GameObjects
  b2Body* body_in_list = world_->GetBodyList();
  while(body_in_list != NULL)
  {
    string sprite_name = json->getCustomString((void*)body_in_list,
      "SpriteName", "");
    if(sprite_name.compare(""))
    {
      // append file extension...sorry we don't have
        spritesheets at the moment! :(
      sprite_name = sprite_name + ".png";

      // see if this game object is a cat
      if(json->getCustomBool((void*)body_in_list,
        "IsCat", false))
      {
```

```
            // create the Cat
            Cat* cat = Cat::create(this);
            // save the body
            cat->SetBody(body_in_list);
            // add & save this Cat
            addChild(cat, E_LAYER_CATS);
            cats_.push_back(cat);
            ++ num_cats_;
          }
          else
          {
            // create the GameObject with the respective
              sprite name
            GameObject* game_object = GameObject::create(this,
              sprite_name.c_str());
            // save the body
            game_object->SetBody(body_in_list);
            // add & save this GameObject
            addChild(game_object, E_LAYER_OBJECTS);
            game_objects_.push_back(game_object);
            ++ num_game_objects_;
          }
        }

        // continue checking
        body_in_list = body_in_list->GetNext();
      }

      // reorder catapult to be above the fish
      reorderChild((CCSprite*)catapult_body_->GetUserData(), E_LAYER_FISH
    + 1);
    }
```

The `CreateGameObjects` function is called when `GameWorld` is created, and accepts a pointer to a `b2dJson` object. We begin by storing references to the bodies of the ground and the catapult, followed by a reference to the catapult's `b2RevoluteJoint` object.

We then extract the world's custom property with the name of `ListOfFish` by calling the `getCustomString` function of the `b2dJson` class. This function accepts a `void*` object, so we can use this very function to get the custom properties for our `b2Body` objects as well. This will return a `std::string` object that we will use when creating the set of `Fish` objects for a particular level.

We then iterate through the list of bodies, looking for bodies that possess the `SpriteName` custom property; this will tell us which bodies need `GameObject` objects created. Within this loop, we also compare the value of the `IsCat` custom property by calling the `getCustomBool` function and, passing in the current `b2Body` object. If this value is `true`, we create an object of the `Cat` class; otherwise, we create an object of the `GameObject` class. We also add the object created to the respective list belonging to the `GameWorld` class. To wind up the `CreateGameObjects` function, we reorder the catapult's sprite so that it is rendered on top of the fish.

Now that we have created the game's physics world and all the `GameObjects`, using the data exported from RUBE, we can define the behavior of the different kinds of fish.

Defining the fish

In *Angry Fish*, we have five different kinds of fish. Since they will share a lot of common behavior, we will define a base `Fish` class and inherit from `Fish` to specialize the behavior wherever required.

The following table describes each fish in brief:

Type of fish	Class	Description
`Simple`	`Fish`	The simplest kind of fish that can be launched from the catapult
`Shooting`	`ShootingFish`	Once launched, tapping the screen boosts this fish's velocity in the direction of motion
`Splitting`	`SplittingFish`	Once launched, tapping the screen causes this fish to split into multiple smaller fish
`Bombing`	`BombingFish`	Once launched, tapping the screen causes this fish to hurl a smaller fish downwards
`Exploding`	`ExplodingFish`	Once launched, this fish automatically explodes after landing or hitting something

The Fish class

We now define the base class for the fish. The `Fish` class will inherit from parent class `GameObject`, which is identical to the one you've seen in *Chapter 5, Let's Get Physical!* This is how the `Fish` class looks inside the `Fish.h` file:

```
class Fish : public GameObject
{
public:
```

```
  Fish() : fish_type_(E_FISH_SIMPLE), radius_(0.0f),
    is_throwable_(false), has_been_fired_(false),
 has_been_touched_(false), has_hit_(false),
 last_position_(b2Vec2_zero)
  {
    type_ = E_GAME_OBJECT_FISH;
  }
  ~Fish();

  static Fish* create(GameWorld* game_world,
    float radius = SIMPLE_FISH_RADIUS, const char* frame_name = NULL);

  virtual bool init(GameWorld* game_world,
    float radius, const char* frame_name);
  virtual void Update();

  virtual void Spawn();
  virtual void Touch();
  virtual void Hit(float check_finish_interval = 1.0f);
  virtual void Finish(float dt);
  virtual void Kill();

  inline EFishType GetFishType() { return fish_type_; }
  inline void SetFishType(EFishType fish_type)
    { fish_type_ = fish_type; }

  inline float GetRadius() { return radius_; }
  inline void SetRadius(float radius) { radius_ = radius; }

  inline bool GetIsThrowable() { return is_throwable_; }
  inline void SetIsThrowable(bool is_throwable)
    { is_throwable_ = is_throwable; }

  void SetHasBeenFired(bool has_been_fired);
  inline bool GetHasBeenFired() { return has_been_fired_; }

protected:
  EFishType fish_type_;
  float radius_;
  bool is_throwable_;
  bool has_been_fired_;
  bool has_been_touched_;
  bool has_hit_;
  b2Vec2 last_position_;
};
```

Let's go over the important member variables of the Fish class:

Variable	Description
fish_type_	This describes the type of this fish. The EFishType enum is defined in GameGlobals.h.
radius_	All the fish bodies will have circular fixtures described by this radius property.
is_throwable_	This flag is true for fish created as a result of being included in the ListOfFish property of the world. This flag is false for fishes that are created by the splitting and exploding fish.
has_been_fired_	This specifies whether or not the fish has been fired from the catapult.
has_been_touched_	This specifies whether or not the player has touched the fish after it has been fired.
has_hit_	This specifies whether or not the fish has hit something after it has been fired.

Let's now take a look at the functions that give the Fish class its angry demeanor, starting with the init function from Fish.cpp:

```
bool Fish::init(GameWorld* game_world, float radius, const char*
frame_name)
{
  if(!GameObject::init(game_world, frame_name))
    return false;

  // every fish must have a radius
  radius_ = radius;
  // fetch a newly created circle fixture body
  b2Body* body = GameGlobals::CreateCircleBody(game_world_-
>GetWorld(), radius_);
  // initially position it outside the left edge of the screen
  body->SetTransform(b2Vec2(SCREEN_TO_WORLD(-SCREEN_SIZE.width *
0.5f), 0), 0);
  // initially no processing is wasted
  body->SetActive(false);
  // save the body
  SetBody(body);
  return true;
}
```

We begin by calling the `init` function of the parent class, passing in the reference to `GameWorld`, and the sprite frame name for this object. We then store the radius property and ask the `GameGlobals` class to create a body with a circle-shaped fixture with the specified radius. This function is pretty basic, so I won't go into the details.

We then set the transform for this body so that it is positioned outside the left-hand side of the screen. We also set this body to inactive before calling the `SetBody` function. Just to remind you, the `SetBody` function simply stores this body's pointer and also saves a reference for this class into the body's user data property.

We now define the functions that compose the life cycle of the fish: `Spawn`, `Touch`, `Hit`, `Finish` , and `Kill`, starting with the `Spawn` function of `Fish.cpp`:

```
void Fish::Spawn()
{
  // reposition the body near the ledge of the catapult
  body_->SetTransform(game_world_->GetFishSpawnPoint() +
    b2Vec2(-radius_, radius_), 0);
  // start physics processing
  body_->SetActive(true);
  // start processing the Update
  setVisible(true);
  // animate the spawn
  setScale(0.0f);
  runAction(CCEaseBackOut::create(
    CCScaleTo::create(0.25f, 1.0f)));
}
```

The preceding function is called from `GameWorld` whenever the game is ready for another fish to be fired. Thus, we set the position of the body at the value returned from the `GetFishSpawnPoint` function from the `GameWorld` class. This function returns nothing but the position at the ledge of the catapult. We also activate the body and set the sprite to visible. We then show a simple spawning animation to wind up the `Spawn` function.

Let's now look at the next function in the list, that is, the `Touch` function of `Fish.cpp`:

```
void Fish::Touch()
{
  // fish can only be touched if it is active,
    has already been fired AND
  // if it has not already been touched
  if(!body_->IsActive() || !has_been_fired_ || has_been_touched_)
    return;

  has_been_touched_ = true;
}
```

Since this is the base class, the `Touch` function just sets the `has_been_touched_` flag to `true`. As you read in the description, a fish can be touched only after it has been fired.

Let's move on to the `Hit` function of `Fish.cpp`:

```
void Fish::Hit(float check_finish_interval)
{
  // fish can only hit something if it is has already
    been fired AND
  // if it has not already hit something
  if(!has_been_fired_ || has_hit_)
    return;

  has_hit_ = true;
  // save last position to find if this fish has stopped moving
  last_position_ = body_->GetPosition();
  // keep checking if fish has finished
  schedule(schedule_selector(Fish::Finish), check_finish_interval);
}
```

The preceding function gets called within the `BeginContact` function from `GameWorld` whenever this fish hits another game object in the world. We begin this function by handling untimely and repeated calls. We also store the previous position of this fish's body into the `last_position_` variable, and then schedule the `Finish` function to be called with the interval specified by the `check_finish_interval` variable. This variable is passed in as an argument to the `Hit` function.

Let's define the `Finish` function of `Fish.cpp`:

```
void Fish::Finish(float dt)
{
  // fish has not finished if it is awake AND
  // if it is moving at a considerable speed
  if(body_->IsAwake() && (body_->GetPosition() -
    last_position_).Length() > radius_ * 3)
  {
    last_position_ = body_->GetPosition();
    return;
  }

  // fish has more or less stopped...unschedule this function
  unschedule(schedule_selector(Fish::Finish));
  // only throwable fish get to spawn other fish
  if(is_throwable_)
  {
```

```
        // ask GameWorld to spawn the next fish
        game_world_->SpawnFish();
    }
}
```

This function is called at regular intervals to check if this fish must "finish". A fish finishes when it has slowed down or its body has fallen asleep. The fish now needs to unschedule the selector for this function and, finally, inform the `GameWorld` class to spawn the next fish from its list.

Notice how we check whether this is a "throwable" fish. If you remember the description of the `is_throwable_` variable, only fish that are created as a result of being on the world's list of fish are "throwable". If we don't perform this check, even fish that are created as a result of the splitting or exploding fish will be able to spawn fish at the catapult's ledge.

Now, let's define the `Kill` function from `Fish.cpp`:

```
void Fish::Kill()
{
  // reposition the body out of the screen
  body_->SetTransform(b2Vec2(SCREEN_TO_WORLD(-SCREEN_SIZE.width *
0.5f), 0), 0);
  // deactivate the body so processing is stopped
  body_->SetActive(false);
  // put the body to sleep...this will help this fish Finish
  body_->SetAwake(false);
  // hide the sprite so Update is stopped
  setVisible(false);
}
```

This function gets called from the `Update` function from the `Fish` class when a given fish has exited the screen. We simply reposition the physics body off the screen, set the physics body to inactive and asleep, and set the sprite to invisible.

Let's take a look at the `Update` function of `Fish.cpp`:

```
void Fish::Update()
{
  // no processing if invisible
  if(!m_bVisible)
    return;

  // Finish & Kill this fish if it has lef the screen
```

```
        if(body_->GetPosition().y < 0 || body_->GetPosition().x >
          SCREEN_TO_WORLD(SCREEN_SIZE.width * 2.0f))
        {
          Kill();
          Finish(0.0f);
        }

        // update the sprite's position
        setPosition(ccp(WORLD_TO_SCREEN(body_->GetPosition().x),
          WORLD_TO_SCREEN(body_->GetPosition().y)));

        // stop rotating after being fired
        if(has_been_fired_)
        {
          // ease the angle from <whatever> to 0
          setRotation(m_fRotationX / 5);

          // fish can't moonwalk...set the correct direction
          if(body_->GetLinearVelocity().x > 0.5f)
            setFlipX(false);
          else if(body_->GetLinearVelocity().x < -0.5f)
            setFlipX(true);
        }
    }
```

We won't waste any processing on this fish when it is not visible. Next we check if this fish has crossed the limits of the screen, and call the `Kill` and `Finish` life cycle functions. Instead of calling the `Update` function of the parent class `GameObject`, we set the position here itself. The reason for this is that we don't want the fish's sprite to rotate along with its physics body. In the last part of the `Update` function, we set the appropriate rotation and flip parameters for the fish's sprite.

With that, we complete defining the base class for our fish. We can now dive into the specializations of each fish, starting with the `ShootingFish` class.

The ShootingFish class

The shooting fish is like a simple fish, except that touching the screen causes it to shoot forward at a high velocity. When I think of it now, I probably should have named this class `DashingFish`. Anyway, we will specialize this fish by overriding the `Touch` function from the `Fish` base class in the `Fish.cpp` file:

```
void ShootingFish::Touch()
{
```

```
    // fish can only be touched if it is active,
      has already been fired AND
    // if it has not already been touched
    if(!body_->IsActive() || !has_been_fired_ ||
      has_been_touched_)
      return;

    // call parent class' Touch
    Fish::Touch();
    // Go faster Fish!
    body_->ApplyLinearImpulse(b2Vec2(10.0f, 0),
      body_->GetWorldCenter());
  }
```

All that we need to do here is apply a linear impulse in the horizontal direction to boost this fish forward. This completely defines our `ShootingFish` class!

The SplittingFish class

The splitting fish spawns three malicious tiny fishes when the player taps the screen. Of course, you can change this to spawn any number of tiny fish, for any amount of destruction! In this case too, we override the `Touch` function from the `Fish` base class in `Fish.cpp`:

```
  void SplittingFish::Touch()
  {
    // fish can only be touched if it is active,
      has already been fired AND
    // if it has not already been touched
    if(!body_->IsActive() || !has_been_fired_ ||
      has_been_touched_)
      return;

    // Call parent class' Touch
    Fish::Touch();
    // Since this Fish's Hit won't be called by default,
      call it here manually
    Fish::Hit(3.0f);

    // spawn "num_splitting_fish_" simple fish
    for(int i = 0; i < num_splitting_fish_; ++i)
    {
      AddSplitFish(i);
    }

    // Kill the splitting fish
    Fish::Kill();
  }
```

We begin by avoiding undesirable processing and then call the base class' life cycle functions. Since this fish is supposed to disappear after spawning the tiny fish, it won't be able to actually hit anything. Thus, we manually call the `Hit` function here and pass in a delay of 3 seconds to check for the finish condition.

We then call the `AddSplitFish` function that will spawn a tiny fish with the desired attributes. To wind this fish up, we call the parent class' `Kill` function. Let's now take a look at how exactly the split fish are created in the `AddSplitFish` function of `Fish.cpp`:

```
void SplittingFish::AddSplitFish(int num_split)
{
  // create a simple fish with a different sprite name & radius
  Fish* split_fish = Fish::create(game_world_, TINY_FISH_RADIUS,
    "fish_03.png");
  // this fish won't spawn so set the visibility to true
  split_fish->setVisible(true);
  // ask GameWorld to add this fish to its list
  game_world_->AddFish(split_fish);

  // find the direction of the mother fish (SplittingFish*)
  b2Vec2 splitting_fish_velocity = body_->GetLinearVelocity();
  splitting_fish_velocity.Normalize();
  // calculate impulse that the mother fish will apply to baby
    fish (Fish*)
  b2Vec2 split_fish_impulse = b2Vec2(
    splitting_fish_velocity.x * 15.0f,
 splitting_fish_velocity.y * 7.5f + num_split * -2);

  // appropriately position the baby fish
  b2Body* split_fish_body = split_fish->GetBody();
  split_fish_body->SetTransform(b2Vec2(
    body_->GetPosition().x + radius_ - (radius_ * num_split),
 body_->GetPosition().y + radius_ - (radius_ * num_split)), 0);
  // activate the fish's body
  split_fish_body->SetActive(true);
  // apply impulse so the baby fish doesn't simply fall to the sea
  split_fish_body->ApplyLinearImpulse(split_fish_impulse,
    split_fish_body->GetWorldCenter());
}
```

We begin by creating an object of the `Fish` class, which is nothing but a simple fish. We pass in a reference to `GameWorld`, and specify the radius for this fish along with the sprite's frame name. You can find the different radii used by the various fish defined in `GameGlobals.h`.

Once created, the fish's sprite must be set to visible and added to the GameWorld. We then proceed to calculate the impulse that must be applied to this tiny fish. Without applying an impulse, this fish would disgracefully fall straight into the sea. We use the num_split argument that is passed to this function to calculate the direction for this impulse and the initial position for this tiny fish.

We finally activate this splitting fish's physics body and apply the impulse we just calculated to set it free. This wraps up our SplittingFish class. The next kind of fish, the bombing fish, is behaviorally similar to the splitting fish so I will skip getting into the details. You can find the BombingFish class defined in the Fish.cpp file after the class definition for SplittingFish.

The ExplodingFish class

The exploding fish is definitely everybody's favorite—who doesn't like blowing things up? Especially so if you have to implement something as funky sounding as a RayCast! Well, in order for the exploding fish to know exactly which bodies to throw and how to throw them, we implement a RayCast function on the b2World object.

As you read in the table describing the various kinds of fish, the exploding fish automatically detonates after it hits something. As such, we will override the Hit function from the parent class Fish and implement an additional Explode function that takes care of the demolition.

Here is the Hit function of Fish.cpp:

```
void ExplodingFish::Hit(float check_finish_interval)
{
  // fish can only hit something if it is has already
    been fired AND
  // if it has not already hit something
  if(!has_been_fired_ || has_hit_)
    return;

  // call parent class' Hit
  Fish::Hit(1.0f);
  // schedule the explosion
  scheduleOnce(schedule_selector(ExplodingFish::Explode), 2.0f);
}
```

As you can see, the Hit function just schedules the Explode function to be called 2 seconds later, and updates the Hit function of the parent class, passing an appropriate interval to check for this fish's finish condition. Before we define the Explode function, we need to understand and implement a RayCast.

Using Box2D's RayCast

To quote Wikipedia, ray casting algorithms are used to render three-dimensional scenes into two-dimensional images. The idea behind ray casting is to trace rays from the eye, one per pixel and find the closest object blocking the path of that ray. This is then the object that the eye sees through that pixel.

Similarly, in a physics engine, ray casting is often used to locate bodies within the physics world. A ray is nothing but a straight line, and we can use a function provided by Box2D to check whether the ray intersects with a fixture. The `RayCast` function looks like this:

```
void RayCast(b2RayCastCallback* callback, const b2Vec2& point1,
  const b2Vec2& point2)
```

The `RayCast` function is a member function of the `b2World` class and accepts three arguments: a class that implements `b2RayCastCallback`, the start point of the ray, and the end point of the ray. We implement the `b2RayCastCallback` class by inheriting our `GameWorld` class from it, as follows:

```
class GameWorld : public CCLayer, public b2ContactListener, public
  b2RayCastCallback
```

The `b2RayCastCallback` class needs us to override just one function:

```
float32 ReportFixture(b2Fixture* fixture, const b2Vec2& point,
  const b2Vec2& normal, float32 fraction);
```

When the `RayCast` function is called on the `b2World` object, each time the ray intersects with a fixture the `ReportFixture` function is called. As you can see, we get plenty of information from this function: the intersected fixture, the point of intersection, the normal at the point of intersection, and the fraction (a confusing bit of information). The fraction is nothing but the ratio of `distance(ray_start_point, intersection_point)` and `distance(intersection_point, ray_end_point)`.

Box2D requires us to return a value from this function so that it knows what we need from the `RayCast` calculation. Now, this is one tricky topic to understand, so I will quote from the man himself. You can take a look at Chris' tutorial on Ray casting at `http://www.iforce2d.net/b2dtut/raycasting` to further your understanding on the topic.

- To find only the closest intersection, return the fraction value from the callback and use the most recent intersection as the result.
- To find all intersections along the ray, return `1` from the callback and store the intersections in a list.
- To simply find if the ray hits anything, if you get a callback, something was hit (but it may not be the closest). So, return `0` from the callback for efficiency.

To complete this pretty picture, let's take a look at how we implement the `ReportFixture` function in `GameWorld.cpp`:

```
float32 GameWorld::ReportFixture(b2Fixture* fixture,
  const b2Vec2& point, const b2Vec2& normal, float32 fraction)
{
  // a fixture has been intersected, save its body & the point
    of intersection
  ray_cast_data_.body_ = fixture->GetBody();
  ray_cast_data_.point_ = point;
  // return the fraction...this will help us find the fixture
    nearest to the start point of the ray
  return fraction;
}
```

As you can see, we return the fraction that is passed as an argument because we need to find the fixture nearest to the start point of the ray (which is the epicenter of the explosion here).

We also maintain a reference to the body of the intersected fixture and also the point of intersection. We store this information in an instance of `struct RayCastData`, which we define in `GameGlobals.h`, as follows:

```
struct RayCastData
{
  b2Body* body_;
  b2Vec2 point_;

  RayCastData() { body_ = NULL; point_ = b2Vec2_zero; }
};
```

The struct simply stores what we need it to store, that is, the body of the fixture with which the ray intersected and the point at which the ray intersected the fixture. With this information in our minds, let's head back to the ExplodingFish class and define the Explode function in Fish.cpp:

```
void ExplodingFish::Explode(float dt)
{
  // find bodies to blow apart
  for(int i = 0; i < num_rays_; ++i)
  {
    // calculate angle based on number of rays
    float angle = CC_DEGREES_TO_RADIANS((i / (float)num_rays_) * 360);
    // calculate direction vector based on angle
    b2Vec2 ray_direction(sinf(angle), cosf(angle));
    // calculate end point of the ray based on blast radius &
   direction vector
    b2Vec2 ray_end = body_->GetWorldCenter() +
   blast_radius_ * ray_direction;

    // perform RayCast on b2World from GameWorld...start point
   is the centre of this fish's body
    game_world_->GetWorld()->RayCast(game_world_,
   body_->GetWorldCenter(), ray_end);
    // query data found by the RayCast
    RayCastData ray_cast_data = game_world_->GetRayCastData();
    // did the ray hit a body?
    if(ray_cast_data.body_)
    {
      // apply a linear impulse at point of contact in the direction
     of this ray
      ray_cast_data.body_->ApplyLinearImpulse(b2Vec2(
     ray_direction.x * blast_magnitude_,
  0.5f * blast_magnitude_), ray_cast_data.point_);
      // reset the data found by the RayCast
      game_world_->ResetRayCastData();
    }
  }
}
```

The num_rays_ variable is a member of the ExplodingFish class and it simply describes the number of rays that we will cast around the center of this fish to find intersecting fixtures. Within the for loop, you will see that we use the counter i as well as the variable num_rays_ to calculate the angle and the direction of the ray.

Since we already know that the center of the fish is the start point of the ray, we can use the blast_radius_ and ray_direction variables to calculate the end point of the ray. We then call the RayCast function on the b2World object of GameWorld, passing in the required parameters.

When the RayCast function has finished executing and the closest intersecting fixture has been found, the RayCastData struct will contain the relevant information. If a body is found as a result of the calculation, we apply a linear impulse at the point of intersection in the same direction as the ray was cast.

Just like that, we implemented explosions in Box2D! We still have a few things to cover before we can call it a day and close this chapter. The Cat class is another important entity that we will define next.

The Cat class

The cats in this game are pretty much like cats in real life—they sit around all day doing absolutely nothing. As such, our Cat class will inherit from GameObject and just add a couple of functions to take care of the cat's death. This is what the Cat class looks like inside Cat.h:

```
class Cat : public GameObject
{
public:
  Cat() : max_impulse_(0.0f), is_dying_(false)
  {
    type_ = E_GAME_OBJECT_CAT;
  }
  ~Cat();

  static Cat* create(GameWorld* game_world);

  virtual bool init(GameWorld* game_world);
  virtual void Update();
  virtual void Die();
  virtual void Dead();

  inline void SetMaxImpulse(float max_impulse)
    { max_impulse_ = (max_impulse_ >
    max_impulse) ? max_impulse_ : max_impulse; }

protected:
  float max_impulse_;
  bool is_dying_;
};
```

The Cat class defines just two variables: max_impulse_, to record the maximum impulse acting on the cat's body, and is_dying_, that is used to prevent multiple deaths (even though cats have nine!).

Let's now describe the lazy behavior of the cat by defining the Update function of Cat.cpp:

```
void Cat::Update()
{
  // no processing if invisible
  if(!m_bVisible)
    return;

  // call parent class' Update
  GameObject::Update();

  // if maximum impulses on cat exceed a threshold, its time to go!
  if(max_impulse_ > 10.0f)
  {
    Die();
  }
}
```

Aside from calling the Update function of the GameObject parent class, we monitor the maximum_impulse_ variable to determine whether this cat is under sufficient pressure to die. The maximum_impulse_ variable is updated inside the PostSolve function of GameWorld. We will take a look at that in a bit. The death of this cat is handled by the Die and Dead functions:

```
void Cat::Die()
{
  // sorry, you can't die more than once!
  if(is_dying_)
  {
    return;
  }

  is_dying_ = true;

  // animate the death & call function Dead afterwards
  CCActionInterval* die = CCEaseBackIn::create(
    CCScaleTo::create(0.5f, 0.0f));
  CCActionInterval* wait = CCDelayTime::create(2.0f);
  CCActionInstant* dead = CCCallFunc::create(this,
```

```
    callfunc_selector(Cat::Dead));
  runAction(CCSequence::create(die, wait, dead, NULL));
}

void Cat::Dead()
{
  // reposition the body out of the screen
  body_->SetTransform(b2Vec2(SCREEN_TO_WORLD(
    -SCREEN_SIZE.width * 0.5f), 0), 0);
  // deactivate the body so processing is stopped
  body_->SetActive(false);
  // hide the sprite so Update is stopped
  setVisible(false);

  // inform GameWorld about dying
  game_world_->CatHasDied();
}
```

When this cat must die, we set the appropriate flag to prevent multiple deaths, and then run a sequence of simple animations terminating in a callback to the `Dead` function. The `Dead` function repositions this cat's physics body outside the screen, makes it inactive, and makes the sprite invisible. Finally, this function also informs `GameWorld` that this cat has died.

The PostSolve function

In this game, we implement another callback function from the `b2ContactListener` class: the `PostSolve` function. This function is called after the solver has finished processing a given contact. We implement this function in our `GameWorld` class in the following way:

```
void GameWorld::PostSolve(b2Contact* contact,
  const b2ContactImpulse* impulse)
{
  b2Body* body_a = contact->GetFixtureA()->GetBody();
  b2Body* body_b = contact->GetFixtureB()->GetBody();

  // only react to contacts involving GameObjects
  if(body_a->GetUserData() == NULL || body_b->GetUserData() == NULL)
  {
    return;
  }

  // cast to GameObject
  GameObject* game_object_a = (GameObject*)body_a->GetUserData();
```

```
    GameObject* game_object_b = (GameObject*)body_b->GetUserData();

    // did this contact involve a cat?
    if(game_object_a->GetType() == E_GAME_OBJECT_CAT ||
      game_object_b->GetType() == E_GAME_OBJECT_CAT)
    {
      // cast to Cat
      Cat* cat = (Cat*)(game_object_a->GetType() ==
     E_GAME_OBJECT_CAT ? game_object_a : game_object_b);

      // save the maximum impulse on this fixture
      for(int i = 0; i < impulse->count; ++i)
      {
        cat->SetMaxImpulse(impulse->normalImpulses[i]);
      }
    }
  }
```

The purpose of implementing the `PostSolve` function is to determine the magnitude of the largest impulse acting on the fixture of the cat's physics body. This seems like the most logical way to determine if a cat should be killed, that is, the cat dies if the amount of impulses acting on its body exceeds a certain threshold.

Thus, we add the necessary conditions such that we only process `GameObjects`, and especially those that are `Cat` objects. We then pass the value of the normal impulse within the `b2ContactImpulse` object into the `SetMaxImpulse` function of the `Cat` class. The `SetMaxImpulse` function will set the `max_impulse_` variable that is queried in the `Update` function in the `Cat` class.

We have now completely defined the behavior for the cats within our *Angry Fish* game. What is left to be discussed is the spawning of the fish, and launching them by pulling and releasing the catapult.

Creating and spawning the fish

We already know the different kinds of fish that will be available to the player within a specific level. We have extracted the value set into the `ListOfFish` custom property of the world and stored it in the `fish_list_` variable of the `GameWorld` class. We now use this variable to create the various fishes in the `CreateFish` function of `GameWorld.cpp`:

```
  void GameWorld::CreateFish()
  {
    Fish* fish = NULL;
```

```
  // get integer list from comma separated string
  vector<int> fish_type_vec = GameGlobals::GetIntListFromString(fi
sh_list_);
  // this list consists of throwable fish
  num_throwable_fish_ = fish_type_vec.size();
  // initially, we will only have throwable fish
  num_total_fish_ = num_throwable_fish_;

  for(int i = 0; i < num_throwable_fish_; ++i)
  {
    // create each type of fish
    EFishType fish_type = (EFishType)fish_type_vec[i];
    switch(fish_type)
    {
    case E_FISH_SIMPLE:
      fish = Fish::create(this);
      break;
    case E_FISH_SHOOTING:
      fish = ShootingFish::create(this);
      break;
    case E_FISH_SPLITTING:
      fish = SplittingFish::create(this);
      break;
    case E_FISH_BOMBING:
      fish = BombingFish::create(this);
      break;
    case E_FISH_EXPLODING:
      fish = ExplodingFish::create(this);
      break;
    }

    if(fish != NULL)
    {
      // tell this fish it is throwable...default is false
      fish->SetIsThrowable(true);
      // initially no Update processing
      fish->setVisible(false);
      // add & save this fish
      addChild(fish, E_LAYER_FISH);
      fish_.push_back(fish);
    }

    fish = NULL;
  }
}
```

We pass in the `fish_list_` string into the `GetIntListFromString` function of the `GameGlobals` class to return a vector of `int`. Since the list contained only the type of fish, we can now simply iterate over the vector and create specific types of fish.

When we defined the `Fish` class, we discussed the use of the `is_throwable_` member variable. We set the fish created within this function as "throwable" fish. Thus, only these fish will be able to ask `GameWorld` to spawn the next fish when they have finished. We finally hide the fish before adding it to `GameWorld` and vector `fish_`.

Let's now look at the `SpawnFish` function that is called every time a fish finishes and when the level is first created:

```
void GameWorld::SpawnFish(float dt)
{
  // DON'T spawn if current_fish_ is out of bounds AND
  // if the current fish has not been fired
  if(current_fish_ >= 0 && current_fish_ < num_throwable_fish_ &&
    fish_[current_fish_]->GetHasBeenFired() == false)
  {
    return;
  }

  // if there are no fish left, its game over!
  if(++ current_fish_ >= num_throwable_fish_)
  {
    GameOver();
    return;
  }

  // spawn the current fish
  fish_[current_fish_]->Spawn();

  // weld the fish to the catapult...else it might fall off
  b2WeldJointDef weld_jd;
  weld_jd.Initialize(fish_[current_fish_]->GetBody(),
    catapult_body_, fish_spawn_point_);
  weld_joint_ = (b2WeldJoint*)world_->CreateJoint(&weld_jd);

  // welding complete, catapult ready
  is_catapult_ready_ = true;
}
```

The first condition ensures that the counter `current_fish_` doesn't violate any bounds and also that the current fish has not been fired before proceeding further. This function must also check to see whether there are any fish left to spawn. If not, it means that the player has run out of fish and has failed the current level.

If all is well, we call the `Spawn` function on the current fish. We then create a weld joint between the `catapult_body_` and the fish's body. A weld joint simply constrains all relative motion between two bodies, thereby welding them together. We need this because when the player pulls the catapult back, we don't want the fish to fall off the catapult. Once the weld joint is created, we set the `is_catapult_ready_` flag to `true`. We can now write the remaining code to pull and release the catapult.

Creating a mouse joint

Since the catapult is a physics body constrained by a revolute joint with a motor and limits enabled, it would be rather complicated to make it move in a non-physics way. Thus, we use the `b2MouseJoint` class provided by Box2D, which is specifically designed for a situation like ours. So, let's define the creation of the `b2MouseJoint` class in the `ccTouchesBegan` function in `GameWorld.cpp`:

```
void GameWorld::ccTouchesBegan(CCSet* set, CCEvent* event)
{
  if(is_catapult_ready_ && !mouse_joint_)
  {
    CCTouch* touch = (CCTouch*)(*set->begin());
    CCPoint touch_point = touch->getLocationInView();
    touch_point = CCDirector::sharedDirector()->
   convertToGL(touch_point);

    // convert from screen to physics co-ordinates
    b2Vec2 touch_world_point = b2Vec2(SCREEN_TO_WORLD(touch_point.x),
   SCREEN_TO_WORLD(touch_point.y));
    // only accept touches to the left of the catapult
    if(touch_world_point.x < catapult_body_->GetPosition().x)
    {
      // define the mouse joint's properties
      b2MouseJointDef mouse_jd;
      mouse_jd.bodyA = boundary_body_;
      mouse_jd.bodyB = catapult_body_;
      mouse_jd.target = touch_world_point;
      mouse_jd.maxForce = 10000;

      // create the mouse joint
      mouse_joint_ = (b2MouseJoint*)world_->CreateJoint(&mouse_jd);
    }
  }
```

```
        // touch the current fish
        if(current_fish_ >= 0)
        {
          fish_[current_fish_]->Touch();
        }
    }
```

We first check to see if the catapult is ready to accept touches, and if the mouse joint doesn't already exist. We then convert the touch point from screen coordinates to physics coordinates using the `SCREEN_TO_WORLD` convenience macro that you have seen in previous chapters.

We do any further processing only if the touch was to the left of the catapult. We now define an object of the `b2MouseJointDef` structure by filling in the `boundary_body_` and `catapult_body_` objects as the two bodies for the joint and—most importantly—the `touch_world_point` as the target for the mouse joint. We must also specify a maximum force for the mouse joint. We then create the mouse joint, like any other joint, by calling the `CreateJoint` factory function of `b2World`.

To move this mouse joint, we simply call the `SetTarget` function of the `b2MouseJoint` class, passing in the physics coordinates of the point touched by the player. Let's now define the `ccTouchesEnded` function to see how the catapult is released:

```
void GameWorld::ccTouchesEnded(CCSet* set, CCEvent* event)
{
  if(mouse_joint_)
  {
    // only release the catapult if it has been pulled
   beyond the minimum angle
    if(catapult_joint_->GetJointAngle() > MINIMUM_CATAPULT_ANGLE)
    {
      is_catapult_released_ = true;

      // destroy the weld joint
      if(weld_joint_)
      {
        world_->DestroyJoint(weld_joint_);
        weld_joint_ = NULL;
      }
    }

    // destroy the mouse joint
    world_->DestroyJoint(mouse_joint_);
    mouse_joint_ = NULL;
  }
}
```

We can only release the catapult if a mouse joint was used to drag it in the first place. We check whether the catapult has been dragged beyond a predefined minimum value. We do this because we don't want the fish falling right in front of the catapult, forcing the player to drag it at least enough to enable the fish to reach the scaffolding.

Based on this condition, we set the `is_catapult_released_` flag to `true` and delete the weld joint that we created in the `ccTouchesBegan` function. Also, now that the player has released the touch, we must destroy the mouse joint.

So far, we have discussed all the main aspects of gameplay and have a fully functional game with a wide variety of fishes, a revolute joint catapult, and a detailed level created with RUBE. I have skipped some code that deals with the creation of the environment and a few minor functions from the `GameWorld` class. I'm sure you can understand them by reading through the code and the comments provided.

I have included plenty of images for the building blocks in the source bundle for this chapter, so you can create as many levels as you need. However, you will have to purchase a licensed version of RUBE to export any of that level information.

Summary

With this chapter, we finish all the physics games in this book. I truly believe we have done quite well in this chapter. You have learned how much work is offloaded from the developers if we use a capable physics editor. You have learned about some of the versatile features of RUBE and created five beautiful levels with it. You have also learned about ray casting in Box2D, and used it to implement some simplistic explosions for our most "physical" physics game yet.

Our next chapter will be our last game in this book. It is a game that I have been personally looking forward to creating for a long time. I hope you will enjoy it as much as I will!

9
The Two Towers

The ninth chapter of this book brings us to the last game that we will develop. What better way to wind up the saga if not with an epic battle between good and evil? In this chapter, we will build a tower defense game. Personally, I really enjoy playing such games and have burned endless hours on them!

In this chapter, you'll learn:

- How to design scalable tower and enemy architecture
- How to implement basic gestures to spawn towers
- How to control the speed of actions and scheduler to speed-up gameplay

Introduction to Pumpkin Defense

If you love tower defense games as much as I do, then you know the sheer multitude and variety of the games available out there. My personal favorites include *Kingdom Rush, Fieldrunners, Plants vs. Zombies, TowerMadness*, and many more. *Pumpkin Defense* is a much simpler version of these games, but it indeed possesses the level design to be scaled up to a much larger and more intricate tower defense game.

The story is the same as always, there are evil creatures trying to cross their limits and reach the good stuff. In this case, the creatures are trying to eat a helpless pumpkin. Our job as players is to build towers along the enemy's path to kill them before they leech off the pumpkin.

We will discuss the following topics in this chapter:

- Define the XML architecture to describe the tower and enemy properties
- Define the XML architecture to describe the various waves in a given level
- Design a simple level describing the enemy's path in Tiled

- Define the behavior of the tower and enemy classes
- Implement a simple lightning bolt effect using `CCDrawNode`
- Implement wave and enemy spawning
- Implement gestures to spawn towers

This is what we will achieve by the end of this chapter:

Defining the properties of the tower

The basic characteristics of a tower can be summarized as follows:

- It will have a specified range
- It will fire at one or more enemies that enter its range
- It will do one or more kinds of damage to its enemies
- It will cost money to build or upgrade, and can be sold

Based on these characteristics, we shall define the following properties for a tower in our game:

- Physical damage
- Magical damage

- Speed damage
- Range of fire
- Rate of fire
- Cost to build

These properties are varied enough to build a simple yet interesting game. With the help of a skilled level designer, you can even make the player enjoy hours of satisfying gameplay.

Let's quickly take a look at the XML structure that is defined to accommodate the data for the towers in this game:

```
<TowerDataSetList>

  <TowerDataSet bullet_name="TD_bullet01.png" is_lightning="false"
    is_rotating="true">
    <TowerData sprite_name="TD_t01gun01.png" range="1.5"
      physical_damage="10" magical_damage="0" speed_damage="1.0"
      speed_damage_duration="0" fire_rate="1.5" cost="100" />
    <TowerData sprite_name="TD_t01gun02.png" range="2"
      physical_damage="25" magical_damage="0" speed_damage="1.0"
      speed_damage_duration="0" fire_rate="1.0" cost="175" />
    <TowerData sprite_name="TD_t01gun03.png" range="3"
      physical_damage="30" magical_damage="0" speed_damage="1.0"
      speed_damage_duration="0" fire_rate="0.5" cost="250" />
  </TowerDataSet>
  .
  .
  .
</TowerDataSetList>
```

The root element of this XML document is titled `TowerDataSetList`, which defines a list of `TowerDataSet` tags. A `TowerDataSet` tag represents nothing but the various levels or upgrades that a given tower can possess. For this game, I have defined that each tower will possess three levels or upgrades, each defined within a `TowerData` tag. The various attributes from the XML file are summarized in the following table:

Tag	Attribute	Description
TowerDataSet	bullet_name	This is the name of the sprite for the bullet shot by this tower
TowerDataSet	is_lightning	This is true if this tower will shoot a bolt of lightning
TowerDataSet	is_rotating	This is true if the tower's sprite will rotate towards its target

Tag	Attribute	Description
TowerData	sprite_name	This is the name of the sprite for this tower
TowerData	range	This is the range for this tower, in multiples of tile size
TowerData	physical_damage	This is the physical damage this tower will do to an enemy
TowerData	magical_damage	This the magical damage this tower will do to an enemy
TowerData	speed_damage	This is the amount by which this tower will slow down an enemy
TowerData	speed_damage_duration	This is the duration for which this tower will slow down an enemy
TowerData	fire_rate	This is the interval at which this tower will fire
TowerData	cost	This is the cost to build/upgrade this tower

For *Pumpkin Defense*, I used this architecture to create just three towers (with three upgrades each): one that does physical damage, one that does magical damage, and one that slows down the enemy for a given period of time. This information is stored in the `tower_data.xml` file inside the source bundle for this chapter. Incidentally, I gave the magical tower a cool ability of casting a lightning bolt at enemies.

All these properties are parsed and stored inside structs `TowerDataSet` and `TowerData` inside our global data class `GameGlobals`. Let's take a quick look at the declaration of these structures, starting with `TowerDataSet` in the `GameGlobals.h` file:

```
struct TowerDataSet
{
  char bullet_name_[256];
  bool is_lightning_;
  bool is_rotating_;
  vector<TowerData*> tower_data_;

  TowerDataSet() : is_lightning_(false),
  is_rotating_(false)
  {
    sprintf(bullet_name_, "%s", "");
    tower_data_.clear();
  }
```

```
    ~TowerDataSet()
    {
      for(int i = 0; i < NUM_TOWER_UPGRADES; ++i)
      {
        delete tower_data_[i];
      }
      tower_data_.clear();
    }
};
```

As you'd expect, the `TowerDataSet` structure mirrors the `TowerDataSet` tag. It contains a `char` array to store the bullet name and two flags to represent if this tower will rotate towards an enemy or if this tower will shoot bolts of lightning instead of bullets.

Finally, you will see a vector holding pointers to the `TowerData` objects. Let's glance at the `TowerData` structure from `GameGlobals.h`:

```
struct TowerData
{
  char sprite_name_[256];
  float range_;
  float physical_damage_;
  float magical_damage_;
  float speed_damage_;
  float speed_damage_duration_;
  float fire_rate_;
  int cost_;

  TowerData() : range_(0.0f),
  physical_damage_(0.0f),
  magical_damage_(0.0f),
  speed_damage_(0.0f),
  speed_damage_duration_(0.0f),
  fire_rate_(0.0f),
  cost_(0)
  {
    sprintf(sprite_name_, "%s", "");
  }
};
```

Once again, the `TowerData` structure is a mirror image of the `TowerData` tag. Its members are identical to the attributes of the `TowerData` tag detailed in the preceding code and hence we will skip discussing them.

What is important to note is that our static class `GameGlobals` maintains a vector named `tower_data_sets_` containing pointers to `TowerDataSet` objects. When the game is launched, the `LoadData` function from `GameGlobals` is called and the `tower_data.xml` file is parsed to fill up the `tower_data_sets_` vector with the relevant information. Whenever the player creates a new tower, that tower reads all its properties from one of the objects within this vector.

In a similar way, let's define the properties of the enemy.

Defining the properties of the enemy

The typical enemy will have the following characteristics:

- It will have health, armor (to prevent physical damage), and magic resistance (to prevent magic damage)
- It will have a certain movement speed
- It will do certain amounts of damage if it reaches the base
- It will have certain rewards on being killed

Based on these characteristics, we will define the following properties for an enemy in our game:

- Health
- Armor
- Magic resistance
- Speed
- Damage
- Reward

Let's now take a look at an excerpt from the `enemy_data.xml` file to see how we define the XML structure for the enemy data:

```
<EnemyDataList>
  <EnemyData animation="enemy_1" health="20" armor="0"
    magic_resistance="0" speed="0.8" damage="1" reward="10" />
  .
  .
  .
</EnemyDataList>
```

The root element of the document titled `EnemyDataList` defines a list of `EnemyData` tags, one for each type of enemy. The only property that we didn't discuss earlier is the one titled `animation`. This is nothing but the name of the sprite animation that will be played on this enemy's sprite.

Just like for the tower data, we have a similar `struct` named `EnemyData` defined in `GameGlobals.h` that will be populated as `enemy_data.xml` is parsed in the `LoadData` function of the `GameGlobals` class when the game is launched. This is what `EnemyData` structure looks like from `GameGlobals.h`:

```
struct EnemyData
{
  char animation_name_[256];
  int health_;
  int armor_;
  int magic_resistance_;
  float speed_;
  int damage_;
  int reward_;

  EnemyData() : health_(0),
    armor_(0),
    magic_resistance_(0),
    speed_(0.0f),
    damage_(0),
    reward_(0)
  {
    sprintf(animation_name_, "%s", "");
  }
};
```

Once again, since this `struct` is a mirror image of the `EnemyData` tag and the `GameGlobals` class maintains a pointer to an `EnemyData` object for each tag in a vector named `enemy_data_`. Let's now take a look at how these enemies are batched into waves and sent out; this is in our next section where we will define the XML structure for a typical level.

Defining the XML file for a level

We could just as easily have used a single XML file that gives us information on the enemy's path as well as the waves that will comprise the level. However, since we already have some experience on Tiled, we will use it to create the enemy path and use our XML file to store details about the waves for a given level.

As such, the XML file for a typical level contains information about waves in which enemies will attack the field and will look like this:

```
<Level cash="150">
  <Wave spawn_delay="2" enemy_list="0,0,0,0,0,0,0,0" />
  <Wave spawn_delay="3" enemy_list="1,0,1,0,1,0,1,0" />
  <Wave spawn_delay="1.5" enemy_list="0,0,1,0,0,1,0,0,1" />
  .
  .
  .
</Level>
```

The root element of the document titled `Level` contains an attribute to describe how much cash the player starts out with. We then have a number of `Wave` tags, each describing a single wave. Each `Wave` tag contains two attributes: `spawn_delay` and `enemy_list`. The `spawn_delay` attribute describes the number of seconds the game will wait before spawning the next enemy in the list. The `enemy_list` attribute describes a list of enemies comprising this wave. The values for the `enemy_list` attribute corresponds directly to the enemy data we defined in the *Defining the properties of the enemy* section. Thus, a value of `0` corresponds to the enemy described by the first tag in `enemy_data.xml`.

A given level's XML file is parsed when the `GameWorld` class is created and added to the scene. But before we look at the code where this happens, we first need to be able to represent a wave. Hence, we define a `struct` titled `Wave` in `GameWorld.h` as follows:

```
struct Wave
{
  int num_enemies_;
  int num_enemies_spawned_;
  int num_enemies_walking_;
  vector<Enemy*> enemies_;
  float spawn_delay_;

  Wave()
  {
    num_enemies_ = 0;
    num_enemies_spawned_ = 0;
    num_enemies_walking_ = 0;
    enemies_.clear();
    spawn_delay_ = 0.0f;
  }
};
```

The struct tiled Wave contains a vector of pointers to Enemy objects and a variable to represent the interval in which the enemies have to be sent out into the field. In addition to this, the struct tiled Wave also maintains various counters to track how many enemies have spawned and how many of them are still walking (ergo, not dead!).

We can now look at the CreateWaves function from GameWorld.cpp, where we parse the level file to create a vector of Wave objects for the given level:

```
void GameWorld::CreateWaves()
{
  // generate level filename
  char buf[128] = {0};
  sprintf(buf, "level_%02d.xml", GameGlobals::level_number_ + 1);

  // read file
  unsigned long size;
  char* data = (char*)CCFileUtils::sharedFileUtils()->
    getFileData(buf, "rb", &size);

  // parse file
  tinyxml2::XMLDocument xml_document;
  tinyxml2::XMLError xml_result = xml_document.Parse(data, size);

  CC_SAFE_DELETE(data);

  // print the error if parsing was unsuccessful
  if(xml_result != tinyxml2::XML_SUCCESS)
  {
    CCLOGERROR("Error:%d while reading %s", xml_result, buf);
    return;
  }

  tinyxml2::XMLNode* level_node = xml_document.FirstChild();
  // save the initial cash for this level
  cash_ = level_node->ToElement()->IntAttribute("cash");

  tinyxml2::XMLElement* wave_element = NULL;
  // loop through each Wave tag
  for(tinyxml2::XMLNode* wave_node = level_node->FirstChild();
    wave_node != NULL; wave_node = wave_node->NextSibling())
  {
    wave_element = wave_node->ToElement();
```

```
        // get list of enemy indices
        vector<int> enemy_list = GameGlobals::GetIntListFromString(
          string(wave_element->Attribute("enemy_list")));

        // createa a new Wave object
        Wave* wave = new Wave();
        // save the spawn delay & list of enemies for this wave
        wave->num_enemies_ = enemy_list.size();
        wave->spawn_delay_ = wave_element->FloatAttribute("spawn_delay");
        // create all enemies in advance
        for(int i = 0; i < wave->num_enemies_; ++i)
        {
          Enemy* enemy = Enemy::create(this, enemy_list[i]);
          wave->enemies_.push_back(enemy);
          addChild(enemy, E_LAYER_ENEMY);
        }

        ++ num_waves_;
        waves_.push_back(wave);
      }
    }
```

After all the `tinyxml2` jargon, the function proceeds to save the initial bounty or cash that the player has to spend. This, of course, is part of the level's XML so a level designer can leverage it. This is followed by a `for` loop that creates a `Wave` object for every `Wave` tag in this level.

A vector of integers named `enemy_list` is generated from the comma-separated string of values using a helper function from `GameGlobals` (as you've seen in previous chapters). The size of this list describes the number of enemies that this wave will spawn. The interval at which they will be spawned is parsed as well.

Finally, an object of type `Enemy` is created and pushed into the `enemies_` vector of `Wave`, before being added onto `GameWorld`. Since this is done for each wave for a given level, all the enemies for all the waves are added onto the node graph right at the start of the level. However, the `Enemy` class takes care that it does not get unnecessarily processed. We'll take a closer look in a later section when we define the enemy behavior.

For now, let's take a look at how the enemy path is designed in Tiled.

Designing the level in Tiled

Since we've already covered Tiled in an earlier chapter, we shall skip straight to the contents of the TMX file for a typical level. So, open up `level_01.tmx` and you should see something like this:

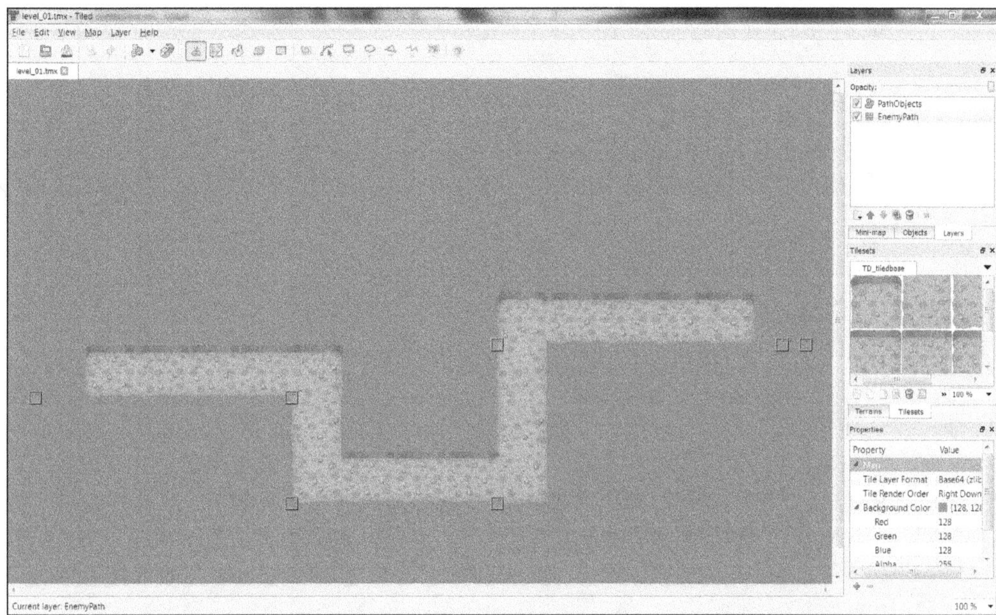

This particular TMX file has a tileset with a tile of size `90` pixels. The tileset is designed in such a way that you can create any path that you wish by simply placing the appropriate tile.

Now you can see in the **Layers** window that there are two layers defined: an object layer named `PathObjects` and a tile layer named `EnemyPath`. The `PathObjects` object layer will provide us with every point where there is a change in the enemy's direction, represented by objects titled `WalkPoint_0`, `WalkPoint_1`, `WalkPoint_2`, and so on.

In addition to this, the object layer also defines another object titled `Pumpkin` that is nothing but the screen position of the pumpkin for this level. Let's now briefly glance at the `CreateWalkPoints` function from `GameWorld.cpp` where the `CCTMXTiledMap` object is queried for the enemy's path:

```
void GameWorld::CreateWalkPoints()
{
```

```
    // parse the list of objects
    CCTMXObjectGroup* object_group =
      tiled_map_->objectGroupNamed("PathObjects");
    CCArray* objects = object_group->getObjects();
    int num_objects = objects->count();
    CCDictionary* object = NULL;

    for(int i = 0; i < num_objects; ++i)
    {
      object = (CCDictionary*)(objects->objectAtIndex(i));
      // save each WalkPoint's position for enemies to use
      if(strstr(object->valueForKey("name")->getCString(),
         "WalkPoint") != NULL)
      {
        enemy_walk_points_.push_back(ccp(
          object->valueForKey("x")->floatValue(),
          object->valueForKey("y")->floatValue()));
      }
    }

    num_enemy_walk_points_ = enemy_walk_points_.size();
  }
```

At the beginning of the function, we query `tiled_map_`; that is nothing but a member of class `GameWorld` and is a reference to the `CCTMXTiledMap` object. We get the object group titled `PathObjects` and consequently loop through each object within it.

All that we actually need from these objects is their position, and we take care of that by storing these positions in a vector named `enemy_walk_points_`. When an enemy is spawned or starts walking, it is passed this vector so it knows exactly what path it needs to follow.

With these sections covered, we have data to create towers and enemies. We have even written code to create a level, store the path that the enemies must follow, as well as create the waves in which they are to attack. We can now focus on the behavior of the towers and enemies by defining the `Tower` and `Enemy` classes, respectively.

The Tower class

Our `Tower` class will inherit from `CCSprite` and will contain all the properties that we saw in the `TowerDataSet` and `TowerData` structures. In addition to that, the `Tower` class will also possess the behavior of targeting and shooting enemies, as well as upgrading itself.

Let's take a look at how the `Tower` class is declared in `Tower.h`:

```
class Tower: public CCSprite
{
public:
  Tower();
  virtual ~Tower();

  static Tower* create(GameWorld* game_world,
    int type, CCPoint position);

  virtual bool init(GameWorld* game_world,
    int type, CCPoint position);
  // copy the data within the TowerDataSet library inside GameGlobals
  void SetTowerProperties();

  // update functions
  virtual void Update();
  void UpdateRotation();

  // functions that take care of upgradation & resale
  void Upgrade();
  void Sell();

  // basic tower behaviour
  void CheckForEnemies();
  void SetTarget(Enemy* enemy);
  void Shoot(float dt);
  void ShootBullet();
  void ShootLightning();

  // show the range for this tower
  void CreateRangeNode();
  void ShowRange();

  // accessors & mutators
  void SetSpriteName(const char* sprite_name);
  void SetIsRotating(bool is_rotating);

  inline void SetBulletName(const char* bullet_name)
    { bullet_name_ = bullet_name; }

  inline void SetIsLightning(bool is_lightning)
    { is_lightning_ = is_lightning; }
```

```
    inline bool GetIsLightning() { return is_lightning_; }

    inline void SetRange(float range) { range_ = range * TILE_SIZE; }
    inline float GetRange() { return range_; }

    inline void SetPhysicalDamage(float physical_damage)
      { physical_damage_ = physical_damage; }
    inline float GetPhysicalDamage() { return physical_damage_; }

    inline void SetMagicalDamage(float magical_damage)
      { magical_damage_ = magical_damage; }
    inline float GetMagicalDamage() { return magical_damage_; }

    inline void SetSpeedDamage(float speed_damage)
      { speed_damage_ = speed_damage; }
    inline float GetSpeedDamage() { return speed_damage_; }

    inline void SetSpeedDamageDuration(
      float speed_damage_duration) {
     speed_damage_duration_ = speed_damage_duration; }
    inline float GetSpeedDamageDuration() {
      return speed_damage_duration_; }

    inline void SetFireRate(
      float fire_rate) { fire_rate_ = fire_rate; }
    inline float GetFireRate() { return fire_rate_; }

    inline void SetCost(int cost) { cost_ = cost; }
    inline int GetCost() { return cost_; }

    inline int GetType() { return type_; }
    inline int GetLevel() { return current_level_; }

  protected:
    GameWorld* game_world_;

    // properties that define the tower
    // these take values straight from the TowerDataSet
      & TowerData structs
    int type_;
    const char* bullet_name_;
    bool is_lightning_;
    bool is_rotating_;
    float range_;
```

```
    float physical_damage_;
    float magical_damage_;
    float speed_damage_;
    float speed_damage_duration_;
    float fire_rate_;
    int cost_;

    // the level of upgrade the tower is currently at
    int current_level_;
    // the tower's current target
    Enemy* target_;

    // a sprite to represent the base for a rotating tower
    CCSprite* base_sprite_;
    // a node to draw the circular range for this tower
    CCDrawNode* range_node_;
};
```

The top half of the declaration of this class deals with the behavior of this tower. You can see the `Upgrade` and `Sell` functions that do exactly what their names suggest, followed by functions `CheckForEnemies`, `SetTarget`, and the shoot functions. You can also see a function that will create and show the range for this tower.

If you look at the bottom half of the class declaration, where all the member variables are declared, you will notice that they are identical to the member variables inside the `TowerDataSet` and `TowerData` structures. The `SetTowerProperties` function of the `Tower` class takes care of filling these member variables with values from `GameGlobals`, based on the `type_` and `current_level_` variables. Let's take a look at how this happens in `Tower.cpp`:

```
void Tower::SetTowerProperties()
{
  // tower properties are set from the TowerDataSet
    & TowerData structs
  SetBulletName(GameGlobals::tower_data_sets_[
    type_]->bullet_name_);
  SetIsLightning(GameGlobals::tower_data_sets_[
    type_]->is_lightning_);
  SetIsRotating(GameGlobals::tower_data_sets_[
    type_]->is_rotating_);
  SetSpriteName(GameGlobals::tower_data_sets_[
    type_]->tower_data_[current_level_]->sprite_name_);
  SetRange(GameGlobals::tower_data_sets_[
    type_]->tower_data_[current_level_]->range_);
  SetPhysicalDamage(GameGlobals::tower_data_sets_[
    type_]->tower_data_[current_level_]->physical_damage_);
  SetMagicalDamage(GameGlobals::tower_data_sets_[
```

```
    type_]->tower_data_[current_level_]->magical_damage_);
  SetSpeedDamage(GameGlobals::tower_data_sets_[
    type_]->tower_data_[current_level_]->speed_damage_);
  SetSpeedDamageDuration(GameGlobals::tower_data_sets_[
    type_]->tower_data_[current_level_]->speed_damage_duration_);
  SetFireRate(GameGlobals::tower_data_sets_[
    type_]->tower_data_[current_level_]->fire_rate_);
  SetCost(GameGlobals::tower_data_sets_[
    type_]->tower_data_[current_level_]->cost_);
}
```

If you remember, each tower is represented by a `TowerDataSet` object inside the `tower_data_sets_` vector. Hence, we use the `type_` variable as an index to access all the properties of a particular tower stored inside `tower_data_sets_`.

Notice how the `current_level_` variable is used to access the appropriate `TowerData` object. This structure makes it a no-brainer for us to implement the upgrades to our towers. We will simply increment the `current_level_` variable and call the `SetTowerProperties` function to equip this tower with the subsequent upgrade. This is exactly what we do in the `Upgrade` function from `Tower.cpp`:

```
void Tower::Upgrade()
{
  // are there any upgrades left?
  if(current_level_ >= NUM_TOWER_UPGRADES - 1)
  {
    return;
  }

  // increment upgrade level and reset tower properties
  ++ current_level_;
  SetTowerProperties();
  // debit cash
  game_world_->UpdateCash(-cost_);

  // reset the range
  range_node_->removeFromParentAndCleanup(true);
  range_node_ = NULL;
  ShowRange();
}
```

At the top of the function, we ensure that the tower doesn't upgrade infinitely. The `NUM_TOWER_UPGRADES` constant is assigned a value of `3` in `GameGlobals.h`. Then we simply increment the `current_level_` variable and call `SetTowerProperties`.

Since upgrades are not free, we must tell `GameWorld` exactly how much this particular upgrade has set the player back by calling the `UpdateCash` function. Finally, since an upgrade may increase the range of the tower, we remove the `range_node_` and call the `ShowRange` function. This will recreate `range_node_` and visually communicate to the player the increase in the tower's range after the upgrade.

Let's focus on the targeting functionality of a tower by defining the `CheckForEnemies` and `SetTarget` functions of the `Tower` class within `Tower.cpp`:

```
void Tower::CheckForEnemies()
{
  // only check the current wave for enemies
  Wave* curr_wave = game_world_->GetCurrentWave();
  if(curr_wave == NULL)
  {
    return;
  }

  // search for a target only when there isn't one already
  if(target_ == NULL)
  {
    // loop through each enemy in the current wave
    for(int i = 0; i < curr_wave->num_enemies_; ++i)
    {
      Enemy* curr_enemy = curr_wave->enemies_[i];
      // save this enemy as a target it if it still
     alive and if it is within range
      if(curr_enemy->GetHasDied() == false && ccpDistance(
     m_obPosition, curr_enemy->getPosition()) <= (
  range_ + curr_enemy->GetRadius()))
      {
        SetTarget(curr_enemy);
        break;
      }
    }
  }

  // check if a target should still be considered
  if(target_ != NULL)
  {
    // a target is still valid if it is alive and
   if it is within range
    if(target_->GetHasDied() == true || ccpDistance(
   m_obPosition, target_->getPosition()) > (
```

```
    range_ + target_->GetRadius()))
      {
        SetTarget(NULL);
      }
    }
}
```

The first thing this function does is query `GameWorld` for the wave that is currently on screen, and returns in the case that there is none. There might be a couple of occasions when the player might place a bunch of towers before the first wave has even started.

If the tower currently has no target, we must loop through each enemy in the current wave in an attempt to find if any are within the tower's range. We must also ensure that the tower doesn't target an enemy that is already dead. Once these two conditions are met, we save the enemy as this tower's target by passing a pointer to the enemy's object into the `SetTarget` function, before breaking from this loop.

In addition to finding enemies within range, the tower must also realize when enemies have escaped its range or have died and stop shooting at them. In the last part of the `CheckForEnemies` function, we check for conditions if an enemy has died or if it has walked out of the tower's range. If these conditions are met, we set the target to `NULL`.

Let's now look at the `SetTarget` function that is called from within the `CheckForEnemies` function in `Tower.cpp`:

```
void Tower::SetTarget(Enemy* enemy)
{
  target_ = enemy;

  if(target_ != NULL)
  {
    // shoot as soon as you get a target
    Shoot(0.0f);
    schedule(schedule_selector(Tower::Shoot), fire_rate_);
  }
  else
  {
    // stop shooting when you lose a target
    unschedule(schedule_selector(Tower::Shoot));
  }
}
```

The SetTarget function simply stores a reference to the enemy and either schedules or unschedules the Shoot function as required. Notice how the fire_rate_ variable is used as the interval for the schedule function. Things are about to get exciting now as we define the Shoot, ShootBullet, and ShootLightning functions.

The Shoot function simply checks the value of the is_lightning_ flag and calls either ShootBullet or ShootLightning. So, we're heading straight into the action with the ShootBullet function of Tower.cpp:

```
void Tower::ShootBullet()
{
  float bullet_move_duration = ccpDistance(m_obPosition,
    target_->getPosition()) / TILE_SIZE * BULLET_MOVE_DURATION;

  // damage the enemy
  CCActionInterval* damage_enemy = CCSequence::createWithTwoActions(
    CCDelayTime::create(bullet_move_duration), CCCallFuncO::create(
 target_, callfuncO_selector(Enemy::TakeDamage), this));
  target_->runAction(damage_enemy);

  // create the bullet
  CCSprite* bullet = CCSprite::create(bullet_name_);
  bullet->setScale(0.0f);
  bullet->setPosition(m_obPosition);
  game_world_->addChild(bullet, E_LAYER_TOWER - 1);

  // animate the bullet
  CCActionInterval* scale_up = CCScaleTo::create(0.05f, 1.0f);
  bullet->runAction(scale_up);

  // move the bullet then remove it
  CCActionInterval* move = CCSequence::create(
    CCMoveTo::create(bullet_move_duration, target_->getPosition()),
    CCRemoveSelf::create(true), NULL);
  bullet->runAction(move);
}
```

The ShootBullet function begins by calculating how long this particular bullet must travel to reach its target. The constant BULLET_MOVE_DURATION is defined in GameGlobals.h with a value of 0.15f and signifies the amount of time a bullet will take to travel a single tile.

Then, we inform the enemy that it must take some damage from this tower by creating a sequence of `CCDelayTime` and `CCCallFuncO`. We pass this tower's object as the `CCObject` pointer as we're using the `callfuncO_selector` selector type. The delay is to ensure that the enemy doesn't get hurt before the bullet has reached it.

We now create a new `CCSprite` for the bullet, using the `bullet_name_` variable as input, then add it to `GameWorld` and run a simple *move-remove* sequence on it. Next up is the function that shoots the bolt of lightning. First, let's take a detour to create a `Lightning` class that we can use inside the `ShootLightning` function.

The Lightning class

The `Lightning` class inherits from `CCDrawNode` because we refrain from using a `CCSprite` for something as electric and random as a bolt of lightning. Also, the length of the bolt of lightning might change over the course of time with the tower being upgraded.

Thus, the `init` function of the `Lightning` class looks like this, from the `Lightning.cpp` file:

```
bool Lightning::init(CCPoint from, CCPoint to,
  ccColor4F color, bool is_animated)
{
  if(!CCDrawNode::init())
  {
    return false;
  }

  color_ = color;
  GenerateKeyPoints(from , to);
  if(!is_animated)
  {
    DrawSegments();
  }
  else
  {
    schedule(schedule_selector(Lightning::DrawNextSegment));
  }

  return true;
}
```

The `init` function takes four arguments: the start and end points for the lightning bolt, the color of the bolt, and another parameter named `is_animated`. If this flag is `true`, the lightning bolt will be shown shooting out from source to destination and the lightning bolt will appear whole if this flag is `false`.

After storing the color, we call the `GenerateKeyPoints` function, passing in the source and destination of the lightning bolt. For a bolt that doesn't need animation, we draw all its constituent segments at once and for a bolt that is not animated, we schedule a function to draw a segment at each tick.

Let's now move on to the `GenerateKeyPoints` function of `Lightning.cpp` to define the shape of our lightning bolt:

```
void Lightning::GenerateKeyPoints(CCPoint from, CCPoint to)
{
  // how many key points do we need?
  float distance = ccpDistance(from, to);
  num_key_points_ = (int)(distance / LIGHTNING_KEY_POINT_DIST);

  CCPoint next_point = CCPointZero;
  // calculate the difference between two key points
  CCPoint delta = ccp( (to.x - from.x) / num_key_points_, (to.y -
from.y) / num_key_points_ );
  for(int i = 0; i < num_key_points_; ++i)
  {
    // add the delta
    next_point = ccpAdd(from, ccpMult(delta, i));
    // randomise the delta
    next_point.x += LIGHTNING_KEY_POINT_DIST * CCRANDOM_MINUS1_1();
    next_point.y += LIGHTNING_KEY_POINT_DIST * CCRANDOM_MINUS1_1();
    // save the key point
    key_points_.push_back(next_point);
  }
}
```

We first calculate the number of key points the lightning bolt will require to interpolate between the source and destination. We calculate the delta between each key point and run a loop to interpolate. In this loop, we also add a random factor to each segment's vertex in order to get the electric feel of a lightning bolt. Let's now take a quick glance at the `DrawSegments` and `DrawNextSegment` functions of `Lightning.cpp`:

```
void Lightning::DrawSegments()
{
  // draw all segments at once
```

```
    for(int i = 0; i < num_key_points_ - 1; ++i)
    {
      drawSegment(key_points_[i], key_points_[i+1], 6, color_);
    }
}

void Lightning::DrawNextSegment(float dt)
{
  // draw one segment at a time
  if(++ last_key_point_ >= num_key_points_ - 2)
  {
    unschedule(schedule_selector(Lightning::DrawNextSegment));
  }

  drawSegment(key_points_[last_key_point_],
    key_points_[last_key_point_+1], 6, color_);
}
```

As you can imagine, both these functions involve calls to the `drawSegment` function with the appropriate vertices for the segment. With this, we have achieved a simple and effortless lightning bolt effect. It's time now to head back to the `Tower` class and finish off the remaining functionalities.

With our shiny new bolt of lightning, the `ShootLightning` function from `Tower.cpp` looks relatively simple:

```
void Tower::ShootLightning()
{
  // damage the enemy
  CCActionInterval* damage_enemy = CCSequence::createWithTwoActions(
    CCDelayTime::create(LIGHTNING_DURATION * 0.5f),
 CCCallFuncO::create(target_, callfuncO_selector(
 Enemy::TakeDamage), this));
  target_->runAction(damage_enemy);

  // create the lightning without animation
  Lightning* lightning = Lightning::create(m_obPosition,
    target_->getPosition(), ccc4f(0.1098f, 0.87059f,
    0.92157f, 1.0f), false);
  game_world_->addChild(lightning, E_LAYER_TOWER - 1);

  // animate the lightning
  CCActionInterval* shake = CCSequence::create(
    CCMoveTo::create(0.01f, ccp(3, 0)), CCMoveTo::create(0.01f,
 ccp(-3, 0)), CCMoveTo::create(0.01f, ccp(0, 3)),
```

```
CCMoveTo::create(0.01f, ccp(0, -3)), NULL);
  lightning->runAction(CCRepeat::create(shake, 5));

  // remove the lightning
  CCActionInterval* wait_remove = CCSequence::createWithTwoActions(
    CCDelayTime::create(LIGHTNING_DURATION),
    CCRemoveSelf::create(true));
  lightning->runAction(wait_remove);
}
```

We begin by creating a sequence of actions so that the enemy is damaged, similar to the `ShootBullet` function. We then create a `Lightning` object with the tower's position as the source and the target enemy's position as the destination, before adding the lightning to `GameWorld`.

We also perform a simple shake effect to make the lightning bolt funkier, while running another action to remove it after a short delay. The last couple of functions in the `Tower` class are `CreateRangeNode` and `ShowRange`, which simply create an object of class `CCDrawNode` to draw a semi-transparent green circle with a border that signifies the range for this particular tower. Since you already know how to do that, we shall conclude the `Tower` class and move on to the next big class: `Enemy`.

The Enemy class

The `Enemy` class inherits from `CCSprite` just like the `Tower` class and will contain all the properties of the `struct` named `EnemyData`. The `Enemy` class defines the functionalities to make the enemy walk along the path dictated by the level, do damage if it reaches the end of the path, take damage from a tower, and die. Let's take a look at the class declaration in the `Enemy.h` file:

```
class Enemy: public CCSprite
{
public:
  Enemy();
  virtual ~Enemy();

  static Enemy* create(GameWorld* game_world, int type);

  virtual bool init(GameWorld* game_world, int type);
  // copy data within the enemy library inside GameGlobals
  virtual void SetEnemyProperties();

  // create & update the progress bar showing health left
  void CreateHealthBar();
```

```
    void UpdateHealthBar();

    // basic enemy behaviour functions
    void StartWalking();
    void FinishWalking();
    void DoDamage();
    void TakeDamage(CCObject* object);
    void Die();
    void TakeSpeedDamage(float speed_damage,
      float speed_damage_duration);
    void ResetSpeed(float dt);

    // accessors and mutators
    inline void SetAnimationName(const char* animation_name) {
      animation_name_ = animation_name; }

    inline void SetHealth(int health) { health_ = health; }
    inline int GetHealth() { return health_; }

    inline void SetArmor(int armor) { armor_ = armor; }
    inline int GetArmor() { return armor_; }

    inline void SetMagicResistance(int magic_resistance) {
      magic_resistance_ = magic_resistance; }
    inline int GetMagicResistance() { return magic_resistance_; }

    inline void SetSpeed(float speed) { speed_ = speed; }
    inline float GetSpeed() { return speed_; }

    inline void SetDamage(int damage) { damage_ = damage; }
    inline int GetDamage() { return damage_; }

    inline void SetReward(int reward) { reward_ = reward; }
    inline int GetReward() { return reward_; }

    inline float GetRadius() { return radius_; }
    inline bool GetHasDied() { return has_died_; }
    inline bool GetIsSlowed() { return is_slowed_; }

    inline void SetWalkPoints(int num_walk_points,
      vector<CCPoint> walk_points) { num_walk_points_ = num_walk_points;
   walk_points_ = walk_points; }

protected:
```

```
    GameWorld* game_world_;

    // properties that define the enemy
    // these take values straight from the EnemyData struct
    int type_;
    const char* animation_name_;
    int health_;
    int armor_;
    int magic_resistance_;
    float speed_;
    int damage_;
    int reward_;

    // more properties that define the enemy
    float radius_;
    int health_left_;
    bool has_died_;
    bool is_slowed_;
    int num_walk_points_;
    int curr_walk_point_;
    vector<CCPoint> walk_points_;

    // the progress bar showing health left
    CCProgressTimer* health_bar_;
};
```

The first half of this class declares the functions that will describe the enemy's behavior. In the second half of the class, you will find the variables that are copied from the `EnemyData` structure.

You can also see a vector of `CCPoint` named `walk_points_`. This vector will copy all the positions stored inside the `GameWorld` class' `enemy_walk_points_` vector we created while parsing the level's TMX file. We also have a `CCProgressTimer` object that we will use to show the enemy's health.

Without further ado, let's begin defining the enemy's behavior with the `init` function from `Enemy.cpp`:

```
bool Enemy::init(GameWorld* game_world, int type)
{
  if(!CCSprite::init())
  {
    return false;
  }
  // save reference to GameWorld & type of enemy
```

```
    game_world_ = game_world;
    type_ = type;
    // set the enemy's properties
    SetEnemyProperties();
    // fetch the first frame of animation so we know
      the size of this enemy
    CCAnimation* animation = CCAnimationCache::sharedAnimationCache()->
      animationByName(animation_name_);
    radius_ = ((CCAnimationFrame*)animation->getFrames()->
      objectAtIndex(0))->getSpriteFrame()->getOriginalSize().width/2;
    // hide the enemy till it starts walking
    setVisible(false);

    CreateHealthBar();

    return true;
  }
```

The `init` function is passed a reference to `GameWorld` and an integer variable named `type`. The wave feeds the value of the variable `type` into its `enemy_list_` vector when `GameWorld` parses the level's XML file. We will use this `type` variable as an index while copying the properties from `GameGlobals` to the `SetEnemyProperties` function.

The `init` function also saves the size of this enemy into a `radius_` variable to be used when being targeted by a tower. Since all enemies from all waves are added to the node graph right at the start of the level, we initially hide the enemies to avoid unnecessary rendering. We finally call the `CreateHealthBar` function to wind up the `init` function.

Since we haven't really covered the use of a `CCProgressTimer` object in previous chapters, let's take a look at the `CreateHealthBar` function of `Enemy.cpp` to see how this is done:

```
  void Enemy::CreateHealthBar(){
    CCPoint position = ccp(radius_, radius_ * 1.75f);
    // sprite behind the progress bar
    CCSprite* red_bar = CCSprite::create("red_bar.png");
    red_bar->setPosition(position);
    addChild(red_bar);
    // create a horizontal progress bar
    health_bar_ = CCProgressTimer::create(CCSprite::create("green_bar.
  png"));
    health_bar_->setType(kCCProgressTimerTypeBar);
    // progress bar takes values from 0 to 100
```

```
    health_bar_->setPercentage( (float)health_left_ / (float)health_ *
  100 );
    health_bar_->setMidpoint(ccp(0, 1));
    health_bar_->setBarChangeRate(ccp(1, 0));
    health_bar_->setPosition(position);
    addChild(health_bar_);
  }
```

We begin the function by calculating the position where this progress timer will be added. We then go ahead and add a background sprite to give us an illustration of the progress timer filling or emptying.

We then create a `CCProgressTimer` object, passing in a `CCSprite`, position it, and add it to the enemy. We set the type of this progress timer as `kCCProgressTimerTypeBar` and set the percentage of the progress timer that must be filled, where `0` is empty, `50` is half full, and `100` is completely full.

The next two lines are very important to understand as they define the behavior of a progress timer. The bar change rate, in the context of a bar type progress timer, controls the direction in which the progress timer will expand. For a vertically expanding progress timer, you'd have to set the bar change rate as (0, 1), and for a horizontally expanding one as (1, 0).

Once the bar change rate has decided whether the progress timer expands vertically or horizontally, the midpoint decides whether it should expand up-to-down or down-to-up for a vertically expanding bar, and left-to-right or right-to-left for a horizontally expanding bar. So if you want the progress timer to expand down-to-up your midpoint would have to be (1, 0).

To summarize the way in which these variables control the behavior of a progress timer, take a look at the following table:

Behavior	**Bar change rate**	**Midpoint**
Vertical (down = 0 percent to up = 100 percent)	(0, 1)	(0, 1)
Vertical (up = 0 percent to down = 100 percent)	(0, 1)	(1, 0)
Horizontal (left = 0 percent to right = 100 percent)	(1, 0)	(0, 1)
Horizontal (right = 0 percent to left = 100 percent)	(1, 0)	(0, 1)

The CreateHealthBar function then positions the progress timer and adds it to the enemy. Let's now look at the movement logic of the enemy in the StartWalking function of Enemy.cpp:

```
void Enemy::StartWalking()
{
  // show the enemy when it starts walking
  setVisible(true);
  // position the enemy at the first walking point
  setPosition(walk_points_[curr_walk_point_]);
  // calculate duration in terms of time taken to walk a single tile
  float duration = speed_ * ENEMY_MOVE_DURATION * (ccpDistance(
    walk_points_[curr_walk_point_ + 1],
 walk_points_[curr_walk_point_]) / TILE_SIZE);

  // walk to the subsequent walk point
  CCActionInterval* walk = CCMoveTo::create(duration,
    walk_points_[curr_walk_point_ + 1]);
  CCActionInstant* finish_walking = CCCallFunc::create(
    this, callfunc_selector(Enemy::FinishWalking));
  CCActionInterval* walk_sequence = CCSequence::createWithTwoActions(
    walk, finish_walking);
  // create a speed action to control the walking speed
  CCAction* walk_action = CCSpeed::create(walk_sequence, 1.0f);
  walk_action->setTag(ENEMY_MOVE_ACTION_TAG);
  runAction(walk_action);

  if(getActionByTag(ENEMY_ANIMATE_ACTION_TAG) == NULL)
  {
    CCActionInterval* animation = CCAnimate::create(
   CCAnimationCache::sharedAnimationCache()->
   animationByName(animation_name_));
    animation->setTag(ENEMY_ANIMATE_ACTION_TAG);
    runAction(animation);
  }
}
```

Remember how we hid the enemy in the init function? We set its visibility to true and position it at the first walk point only when it is commanded to start walking. This vector of walk_points_ is filled when the enemy is spawned by GameWorld.

We must now calculate the amount of time the enemy will take, walking at its current speed (speed_), to reach the next walk point. We create a simple CCMoveTo action and sequence it with CCCallFunc to call the FinishWalking function.

Here is the interesting part: we use CCSpeed to control the execution speed of the walk_sequence action interval. Thus, we pass walk_sequence into the CCSpeed::create function along with the default speed at which we want this action to run. Now, by calling the setSpeed function of the CCSpeed class, we can slow down or speed up the action passed to it. We also set the tag of this CCSpeed action to ENEMY_MOVE_ACTION_TAG so that we can fetch it later. Why would we need to control the speed of the enemy's movement? Well, because we have towers that can slow down enemies!

As you can see, we don't run really run the walk_sequence action (of type CCSequence) that we created, but instead run walk_action action (of type CCSpeed). This is because the CCSpeed action will internally step whatever action it is created with. Consequently, the CCSpeed action will end when its inner action ends.

With the movement logic figured out, we simply run a CCAnimate to animate this enemy and finish the StartWalking function. We shall now move to the function that gets called when the enemy reaches the destination walk point, that is, the FinishWalking function of Enemy.cpp:

```
void Enemy::FinishWalking()
{
  // can't stop walking if already dead
  if(has_died_)
  {
    return;
  }

  // move to the subsequent walk point
  ++ curr_walk_point_;
  if(curr_walk_point_ < num_walk_points_ - 1)
  {
    StartWalking();
  }
  // enemy has reached the pumpkin
  else
  {
    DoDamage();
  }
}
```

We first check if the enemy is still alive and return from the function if the enemy has died while walking from one walk point to the next. We then increment the current_walk_point_ counter and check whether there are any more walk points left.

If there is a subsequent walk point, we simply call the StartWalking function so that the enemy starts moving towards the next walk point. If there are no walk points left, it means the enemy has reached the pumpkin and we call the DoDamage function.

We have completed the movement logic for the Enemy class. Now we need to define the way in which the enemy damages the pumpkin, and the way in which the enemy takes damage from the towers. So let's begin with the DoDamage function of Enemy.cpp:

```
void Enemy::DoDamage()
{
  // inform GameWorld that damage must be done
  game_world_->EnemyAtTheGates(this);

  stopAllActions();
  // hide the enemy
  setVisible(false);
}
```

This is a very lazy enemy indeed. It uses CCMoveTo to walk and makes GameWorld do all the work. The enemy simply informs GameWorld that it has reached the pumpkin and passes in a reference to itself. It then hides itself, so no further processing is wasted on it.

Now, an enemy is damaged whenever a tower shoots a bullet or lightning bolt at it. This happens in the ShootBullet and ShootLightning functions (as we saw when defining the Tower class). These functions run a CCCallFuncO action to call the TakeDamage function of the Enemy class. So let's look at the way in which an enemy takes damage inside the TakeDamage function of Enemy.cpp:

```
void Enemy::TakeDamage(CCObject* object)
{
  // sometimes a dead enemy might get shot
  if(has_died_)
  {
    return;
  }

  Tower* tower = (Tower*)object;
  // calculate total damage taken by this enemy from a given tower
  float physical_damage = tower->GetPhysicalDamage() - armor_;
  float magical_damage = tower->GetMagicalDamage() - magic_
resistance_;
  float total_damage = (physical_damage > 0 ? physical_damage : 0) +
    (magical_damage > 0 ? magical_damage : 0);
```

```
    health_left_ -= total_damage;

    // slow the enemy if not already being slowed &
      if the tower has speed damage
    if(is_slowed_ == false && tower->GetSpeedDamage() < 1.0f)
    {
      TakeSpeedDamage(tower->GetSpeedDamage(),
     tower->GetSpeedDamageDuration());
    }

    // check if enemy should die
    if(health_left_ <= 0)
    {
      Die();
    }

    // update the health bar
    health_bar_->setPercentage( (float)health_left_ /
      (float)health_ * 100 );
}
```

This enemy cannot be damaged if it has already been killed. There may be times when multiple towers are simultaneously targeting this particular enemy. Then, the enemy might die by the first tower alone, and subsequent attacks must be ignored.

We now extract the `Tower` object passed to this function with the `CCCallFuncO` action that was run on this enemy object. We can then use this `Tower` object to calculate the total damage that this enemy must suffer. The total damage is the sum of all physical and magical damage levied upon this enemy, with the quantities of armor and magic resistance subtracted. We subtract this total damage from the enemy's remaining health.

Now, if the tower has the capability to slow the enemy, we must call the `TakeSpeedDamage` function, passing in the quantity of speed damage and the duration for which the enemy must be slowed. If the enemy has no health left, we must call the `Die` function. Finally, we update the progress timer used to display the enemy's health.

We saw two new functions in the `TakeDamage` function: `TakeSpeedDamage` and `Die`. Let's see how the enemy dies in the `Die` function of `Enemy.cpp`:

```
void Enemy::Die()
{
  // inform GameWorld that an enemy has died
```

```
    has_died_ = true;
    game_world_->EnemyDown(this);

    stopAllActions();
    runAction(CCSequence::createWithTwoActions(
      CCEaseBackIn::create(CCScaleTo::create(0.2f, 0.0f)),
  CCHide::create()));
}
```

We first set the `has_died_` flag and then inform the `GameWorld` that an enemy has died, passing in a pointer to this enemy's object. Then we must stop all actions running on this enemy and run one last action to animate this enemy's death and finally hide it.

Moving on to the `TakeSpeedDamage` function of `Enemy.cpp`:

```
void Enemy::TakeSpeedDamage(float speed_damage,
  float speed_damage_duration)
{
  // reduce the walking speed
  is_slowed_ = true;
  CCSpeed* walk_action = (CCSpeed*)getActionByTag(
    ENEMY_MOVE_ACTION_TAG);
  if(walk_action != NULL)
  {
    walk_action->setSpeed(speed_damage);
    // walking speed must return back to normal after
   certain duration
    scheduleOnce(schedule_selector(Enemy::ResetSpeed),
   speed_damage_duration);
  }
}
```

We begin by setting the `is_slowed_` variable to `true` so that the enemy isn't slowed more than once at a time. We then fetch the `CCSpeed` action and call its `setSpeed` function. This manipulates the speed of its inner action, which in our case is the enemy's walking sequence. We also schedule a function to return the enemy's walking sequence to normal speed after the specified duration in the `ResetSpeed` function.

So far, we have defined the movement, take damage, and do damage behaviors of our enemy—thereby completing the `Enemy` class. We still have a decent amount of work left. We need to stitch everything together in our `GameWorld` class, implement a simple gesture recognition mechanism to spawn our towers, and discuss a special feature at the end!

Spawning waves of enemies

Before we discussed the tower and enemy behaviors, we parsed an XML file containing the various hordes or waves of enemies that the player would have to face in a given level. Now it's time to code in the logic of actually spawning a wave and its constituent enemies. A wave may be spawned after any previous wave has completed or when the level has just begun. Let's take a look at the spawning of a wave in the `StartNextWave` function of `GameWorld.cpp`:

```
void GameWorld::StartNextWave(float dt)
{
  // increment the current wave index
  ++ curr_wave_index_;
  // are there any waves left?
  if(curr_wave_index_ >= num_waves_)
  {
    // level has completed
    GameOver(true);
  }
  else
  {
    // start the next wave in a few seconds
    curr_wave_ = waves_[curr_wave_index_];
    schedule(schedule_selector(GameWorld::SpawnEnemy),
      curr_wave_->spawn_delay_);
    UpdateHUD();

    GameGlobals::ScaleLabel(waves_label_);
  }
}
```

The reason that the `StartNextWave` function gets a `float dt` parameter is because this function is scheduled by `GameWorld` with a delay of a couple of seconds. If we don't do this, the waves would start immediately after one another and the player wouldn't really know the difference between first and second waves.

We begin the `StartNextWave` function by incrementing the counter pointing to the currently running wave. We then check if there are any waves left for the given level and if there are none then the level has been completed successfully.

If there are any waves left, we save a reference to the current wave into a pointer of type `Wave` named `curr_wave_`. We then schedule the enemies to be spawned with the delay that has been predefined for this given wave. We finally update the HUD that gives the player information on the number of waves left.

An important aspect of implementing waves is to check when a wave has finished. Now, if you remember the definition of the Wave structure, we have maintained counters to track the number of enemies spawned and the number of enemies that are walking. We will use the same variables to check whether the current wave has finished spawning its enemies. This happens in the CheckWaveCompletion function in GameWorld.cpp:

```
void GameWorld::CheckWaveCompletion()
{
  // wave has completed when all enemies have been spawned AND
  // when there are no enemies walking (cuz they're all dead!)
  if(!is_wave_starting_ && curr_wave_ && curr_wave_->
    num_enemies_spawned_ >= curr_wave_->num_enemies_ &&
 curr_wave_->num_enemies_walking_ <= 0)
  {
    // start the next wave
    is_wave_starting_ = true;
    scheduleOnce(schedule_selector(GameWorld::StartNextWave), 2.0f);
  }
}
```

As you can read in the comment at the start of the function, a wave ends when all the enemies have spawned and if none of them are still walking. These conditions are exactly what we check in the if conditional defining this function.

We also ensure that we don't check for wave completion when there isn't a current wave in memory or the current wave has not started (since the counters will be 0 and we'd get a fake positive). If the conditions are met, we schedule the next wave to start in a couple of seconds.

With the functionalities of the wave starting and wave ending covered, we can take a quick look at the SpawnEnemy function that is scheduled whenever a new wave starts. Let's take a look at the SpawnEnemy function in GameWorld.cpp:

```
void GameWorld::SpawnEnemy(float dt)
{
  // have all enemies of this wave been spawned?
  if(curr_wave_->num_enemies_spawned_ >= curr_wave_->num_enemies_)
  {
    // wave has finished starting
    is_wave_starting_ = false;
    // stop spawning enemies
```

```
        unschedule(schedule_selector(GameWorld::SpawnEnemy));
        return;
      }
      // fetch the next enemy in the list
      Enemy* enemy = curr_wave_->enemies_[
        curr_wave_->num_enemies_spawned_ ++];
      // tell the enemy where to go
      enemy->SetWalkPoints(num_enemy_walk_points_,
        enemy_walk_points_);
      // tell the enemy to start walking
      enemy->StartWalking();
      curr_wave_->num_enemies_walking_ ++;
    }
```

We begin the function by checking if all the enemies from this wave have already been spawned, in which case the wave has finished spawning its enemies. Then, we set the `is_wave_starting_` flag to `false` and unschedule the `SpawnEnemy` function before returning.

However, if there are any enemies left, we fetch the next one from the `enemies_` vector belonging to the current wave. Then we inform the enemy of the path it must follow by passing the vector of points (`enemy_walk_points_`) of `GameWorld` to the `SetWalkPoints` function of the `Enemy` class. We then instruct the enemy to start walking and increment the variable counting the number of enemies walking, before returning from the `SpawnEnemy` function.

This takes care of the enemy behavior throughout the game. We are now left with spawning the towers, for which we will write a simple class that recognizes gestures.

The GestureLayer class

For the scope of this game, we will observe just a few basic gestures. These are defined by an enum `EGestureType` in `GameGlobals.h` as follows:

```
enum EGestureType
{
  E_GESTURE_NONE = 0,
  E_GESTURE_TAP,
  E_GESTURE_SWIPE_UP,
  E_GESTURE_SWIPE_DOWN,
  E_GESTURE_SWIPE_LEFT,
  E_GESTURE_SWIPE_RIGHT,
};
```

As you can see, we will observe the player's touches for taps and swipes in four directions: up, down, left and right. A lot of developers have written great code that observes multiple taps, pinch-zoom gestures, panning gestures, and so on. I encourage you to plug them into this class and increase its capabilities.

Without further ado, let's take a look at the class declaration of `GestureLayer` from the `GestureLayer.h` file:

```
class GestureLayer : public CCLayer
{
public:
  GestureLayer();
  ~GestureLayer();

  static GestureLayer* create(CCObject* target, SEL_CallFuncO
handler);

  virtual bool init(CCObject* target, SEL_CallFuncO handler);

  // touch listeners
  virtual void ccTouchesBegan(CCSet* set, CCEvent* event);
  virtual void ccTouchesMoved(CCSet* set, CCEvent* event);
  virtual void ccTouchesEnded(CCSet* set, CCEvent* event);

  // accessors and mutators
  inline CCPoint GetTouchStart() { return touch_start_; }
  inline CCPoint GetTouchEnd() { return touch_end_; }
  inline EGestureType GetGestureType() { return gesture_type_; }

protected:
  void HandleTouch();

  // target to pass the gesture event to
  CCObject* target_;
  // function to call when gesture event occurs
  SEL_CallFuncO handler_;
  // member variables
  bool is_touch_active_;
  CCPoint touch_start_;
  CCPoint touch_end_;
  EGestureType gesture_type_;
};
```

Our `GestureLayer` class publicly inherits from `CCLayer`, and needs a target object and a callback function to be created. The target object will be the node that will be listening for gestures, and the callback function is the function that must be called when a gesture is detected. Before we move further, let me show you how this class is created in the `CreateGame` function of `GameWorld.cpp`:

```
void GameWorld::CreateGame()
{
    .
    .
    .
// create & add the gesture layer
  gesture_layer_ = GestureLayer::create(this,
    callfuncO_selector(GameWorld::OnGestureReceived));
  addChild(gesture_layer_);
    .
    .
    .
}
```

While creating the `GestureLayer` object, we pass in a reference to `GameWorld` as the target and a function callback to the `OnGestureReceived` function of `GameWorld`. Now, let's take a look at the touch callback functions of `GestureLayer.cpp`:

```
void GestureLayer::ccTouchesBegan(CCSet* set, CCEvent* event)
{
  CCTouch* touch = (CCTouch*)(*set->begin());
  CCPoint touch_point = touch->getLocationInView();
  touch_point = CCDirector::sharedDirector()->convertToGL(touch_
point);

  // first reset variables
  gesture_type_ = E_GESTURE_NONE;
  touch_end_ = CCPointZero;
  // start observing touch
  is_touch_active_ = true;
  // save first touch point
  touch_start_ = touch_point;
}

void GestureLayer::ccTouchesMoved(CCSet* set, CCEvent* event)
{
```

```
    CCTouch* touch = (CCTouch*)(*set->begin());
    CCPoint touch_point = touch->getLocationInView();
    touch_point = CCDirector::sharedDirector()->convertToGL(
      touch_point);

    // save subsequent touch
    touch_end_ = touch_point;
    HandleTouch();
}

void GestureLayer::ccTouchesEnded(CCSet* set, CCEvent* event)
{
    CCTouch* touch = (CCTouch*)(*set->begin());
    CCPoint touch_point = touch->getLocationInView();
    touch_point = CCDirector::sharedDirector()->convertToGL(
      touch_point);

    // save subsequent touch
    touch_end_ = touch_point;
    HandleTouch();

    // stop observing touch
    is_touch_active_ = false;
}
```

As you can see, these functions are run-of-the-mill touch functions that store the initial and subsequent touches while calling the `HandleTouch` function. The `HandleTouch` function recognizes all the gestures:

```
void GestureLayer::HandleTouch()
{
    // don't do anything if not observing touch
    if(is_touch_active_ == false)
    {
      return;
    }

    // check for a single tap
```

```
    if(ccpFuzzyEqual(touch_start_, touch_end_, 1))
    {
      gesture_type_ = E_GESTURE_TAP;
      (target_->*handler_)(this);
      is_touch_active_ = false;
      return;
    }

    // calculate distance between first and last touch
    CCPoint touch_difference = ccpSub(touch_end_, touch_start_);
    // horizontal swipe
    if(fabs(touch_difference.x) > MIN_GESTURE_DISTANCE)
    {
      gesture_type_ = (touch_difference.x > 0) ? E_GESTURE_SWIPE_RIGHT
  : E_GESTURE_SWIPE_LEFT;
      (target_->*handler_)(this);
      is_touch_active_ = false;
      return;
    }
    // vertical swipe
    if(fabs(touch_difference.y) > MIN_GESTURE_DISTANCE)
    {
      gesture_type_ = (touch_difference.y > 0) ? E_GESTURE_SWIPE_UP :
  E_GESTURE_SWIPE_DOWN;
      (target_->*handler_)(this);
      is_touch_active_ = false;
      return;
    }
  }
```

The first type of gesture we check is a single tap. Quite simply, this would happen if the touch start and end points are at the same point. Yet we've given the comparison a slight tolerance.

In the swipe gestures, we fetch the distance between the first and last touch and compare with a predefined constant, `MIN_GESTURE_DISTANCE` (defined as `10` pixels in `GameGlobals.h`). If the distance is greater, we have a swipe. The code that follows that condition basically narrows it down to one of four directions.

All these conditionals call the same callback function that is passed to this class at the time of creation. Also, the callback function is passed a reference to this `GestureLayer` class as an argument, since this was a callback of type `SEL_CallFuncO`. This sums up our gesture `recognition` class, but we still have to implement the spawning of towers based on these gestures. Before we move forward, let's take a quick look at the function passed to `GestureLayer` when `GameWorld` created the `OnGestureReceived` function:

```
void GameWorld::OnGestureReceived(CCObject* sender)
{
  GestureLayer* gesture_layer = (GestureLayer*)sender;
  // call the respective gesture's handler
  switch(gesture_layer->GetGestureType())
  {
  case E_GESTURE_TAP:
    HandleTap(gesture_layer->GetTouchStart());
    break;

  case E_GESTURE_SWIPE_UP:
    HandleSwipeUp();
    break;

  case E_GESTURE_SWIPE_DOWN:
    HandleSwipeDown();
    break;

  case E_GESTURE_SWIPE_LEFT:
    HandleSwipeLeft();
    break;

  case E_GESTURE_SWIPE_RIGHT:
    HandleSwipeRight();
    break;
  }
}
```

The `OnGestureReceived` function first casts from `CCObject` to `GestureLayer`, so we have all the information we require to handle the gesture detected. Based on the type of gesture, we have a function to handle each type. Rest assured, we shall discuss them in detail in our next section when we write the logic to spawn our towers.

Spawning the towers

To spawn a tower, the player must first tap somewhere on the map to select the location where they want the tower placed. Once an area of the map has been tapped, the following tower selection menu will be shown:

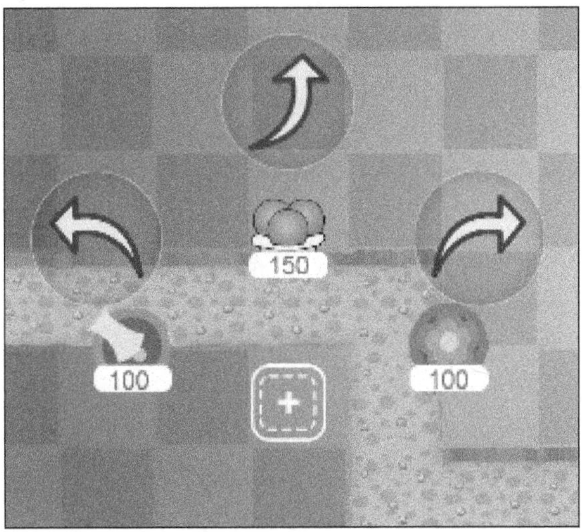

As you can see in the previous screenshot, the player is shown an arrow for each tower. This indicates the direction in which the player must swipe in order to spawn the tower at the specified location. The player can swipe anywhere on the screen and the respective tower will be spawned at the location.

The class responsible for creating that menu, as well as the tower upgrade menu, is defined in the `TowerMenu.h` and `TowerMenu.cpp` files. I will skip discussing this class, since it is quite a straightforward class that I'm sure you will be able to wrap your head around with ease.

Now, the tower selection menu shows up when the player taps on the map. Tap gestures are forwarded to the `HandleTap` function of the `GameWorld` class:

```
void GameWorld::HandleTap(CCPoint position)
{
  // get the touch coordinates with respect to the tile map
  CCPoint touch_point = tiled_map_->convertToNodeSpace(position);
  CCPoint tile_coord = ccp(GET_COL_FOR_X(touch_point.x),
    GET_ROW_FOR_Y(touch_point.y, MAX_ROWS));
  touch_point = ccpMult(tile_coord, TILE_SIZE);
```

```
touch_point.y = SCREEN_SIZE.height - touch_point.y;

// check if the touched tile is empty
int tile_GID = tmx_layer_->tileGIDAt(tile_coord);
// if the touched tile is empty, show the tower placement menu
if(tile_GID == 0)
{
  // check to ensure only one menu is visible at a time
  if(tower_menu_->placement_node_->isVisible() == false &&
 tower_menu_->maintenance_node_->isVisible() == false)
  {
    tower_menu_->ShowPlacementMenu(touch_point);
    // show the grid
    grid_node_->setVisible(true);
  }
}
// a tower exists on the touched tile
else if(tile_GID >= TOWER_GID)
{
  int tower_index = tile_GID - TOWER_GID;
  // first check bounds and then check to ensure only one
 menu is visible at a time
  if(tower_index >= 0 && tower_index < num_towers_ &&
 tower_menu_->maintenance_node_->isVisible() == false &&
 tower_menu_->placement_node_->isVisible() == false)
  {
    // show the tower's current range
    towers_[tower_index]->ShowRange();
    tower_menu_->ShowMaintenanceMenu(touch_point, tower_index,
   towers_[tower_index]->GetType(),
towers_[tower_index]->GetLevel());
  }
}

// hide the tower placement menu if it is visible
if(tower_menu_->placement_node_->isVisible())
{
  tower_menu_->HidePlacementMenu();
  grid_node_->setVisible(false);
}
// hide the tower maintenance menu if it is visible
if(tower_menu_->maintenance_node_->isVisible())
```

```
        {
          tower_menu_->HideMaintenanceMenu();
        }
    }
```

In the preceding code, we take the location of the touch (that is, screen coordinates), convert into coordinates local to the Tiled map, and store it into the `touch_point` variable. We then calculate the tile coordinate where the preceding tap occurred. Now we know exactly where we need to place our tower.

With the tile coordinates in hand, we first query the Tiled map to see if the requested tile is free. The requested tile won't be free if there is an enemy path tile or another tower placed at that tile coordinate. Thus, if the GID at the requested tile is `0` we know that the tile is empty, and we show the tower selection/placement menu.

If the GID at the requested tile is not 0, it could mean that an enemy path tile or a tower exists there. To find out if there is a tower placed at the tile, we compare the GID with the `TOWER_GID` constant that is defined as `100` in `GameGlobals.h`.

Whenever we place a tower at a certain tile, we save a certain GID at that tile. We shall look into this in more detail when we discuss the `PlaceTower` function from `GameWorld`. For now, all we need to know is that the GID will point us to the tower placed at the requested tile.

Once we fetch the index of the tower from within `GameWorld` class' `towers_` vector, we simply show the tower maintenance menu. From the tower maintenance menu, the player can choose to either upgrade or sell the respective tower. Lastly, we hide any menus that might have been enabled in any previous taps on the screen.

Now that we've discussed what happens on a tap gesture, let's take a look at the `HandleSwipeUp` function that is called when an upward swipe is detected:

```
void GameWorld::HandleSwipeUp()
{
  // return if the tower placement menu is not active
  if(tower_menu_->placement_node_->isVisible() == false)
  {
    return;
  }

  // place the tower with specified type at specified position
  PlaceTower(1, tower_menu_->placement_node_->getPosition());
  tower_menu_->HidePlacementMenu();
  grid_node_->setVisible(false);
}
```

The player can only place a tower if the tower selection menu is visible; swipes at other times must simply be ignored. This function internally calls the `PlaceTower` function, passing in the type of tower that needs to be placed along with the location at which it needs to be placed. Without further ado, let's look at the `PlaceTower` function from `GameWorld.cpp` to wrap up our tower spawning section:

```
void GameWorld::PlaceTower(int type, CCPoint position)
{
  // can the player afford this tower?
  if(cash_ < GameGlobals::tower_data_sets_[type]->tower_data_[0]-
>cost_)
  {
    return;
  }

  // create a new Tower object & add it into the vector of towers
  Tower* tower = Tower::create(this, type, position);
  addChild(tower, E_LAYER_TOWER);
  ++ num_towers_;
  towers_.push_back(tower);

  // save tower's information into the tile map
  position = tiled_map_->convertToNodeSpace(position);
  CCPoint tile_coord = ccp(GET_COL_FOR_X(position.x), GET_ROW_
FOR_Y(position.y, MAX_ROWS));
  tmx_layer_->setTileGID(TOWER_GID + (num_towers_ - 1), tile_coord);

  // debit cash
  UpdateCash(-tower->GetCost());
  UpdateHUD();
  // show the range for this tower
  tower->ShowRange();

  // hide the grid now that the tower has been placed
  grid_node_->setVisible(false);
}
```

First off, we return from the `PlaceTower` function if the player cannot afford to place the selected tower. We then create a brand new `Tower` object, passing in a reference to `GameWorld`, the type of the tower, and its position. We then add it both to the node graph as well as the `GameWorld` class' vector by the name `towers_`.

We then calculate the position of the tower with respect to the Tiled map and then use that quantity to calculate the tile coordinates at that point. With the tile coordinates in place, we save this tower's index into the Tiled map. Since Tiled will save the tileset for this tile layer from `0 -> number of tiles`, we offset our tower's index by the constant `TOWER_GID`. That is why we use the following line in the `HandleTap` function:

```
int tower_index = tile_GID - TOWER_GID;
```

Now that we've saved this tower's index safely into the Tiled map for later, we only need to debit the player's cash and update the HUD. We also show the newly placed tower's range.

With this, we wind up our tower placing logic. By now, we have a functional and enjoyable tower defense game—complete with upgradable towers and levels with configurable paths and limitless waves of enemies. We can add one more neat little feature though—a feature that is not uncommon in tower defense games—the fast-forward feature!

Fast forwarding the gameplay

Well, this could be quite a complicated task to achieve based on the exact type of result you wish to achieve. If you have schedulers that you want to speed up, you'd have to adjust each of your scheduler's delays by scheduling them yet again (with the adjusted delay) on each of your nodes. Secondly, you would have to speed up each running animation on each of your game's entities, either by using `CCSpeed` on each action or by using the same logic as the schedulers.

Fortunately, there is an unbelievably painless way to accomplish a fast-forward effect with Cocos2d-x, but it comes with a slight drawback. We can actually control the main scheduler's time scale. The main scheduler that resides within `CCDirector`, the one that is responsible for scheduling each scheduler within the application (including the `CCActionManager`), can have its speed controlled by a single function!

Let's just see how it's done:

```
CCDirector::sharedDirector()->getScheduler()->
  setTimeScale(2.0f);
```

The `CCScheduler` class internally multiplies time scale with the delta time, on each tick of the engine. The time scale for a `CCScheduler` class possesses a default value `1.0f`. When we pass it a value `2.0f`, the resultant delta time variable within the main update loop of `CCScheduler` is doubled.

Thus, by doubling the time scale, you're not really calling twice as many update functions at each tick. You're just telling each scheduler and action that time is moving twice as fast. If you've looked at the code of any of the `CCAction` subclasses, you will know that the delta time variable is key to each calculation within each action. Thus, by doubling the value of delta time, we double the result of each calculation within the engine—be it movement, scaling, rotating, or sprite animations.

This is also the drawback of using this method to speed-up the gameplay. Along with our enemies and towers, even our HUD animates twice as fast, just as our tower menus. But for this game, that is a small trade-off to achieve a really handy feature that most tower defense players have come to expect.

With that little section, we have come to the end of our chapter and sadly the last game of this book. I have skipped discussing a few sections, such as the tower placement and maintenance menus, the HUD, and loading of data. I suppose you should be able to figure these things out for yourself by now.

What you have achieved is a primer to implement an enjoyable tower defense game. I've even included two sample paths in the source bundle so you can create and add a couple of more levels and see how easily you can scale the game.

Also, if you like developing tower defense games, I have a few suggestions to make your towers a bit more diverse. You could add an area of effect type of tower that damages all enemies within a range. You could also add properties to bullets so that they cause damage over time.

Similar improvisations could be made to enemies as well. For example, you could give enemies a property to suddenly speed up while walking.

Summary

With this chapter, we finish all the games of this book. We used a bunch of things you learned in the previous chapters, including parsing XMLs and TMXs. We created simple, yet scalable, tower and enemy designs, complete with tower upgrades. We wrote a basic gesture recognition mechanism to spawn the towers in the game and did some good old-fashioned drawing. Finally, you have learned how easily you could do something as complicated as speeding up gameplay. This being our last game, I had some great fun developing and writing about it. I hope you did too!

In the next chapter, we will use this amazing cross-platform engine of ours to build one of our games on Android and Windows Phone 8!

10
Cross-platform Building

In the previous chapters, you learned how to leverage the power and versatility of Cocos2d-x to create an array of games. However, one of the reasons Cocos2d-x became so famous and versatile—aside from the fact that it is fast, powerful, and open source—is the fact that it is cross-platform. In this chapter, we'll leverage this awesome aspect of Cocos2d-x to build one of our games on Android and Windows Phone 8!

In this chapter, you'll learn about the following topics:

- Setting up the environment for Android
- Building one of our existing games on Android
- Setting up the environment for Windows Phone 8
- Building one of our existing games on Windows Phone 8

Setting up the environment for Android

At this point in the timeline of technological evolution, Android needs no introduction. This mobile operating system was acquired by Google, and it has reached far and wide across the globe. It is now one of the top choices for application developers and game developers. With octa-core CPUs and ever-powerful GPUs, the sheer power offered by Android devices is a motivating factor!

While setting up the environment for Android, you have more choices than any other mobile development platform. Your workstation could be running any of the three major operating systems (Windows, Mac OS, or Linux) and you would be able to build to Android just fine. Since Android is not fussy about its build environment, developers mostly choose their work environment based on which other platforms they will be developing for.

As such, you might choose to build for Android on a machine running Mac OS since you would be able to build for iOS and Android on the same machine. The same applies for a machine running Windows as well. You would be able to build for both Android and Windows Phone. Although building for Windows Phone 8 requires you to have at least Windows 8 installed. We will discuss more on that later. Let's begin listing down the various software required to set up the environment for Android.

Java Development Kit 7+

Since you already know that Java is the programming language used within the Android SDK, you must ensure that you have the environment set up to compile and run Java files. So go ahead and download the **Java Development Kit (JDK)** version 6 or later. You can download and install a **Standard Edition (SE)** version from the page available at the following link:

`http://www.oracle.com/technetwork/java/javase/downloads/index.html`

Mac OS comes with JDK installed and as such, you won't have to follow this step if you're setting up your development environment on a Mac.

The Android SDK

Once you've downloaded JDK, it's time to download the Android SDK from the following URL:

`http://developer.android.com/sdk/index.html`

If you're installing the Android SDK on Windows, a custom installer is provided that will take care of downloading and setting up the required parts of the Android SDK for you. For other operating systems, you can choose to download the respective archive files and extract them at the location of your choice.

Eclipse or the ADT bundle

Eclipse is the most commonly used IDE when it comes to Android application development. You can choose to download a standard Eclipse IDE for Java developers and then install the ADT plugin into Eclipse, or you can download the ADT bundle, which is a specialized version of Eclipse with the ADT plugin preinstalled.

At the time of writing this chapter, the Android developer site had already deprecated ADT in favor of Android Studio. As such, we will choose the former approach for setting up our environment in Eclipse.

You can download and install the standard Eclipse IDE for Java Developers for your specific machine from the following URL:

http://www.eclipse.org/downloads/

ADT plugin for Eclipse

Once you've downloaded Eclipse, you must now install a custom plugin for Eclipse: **Android Development Tools (ADT)**. Visit the following URL and follow the detailed instructions that will help you install the ADT plugin into Eclipse:

http://developer.android.com/sdk/installing/installing-adt.html

Once you've followed the instructions on the preceding page, you will need to inform Eclipse about the location of the Android SDK that you downloaded earlier. So, open up the **Preferences** page for Eclipse and go to the location where you've placed the Android SDK in the **Android** section.

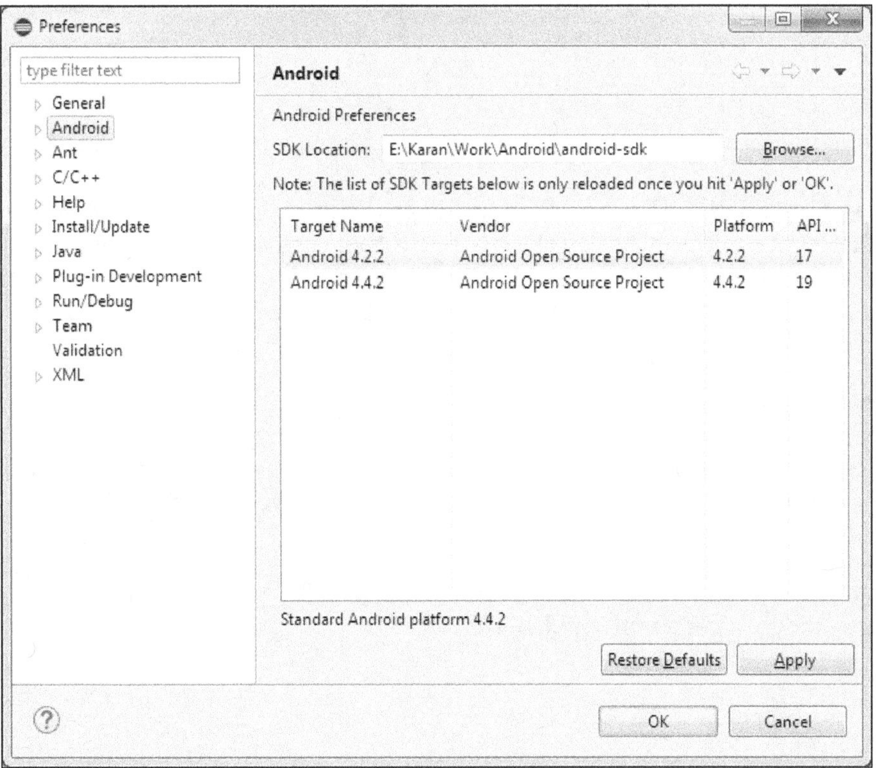

With that done, we can now fire up the SDK Manager to install a few more necessary pieces of software. To launch the Android SDK Manager, select **Android SDK Manager** from the **Windows** menu in Eclipse. The resultant window should look something like this:

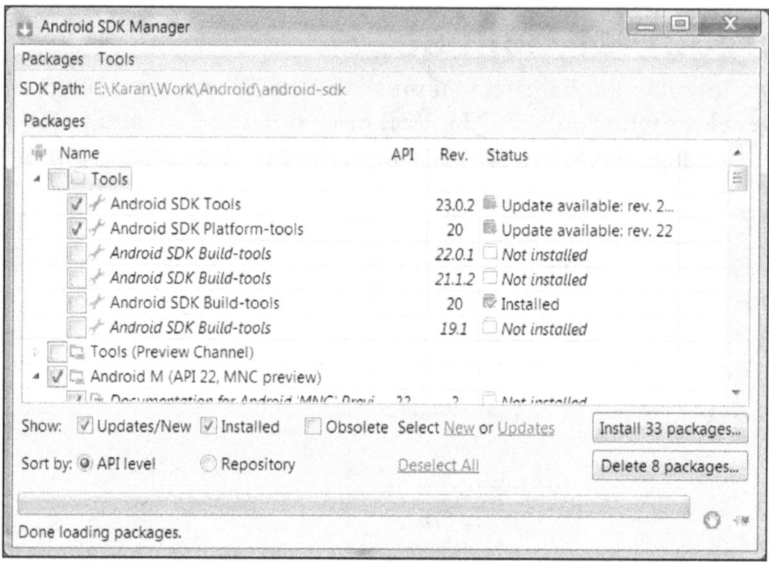

By default, you will see a whole lot of packages selected, out of which **Android SDK Platform-tools** and **Android SDK Build-tools** are necessary. From the rest, you must select at least one of the target Android platforms. An additional package will be required if you're target environment is Windows: **Google USB Driver**. It is located under the **Extras** list.

I would suggest skipping downloading the documentation and samples. If you already have an Android device, I would go one step further and suggest you skip downloading the system images as well. However, if you don't have an Android device, you will need at least one system image so that you can at least test on an emulator.

Once you've chosen from the various platforms needed, proceed to install the packages and you get a window like this:

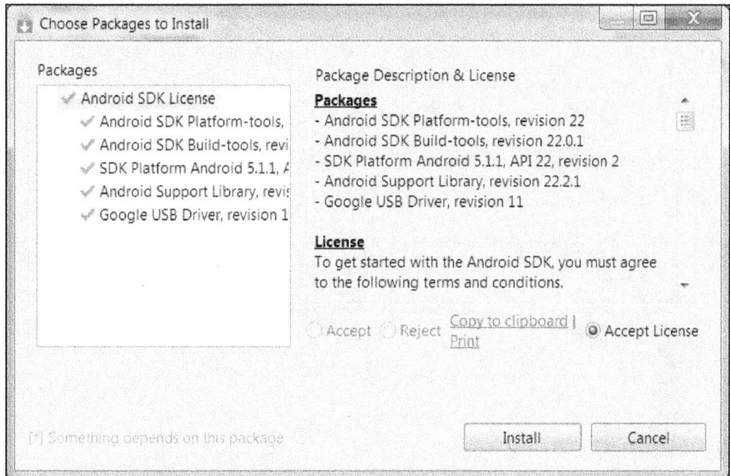

Now, you must select **Accept License** and click on the **Install** button to install the respective packages. Once these packages have been installed, you have to add their locations to the path variable on your respective machines.

For Windows, modify your path variable (go to **Properties** | **Advance Settings** | **Environment Variables**) to include the following:

```
;E:\Android\android-sdk\platform-tools
```

For Mac OS, you can add the following line to the `.bash_profile` file found under the home directory:

```
export PATH=$PATH:/Android/android-sdk/platform-tools/
```

The preceding line can also be added to the `.bash_rc` file found under the home directory on your Linux machine. At this point, you can use Eclipse for Android development.

Installing Cygwin for Windows

Developers working on Linux can skip this step as most Linux distributions come with the `make` utility. Also, developers working on Mac OS may download Xcode from the Mac App Store, which will install the `make` utility on their respective Macs.

We need to install Cygwin on Windows specifically for the GNU `make` utility. So, go to the following URL and download the installer for Cygwin:

`http://www.cygwin.com/install.html`

Once you've run the `.exe` file that you downloaded and get a window like this, click on the **Next** button:

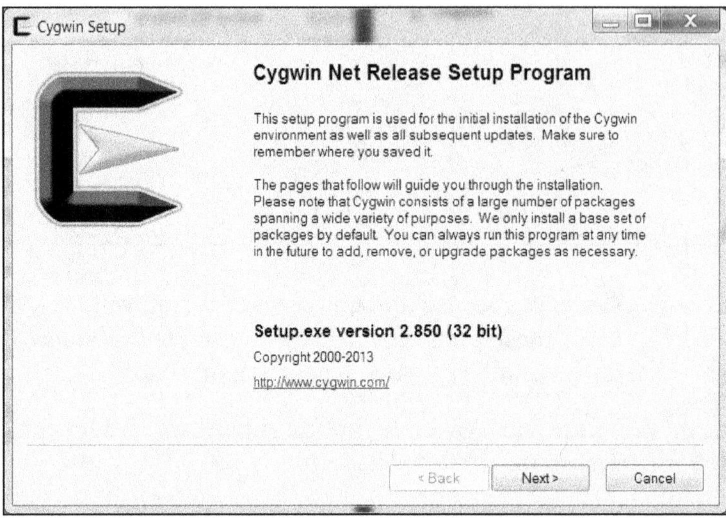

The next window will ask how you would like to install the required packages. Here, select option **Install from Internet** and click on **Next**:

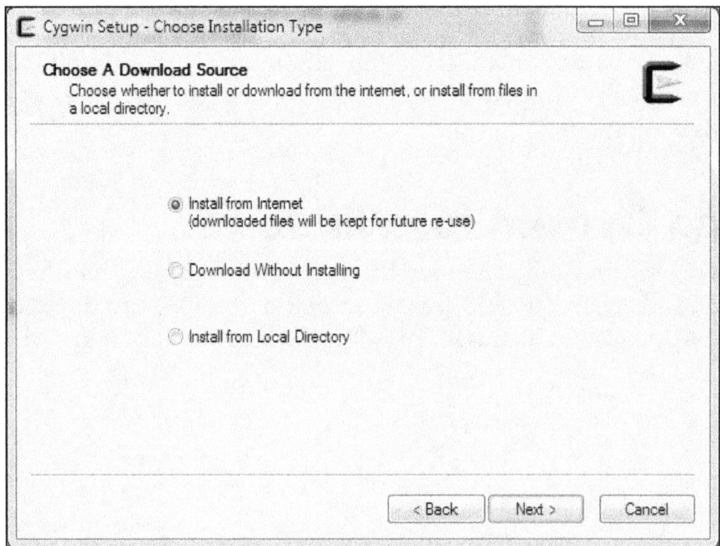

The next window will ask where you would like to install Cygwin. I'd recommend leaving it at the default value unless you have a reason to change it. Proceed by clicking on **Next**.

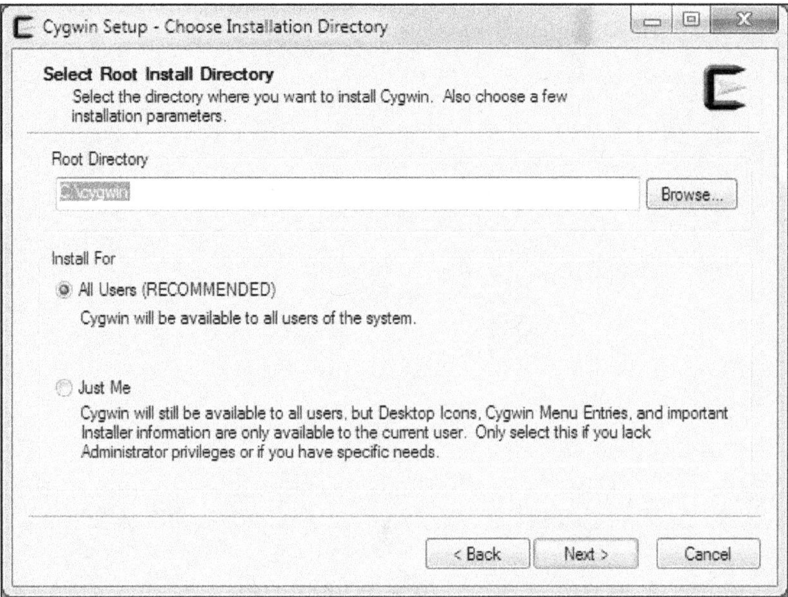

In the next window, you will be asked to specify a path where the installation can download the files it requires. You can fill in a suitable path of your choice in the box and click on **Next**.

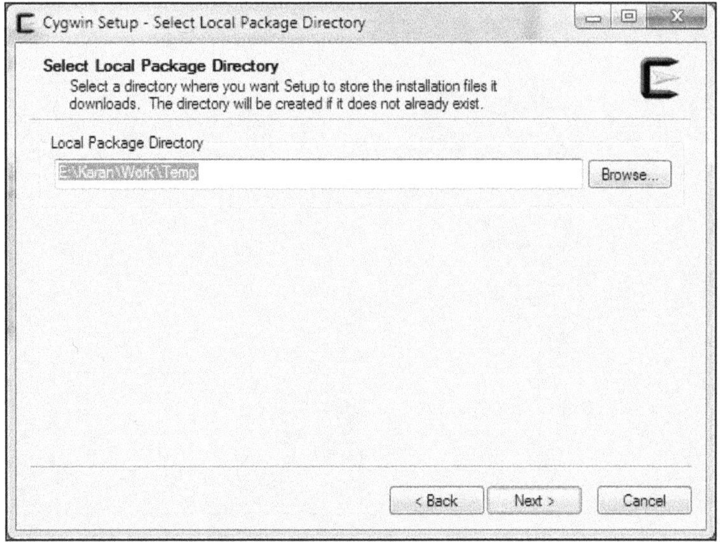

In the next window, you will be asked to specify your Internet connection. Leave it at the **Direct Connection** option and click on **Next**.

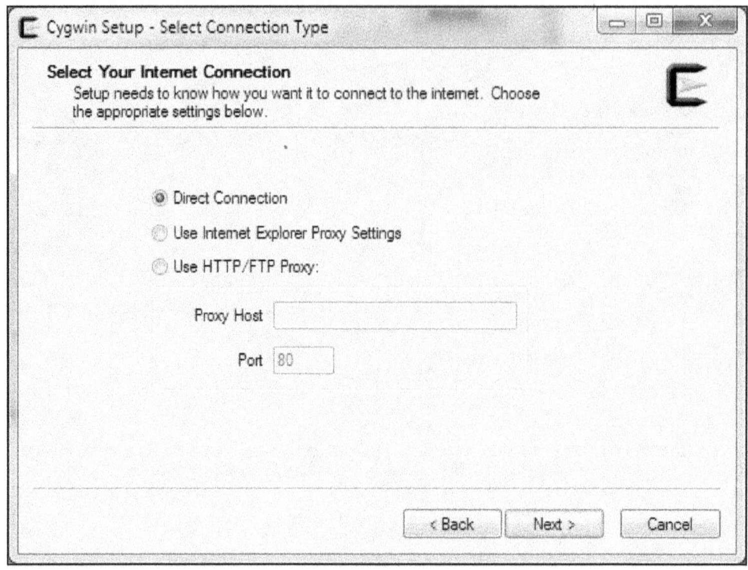

In the next window, you will be asked to select a mirror location from where to download the installation files. Here, select the site that is geographically closest to you and click on **Next**.

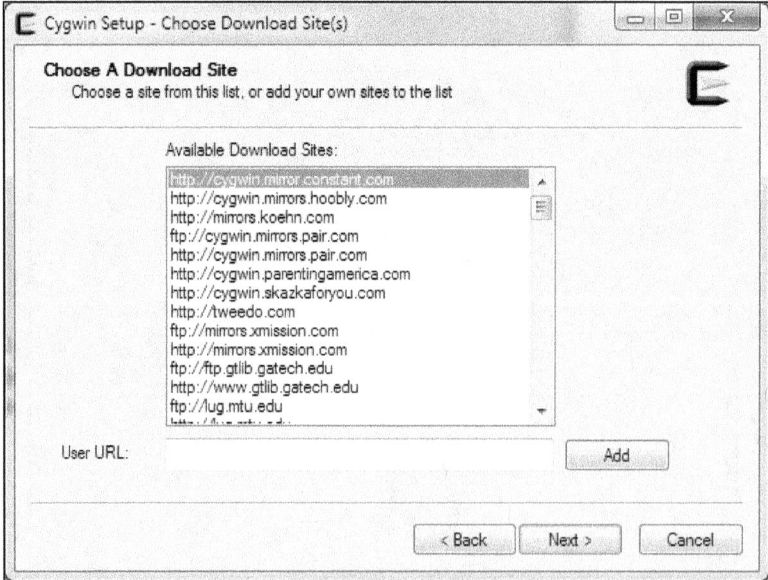

In the window that follows, expand the **Devel** section and search for **make: The GNU version of the 'make' utility**. Click on the **Skip** option to select this package. The version of the `make` utility that will be installed is now displayed in place of **Skip**. Your window should look something like this:

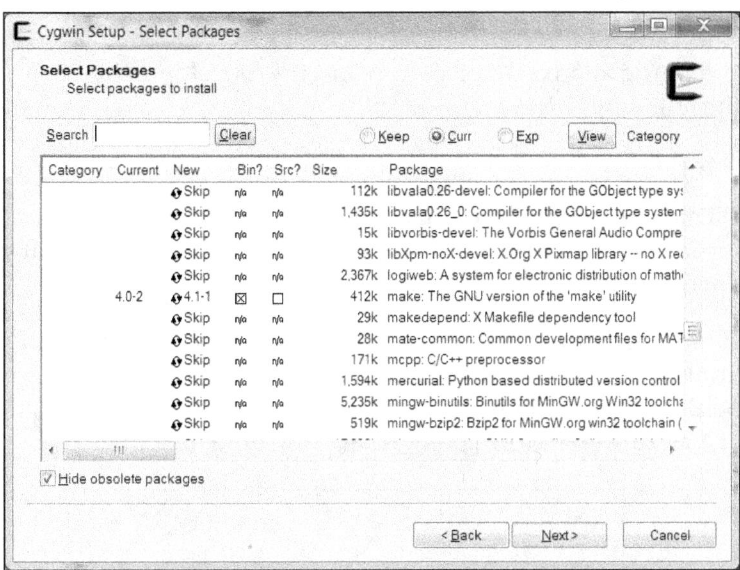

You can now go ahead and click the **Next** button to begin the download and installation of the required packages. The window should look something like this:

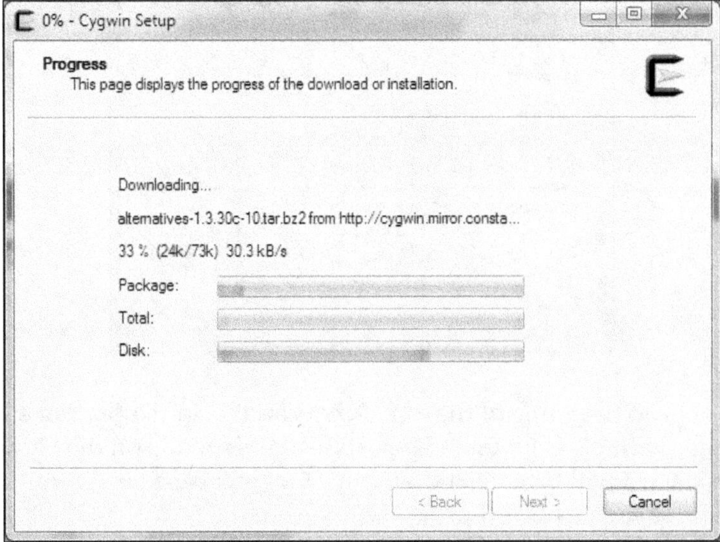

Once all the packages have been downloaded, click on **Finish** to close the installation. Now that we have the `make` utility installed, we can go ahead and download the Android NDK, which will actually build our entire C++ code base.

The Android NDK

To download the Android NDK for your respective development machine, navigate to the following URL:

`https://developer.android.com/tools/sdk/ndk/index.html`

Unzip the downloaded archive and place it in the same location as the Android SDK. We must now add an environment variable named `NDK_ROOT` that points to the root of the Android NDK.

For Windows, add a new user variable `NDK_ROOT` with the location of the Android NDK on your filesystem as its value. You can do this by going to **Properties** | **Advance Settings** | **Environment Variables**. Once you've done that, the **Environment Variables** window should look something like this:

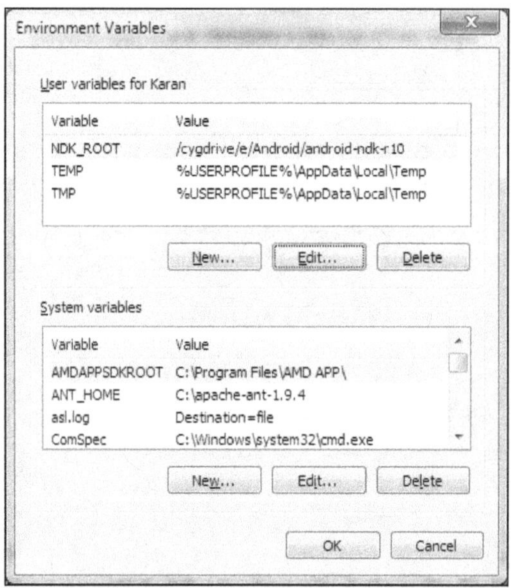

I'm sure you noticed the value of the `NDK_ROOT` variable in the previous screenshot. The value of this variable is given in Unix style and depends on the Cygwin environment, since it will be accessed within a Cygwin bash shell while executing the build script for each Android project.

Mac OS and Linux users can add the following line to their `.bash_profile` and `.bashrc` files, respectively:

```
export NDK_ROOT=/Android/android-ndk-r10
```

We have now successfully completed setting up the environment to build our Cocos2d-x games on Android. To test this, open up a Cygwin bash terminal (for Windows) or a standard terminal (for Mac OS or Linux) and navigate to the Cocos2d-x test bed located inside the `samples` folder of your Cocos2d-x source. Now, navigate to the `proj.android` folder and run the `build_native.sh` file. This is what my Cygwin bash terminal looks like on a Windows 7 machine:

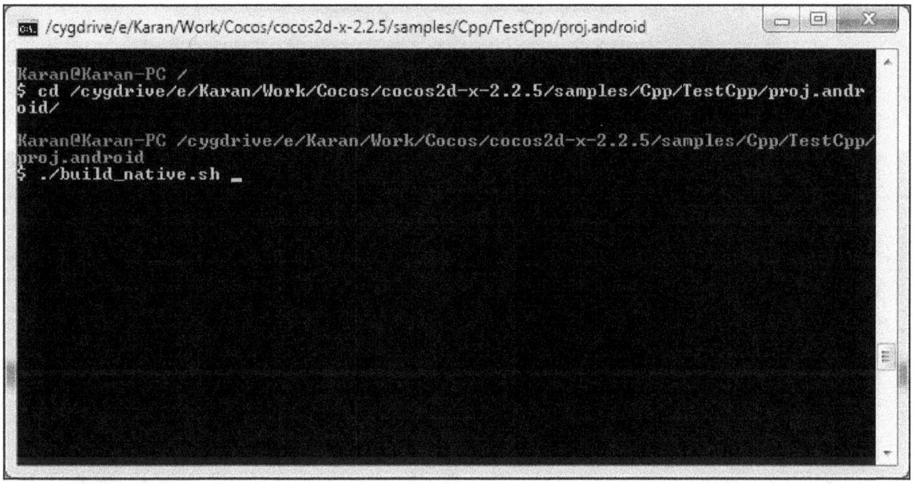

If you've followed the aforementioned instructions correctly, the `build_native.sh` script will then go on to compile the C++ source files required by the `TestCpp` project and will result in a single shared object (`.so`) file in the `libs` folder within the `proj.android` folder.

Building Pumpkin Defense on Android

We will now build one of our own games to further our understanding of how the Android environment works. The game we will build is the one we created last, that is, *Pumpkin Defense*. Before you proceed, extract the source bundle for *Pumpkin Defense* and place it inside the projects folder inside your copy of the Cocos2d-x source.

Fire up your swanky new Eclipse and when you're asked to select a workspace, set it as the `projects` folder in your Cocos2d-x source. This is shown in the following screenshot:

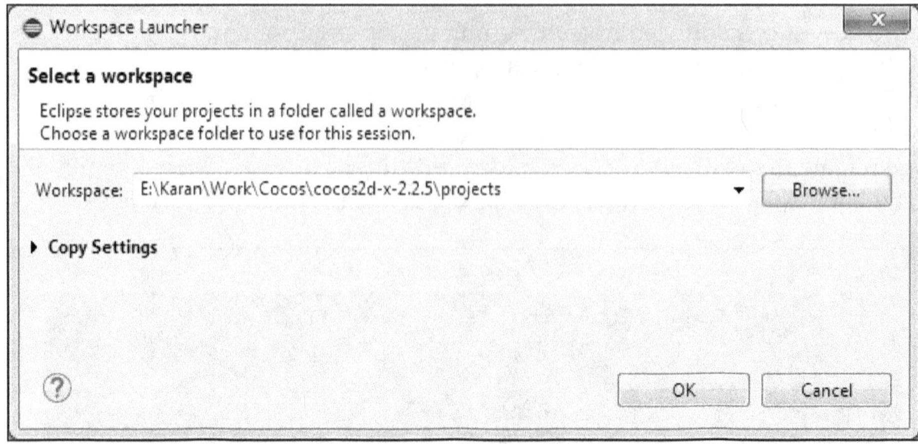

Now, import the Pumpkin Defense Android project into Eclipse by selecting **File** | **Import...**. In the following window, select **Existing Projects into Workspace** under the **General** setting and click on **Next**:

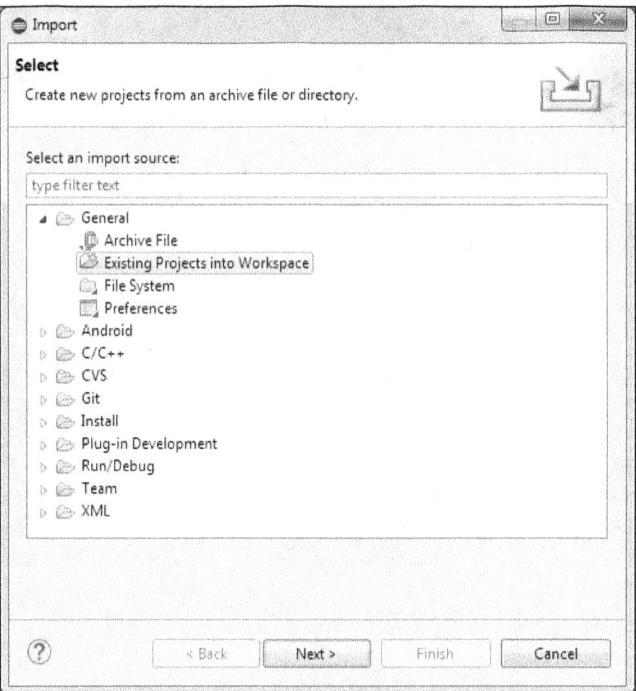

In the next window, browse to the `proj.android` folder within the *Pumpkin Defense* source bundle and click on **Finish**:

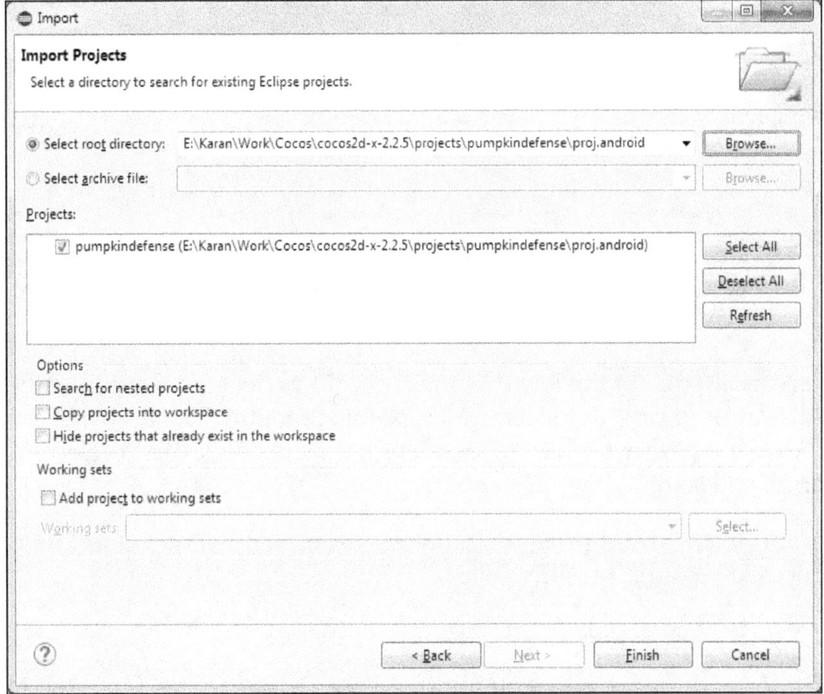

Once it is imported, you can find the `pumpkindefense` project under the **Package Explorer** view. It should look something like this:

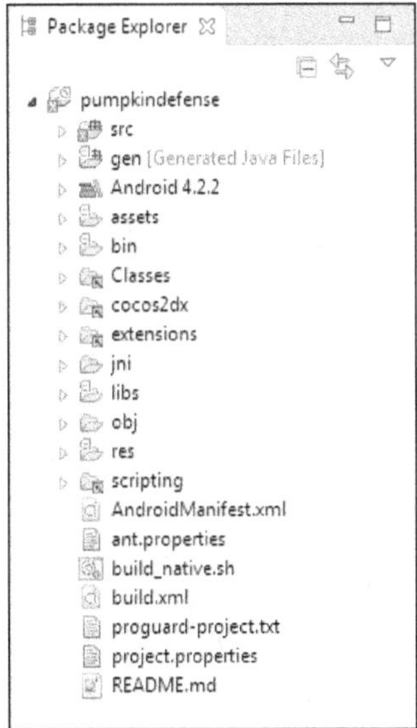

As you can see, there are a few errors in the project. If you look at the **Problems** view (**Window** | **Show View** | **Problems**) located on the bottom half of Eclipse, you might see something like this:

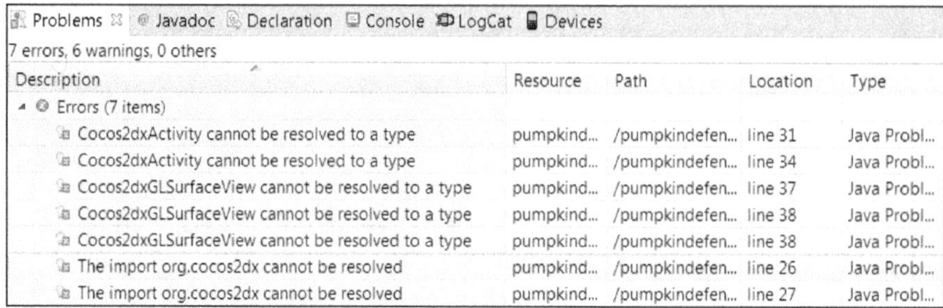

All these errors are due to the fact that the Android project for our game depends on Cocos2d-x's Android project for Android-specific functionality: things like the actual OpenGL surface where everything is rendered, the music player, accelerometer functionality, and so on.

So let's import the Android project for Cocos2d-x located inside the following path in your Cocos2d-x source bundle:

```
cocos2d-x-2.2.5\cocos2dx\platform\android
```

You can import it the same way you imported `pumpkindefense`. Once the project has been imported, it will be titled `libcocos2dx` in the **Package Explorer** view. Now select **Clean...** from the **Project** menu.

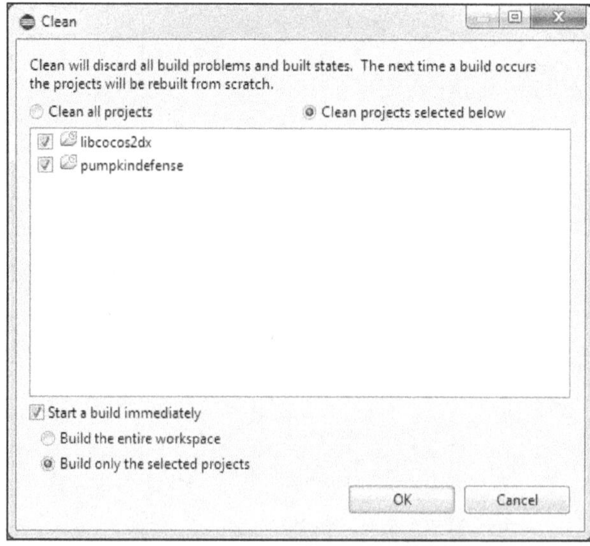

You will notice that when the clean operation has finished, the dependency `pumpkindefense` had on `libcocos2dx` is taken care of, and the project for `pumpkindefense` builds error free.

Creating an Android Virtual Device

We're close to running the game, but we need to create an **Android Virtual Device (AVD)** before we proceed. If you have an actual Android device, you can skip to the next section. If not, open up the **Android Virtual Device Manager** from the **Windows** menu and click on **Create**.

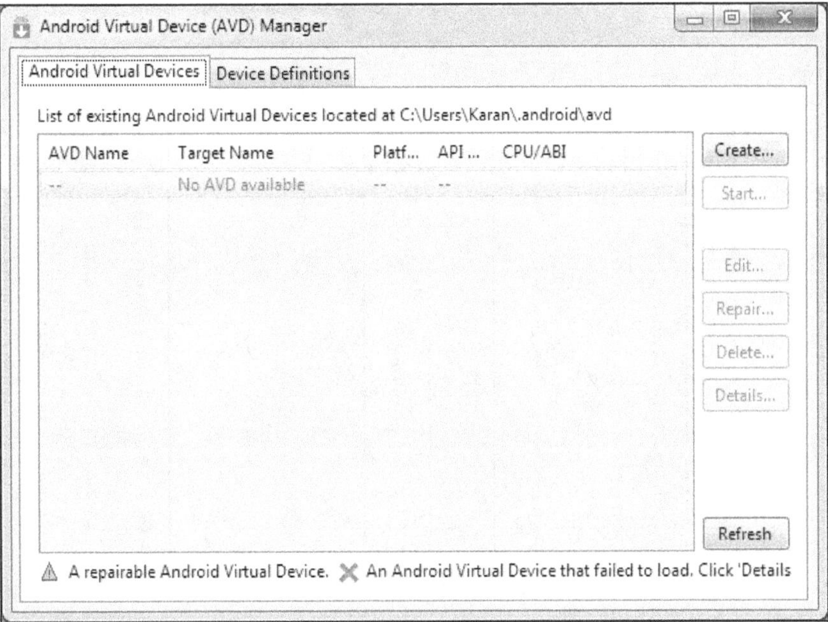

In the next window, fill in the required details as per your requirements and configuration and click **OK**. This is what my window looks like with everything filled in:

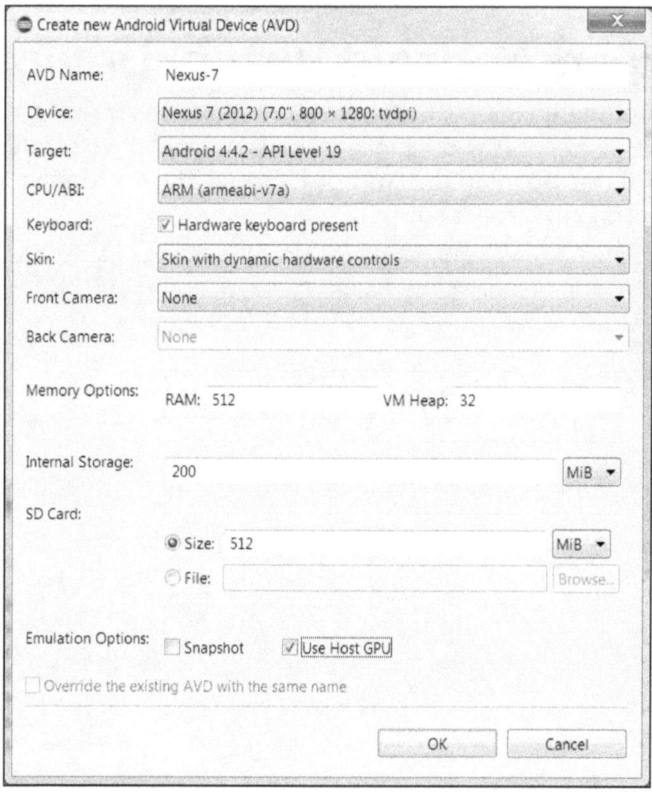

From the **Android Virtual Device Manager** window, select the newly created AVD and click on **Start** to boot it.

Running Pumpkin Defense on Android

Now that we have a device set up, we can run Pumpkin Defense on it and realize how easy it is to port an existing Cocos2d-x game to Android. Without further ado, right-click on the `pumpkindefense` project in **Package Explorer**, select **Run As**, and select **Android Application**. It might take a bit more time to start running on an emulator as compared to an actual device, but ultimately you will have something like this:

With that, we have managed to set the Android environment to work with Cocos2d-x and run one of our games on an AVD. It's time to move on to the next section, which involves setting up and building for Windows Phone 8.

Setting up the environment for Windows Phone 8

In order to develop for Windows Phone 8, you will need to have Windows 8 running on your development machine. The first thing to do would be installing Windows 8 on your machine and then proceed with the rest of this section.

Once you have Windows 8 set up, you can begin installing the various pieces of software required to build for Windows Phone 8. You can choose either Visual Studio Express 2012 or Visual Studio Community 2013. They're both free and can be used in conjunction with the Windows Phone 8 SDK. My setup has Visual Studio Community 2013 and Windows Phone 8 SDK.

You can download your preferred version of Visual Studio from the following URL:

`https://www.visualstudio.com/en-us/downloads/download-visual-studio-vs.aspx`

From the preceding link, you can choose to download an installer or an ISO. Either way, once you've downloaded and installed your preferred version of Visual Studio, download the Windows Phone 8 SDK from the following URL:

`https://dev.windows.com/en-US/develop/download-phone-sdk`

Note that the setup for the preceding software is quite large and might take a while so plan your day accordingly!

Once you've installed both Visual Studio and the Windows Phone SDK, double-click the `cocos2d-wp8.vc2012` file from your Cocos2d-x source to open up the project in Visual Studio. Your **Solution Explorer** window should look something like this:

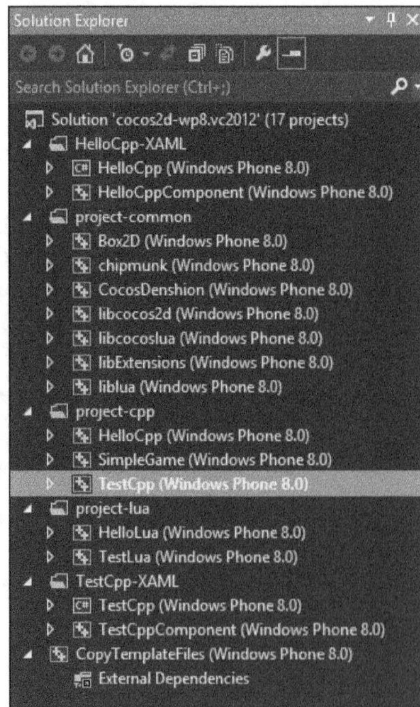

Now, right-click on the `TestCpp` project and select **Set as StartUp Project**. Next, select **Emulator** to run the project and voila!

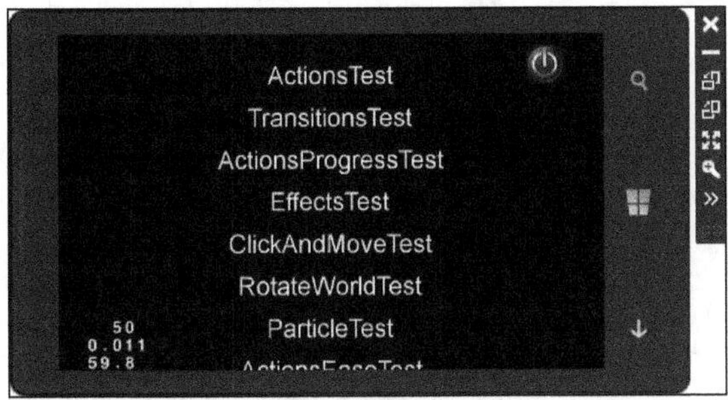

Now that we've run the Cocos2d-x test bed, let's build one of our games in the next section.

Building Pumpkin Defense on Windows Phone 8

To build Pumpkin Defense, we'll open up the solution located inside the `proj.wp8-xaml` folder in the source bundle, since `proj.wp8` will be deprecated soon.

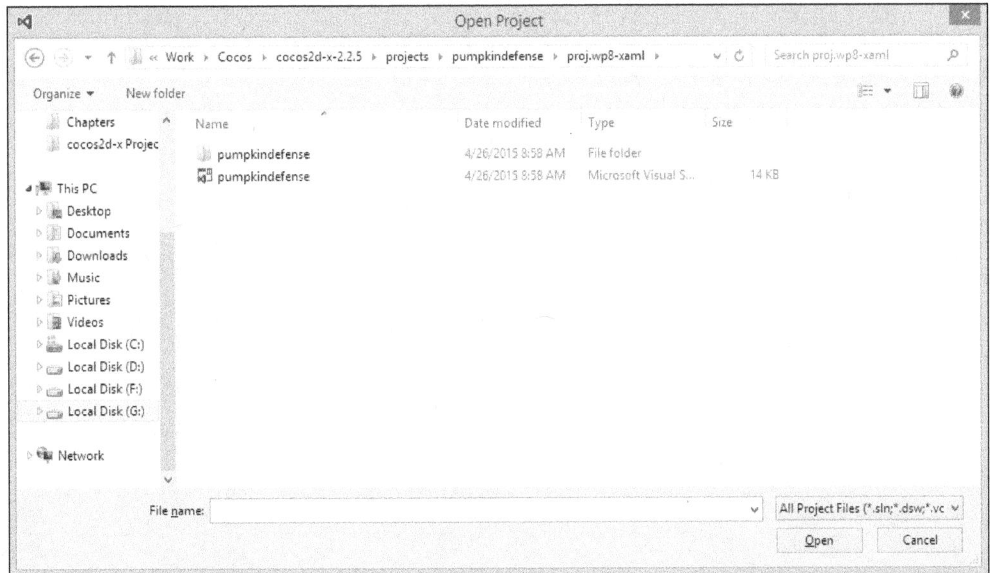

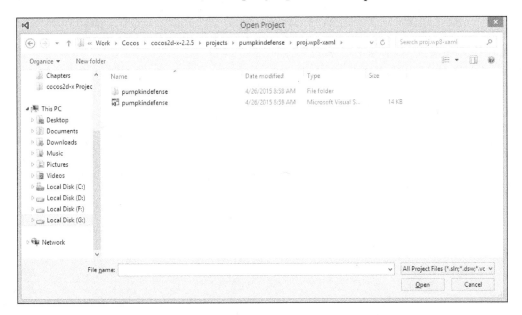

Once we have imported the project, the **Solution Explorer** shows you the various other projects that `pumpkindefense` depends on. This is quite similar to the win32 builds we've been following throughout the book.

However, one important difference here is that along with the `pumpkindefense` project, there is another project titled `pumpkindefenseComponent`. If you look closely, you will notice that `pumpkindefense` is a C# project and it is used to provide the primary application framework for a Windows Phone 8 project. The `pumpkindefenseComponent` project is a C++ project that contains all the source files for our project.

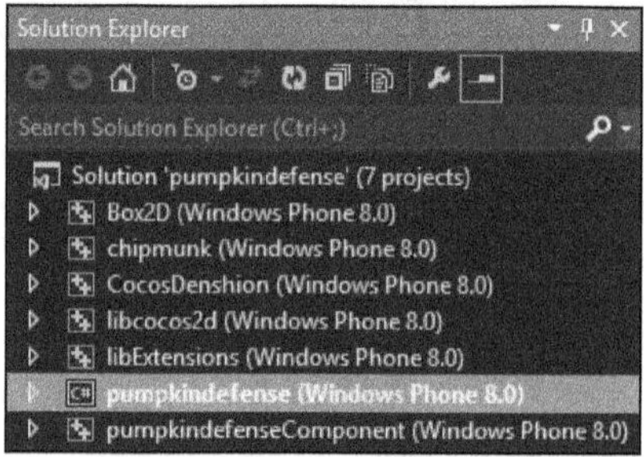

If you expand the `Classes` folder inside `pumpkindefenseComponent`, you will notice that the actual sources are missing. So, delete the default class files listed there and then right-click on the `Classes` folder, select **Add**, and select **Existing Item...**.

In the window that follows, select all the source files for *Pumpkin Defense* and add them to the `Classes` folder inside `pumpkindenfenseComponent`.

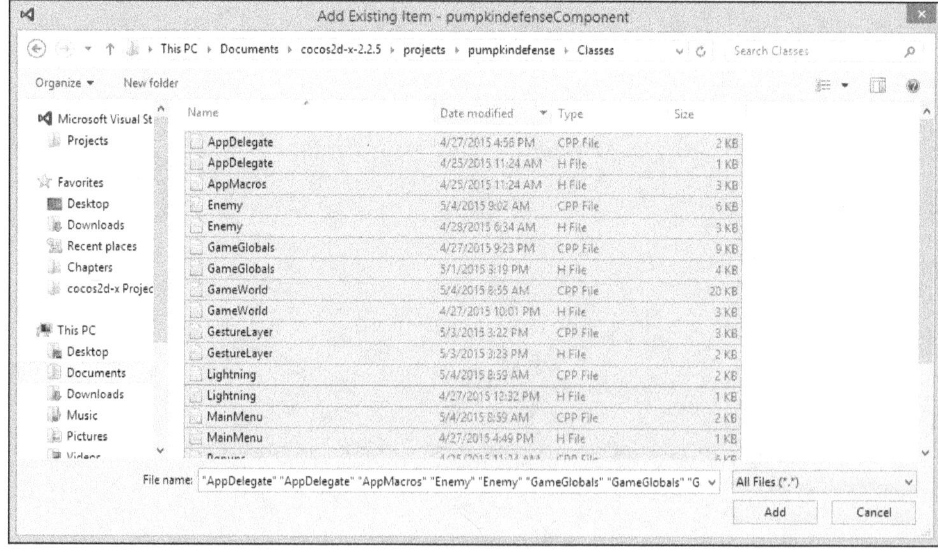

Now that we have our classes in place, all we need to do is click on that little green arrow and run the project.

A few customizations for audio and fonts are required while building for Windows Phone 8. Windows Phone 8 does not support MP3 audio files, so ensure that all your audio files are converted to WAV. You could use Audacity (`http://sourceforge.net/projects/audacity/`), which is an open source utility to convert your audio.

With regard to fonts, you only need to worry if you're using true type fonts or TTF labels in your code. If so, you must check the list of supported fonts (`http://msdn.microsoft.com/en-us/library/windowsphone/develop/cc189010(v=vs.105).aspx#silverlight_fonts`). If your font is not in that list, you must include the `.ttf` file for the respective font in the resource bundle for the given project.

What to do next?

Well you may want to port your game to more than just Android and Windows Phone platforms. The biggest advantage of developing in C++ is the number of platforms one can reach. As such, Cocos2d-x supports a sleuth of platforms such as the ones listed next. I have provided links to a few tutorials that can help get you started with some of the unfamiliar/newer platforms:

- iOS
- Android
- Windows Phone 8
- Windows PC
- Mac OS
- Linux
    - `http://voidfuture.com/2013/10/08/building-cocos2d-x-on-rhel-fedora-centos-linux/`
    - `http://www.cocos2d-x.org/wiki/Linux_Installation_and_Setup`
- Blackberry OS
    - `http://www.cocos2d-x.org/wiki/How_to_run_HelloWorld_and_Tests_on_BlackBerry_Tablet_OS`
    - `http://boredwookie.net/index.php/blog/blackberry-10-getting-the-cocos2d-x-hello-world-app-to-build/`

- Marmalade (cross-platform development tool for mobile, TV, and desktop)
    - `https://www.madewithmarmalade.com/`
- Tizen (Linux-based operating system targeting mobile, in-vehicle infotainment, TV, PC, cameras, wearable computers, smart home appliances and so on)
    - `https://www.tizen.org/`
    - `http://www.cocos2d-x.org/wiki/How_to_run_HelloWOrld_and_tests_of_cocos2d-x_on_Tizen`
    - `https://developer.tizen.org/documentation/articles/using-cocos2d-x-tizen-native-applications`
- Emscripten (a type of compiler that converts LLVM code produced by C/C++ into JavaScript)
    - `https://github.com/kripken/emscripten`
    - `http://www.cocos2d-x.org/wiki/Emscripten_usage`

Summary

In our last chapter, we used the cross-platform versatility that Cocos2d-x offers and set up environments for Android and Windows Phone 8. We then ported one of our own games to the respective environments.

This entire book has been an attempt at showing you the ease with which good quality games can be created using Cocos2d-x. All the games we've made are prototypes of the genres they represent, and I have tried my best to develop them in a way that might enable you to scale them up to exciting altitudes.

I learned more in the process of writing this book than in any other task I have undertaken and I enjoyed every bit of it. Now, I'm excited at the prospect of seeing what you will create with the knowledge gained from this book. Godspeed to you dear reader!

Index

Symbols

A

B

C

D

E

F

G

H

I

J

K

L

M

O

P

R

S

T

U

V

W

X

Thank you for buying
Cocos2d-x Game Development Blueprints

About Packt Publishing

Packt, pronounced 'packed', published its first book, *Mastering phpMyAdmin for Effective MySQL Management*, in April 2004, and subsequently continued to specialize in publishing highly focused books on specific technologies and solutions.

Our books and publications share the experiences of your fellow IT professionals in adapting and customizing today's systems, applications, and frameworks. Our solution-based books give you the knowledge and power to customize the software and technologies you're using to get the job done. Packt books are more specific and less general than the IT books you have seen in the past. Our unique business model allows us to bring you more focused information, giving you more of what you need to know, and less of what you don't.

Packt is a modern yet unique publishing company that focuses on producing quality, cutting-edge books for communities of developers, administrators, and newbies alike. For more information, please visit our website at `www.packtpub.com`.

About Packt Open Source

In 2010, Packt launched two new brands, Packt Open Source and Packt Enterprise, in order to continue its focus on specialization. This book is part of the Packt Open Source brand, home to books published on software built around open source licenses, and offering information to anybody from advanced developers to budding web designers. The Open Source brand also runs Packt's Open Source Royalty Scheme, by which Packt gives a royalty to each open source project about whose software a book is sold.

Writing for Packt

We welcome all inquiries from people who are interested in authoring. Book proposals should be sent to `author@packtpub.com`. If your book idea is still at an early stage and you would like to discuss it first before writing a formal book proposal, then please contact us; one of our commissioning editors will get in touch with you.

We're not just looking for published authors; if you have strong technical skills but no writing experience, our experienced editors can help you develop a writing career, or simply get some additional reward for your expertise.

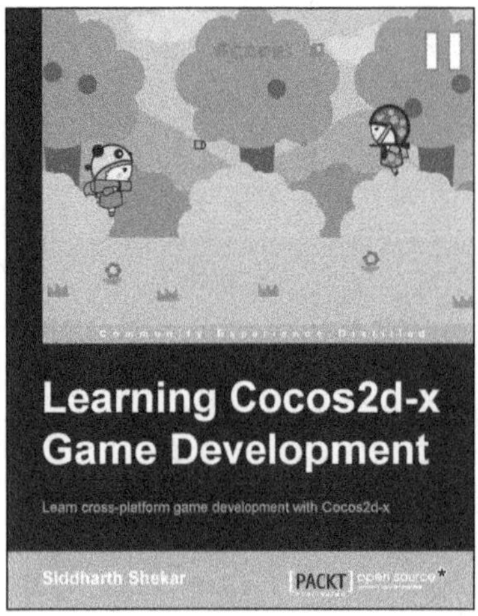

Learning Cocos2d-x Game Development

ISBN: 978-1-78398-826-6 Paperback: 266 pages

Learn cross-platform game development with Cocos2d-x

1. Create a Windows Store account and upload your game for distribution.
2. Develop a game using Cocos2d-x by going through each stage of game development process step by step.

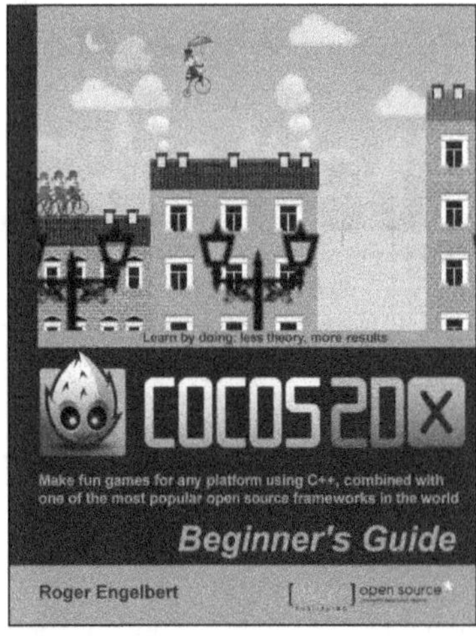

Cocos2d-X by Example Beginner's Guide

ISBN: 978-1-78216-734-1 Paperback: 246 pages

Make fun games for any platform using C++, combined with one of the most popular open source frameworks in the world

1. Learn to build multi-device games in simple, easy steps, letting the framework do all the heavy lifting.
2. Spice things up in your games with easy to apply animations, particle effects, and physics simulation.
3. Quickly implement and test your own gameplay ideas, with an eye for optimization and portability.

Please check **www.PacktPub.com** for information on our titles

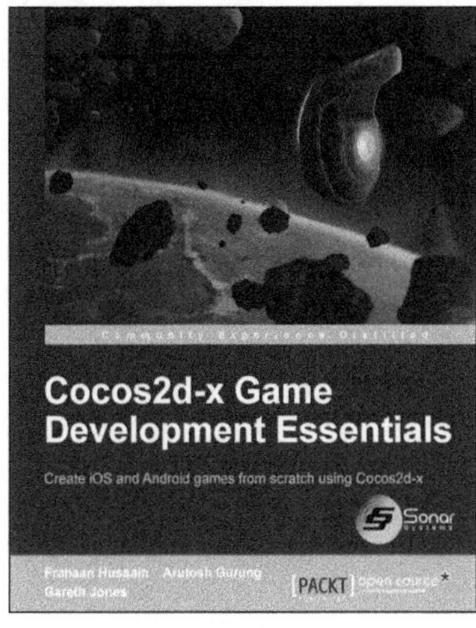

Cocos2d-x Game Development Essentials

ISBN: 978-1-78398-786-3 Paperback: 136 pages

Create iOS and Android games from scratch using Cocos2d-x

1. Create and run Cocos2d-x projects on iOS and Android platforms.
2. Find practical solutions to many real-world game development problems.
3. Learn the essentials of Cocos2d-x by writing code and following step-by-step instructions.

Creating Games with cocos2d for iPhone 2

ISBN: 978-1-84951-900-7 Paperback: 388 pages

Master cocos2d through building nine complete games for the iPhone

1. Games are explained in detail, from the design decisions to the code itself.
2. Learn to build a wide variety of game types, from a memory tile game to an endless runner.
3. Use different design approaches to help you explore the cocos2d framework.

Please check **www.PacktPub.com** for information on our titles

www.ingramcontent.com/pod-product-compliance
Lightning Source LLC
LaVergne TN
LVHW081330050326
832903LV00024B/1103

* 9 7 8 1 7 8 3 9 8 5 2 6 5 *